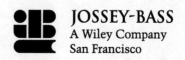
JOSSEY-BASS
A Wiley Company
San Francisco

# Angel Investing

# Angel Investing

Matching Start-up Funds with Start-up Companies—The Guide for Entrepreneurs, Individual Investors, and Venture Capitalists

Mark Van Osnabrugge

Robert J. Robinson

JOSSEY-BASS
A Wiley Company
San Francisco

Jossey-Bass books and products are available through most bookstores. To contact Jossey-Bass directly, call (888) 378-2537, fax to (800) 605-2665, or visit our website at www.josseybass.com.

Substantial discounts on bulk quantities of Jossey-Bass books are available to corporations, professional associations, and other organizations. For details and discount information, contact the special sales department at Jossey-Bass.

 Manufactured in the United States of America on Lyons Falls Turin Book. This paper is acid-free and 100 percent totally chlorine-free.

**Library of Congress Cataloging-in-Publication Data**
Van Osnabrugge, Mark, date.
   Angel investing : matching startup funds with startup companies : the guide for entrepreneurs, individual investors, and venture capitalists / Mark Van Osnabrugge and Robert J. Robinson.—1st ed.
      p.   cm.—(The Jossey-Bass business & management series)
Includes bibliographical references and index.
   ISBN 0-7879-5202-8 (acid-free paper)
   1. New business enterprises—Finance.   2. Small business—Finance.   3. Venture capital.   I. Robinson, Robert J., date.   II. Title.   III. Series.
   HG4027.6 .V36 2000
   658.15'224—dc21

00-008230
FIRST EDITION
*HB Printing*   10  9  8  7  6  5  4  3  2  1

The Jossey-Bass
Business & Management Series

*Mark dedicates this book to his parents and Kristine.*
*Rob dedicates this book to Eileen and the twins.*

# Contents

to Your Start-up Firm**                                      **213**

12    Valuing Your Firm                                      215
13    Negotiating the Funding Agreement                      224

**Part Five: Becoming a Successful Business
Angel Investor**                                             **233**

14    Steps in Effectively Making Your First Investment
      in an Entrepreneurial Firm                             235

**Part Six: The Future of the Business Angel Market**        **247**

15    The Business Angel Market in the
      New Millennium                                         249

**Part Seven: Putting the Wheels in Motion**                 **255**

      Appendix One: A Detailed List of More Than
      Seventy Matching Services in the United States         257
      Appendix Two: Further Helpful Resources                339
      Appendix Three: Writing a Winning Business Plan        359
      Glossary                                               373
      Bibliography                                           383
      Name Index                                             407
      Subject Index                                          411

# Preface

Delivering more funding to more entrepreneurs than any other source, business angels are some of the most important (though least understood) players in our entrepreneurial landscape today. Their influence has shaped our nation since before its founding, and their economic importance continues to be immeasurable. Since little has been written about such individuals investing privately in entrepreneurial firms (partly because of their preference for anonymity and being difficult to locate), *Angel Investing* dispels the myths to give the most comprehensive and best-researched discussion available of who business angels are, how they operate, and how to find them, especially relative to their better-known counterparts, the venture capitalists. This book should be read by anyone who is starting a firm, seeking funds to grow his or her existing venture, considering investing in an entrepreneurial opportunity, or even pondering how best to position the firm so that it can attain quotation on the stock market through an initial public offering (IPO).

*Angel Investing* is the product of more than four years of rigorous research and many years of personal, hands-on experience in the field. Unlike a small number of other offerings that base their business angel discussion solely on small-scale anecdotal evidence or dedicate only a few pages to the subject, this book is the first to present the latest, large-scale, empirical evidence (from the United States and abroad)—more than three hundred empirically validated academic research studies; personal interviews with business angels, venture capitalists, entrepreneurs, academics, and intermediaries; as well as anecdotal evidence, all offering an illuminating account of these private investors. You will gain knowledge that you can put to good use, whether you are (or want to be) an entrepreneur or an investor, since it gives entrepreneurs all the

knowledge they need to effectively secure business angel investments for their growing firms, and private investors the insights to
successfully buy a slice of a small firm before it potentially grows to
be worth millions.

## How This Book Is Organized

*Angel Investing* is divided into seven major sections, each dealing with one aspect of our diverse entrepreneurial funding
environment.

Part One, "Financing Options for Start-up Firms," reviews the
financing choices available to entrepreneurs of start-up and growing firms and the challenges they must learn to overcome. We detail how entrepreneurs can best finance their firms initially
through internal means (such as bootstrapping and business alliances) as well as the types of outside investor they can best approach as their firms evolve.

Part Two, "The Two Main Sources of Funding: Business Angels
and Venture Capitalists," is a thorough review of the traits and investment power of business angels and venture capitalists and how
entrepreneurs can best tap into the vast wealth potential of business angels. Knowing exactly who the investors are and how (and
why) they operate is critical, so we end Part Two by comparing how
angels differ from venture capitalists.

Part Three, "Business Angel and Venture Capitalist Differences Throughout the Investment Process," compares business
angels and venture capitalists throughout their full investment activities, from initial investment motivations to exit strategies and
postinvestment regrets. This gives you an unprecedented look at
how these two investors think and operate—vital information if
you hope to secure financing from either source. If you are an investor, this same information provides many insights that may
help you improve your own investment procedures.

Part Four, "Attracting Business Angel Funds to Your Start-up
Firm," extends valuable tips to entrepreneurs on how they can use
the information they have acquired to obtain funds from business
angels and venture capitalists. We review in detail how to value a
young firm and negotiate effectively for funds with investors, plus
many other helpful insights.

Part Five, "Becoming a Successful Business Angel Investor," guides potential investors through the steps they need to take to become successful private investors in young entrepreneurial ventures.

Part Six, "The Future of the Business Angel Market," chronicles our predictions for the future of the business angel market and the variety of exciting changes and opportunities that will emerge.

Part Seven, "Putting the Wheels in Motion," comprises three appendixes that list valuable resources to allow entrepreneurs and private investors to start the process of becoming successful players in the world of entrepreneurial financing. In particular, we have compiled the largest and most detailed list to date of U.S. matching services (more than seventy). These beneficial organizations match entrepreneurs looking for funds with investors looking for ventures in which to invest. We have taken great time and care to collect this information since it gives us all the means to put the information learned in this book to work in the real world. We also present a detailed discussion of how to write a winning business plan.

Specifically, here are just some of the facts you will learn in this book:

- Business angels are the oldest, largest, and most often used source of outside funds for entrepreneurial firms.
- The United States has close to three million angels, investing more than $50 billion in entrepreneurial firms each year. With the right incentives, this market could become many times larger.
- Angels already fund thirty to forty times as many entrepreneurial firms as the formal venture capital industry does, investing three to five times more money.
- Many of our most influential firms, such as Ford, Apple, and Amazon.com, were initially angel-funded. More and more firms over the coming years will also be angel-supported.
- An increasing number of today's most successful high-tech and Internet entrepreneurs, such as former Apple CEO John Sculley, Netscape's Jim Barksdale, and Microsoft's Paul Allen, have cashed out and become angel investors.

- Angels fund 60 percent of all new technology firms in the United States.
- There are ten distinct advantages that business angels bring to their investments (listed in Chapter Four).
- Angel investing is one of the most important of a number of financing options available to entrepreneurs trying to grow their ventures.
- Though business angels are difficult to locate, there are ten effective ways for entrepreneurs to find them (listed in Chapter Five).
- Angels have investment criteria and behaviors distinct from those of venture capitalists. Understanding these differences is vital for entrepreneurs, investors, and anyone interested in entrepreneurship.
- Many Americans have already invested a small part of their portfolios in entrepreneurial firms. We give ten tips for those who also want to become angels (listed in Chapter Fourteen).
- The U.S. business angel market is exploding and will most likely double within the next decade.

## Who Should Read This Book?

As our economy and the outside world continue to change, promoting entrepreneurship at home may be America's best chance of realizing a natural competitive advantage in the twenty-first century (Bygrave and Timmons, 1992). This book's main value, therefore, is its usefulness for readers; our intent is to enlighten and increase understanding of investment techniques and procedures for the diverse groups of practitioners currently in our entrepreneurial marketplace.

### Entrepreneurs

Every entrepreneur should read this book, since raising external finance to grow a firm is often very challenging. Finding the right investor is frequently an uphill battle. This book gives entrepreneurs a number of particular advantages. First, greater understanding of investors' investment criteria and processes enables entrepreneurs to create better funding proposals and so increase their chances of success. This allows them to assess how their ventures compare with investors' criteria, permitting them to identify the steps necessary to resolve any major flaws in their proposals before submitting them. In fact, many viable proposals are rejected because they have flaws that can be removed if entrepreneurs are alerted to them before they are submitted (MacMillan, Siegel, and Subbanarasimha, 1985).

Second, gaining greater understanding of investors allows entrepreneurs to form realistic expectations of what they can demand from an investor and what they should forfeit in return. Currently, this area is not well understood by either investors or entrepreneurs; as a result, offers of investment are often rejected.

Third, with greater understanding of investors, entrepreneurs are better able to assess how suitable the types of finance provider are and thus better target those that are most sympathetic to their type of firm and most capable of adding the financial and non-financial input desired.

Fourth, knowing what criteria investors look for as a measure of potential success allows entrepreneurs to emphasize these factors in their ventures, in the hope of aiding their performance focus. This may also give potential entrepreneurs knowledge of what they should be looking for in prospective opportunities they wish to start and grow.

## Private Investors (Business Angels)

This book teaches private investors, or anyone with some money to invest, how to make better investments. By learning how venture capitalists and other business angels make investments, and which criteria they find important, investors have a head start over the competition. This is particularly beneficial since research has shown that many private investors are inefficient, or insufficiently experienced, in identifying proposals worthy of serious consideration. Advice on how to conduct due diligence and how to be more successful in the investment process may be helpful for many private investors.

For wealthy private individuals with a business background who are interested, but have not yet invested, in entrepreneurial firms (such potential business angel investors are known as "virgin angels"), this book raises awareness of informal venture capital as a viable funding option; we hope the book also offers insights to motivate them to get involved. At the very least, this book shows them what they should look for in an entrepreneurial investment opportunity before committing financial capital—which should also aid their analysis of larger firms, even those quoted on a stock exchange.

## Venture Capitalists

This book should be required reading for venture capitalists because it presents unbiased information about their investment practices and about the practices of business angels—those investors who may soon be their competitors (as well as co-investors) as the investment power of angels and their preference for co-investing continue to grow. This book offers a number of significant insights.

First, venture capitalists will find it useful to compare their investment practices to those of other venture capitalists in the market, especially since, for venture capital firms, knowledge of the practices of others could prove useful in selecting their domain, planning their portfolio, choosing which competencies to develop, and setting operating policies (Sapienza, Manigart, and Vermeir, 1996).

Second, since the success rate of venture capital–backed companies tends to be higher than for new ventures in general (Hall and Hofer, 1993), better understanding of the investment criteria used by venture capitalists may produce greater understanding of the reasons for their success.

Third, *Angel Investing* highlights the sometimes forgotten area of early-stage financing; empirical results may induce some venture capitalists to reconsider focusing more on this area.

Fourth, since venture capitalists have increasingly looked abroad to other countries to diversify their investment activities, we display information from a number of nations to garner further insight into foreign investment practices and potential. Similarly, just as the older venture capital market in the United States has acted as a guide for the UK venture capital industry, so too do these venture capital communities influence the growing venture capital culture in Europe. Clearly, this book is of particular interest to the less developed institutional venture capital market in Europe and elsewhere.

Lastly, the greater understanding that this book provides about the full investment process of venture capitalists, and how this differs from the processes of other types of investor, may offer a good starting point for evaluating (and possibly improving) the efficiency and effectiveness of the venture capital investment process (Hall and Hofer, 1993; Carter and Van Auken, 1994).

This book is also insightful for intermediaries and secondary players in the market for entrepreneurial finance.

## Investor-Entrepreneur Matching Services

This book is vital for matching services since research has shown that they have only a partial view of the business angel market and research is important to them in broadening the picture. Matching services are organizations scattered around our nation that help to match (often for a fee) entrepreneurs looking for investors with potential private investors seeking investment opportunities. For these organizations, procuring more knowledge about their market (offered in this book) may help them develop relevant and effective services. As one manager of a matching service recently told us: "We really don't know the answers because there hasn't been enough research. It's good that you are doing the research now."

This book has significant implications for matching services. First, greater knowledge of business angels' investment processes allows matching services to effectively tailor the structure and content of the information on investment opportunities to meet the needs of investors.

Second, the findings in this book help matching services identify potentially deficient areas where advice, training, and counseling can be extended to business angels and entrepreneurs, either through workshops or literature. This book highlights the need for extensive due diligence by business angels, an area in which matching services can provide valuable advice.

Third, *Angel Investing* allows matching services to combat a misconception held by many business angels, entrepreneurs, and other players in the market: that matching services are a source of last-resort funding with low-quality investment opportunities and few value-added activities.

Fourth, if venture capitalists have better insight as to the potentially valuable role of business angels in supporting the start-up entrepreneurial ventures that may eventually be funded, venture capitalists might be induced to refer some early-stage investment opportunities (that they have rejected) to matching services to seek business angel funding.

Although matching services are no panacea for the funding gap of small firms (less than $500,000 sought, which is too small for institutional investors), they do effectively address some inefficiencies in the entrepreneurial investment market. This book helps them examine their own services to make the matching process potentially more effective and efficient.

## Corporate Managers

For managers of large corporations, the themes of this book have some important implications. First, by providing details of how venture capitalists allocate their funds, *Angel Investing* gives insights that are also valuable to managers in large companies who wish to improve their allocation of resources to internal ventures competing for new business development funds (Tyebjee and Bruno, 1984).

Second, this book also raises awareness of corporate venturing as a viable means of investment for large firms. In corporate venturing, large companies fund entrepreneurial firms directly or indirectly as an effective means of using this alliance for potential gains and access to leading-edge technologies. Such forms of business alliances may also offer a valuable alternative source of finance for entrepreneurial firms.

## Banks

Small-business loan officers should read this book since it empowers them to discuss a wider array of funding options with their entrepreneurial start-up clients. It offers valuable information that banks should pass on to their customers as yet another service provision. This is particularly important since banks are a major source of information and advice to small firms and are ideally placed to educate their small-business customers on the role of equity finance, encouraging them, where appropriate, to consider the possibility of raising external equity and to provide information on how to find business angels. At present, banks play a very minor role in networking between the small-business sector and the business angel community. This book also gives them better understanding of how they should evaluate established entrepreneurial firms that approach them for funding; by reviewing the fund providers, this book clarifies the role that banks play in funding small entrepreneurial firms. Thanks to their regulatory environment and investment limitations, there is a general misconception that banks play a lead role in start-up finance for small firms.

## Institutional Investors

This book is insightful for managers of pension funds and other large organizations and trusts that extend funding to venture capitalists. In particular, it details how the investment procedures of venture capitalists are formulated to comply with the demands and concerns of their fund investors, and it offers a valuable perspective for fund providers (limited partners) to complement the venture capitalists' provision of timely investment information. This may be especially important since Robbie, Wright, and Chiplin (1997) claim that there is a continuing need to educate fund providers on venture capital activity.

## Policymakers

This book offers policymakers additional information and perspective that will assist them in effectively promoting the economic power of this country's millions of individual business angel investors. The use of government policy can be "a powerful—probably the most powerful—promoter or inhibitor of venture capital–backed entrepreneurship. It is a long-term process; policy initiatives taken in the 1990s will have an effect on entrepreneurship well into the next century" (Bygrave and Timmons, 1992, p. 285). There may therefore be a legitimate role for government policy in shaping national and local economic development and promoting the appropriate elements of capital formation. However, designing policy which is well tailored to all objectives is extremely difficult (Wetzel, 1986a). New research is constantly needed on entrepreneurship issues since "the better we understand this market, the better we can fix it" (Wetzel, 1993, p. 10). Unfortunately, though, we should caution that forming and implementing policy often runs ahead of knowledge, and so more empirical evidence is needed (Mason, 1996a).

This book focuses on investments in early-stage and high-growth firms, two areas where academics believe particular policy attention should be paid. In addition, it sheds some light on a number of policy changes proposed to boost the market for entrepreneurship, such as government subsidies for matching services, encouragement of the IPO market (Bygrave and Shulman, 1988), special policies that consider the heterogeneity of individual investors (Mason and Harrison, 1996a), creation of public sector venture capital funds for early-stage deals (Lonsdale, 1996), and government support for "risk rating" entrepreneurial firms.

## Students of Entrepreneurship

This book is ideal for the thousands of students taking classes on entrepreneurship. Over the last decade, with so many entrepreneurial success stories in the media, interest in entrepreneurship has seen an explosion. This book is particularly noteworthy since it chronicles the most important supporters of those firms that drive our entrepreneurial economy and interest. Best of all, we give students the tools and insights they need in becoming successful entrepreneurs themselves.

• • •

As we start the new millennium, entrepreneurship is destined to become an even greater force in the well-being of our economy and its competitive position in the global marketplace. Although the entrepreneurial process can be highly dynamic and complex, *Angel Investing* adds some structure and clarity to this important area. By offering comprehensive analysis of the entrepreneurial environment and the investment procedures of the two most important types of financier that spark the growth of entrepreneurial firms, we hope that this book helps us all add more fuel to the flames of entrepreneurship.

Harvard Business School          MARK VAN OSNABRUGGE
March 2000                       ROBERT J. ROBINSON

# Acknowledgments

First and foremost, we would like to thank Michal Sobieszczyk for his many months of excellent research assistance. His motivation, insights, and hard work are evident throughout this book. We would also like to express our gratitude to the people at Jossey-Bass who worked so diligently to get this to press. In particular, we thank Cedric Crocker, Kathe Sweeney, Danielle Neary, Pamela Berkman, and Tom Finnegan.

Our appreciation also goes to our many colleagues and students at the Harvard Business School who reviewed drafts of this book and offered their valuable advice. In particular, we would like to thank Jim Sebenius, Howard Stevenson, and Bill Sahlman, as well as Harvard Business School's Division of Research for funding much of the work underlying this project. Also, Colin Mayer and Keith Grint offered much helpful advice and assistance, which planted the seeds for this book.

In addition to the many practitioners who shared their experiences with us, this book would not have been possible without the pioneering research that a number of individuals have conducted over the last decade on business angels. They helped to first formally identify this most important type of entrepreneurial investor and pave the way for many aspects of the angels' research we have conducted over the last few years. In particular, we would like to thank Jeff Sohl, Bill Wetzel, John Freear and James Fiet from the United States, Colin Mason and Richard Harrison from the UK, Hans Landstrom from Sweden, and Allan Riding from Canada, to name but a few.

However, when writing a book on entrepreneurship and venture capital investing, the most important and illuminating insights come from the many successful entrepreneurs and investors you meet. We were certainly very lucky to have hundreds of entrepreneurial investors participate in our data collection process and countless dozens who took considerable time out of their busy schedules to share their great entrepreneurial success stories and wisdom with us. We hope that this book may, in some small way, help to foster many more such adventurous supporters of tomorrow's trend-setting corporations. It is the entrepreneurial spirit of these investors that we have tried to capture in the pages of this book.

# The Authors

*Mark Van Osnabrugge* recently completed a fellowship at the Harvard Business School. He is now a management consultant at Marakon Associates, an international consulting firm. He earned his B.B.A. degree (1994) in finance and marketing from the University of Wisconsin-Madison and his Ph.D. (1998) from Oxford University, where he also taught finance at the undergraduate and M.B.A. levels.

Van Osnabrugge has spent many years studying the business angel and venture capital markets, but he has also encountered them firsthand as a consultant for a large venture capital firm, as a project coordinator for a matchmaking service that helps entrepreneurs find investment funds, and as an advisor to start-up firms. He has written many articles about entrepreneurial finance, and he recently received the Academy of Management's prestigious Heizer Award for the best dissertation in the field of entrepreneurship, as well as the Taylor & Francis Publishers Prize for venture capital research.

*Robert J. Robinson* is an associate professor at the Harvard Business School and a faculty member of the Harvard Program on Negotiation (PON). He earned his B.A. (1984) and M.A. (1987) degrees in organizational psychology from the University of Cape Town and his Ph.D. (1991) in social psychology from Stanford University.

Robinson teaches a required first year M.B.A. course called Negotiation, and a second-year M.B.A. elective, Entrepreneurial Negotiations, that covers important issues entrepreneurs need to consider in negotiating with business angels, venture capitalists, and other investors. He has served as codirector of the PON project on psychological processes in negotiation; authored numerous academic and business articles in the fields of social cognition, negotiation, conflict analysis, ethics, entrepreneurship, and venture capital; and has been awarded several international academic writing prizes, including prizes for best paper from the Academy of Management and the International Association of Conflict Management (the latter twice).

Robinson is currently heading an active applied-research program on issues of negotiation and conflict, with particular emphasis on high-tech start-up companies and their entrepreneurial negotiations. This runs the gamut from negotiating with potential partners for equity, to negotiations with venture capital firms, and selling or taking the company public.

In addition to his academic work, Robinson has been a successful entrepreneur, a business angel investor in two start-up ventures, and a consultant for numerous entrepreneurial ventures large and small. A number of these consultant interactions have been chronicled in Harvard Business School case studies, which he uses as teaching tools in his classes.

# Angel Investing

# Part One

# Financing Options for Start-up Firms

# Chapter One

# Funding Entrepreneurial Firms

We begin with a tale of two entrepreneurs and their angels. The names and identifying circumstances are disguised or otherwise altered.

In 1998, Jeff Shaw, twenty-eight and a recent graduate of Harvard Business School, started a business recycling used computers. By the time he had completed a business plan, recruited his immediate team, contracted with the necessary vendors, and made contact with potential customers, he was $100,000 in debt. He had also taken close to $50,000 from his parents, and another $35,000 from classmates. Jeff was in a classic funding bind. Having exhausted the "three Fs" (founders, family, and friends) as sources of cash, he needed about $300,000 to get his company rolling. Fortunately, one of his professors introduced him to Andy Bell, a wealthy investor in the Boston area. After reviewing Jeff's plan, the two structured a deal whereby Andy took 30 percent of Jeff's business in exchange for $200,000 in cash, and a credit line of another $150,000. Today Jeff is doing well; he projects a net profit of $1.5 million for financial year 2000.

Also in 1998, Freddy LeBeque, forty-two and a caterer in New Orleans, decided to start a high-end chain of dessert and coffee shops, beginning with one shop but with plans to expand to a dozen within three years. Despite decades of experience in the food industry, Freddy lacked financing for his new enterprise. Recognizing that he needed help, he approached a local small-business incubator, where he was put in touch with a matching service that helped him advertise his project to potential investors. One such individual was Ryan Davis, a retired orthodontist in Boise, Idaho. Ryan was looking for an investment that was more interesting and personal than the mutual fund market. One of several people to invest in Freddy's Café Crème restaurants, Ryan invested $35,000 for about 1.8 percent of the equity of the new enterprise. Thus far the chain has opened three stores and is breaking even financially.

Both these stories are celebrations of the informal venture capital market, and in particular the role of Andy Bell and Ryan Davis—two very different people, but both of them business angels. Andy is an experienced investor with a net worth of a few million dollars; as we shall discuss, he fits the traditional definition of a business angel. Ryan has less net worth and was making his first investment of this sort, motivated as much by the romance of New Orleans and the food industry as by any hard business analysis. This book shows that Ryan represents a growing phenomenon in the U.S. economy: an upper-middle-class individual (rather than a member of the very rich) looking to invest directly in start-ups rather than just in the stock or mutual fund markets. We examine angels running the gamut from Andy to Ryan as well as entrepreneurs like Jeff Shaw and Freddy LeBeque; the deals that are struck between these two sides; and the relationship between entrepreneurs, angels, and the more formal venture capital market.

Today, we stand at the brink of an explosion in entrepreneurship. Business angels such as Andy and Ryan have been one of the most important catalysts in this change, and their influence continues to escalate. These private investors have usually started their own successful firms in the past and are now looking to invest some of their money and experience in small entrepreneurial ventures. They do this in the hope of financial returns, but also for the fun of being involved again in the entrepreneurial process. This type of investor was originally referred to as "Aunt Agatha" and "the rich uncle" (Mason and Harrison, 1990) but is now commonly called a *business angel* because many perceive that they save struggling firms with both finance and know-how when no one else will. In fact, the term *angel* was originally coined at the turn of the century to describe the wealthy backers of Broadway shows who made risky investments in those productions (Benjamin and Margulis, 1996).

In recent years, we have witnessed an extraordinary phenomenon in the marketplace. Venture capitalists get all the press, but the vast majority of entrepreneurial firms are actually funded by business angels, especially those firms in their earliest stages. A good analogy might be to equate this to looking at a forest of trees and—though we realize that only a small percentage of seedlings make it to maturity—acknowledging just those trees that are over six feet high and growing. This shows little concern for the seedlings and the germination process. In our real-life forest of entrepreneurial firms, it is the business angels who are the gardeners caring for the seedlings. In fact, few know that U.S. business angels collectively invest more money, in more entrepreneurial firms, than any other investor type. *Business angels fund thirty to forty times more ventures each year than venture capitalists,* their better-known counterparts. Undeniably, business angel funds are the oldest, largest, and most frequently used source of external equity for entrepreneurial firms. Unfortunately, this is a story not well told (even though well understood and acknowledged by those in the venture capital industry).

In this book, we show that

- Business angels are the most important means by which entrepreneurial firms get outside funds.
- The entrepreneurial environment is exploding, especially in the United States, and the number of investors needed to support this growth is dramatically increasing.
- The number of potential business angel investors is at an all-time high, spanning the very rich and the upper-middle class, and rapidly expanding.

As fascinating a concept as the business angel is, it exists within the context of the economy. Business angel investors, such as Andy and Ryan, are the focus of this book, but we also discuss the environment around them. Here are the main segments of the environment that we deal with, as they correspond to the seven parts of this book:

1. Financing options in the entrepreneurial landscape
2. Comparison of business angels and venture capitalists

3. The differences between them throughout the investment process
4. Attracting business angel funds to your start-up firm
5. Becoming a successful business angel investor
6. The future of the business angel market
7. Putting the wheels in motion: valuable resources for entrepreneurs and investors

To make this the most comprehensive and helpful book to date on business angels and securing finance for growing entrepreneurial firms, these sections expand upon the book's four main themes, as shown in Figure 1.1.

## This Book and the Entrepreneur's Funding Problem

For entrepreneurs, it is crucial to gain the most comprehensive information about their various funding options as they attempt to start and grow their ventures. From internal funding options that they can employ initially without external assistance to the types of outside investors most willing to offer funds, entrepreneurs should learn how to most effectively lure the financial investors they so desperately need. This involves knowing how business angels and venture capitalists compare across their full investment processes, from what motivates them to invest (and the criteria they use) to how they structure deals and help firms grow. This book gives entrepreneurs everything they need to know to locate and secure such investors for their firms.

## This Book and the Angel Investor

Investors with an appetite for getting involved in growing entrepreneurial firms—either to complement their existing stock portfolio or to satisfy their entrepreneurial ambitions—should also understand how to invest their money most effectively and learn how the professionals do it. For many others, business angel investing is a suitable, and potentially very profitable, investment option that they should consider. As we shall discuss, there are literally millions of Americans who are potential business angels but may not yet have considered making an angel investment. We

**Figure 1.1. The Four Main Themes of This Book.**

## Players in Our Entrepreneurial Economy

*Chapters 1–6*

- An overview of our new "entrepreneurial age" and its rewards
- A summary of the many financing options available to entrepreneurs
- The vital role played by business angels and venture capitalists
- The two most important financial supporters of entrepreneurial firms today
- Steps entrepreneurs need to take to tap into the $50 billion invested annually by private investors

## How Investors Really Invest in Growth Ventures

*Chapters 7–11*

- First-time insights on how business angels and venture capitalists make investments
- A unique review of every stage of investors' investment processes, from finding to successfully exiting deals
- Important insights on each investment stage particularly vital to entrepreneurs hoping to court investors, and to investors wishing to make better entrepreneurial investments

## Practical Advice for Securing and Investing Funds

*Chapters 12–15*

- Important practical step-by-step advice for entrepreneurs hoping to attract outside investors
- The steps wealthy individuals should follow to help them make their first investment in an entrepreneurial firm
- Negotiation and valuation methods to follow with entrepreneurial ventures
- Taking advantage of opportunities in the changing angel marketplace

## Resources to Help Make and Find Investments

*Appendixes 1–3*

- Resources to help turn knowledge into entrepreneurial action
- The first-ever listing of U.S. matching services that entrepreneurs can use to find investors, and investors can employ to locate investment opportunities
- Appendix two lists countless organizations, literature, and websites for finding funds, advice, and investment deals
- Appendix three details how to write a winning business plan

hope to encourage some of those people to join the active angels already making an important difference in our marketplace.

## This Book and Participation in the Entrepreneurial Dream

There is currently much confusion in our entrepreneurial marketplace about business angels, and little is known about how they operate, especially compared to venture capitalists. This book dispels myths and presents well-researched facts that every entrepreneur and investor should know about the most important financial supporters of entrepreneurial firms today. In fact, in today's high-tech environment of day trading of stocks on the Internet, it seems as if there are too many people with lots of money to invest chasing too few opportunities. Any rational investor would have difficulty explaining the overinflated prices of many Internet stocks—with such start-ups as eBay, for instance, realizing market capitalization many times that of Wal-Mart, which was one of the most respected and profitable firms in quite recent years! Rather than investing exclusively in such Internet "lottery tickets," investing a small proportion of your wealth in a start-up or early-stage entrepreneurial firm located in your neighborhood may be a more stable and sustainable way to invest. Instead of your investment relying on market-driven hysteria, private investors in local entrepreneurial firms can use their own skills to make the investment profitable. As this book shows, such business angel deals have a number of advantages that should make them a valid investment option for many:

- Business angel investments are a good hedge against fluctuations in the stock market.
- Investors do not pay astronomical prices to invest in entrepreneurial firms.
- Investors can leverage their previous experience by funding and helping firms in areas they know quite a bit about, and thereby actually make a difference directly.

The popularity of business angel investing has increased dramatically over the last decade and is expected to become even more pervasive over the next few years as our growing entrepreneurial economy continues to have an increasingly significant effect on our daily lives, offering investors more and more profitable investment opportunities.

## Clarifying Common Misconceptions

Throughout this book, we set the record straight on a number of common misconceptions about our entrepreneurial economy. Most of them were first clarified by Bill Wetzel, a pioneer in the business angel field, in testimony before the Congressional House Banking Committee in 1993, although —according to his colleague, Jeffrey Sohl—they still hold true today (Sohl, 1999).

### Misconception One: Jobs Are Created Primarily by Fortune 500 Companies

The truth: most new jobs are created by a small percentage of firms growing at a rate of at least 20 percent per year, the so-called *entrepreneurial firms*. Since 1979, more than 75 percent of net new jobs have been created by around 8 percent of small businesses. These firms are started and driven by true entrepreneurs, not small businessmen or businesswomen.

### Misconception Two: Access to Credit Is the Major Financial Obstacle to Job Creation

The truth: access to equity capital, not credit, is the major financial obstacle to job creation. The business history of the United States is the history of equity financing. Entrepreneurial firms, especially those in their earliest stages, need high-risk, patient, value-added equity financing to supplement internal cash flows. U.S. entrepreneurs face an annual equity financial shortfall of more than $45 billion. This is our nation's real capital formation challenge.

(*continued*)

## Misconception Three: Venture Capital Comes from the Venture Capital Funds Listed in *Pratt's Guide to Venture Capital Sources*

The truth: business angels, rather than formal venture capitalists, make the most venture capital–style investments to young entrepreneurial firms. Business angels—the invisible segment of the venture capital markets—fund thirty to forty times as many entrepreneurial ventures as do venture capitalists, the market's visible segment. Angels tend to play complementary roles in financing young firms, since they support those start-up firms that later become candidates for formal venture capital.

## Misconception Four: Private Investors (Business Angels) Invest in Small Businesses

The truth: business angels usually back only entrepreneurial firms—those ventures offering the prospect of long-term capital gains sizable enough to offset the short-term risks and illiquidity. Classic small businesses with annual growth rates projected below 20 percent are of little interest to outside investors.

## Misconception Five: All Venture Investors Are Equally Venturesome

The truth: business angels are the real venture capitalists since they bankroll entrepreneurial ventures in their earliest stages, when the risks are the greatest. Early-stage deals receive around 60–70 percent of angel funds invested, but only around 28 percent of venture capital invested.

## Misconception Six: Limited Access to Credit Is the Most Serious Financial Obstacle Confronting High-Growth Established Firms

The truth: limited access to equity capital is the most serious problem. For high-growth ventures, credit constraints usually are due to an inadequate capital base. Profitable firms growing in excess of 20 percent annually are typically unable to sustain growth with retained earnings and cash flow; the more rapid their growth, the more severe their equity and cash problems.

## Misconception Seven: Capital Gains Taxes Are a Tax on the Wealthy

The truth: capital gains taxes are a tax on *creation* of wealth. They are a tax on America's real competitive edge: creative risk taking, the creation of jobs, innovation, and new technology-based ventures. Reducing the tax on capital gains—which are the investor's reward for risk taking—should increase the availability of equity financing for our nation's entrepreneurs.

## Our New Entrepreneurial Economy

The United States is increasingly an entrepreneurial nation, in which the economy and jobs are significantly more dependent on the initiatives of the nation's entrepreneurs than on corporate titans. The beginnings of this transformation to a true land of entrepreneurs was evident by about 1979, when the U.S. economy formally passed a milestone of great importance: the shift from a decaying industrial and manufacturing economy composed of large firms to an entrepreneurial economy driven by information and innovative technology (Freear, Sohl, and Wetzel, 1996):

First of all, Fortune 500 companies lost more than four million jobs between 1979 and 1995, but more than twenty-four million jobs were created by the entrepreneurial economy as the total number of businesses skyrocketed by 200 percent (Freear, Sohl, and Wetzel, 1996; Dennis, 1997; Sohl, 1999). When compared to the 17 percent increase in its population over that same time period, the United States is clearly becoming more entrepreneurial (SBSC, 1998). Today, 6.8 million U.S. households (or 7.2 percent of the country's total) include someone who is currently trying to start a business; in any given year, small businesses create anywhere from 66 percent to 100 percent of net new jobs, as large firms shed employees (Usem, 1997; SBSC, 1999). In 1997, new business incorporations in this country hit a record 798,917, which may shed light on a new estimate from the Small Business Administration (SBA) that small businesses now account for 51 percent of private sector output.

Second, innovative and high-growth entrepreneurial firms have been viewed well by public equity markets in the United States (Sohl, 1999). The volume of shares traded on the NASDAQ market in 1979 was less than half that of the NYSE. In 1994 the share volume of NASDAQ overtook that of the NYSE for the first time, and this trend has continued since (Sohl, 1999).

Third, the primary source of wealth for the richest Americans has shifted with the evolution of the entrepreneurial economy. Today, many first-generation entrepreneurs are among the wealthy elite (Sohl, 1999). With such potential for generating jobs, economic growth, and wealth, it is not surprising that greater attention has been paid to small entrepreneurial firms in recent years. A similar shift has also been witnessed in a number of European countries, especially the UK, where it is now accepted government policy that the small-firm sector should constitute the main vehicle for recovery from recessions and be the main provider of jobs for many years to come (Deakins, 1996).

Entrepreneurship is a hot topic these days, with more people than ever trying their hand at this particular brand of free-market capitalism. Entrepreneurial optimism has prevailed, playing a significant part in the explosion of the Dow Jones industrial average—an increase of more than 1,100 percent in nominal terms since 1982—the annual increase in the economy of 3.2 percent, the annual expansion in corporate profits of 6 percent, and the drop in unemployment from 11 percent to 4.4 percent (Kudlow, 1999). Household wealth has also increased, up roughly $25.7 trillion in these years of economic expansion, giving more people than ever before the means to become business angels.

Along with a sharp reduction in interest rates, the increase in wealth has further revived the risk taking and entrepreneurship that is so vital to our economy (Kudlow, 1999). The chief economist of the Small Business Survival Committee recently stated that "entrepreneurs and investors continue to take risks that drive our economy forward. Innovation runs at a rapid clip, as we continue to live amidst perhaps the greatest economic revolution in the history of mankind" (Keating, 1999). Not surprisingly, a recent Ernst and Young survey of leading Americans concluded that entrepreneurship will emerge as the defining trend of the business world in the twenty-first century ("Next Millennium . . .," 1998). Just as the nineteenth century is associated with the industrial age and the twentieth century with the corporate age, the twenty-first century may very well be remembered as the entrepreneurial age. It appears that the entrepreneur is slowly replacing the corporate leader as business hero; the dream of the past—to own one's own home—has been replaced by the desire to own one's own business (Sohl, 1999).

Driving this growth in entrepreneurship are new technology, a favorable economic climate, social conditions (the rise of two-income families), the advent of the global economy, government deregulation, and the inability of many larger companies to innovate ("Next Millennium . . .," 1998). But in addition to such incentives as lower taxes, less bureaucracy, and more flexibility, one of the greatest constraints against company formation may be related less to success and more to failure: a nation's bankruptcy laws (Surlemont, Leleux, and Denis, 1999). In this respect, the United States offers some of the most effective personal bankruptcy laws in the world as well as consistent implementation systems. In American society, it is certainly better to have tried and lost than not to have tried at all. There is little social shame in failure; unlike many other countries, bankruptcy in the United States is not a permanent scar on an entrepreneur's professional career.

This lessening of risk is also partly responsible for the tremendous increase in entrepreneurship that America has witnessed over the last few decades. In European countries, there is a recent trend to revamp bankruptcy legislation to promote entrepreneurship as well. However, despite the lavish praise our legislators in Congress give to small firms, only one U.S. senator and just fifteen members of the House scored a perfect 100 percent voting record on small-business support in the 105th Congress (SBSC, 1999). With continued downsizing, advances in technology, and the global marketplace, the small-business agenda will increasingly dominate policy debates on Capital Hill and in state capitals, as entrepreneurship is further acknowledged to be the foundation for our future growth. As the chief financial and hands-on supporters of entrepreneurship today already, business angels can only become more important to our nation's well-being in the future.

## The Rewards of Entrepreneurship

For most entrepreneurs, entrepreneurship is a means to financial wealth, and the fun of getting there. The fact that of the richest 1 percent of Americans more than nine in ten are entrepreneurs who made their fortunes themselves, rather than through inheritance, motivates many others to flex their entrepreneurial muscles (Weicher, 1997). In fact, the percentage of millionaires in the U.S. population has tripled over the last decade; around three-quarters of those on the Forbes 400 Richest People list are self-made, and more than half have at least a billion dollars each ("The First Billion . . .," 1999). Such entrepreneurial wealth is to be found not only in the United States but also in the UK, for instance, where the majority of the four hundred wealthiest individuals are also self-made.

Even historically, the richest Americans have been entrepreneurs, from John D. Rockefeller in the late 1800s (whose wealth was 1.54 percent of the economy) to Bill Gates today (with wealth of 0.58 percent of the economy; "Richest Americans . . .," 1998). Yet such rankings should serve more as a source of inspiration for new entrepreneurs than as reality. Although many try, only a very few actually become successful entrepreneurs able to amass a fortune worth more than a million dollars. As a better measure of reality, the average self-employed entrepreneur in the United States earns only around $24,000 per year, and only 5 percent earn more than $100,000 (SBSC, 1999).

## The Internet Revolution

In today's Internet age, the rules of amassing wealth have been changing. It used to take decades for the lucky few to acquire a billion-dollar fortune, but today with the right Internet company it can take only a few years—or months ("The First Billion . . .,"

1999). Very recent winners on the Internet wealth bandwagon who have earned billions in a matter of a few years are eBay founder Pierre Omidyar ($6.7 billion), Yahoo founders Jerry Yang and David Filo ($4 billion each), Amazon.com founder Jeffrey Bezos ($8.9 billion), and Broadcom founder Henry Nicholas ($2.7 billion) ("The First Billion . . .," 1999). In fact, in terms of how many "millions of dollars per hour" during 1999, Bill Gates made 5.4 "mph," Jeffrey Bezos 0.9 mph, and Michael Dell 0.8 mph ("The First Billion . . .," 1999)!

But even young and junior employees of many Internet firms are leaving as multimillionaires before they turn thirty, especially with Internet-related initial public offerings (IPOs) gaining an average of 242 percent last year, while the average non-Internet-related counterpart actually finished the year below its first-day close (Sareen, 1999). The Forbes 500 list of the five hundred largest U.S. corporations in 1998 now has sixty technology and telecommunications-related firms, up from only three in 1969, and many more are expected in the next few years (Malik, 1999b). Understandably, thanks to the Internet's winning theme on Wall Street, venture capitalists, business angels, and large corporations have taken much interest in this area of investment.

The importance of the Internet is not just its ease of communication; there is its vast scale. With more than 58 percent of Americans already online and many more joining the ranks daily (Malik, 1999a), the reach of the Internet looks certain to expand much further. From 1995 to 1998, the Internet economy grew 174.5 percent, compared with worldwide economic growth of 3.8 percent and the increase in the U.S. GDP of 2.8 percent during that same period. In the United States, this economy generated around $301.4 billion in revenue in 1998, of which a third came from electronic commerce ("Internet Economy Surges . . .," 1999). Not surprisingly with such opportunities, 56 percent of the first-round capital funds invested by the venture capital industry in 1998 and 54 percent of the firms receiving first-time funds were in information technology and Internet-related areas (NVCA, 1999). Only 28 percent of these funds went to early-stage Internet companies, while 66 percent was received by expansion-stage firms.

With such wealth creation in the wake of the frenzy of Internet start-ups, the number of new "dot com" firms born in the last few

years has been startling. In the last five years, the number of software companies in the Boston area alone has more than tripled
(Blanton,1998). M.B.A. students here at the Harvard Business
School have also been caught up in this entrepreneurial trend. In
the class of 1999, 343 of the 880 graduates (or 39 percent) say they
plan to either launch or join high-tech start-up firms, or join the
venture capital firms that support them, to cash in on the Internet
boom (Wilmsen, 1999b). This is triple the number of four years
ago, while the number of graduates seeking consulting or Wall
Street jobs has dropped by nearly half.

One role model for this year's Harvard graduates is a very recent alumnus, Stig Leschley, who started an online seller of used
books, Exchange.com, and sold it seven months later to Amazon
.com for $200 million. Such stories are sparking interest nation-
wide. In five other top business schools, ranging from Kellogg to
Wharton, student enrollment in entrepreneurship classes has increased 92 percent over the last three years (from a total of 3,078
to 5,913) as the number of entrepreneurship classes offered by
these schools increased 74 percent (Foote, 1999).

With so many new M.B.A. graduates and other technology-
loving entrepreneurs seeking funds to jump-start their entrepreneurial dreams of riches and business success, business angels will
have even greater economic impact than ever before. They currently fund about 60 percent of those new technology firms seeking $1 million or less in start-up capital (Chan, 1999), making this
book an invaluable source of guidance for the new generation of
Internet entrepreneurs.

## Succeeding with Limited Funding Options

The struggle to grow an idea into a smoothly operating entrepreneurial entity is not for those who lack courage and the conviction
of their ideals. Many people try each year, but only a small minority succeeds in the long run, and even fewer realize vast wealth by
becoming publicly traded entities. Such are the perils and hurdles
of entrepreneurship; the risks as well as the rewards are high. Although luck naturally has some say in the outcomes, perseverance
and making smart moves are key ingredients. Yet even with these
contributing factors, entrepreneurial dreams often come to an end

for want of the thousands (if not millions) of dollars each needs as fuel to run and propel itself forward. Unfortunately, as we discuss in the next few chapters, funding sources (even for Internet firms) are limited, and every entrepreneur needs to be aware of how best to exploit the available options. This broadens his or her ability (and chances) to secure financial backing under the right conditions. But doing so also requires awareness of the role that the small firms and the entrepreneurial economy play in our lives, and knowing how to distinguish among the types of small firm.

## The Role of Small Firms

It is easy to wonder: Why should we really focus so much attention on small firms? What, in particular, do they really offer us, beyond rewards for their founders? In truth, there are actually five types of economic benefit produced by small businesses that are especially noteworthy: innovation, employment, a shock-absorber role in declining sectors, increased competition, and flexible specialization.

First, small firms produce many important innovations vital to economic growth. Out of sixty-one important U.S. inventions and innovations this century, more than half came from small firms and independent investors (Wetzel, 1982b). Small firms (those with fewer than one thousand employees) also produce twenty-four times as many innovations per dollar of research and development (R&D) spending as do large firms (more than ten thousand employees), and four times more than medium-sized firms (Wetzel, 1982b). Indeed, innovation and its diffusion were estimated by the 1989 Economic Report of the President (cited in Wetzel and Freear, 1994) to have accounted for half the historical increase in the U.S. standard of living! The innovation process clearly has many social benefits, such as technology spin-off and increased tax revenues (Freear and Wetzel, 1991; Tewksbury, Crandall, and Crane, 1980).

Second, small firms are also beneficial as effective means of reducing unemployment and fostering job creation. While large and medium-sized firms were decreasing their payrolls by more than 25 percent and 5 percent respectively between 1979 and 1993, small firms created twenty million new jobs (Huey, 1994; Hale,

1992; Freear, Sohl, and Wetzel, 1995a), twelve million alone in the 1980s (Eglin, 1994). Most of the new jobs attributed to small firms are actually created by the minority of companies that are the fastest-growing (as we will see in the next section). Some may argue that the static share of employment in small and medium-sized firms has remained close to 50 percent, but this is misleading since some small firms grow into large firms, and some large firms decline into small ones. This only demonstrates that small firms have great job creating power (Acs and Phillips, 1997). In particular, U.S. small firms have dominated job creation in about 40 percent of growing industries, and almost 80 percent of the 2.6 million new jobs in the computer programming, restaurant, and social service sectors (Acs and Phillips, 1997). In fact, Acs and Phillips (1997) conclude that "it is highly likely that small firms and entrepreneurs probably employ a much larger share of the U.S. labor force than is commonly believed" (p. 9). Indeed, in its first year the average new firm creates six jobs (including two for the founders), and by the time they reach the end of their working lives about two-fifths of the workforce will have had at least one spell of self-employment (Reynolds and White, 1997).

Third, small firms play the shock-absorber role of job creation, since they create jobs in declining industries where most of the lost jobs are terminations by large firms (Acs and Phillips, 1997). Certainly, with the high number of corporate layoffs in the 1980s, many of those former corporate employees founded their own niche ventures (often in the same industry) or joined other small firms already in the field. Furthermore, when large firms lay off internal employees, more work has to be outsourced, often to small businesses. If the economy grows, these small firms flourish, and if the economy is weak, it is easier for them to attract new employees and to reinvent themselves.

Fourth, small firms often complement large firms in an industry, thereby increasing competition that may also make the economy more competitive (Mitchell, 1980). With many small firms, there may be less inclination to collude and accept restrictive practices, which often erode competition in industry sectors where only a few large firms operate.

Fifth, small firms are of increased importance because of their ability to quickly respond to change ("flexible specialization") in market conditions. With increased globalization and increased competition thanks to advancing technology, it is possible that the structure of the economy has changed in favor of these small and flexible firms.

Clearly, the economic benefits of small businesses are well documented, especially in comparison to large firms. A leading academic even concluded that, "relative to their larger, established counterparts, small technology based firms are more effective contributors to the generation of new jobs, innovative technology, productivity, price stability and favorable international trade balances" (Wetzel, 1982b, p. 336).

The economic potential and power of entrepreneurship was even clearer on a smaller scale in a BankBoston study analyzing the worldwide impact of graduates and faculty of the Massachusetts Institute of Technology (MIT). It revealed that, since 1994, MIT alumni founded four thousand companies, which employed 1.1 million people and had $232 billion in world sales. If these MIT-related firms constituted a separate country, its national economy would rank twenty-fourth in the world (*International Herald Tribune,* 1997)!

## The Stages of Firm Development

Of course, small firms come in many sizes and stages of development:

*Seed stage:* the entrepreneur has only a concept for a potentially profitable business opportunity that still has to be developed and proven.

*Start-up stage:* the newly formed business is completing product development and initial marketing. It is typically one year old or younger.

*Early stage:* the firm is usually expanding, and producing and delivering products or services. Often less than five years old, it may not yet be profitable.

*Later stage:* also called the expansion stage, at this level of development the firm is mature and profitable, and often still expanding. With a continued high-growth rate, it may go public within six months to a year.

(Source: partially adapted from Sohl, 1999)

## Growth Categories of Small Firms

Since small firms vary in management structure, legal form, ro-
bustness, and sophistication, they are clearly diverse. Rather than
categorizing small firms by their size or stage of development, one
of the best ways to distinguish the types is by growth potential
(Wetzel and Freear, 1994). In fact, there are three general types of
small firm every entrepreneur and investor should be familiar
with: lifestyle, middle-market, and high-potential ventures (Bygrave, 1994; Wetzel and Freear, 1994; Sohl, 1999). The last two are
considered entrepreneurial firms.

*Lifestyle firms* are those ventures that provide only a reasonable
living for their founders, rather than incurring the risks that come
with prospects of high growth. Constituting more than 90 percent
of all start-ups, it is unlikely that these firms will attract equity
funding from external parties; instead they have to rely on internal funds (Wetzel and Freear, 1994). These ventures have five-
year revenue projections under $10 million and are the classic
small business (Sohl, 1999). Unfortunately, the "bonsai syndrome"
is much too common with small firms, since many show no willingness to grow over the next few years.

*Middle-market firms* have growth prospects of more than 20 percent annually and five-year revenue projections between $10 and
$50 million. These firms are attractive to business angel investors,
but they also depend heavily on bootstrapping to fund initial
growth (Wetzel and Freear, 1994, Sohl, 1999). As we see in the
next chapter, bootstrapping is a form of finance involving internal
generation of funds through using personal savings, credit cards,
second mortgages, customer advances, and vendor credit (Freear,
Sohl, and Wetzel, 1995b; Winborg and Landstrom, 1997). These
firms are the backbone of the U.S. economy.

*High-potential firms* are those with a vision for growth that are
also innovative, risk-taking, and able to change (Wetzel, 1993;
Freear, Sohl, and Wetzel, 1994a). They typically plan to grow into
a substantial firm with fifty or more employees within five to ten
years, have five-year revenue projections in excess of $50 million,
and anticipate annual growth rates in excess of 50 percent (Sohl,
1999). These "big-time-winning" firms are often the primary re-
cipients of a couple of rounds of external equity finance, early on
from business angels and later from venture capitalists (Wetzel

and Freear, 1994). Making up less than 1 percent of all start-ups, these firms are among the Microsofts, Disneys, Blockbuster Videos, and Dell Computers of the next millennium.

The last two growth categories offer the greatest economic contribution of all the firm types; one economist even observed that "our country's ace in the hole is our ability to spawn a lot of high growth, entrepreneurial firms" (Freear, Sohl, and Wetzel, 1996, p. 1). This book chronicles the financing of entrepreneurial firms—those that are either middle-market or high-potential ventures, as Figure 1.2 clarifies—since these are the only company types with the growth potential to be able to attract the funding interest of angels, and some even of venture capitalists.

## The Economic Importance of Entrepreneurial Firms

Small entrepreneurial firms are those with the opportunity to have a significant impact on our lives and to reshape our industries as we know them. Even though these high-flying firms have the greatest ability, through their rapid growth, to generate jobs and high returns for potential investors, it is important to remember that only a minority of small firms can grow into large ones.

**Figure 1.2.  The Three Types of Start-up Firms**

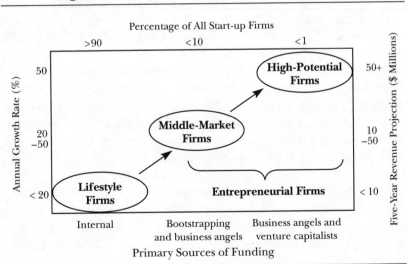

However, this small minority of growth firms is much more important than their numbers suggest. It is these ventures that most represent the dynamism and potential for innovation claimed for small business in general. They create jobs and help to keep fixed capital going. These dynamic small firms can show rates of growth that large firms can match only by resorting to acquisitions and mergers (Mitchell, 1980).

Entrepreneurial firms represent fewer than 10 percent of the one million start-ups in the United States per year (Wetzel and Freear, 1994). Since 1979, these job-generating firms have represented only about 4–8 percent of all small businesses but have accounted for 70–75 percent of net new jobs (Wetzel, 1993, 1996; Birch, Haggerty, Parsons, and Rossel, 1993). In particular, one-fifth of this small minority of high growth firms are responsible for about half of all jobs generated by autonomous new firms (Reynolds and White, 1997).The true engine of job growth is the Inc. 500 of the nation, not the Fortune 500; over the last four years, these high-growth start-up firms were responsible for adding 6 million of the total 7.7 million jobs that were created in the economy (Sohl, 1999). Similarly in the UK, it is the 4 percent of all start-ups (with, naturally, the highest growth) that will generate 50 percent of employment out of all surviving firms in ten years' time (Storey, 1994).

When we think about starting a successful firm, these are the types that we hope ours will become. They are the firms that make their founders multimillionaires within a matter of years. They are the same entrepreneurial dreams that the Michael Dells, Steve Jobses, and Bill Gateses of this world started only a decade or two ago. Since most of us would like our firms to become entrepreneurial firms of success, this book is dedicated to explaining in detail how best to finance the growth of such ventures. Bootstrapping—funding growth internally using credit cards and so on—is a good way to further the power of the founders' own cash infusion into the firm (as we see in the next chapter), but it often does not generate enough finance to support rapid growth. The best means of obtaining this necessary financing early on may be by courting private investors (business angels) since they fund more money to more young entrepreneurial firms than any other type of fund provider, while venture capital funds may be more appropriate later on.

# Chapter Two

# Bootstrapping Internally and the Challenges to Securing Outside Finance

Funding is particularly critical to the success of a start-up firm, although ironically it is at this early stage that funding options are most limited because of the high risks involved. Business angels specialize in supporting a significant proportion of such young firms (as we see in Chapter Three), but especially in comparison to the venture capital industry most firms are not so fortunate as to attract outside equity capital at the outset; they have no option but to rely primarily on personal savings and bootstrapping to survive and grow initially. In fact, bootstrapping is the most likely source of initial equity for 94 percent of new technology-based firms (Freear, Sohl, and Wetzel, 1991); it was initially used by more than 80 percent of the five hundred fastest-growing privately held entrepreneurial firms in the United States (Bhide, 1992).

In part, venture capitalists are rarely able to fund small start-up firms seeking less than $5 million, regardless of the quality of the venture, because of their very specific investment criteria and high costs of due diligence, negotiating, and monitoring. Bootstrapping offers many advantages for entrepreneurs and is probably the best method to get an entrepreneurial firm operating and well positioned to seek equity capital from outside investors at a later time. For this reason, it is worth examining the strategies of bootstrapping, before turning specifically to matters relating to angel investors and venture capitalists.

## Bootstrapping

In a word, bootstrapping is a means of financing a small firm through highly creative acquisition and use of resources without raising equity from traditional sources or borrowing money from a bank (Freear, Sohl, and Wetzel, 1995b). This entails both reduction in expenses and acquisition of capital (Sohl, 1999). It is characterized by high reliance on any internally generated retained earnings, credit cards, second mortgages, and customer advances, to name but a few sources. The methods of bootstrapping are diverse and difficult to identify, which explains why not enough has been written about this important internal approach to financing (Freear, Sohl, and Wetzel, 1995b). Bootstrapping should not always be considered mutually exclusive with outside equity funding, but as a means to getting such outside funds at a later time.

### Benefits and Disadvantages of Bootstrapping

If effectively used, bootstrapping can present entrepreneurs with a wealth of new and alternative options to grow their firms while lessening or postponing the need for large cash infusions. Since "entrepreneurial firms" are really the main contenders for the business angel, and especially the venture capitalist, most young firms have to rely on personal savings and bootstrapping to survive. Even entrepreneurial firms sometimes opt to rely on bootstrapping first (and outside investors later), because of its advantages:

• Waiting as long as possible to seek equity financing postpones the entrepreneur's surrendering a significant share portion of his or her equity stake. This permits getting financial assistance on better terms and retaining more of the final fruits of hard work.
• By waiting until the firm is more developed, entrepreneurs have greater authority and overall control to subdue investor pressure, as opposed to having investors monitoring the firm from early on and compromising the entrepreneur's flexibility to make alterations (Bhide, 1992).
• Deciding from day one to bootstrap the initial growth of a firm enables the entrepreneurs to allocate all their time and re-

sources to growing the firm, rather than spending many hours and much money in an often futile attempt to court potential investors. The biggest challenge may not be raising money "but having the wits and hustle to do without it" (Bhide, 1992, p. 110). Although the odds of getting angel finance are quite healthy, the chances of getting a venture capitalist's interest, let alone investment, are very slim. Recognizing this early on can save the entrepreneur valuable time and energy.

• It is also possible to experience problems associated with raising too much money (Bhide, 1992). Since venture capitalists prefer to make a small number of large investments, rather than overseeing many small ones, raising $5 million is often easier than raising just a fraction of that. However, if a firm only needs $1 million, for instance, this means that the recipient firm is left with $4 million that it doesn't truly need and has to figure out how to spend anyway (Bhide, 1992). Although this may seem like a welcome problem, entrepreneurs in such a position often spend the money freely, without creating much additional value for the firm. This can instill an underlying sentiment in the firm that more money is perpetually needed, rather than encouraging analysis of the firm's operations and determining how existing money can be spent wisely.

• Hidden problems can be revealed. As Bhide (1992) eloquently states it, "bootstrapping in a start-up is like zero inventory in a just-in-time system: it reveals hidden problems and forces the company to solve them" (p. 112). Taking such a careful and well-disciplined approach early on can increase the chances of a start-up firm's success in the years to come; it certainly increases attractiveness to outside investors.

The main disadvantage of using bootstrapping in a start-up or early-stage firm is clearly that it may not generate enough money to grow the firm at the desired rate. This can result in the firm competing poorly against its financially endowed competitors, limiting potential grasp on sales, market share, and overall competitive position within its target market. Although bootstrapping is a very effective means of financing the inception and early development of a firm, it may offer only limited support for high-growth prospects, which are what increase the firm's valuation, make it a potential candidate for a stock market listing, and ensure that the entrepreneurs (and investors) are in the end compensated generously for their efforts. This is clearly why business angels are often such an attractive funding option for fast-growing entrepreneurial firms—a source that many can not do without.

## Bootstrapping Methods

We divide the many bootstrapping options available to entrepreneurs into four categories (Freear, Sohl, and Wetzel, 1995b; Winborg and Landstrom, 1997), depending on their suitability for (1) product development, (2) business development, (3) minimization of capital needed, and (4) meeting the need for capital. Of course, the bootstrapping methods have various levels of value potential and applicability for each individual entrepreneur.

## Bootstrapping Options for Product Development

Developing the entrepreneurial firm's specific product can make or break a young venture, depending on the level of acceptance by the target consumer. Freear, Sohl, and Wetzel (1995b) identified a number of effective bootstrapping methods. Most of these involve using existing relationships with customers and suppliers effectively to make ends meet and roll out the product:

*Important Bootstrapping Techniques for Product Development*

- Prepaid licenses, royalties, or advances from customers
- Special deals on access to product hardware
- Development of product at night and on weekends while working elsewhere
- Customer-funded research and development
- Free or subsidized access to general hardware
- Turning a consultant project into a commercial product

Among the least important ways identified to bootstrap product development are attempting to obtain research grants and commercializing university-based research (Freear, Sohl, and Wetzel, 1995b).

## Bootstrapping Options for Business Development

To grow the firm as a whole, a different array of bootstrapping techniques have proven to be effective (Freear, Sohl, and Wetzel, 1995b):

*Important Bootstrapping Techniques for Business Development*

- Forgone or delayed compensation
- Reduced compensation
- Personal savings
- Working from home
- Deals with professional service providers at below-competitive rates
- Space at below-market or very low rent
- Personal credit cards and home equity loans

The least important bootstrapping techniques used in business development include SBA guarantees, the entrepreneur's severance and parachute payments, barter arrangements, and special terms with customers (Freear, Sohl, and Wetzel, 1995b).

## Bootstrapping Options to Minimize the Need for Capital

To lessen the need for capital, whether it is generated internally by the firm or raised from outside, Winborg and Landstrom (1997) identified a number of feasible bootstrapping methods to minimize the level of monetary expense for the young firm:

*Important Bootstrapping Techniques
to Minimize the Need for Capital*

- Buy used equipment instead of new
- Borrow equipment from other businesses for short-term projects
- Use interest on overdue payments from customers
- Hire personnel for shorter periods instead of employing permanently
- Coordinate purchases with other businesses (mutual purchasing of goods)
- Lease equipment instead of buying

- Use routines to speed up invoicing
- Cease business relations with customers who frequently pay late
- Offer same conditions to all customers (that is, no expense on preferential treatment to some)
- Buy on consignment from suppliers
- Obtain trade credit from suppliers
- Deliberately choose customers who pay quickly
- Share business premises with others
- Employ relatives or friends at nonmarket salaries
- Run the business completely from your home

Interestingly, a 1996 survey conducted for the *American Banker* magazine showed that small businesses have increased their reliance on leases and credit lines at the expense of traditional bank loans ("Bank and Nonbank Competition . . .," 1996). In fact, trade credit is used by 61 percent of small businesses ("Financial Services Used . . .," 1995), and leasing is often a sound means of acquiring equipment without borrowing. One of the least used methods to minimize the need for capital is constant sharing of equipment and employees with other local businesses to reduce fixed commitments.

## Bootstrapping Options to Meet the Need for Capital

The bootstrapping methods in the last subsection minimize the need for capital flow, but Winborg and Landstrom (1997) state that other options may be employed to swiftly *raise* a certain amount of money to run the firm or to meet short-term material costs:

*Important Bootstrapping Techniques to Meet the Need for Capital*

- Withhold entrepreneur's salary payment for short or long periods of time
- Seek out best purchasing conditions with suppliers
- Deliberately delay payment to suppliers
- Use the entrepreneur's private credit card for business expenses
- Obtain capital via the entrepreneur's assignments in other businesses
- Obtain loans from relatives and friends

Credit cards in particular are becoming a popular substitute for loans for those start-up firms with little experience or credit history ("Financial Services Used . . .," 1995). In fact, the percentage of small businesses using credit card financing has increased dramatically over the last five years, from 16 percent to 47 percent; three-fifths of these firms pay off the balance in full each month to keep debt from mounting (Small Business Administration, 1999; "Small Business Entrepreneurship 101," 1998).

Raising capital from a factoring company (through selling the firm's accounts receivable to the lender) and obtaining federal or state subsidies are among some of the least employed bootstrapping methods used to meet the need for capital. Factoring can be quite expensive, subsidies are not always easy to obtain, and they may entail certain restrictions. Because of the tightening of lending policies by banks, nontraditional finance companies have significantly increased their share of small-business loans in the last decade (Posner, 1993).

Some alternative methods of bootstrapping that entrepreneurs may also wish to explore, include bartering underused products or services with other firms, franchising or licensing the product or business idea to others for a royalty fee, and paying employees with company stock; this last suggestion saves on cash expenditures and gives the employees some ownership and additional motivation to work hard.

## Strategies for Successful Bootstrapping

Employing bootstrapping measures to grow a small firm clearly relies greatly on networks, trust, cooperation, and (especially) wise use of the firm's existing resources, rather than collecting new financial resources from outside. This takes real entrepreneurial skill and involves significant challenges. Bhide's *Harvard Business Review* article (1992) lists seven recommendations for successful bootstrapping:

1. *Get operational quickly.* Use a copycat idea in a small target market to get a firm off the ground fast. Imitation products avoid research costs, and a small market offers little competition. The idea is to get the firm up and running rather than waiting passively

for a big idea to appear. New and bigger opportunities are certain to develop once the firm is in business.

2. *Look for quick, break-even, cash-generating products.* Firms that are making money build credibility in the eyes of customers, employees, and competitors. Therefore bootstrapped firms may wish to take on profit opportunities that large firms regard as distractions. Although large firms have to stick to their underlying strategic plan, bootstrapped small firms often do not have that obligation.

3. *Offer high-value products or services that sustain direct personal selling.* Since it is usually difficult and costly to persuade customers to switch from a familiar product or service to a substitute offered by a new firm, successful entrepreneurs usually choose high-ticket products and services where their individual passion and sales tactics can substitute for a large marketing budget. Of course, convincing customers to change is considerably easier if the product being sold offers some tangible advantage over its competitors.

4. *Forget about the crack team.* Small bootstrapped firms do not have the financial means to afford and recruit a well-balanced management team of seasoned veterans. Reliance on inexperienced personnel is common—and not always a disadvantage. Learning how to motivate diamonds in the rough should be part of every bootstrapper's repertoire.

5. *Keep growth in check.* Since bootstrapping supplies only limited financial means for growth, bootstrapped firms should take care to expand at a rate they can control. Too many start-ups fail because they grow beyond their financial means. This is clearly a major limitation for those entrepreneurial firms with growth rates of more than 20 percent per year. These firms may certainly elect to rely less on bootstrapping and instead finance growth using their rosy future earnings potential to attract business angel funds.

6. *Focus on cash (not on profits, market share, or anything else).* Because of their limited financial means, bootstrapped firms cannot afford to pursue a number of strategic goals. Unlike those counterparts funded by business angels and venture capitalists, bootstrapped firms must focus on healthy margins from day one, to cover costs but also to fund growth. They cannot pursue loss-making strategies to build market share or a customer base. Having a healthy cash flow is critical to survival, so their sales strategies

must ensure healthy returns from the outset. Again, for many firms this may not be feasible and reliance on outside equity capital can be crucial.

7. *Cultivate banks before the business becomes creditworthy.* For those small firms without the growth prospects that attract outside investors, gaining bank financing is one of the few remaining funding options. Bank financing is usually unavailable to start-up firms, especially if little or no collateral is offered. However, bank financing is quite important for all small firms once they are established and making some profit. Therefore, the foundation for a healthy relationship with your banker should be laid with careful preparation and timing. Keeping good books, immaculate records, and sound balance sheets from day one allows you to approach your banker with confidence once the firm has been in operation for a few years and is creditworthy.

## Business Alliances

Very closely related to bootstrapping is the process of forming a business alliance with another firm to generate revenues and reduce costs. Such business alliances are defined as "cooperative agreements with one or more firms to utilize complementary resources for mutual benefit" (Freear, Sohl, and Wetzel, 1995b, p. 398). A study found that 77 percent of U.S. software companies in their start-up or early stages form some sort of business alliance, that those firms in an alliance have an overall higher success rate (around 71 percent, compared to a 46 percent average overall) and 67 percent of these firms believe that their primary business alliance was a "very important" or "important" factor in the initial success of their company. These firms state that their primary business alliance accounts for more than 30 percent of revenues, while 25 percent claim that they account for more than 50 percent (Freear, Sohl, and Wetzel, 1995b). Alliances give your firms some competitive protection and infusion of shared know-how; nevertheless, forming too many business alliances (and thus assuming too many obligations) can also lower performance for a new venture. Here are the primary reasons for forming a business alliance (Freear, Sohl, and Wetzel, 1995b):

## Reasons for Forming a Business Alliance

- Market penetration
- Sales and marketing channels
- Common views of customers and market
- Inadequate resources to go it alone
- Product development
- Complementary products
- Teaming up versus competing
- Joint bidding on projects
- Accelerate time to market
- Geographic expansion
- Access to customer lists
- Customer request
- Build product credibility
- Enhance company status
- Take advantage of economies of scale
- Gain business experience
- Lack of expertise

Though reasons for forming an alliance abound, doing so usually involves some effort on the part of the entrepreneur. This is often worthwhile since he or she typically has inadequate resources to go it alone and few other choices. As the next list shows, most alliances are formed after an active search for a partner and some use of industry networks and contacts (Freear, Sohl, and Wetzel, 1995b). In fact, more alliances are formed through chance encounters than through attorneys, accountants, bankers, and investors combined.

## How Business Alliance Partners Are Found

- Active search based on industry knowledge
- Industry networks and contacts
- "They called us"
- Trade shows
- Chance encounters
- Friends
- Professional associations
- Cold calls
- Attorneys
- Accountants
- Bankers
- Investment forums and gatherings

Upon finding and evaluating a potential partner, firms seal the alliance with tight documentation, a legal agreement, or a memorandum of understanding in 73 percent of cases (Freear, Sohl, and Wetzel, 1995b). Although another 7 percent rely on an exchange of letters to protect themselves from future liabilities, a surprising 2 percent of all firms that enter into an alliance use no documentation and instead rely on verbal commitment. Most alliances do not involve any cash financing.

An effective business alliance can often be very beneficial to a start-up or early-stage firm with inadequate resources to go it alone, but these alliances do not always make sense once the firm has grown, is healthy, and reaches self-sufficiency. Although there may be many reasons for terminating an alliance, strategic reasons dominate: maturation of the product life cycle, divergence of business interests, appearance of more profitable strategies (including internal solutions), and failing to realize the objectives of the alliance (Freear, Sohl, and Wetzel, 1995b).

Like bootstrapping, alliances increase the availability of resources beyond those belonging to just the small firm, which in turn may increase the chances of success for the participating ventures. Alliances do not vastly increase available resources, but they are a good alternative for funding whenever outside equity investors are not readily forthcoming or have been reserved for a later round of growth financing. Furthermore, a strategic alliance with a larger company, on such things as marketing or manufacturing, might be a sound way to formulate an exit strategy for your company in the future (Posner, 1993). Getting to know, and creating synergy with, a potential acquirer may result in a ready buyer and a strong selling price once you are ready to sell your firm.

## When Bootstrapping and Alliances Won't Do: Inherent Challenges

Although personal funds, internally generated bootstrapping, and business alliances may be sufficient sources of capital for the majority of small firms in our economy growing modestly at 20 percent or less per year, unfortunately these methods are often insufficient after only a short time for fast-growth firms, those looking to double in size within a matter of a few years. These are the firms that often make it to a publicly quoted stock market, generating untold millions for their founders. Raising external equity financing, from business angels or venture capitalists, is often the best means for these firms to reach their potential. In fact, those with an annual growth rate of 40 percent are about twice as likely to seek external equity finance as those firms with growth of less than 20 percent (Wetzel and Wilson, 1985). Indeed, the choice of equity finance that a firm makes is related to its growth expectations and whether the firm has raised external financing before

(Freear, Sohl, and Wetzel, 1991). Some entrepreneurs may decide not to seek external funding (possibly preferring debt) because of the prospect of having to surrender part of the equity, but they often do so at the cost of limiting their firm's growth (Landstrom, 1992; Alvarez and others, 1997). A recent U.S. study found that start-ups having substantially more financing than average make a significantly larger contribution to economic growth than other firms (Reynolds and White, 1997).

Many of the entrepreneurial firms seeking external funding unfortunately have difficulty locating it thanks to their higher risks and higher cost of financing (Wetzel and Wilson, 1985; Harrison and Mason, 1996a; Wetzel, 1993), particularly from more conventional sources such as banks. It is usually not the entrepreneur who bears the ultimate risk or uncertainty, but the person who provides the financing (Schumpeter, 1951), which limits the supply of funds. Indeed, the SBA claims that five out of six start-up companies in general do not last beyond their fifth year (Cullen, 1998). Start-up and early-stage firms certainly have many inherent challenges that limit their ability to raise necessary outside equity funds. In particular, young firms usually have (to name but a few) specific characteristics:

- Short performance histories
- Small-scale operations
- Weak access to supply and distribution markets
- Illiquidity
- Long development times
- Uncertain growth rates
- No collateral
- Relatively high transaction costs for the size of the investment
- Potentially high information asymmetries between entrepreneurs and potential investors
- Low survival rates
- Involvement of an innovation that further increases already high risk

Not surprisingly, many fast-growing unquoted firms self-report that financing is the most frequent obstacle to growth.

Even three of the leading academics in the field—Freear, Sohl, and Wetzel—found that the equity financing *need* of high-growth start-up firms in the United States in the early 1990s was over $60 billion a year, stating that this "is one measure of the capital formation challenge confronting the U.S. economy" (1995a, p. 86). Unfortunately, this number is probably much higher today. Indeed, despite compelling evidence of their job-generating capacity, the entrepreneurs of today often "face a daunting task in their search for equity financing, the fuel for the engine that created jobs and moves technology from the laboratory to the marketplace" (Freear, Sohl, and Wetzel, 1992b, p. 2).

Since entrepreneurial firms commonly face funding hurdles, despite their sizable economic impact potential, the next chapter examines the types of external fund provider that do fund a percentage of these entrepreneurial firms through the various stages of their growth.

*Chapter Three*

# Types of Outside Investors Willing to Finance Growing Firms

Although the majority of entrepreneurial firms at some point try to raise external finance to help them grow, not all are successful. Knowing what type of investor to approach, and when, is critical. In fact, demand for external equity funds by entrepreneurial growth firms is much greater than commonly thought (Mason and Harrison, 1996b), in part because obtaining external equity usually benefits the firm in the long run. In a 1991 study of firms receiving money from outside investors, it was found that over the following years they tended to have higher forecast growth rates, held a more international focus, and expected to have larger market share than those not receiving external equity support (Freear, Sohl, and Wetzel, 1991). Such financial capital input levels are strong determinants of the survival prospects for a small business (Bates, 1990).

## Likely Financiers During the Evolution of a Firm

This chapter presents a model of the providers of financing to entrepreneurial firms. The amount of money required and the stage of growth are the best indicators of likely sources of outside equity funds, as Figure 3.1 demonstrates.

The amount of funding usually increases with each progressive stage of financing (Freear and Wetzel, 1990); as a firm becomes

**Figure 3.1.  Model of the Main Providers of External Finance Throughout the Evolution of the Entrepreneurial Firm.**

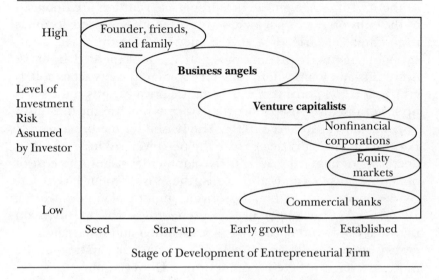

more mature and larger in size (that is, its inherent riskiness decreases), the problems of securing finance normally decrease (Wetzel and Wilson, 1985). Ironically, a small firm's dependence on outside funds for survival also lessens (Moore and Segaghat, 1992). Obviously, not every firm uses every funding source. Only when one source has been fully exploited is the next form of financing best courted and used, although few firms actually go beyond the bank stage, that is, get listed on the stock market through an IPO or sold in a trade sale). Thus as an entrepreneurial firm develops, its most likely sources of outside finance (in descending order of probability) are

1. The founder, family, and friends (the three Fs)
2. The equity gap (a stage void of finance)
3. Business angels
4. Venture capitalists
5. Banks
6. Nonfinancial corporations
7. IPOs and the equity markets

## Founder, Family, and Friends (The Three Fs)

At the start-up stage, most entrepreneurial ventures are financed by the entrepreneur's personal savings; if more is needed, it comes from family and friends—"love money." During this stage, bootstrapping methods predominate, often supplemented by bank overdrafts and loans where the entrepreneur's assets act as collateral. Indeed, 74 percent of U.S. firms use private funds at the start-up stage, and this is used more than twice as much as the next most popular source (Roberts, 1991). The reason for the popularity of personal financing is clear. Since the perceived riskiness of a firm decreases dramatically over its developmental stages, the cost of obtaining outside funds also drops (the entrepreneur has to surrender less equity to obtain a given amount of funds; Wetzel, 1983). Clearly, the longer an entrepreneur is be able to survive on personal funds and hard work (sweat equity) and internally generated funds, the lower the cost of external risk capital and the more sovereignty the entrepreneur has. However, once these resources of support have been exhausted, it is necessary to seek external finance (Wetzel and Freear, 1994).

## The Equity Gap (A Stage Void of Finance)

Unfortunately, seeking and locating external finance at the very early stages of a business venture may be extremely difficult (Wetzel, 1983), as we saw in the last chapter. This is principally due to the equity gap that exists in the market for entrepreneurial finance (Wetzel, 1986a; Wetzel and Freear, 1994; Mason and Harrison, 1996a). This equity gap is best defined as "the absence of small amounts of risk capital from institutional sources for companies at the seed, start-up and early-growth stages which arises because the fixed costs of investment appraisal and monitoring make it uneconomic for venture capital funds to make small investments, and also because of the reluctance of banks to make unsecured lending" (Mason, 1996a, p. 4).

This financing gap exists in the United States in seeking less than $500,000 (Alvarez and others, 1997). Such an equity gap is also prominent in many other countries. The UK, for example, has an equity gap for funds below the £250,000–400,000 level (Mason, 1996a; Lonsdale, 1996). The gap is not a recent phenomenon. More than sixty years ago, the difficulty small firms had in raising loan and equity finance was first formally identified, and it has been a continuously recognized cause for concern since.

Although its presence is clear, its cause is ambiguous. Traditionally, the gap has been attributed to a shortage of capital in the marketplace (Freear and Wetzel, 1991; Duxbury, Haines, and Riding, 1996; Wetzel, 1983). Within the last ten to twenty years the explanation has been modified, and the gap is now attributed to fragmentation of the marketplace, where financial markets cannot freely provide all relevant information about fund sources and investment opportunities to the buyers and sellers of capital (Wetzel, 1983; Wetzel and Wilson, 1985). This market inefficiency has led suppliers of financing to claim that the gap is a demand-side problem, since many claim (slightly unfairly) that investment proposals and entrepreneurs are often of a low quality (that is, there's a management gap). Others believe it is more of a supply-side problem, where the preferences and lending practices of institutional investors restrict investment regardless of the level of available funds (Mason and Harrison, 1992). Indeed, these restrictive practices may be due to the small size of the desired investments, and to the fact that the transaction and monitoring costs alone may make it unfeasible for venture capital firms and banks to offer funding (Alvarez and others, 1997).

The development of the venture capital industry has helped somewhat to reduce the top portion of the equity gap, but it remains to this day. In fact, in the 1990s concern about the equity gap increased thanks to changes in banking practice concerning small-firm lending and growing evidence that private and public sector initiatives to close the gap have failed. Obtaining external finance is therefore still a genuine problem for small U.S. firms looking to grow and expand.

## Business Angels

As the only investors who invest primarily in the entrepreneurial high-growth areas that are cited as gaps in the market for funding, business angels support the firms that other investors are reluctant to fund (Wetzel, 1983; Mason and Harrison, 1995). They use their financial wealth and entrepreneurial experience to help young entrepreneurial firms grow, often by working side by side with their entrepreneurs. Collectively, they are the oldest, largest, and most-often-used source of outside funds for young high-growth firms. Business angels are active, in one way or another, in every country worldwide and have been formally studied in the United States, Great Britain, Canada, Brazil, Sweden, Finland, Norway, Denmark, France, Germany, Portugal, the Netherlands, Belgium, Saudi Arabia, South Korea, Japan, and Australia.

Business angels are known to partially ease the equity gap problem in these countries in a number of ways.

### *The Benefits of Angels*

First, business angels prefer funding high-risk entrepreneurial firms in their earliest stages (Freear, Sohl, and Wetzel, 1991). In the United States, they invest more funds, in more rounds, in more firms than any other source of early-stage firm finance (Freear, Sohl, and Wetzel, 1992b). Similarly in the UK, they are the most important source of external equity after family and friends, funding about 5 percent of small firms while venture capitalists fund less than 1 percent (Mason and Harrison, 1990). Roberts (1991) found that U.S. business angels are the major source of external funds for start-ups with high growth potential, as Table 3.1 illustrates.

In particular, business angels prefer investments with deal size under $1 million and that generally have fewer than one hundred

**Table 3.1.  Primary Sources of Initial Capital
for Small High-Growth Firms.**

| Source | Percentage of Finance |
|---|---|
| Entrepreneur's personal savings | 74 |
| Family and friends | 5 |
| Business angels | 7 |
| Venture capitalists | 5 |
| Nonfinancial corporations | 6 |
| Commercial banks | 0 |
| Public stock issues | 3 |

*Source:* Roberts (1991).

employees, less than $5 million in annual sales, and growth rates under 40 percent but still above 20 percent (Freear and Wetzel, 1988, 1990, 1991; Wetzel and Wilson, 1985). Indeed, some claim that because 60 percent of business angel deals are early-stage, compared to around a quarter of all deals for venture capitalists, it is actually the business angel who is the real venture capitalist. Clearly, business angels fill the so-called equity gap by making those investments exactly in those areas in which institutional venture capital providers are reluctant to invest.

Second, business angels prefer funding the small amounts (falling within the equity gap) needed to launch new ventures (Freear and Wetzel, 1991). In fact, business angels provide 84 percent of rounds under $250,000, and 58 percent between $250,000 and $500,000, while overall in rounds of less than $500,000 business angels offer, in dollar terms, four times as much as venture capitalists (Freear, Sohl, and Wetzel, 1992b). Since angels normally invest a small proportion of their wealth—typically less than 15 percent—in entrepreneurial firms, the amount they each have to invest is relatively small compared to venture capital firms, though collectively it is massive.

Third, business angels tend to have less risk aversion and lower expectations of return than other types of investors (Freear, Sohl, and Wetzel, 1991; Freear and Wetzel, 1991). Also, their cost of finance is often cheaper for the entrepreneur, and their funding is received more quickly than from other finance sources (Freear, Sohl, and Wetzel, 1990).

Unfortunately, business angels are often overlooked by entrepreneurs and by the equity gap debate as a source of capital (Freear and Wetzel, 1991; Wetzel and Wilson, 1985); Mason and Harrison (1996a) found that 34 percent of entrepreneurs were unaware of them. But business angels are a plentiful source of finance and are especially valuable since they are located almost everywhere and can add value through direct involvement (Haar, Starr, and MacMillan, 1988; Wetzel, 1983).

### A History of Angels

The value of business angels has been evident for many years. In 1874, Alexander Graham Bell used angel money to found Bell Telephone; in 1903, five business angels launched Henry Ford's auto empire with a $40,000 investment; in 1977, an angel invested

$91,000 in Apple Computer; and in 1978, a business angel initiated the launch of the Body Shop retail chain. More recently, Pete's Brewing Company (brewer of Pete's Wicked Ale) and a number of Internet-related successes, such as Amazon.com, the Mining Company, Go2Net (one of many firms funded by Paul Allen), and Firefly (recently acquired by Microsoft) among countless others, owe their existence to business angel funds. Even the $6 million construction cost of the Golden Gate Bridge was financed by a business angel, A. P. Giannini, discovered by the architect, Joseph Strauss, after a nineteen-year search for funding (Benjamin and Margulis, 1996). In recent years, the status of being a business angel has increased dramatically, especially in the media and business circles. Recent U.S. research confirms that angels are widespread: at least 2.8 percent of U.S. households have at least one angel in the family (Usem, 1997).

It is clear that business angels are seeding start-up firms, of which some subsequently receive funding from more formal sources of finance such as venture capitalists, while the majority never need to raise further funds (Freear and Wetzel, 1990; Freear, Sohl, and Wetzel, 1995a). A potentially complementary relationship exists between business angels and venture capitalists, where the angels act as the farm system for the venture capitalists, since angels invest in and nurse small firms with growth potential into large firms that then interest venture capitalists for further rounds of investment (Timmons and Sapienza, 1992; Wetzel and Wilson, 1985; Freear and Wetzel, 1988, 1989, 1991; Freear, Sohl, and Wetzel, 1991, 1996; Roberts, 1991). In the UK, 23 percent of venture capital–funded firms had previously received funding from business angels (BVCA, 1993). It is clear that a healthy informal venture capital market is required for the institutional venture capital market to thrive (Mason and Harrison, 1995). Some business angels (especially those with experience) are even investing alongside venture capital firms, and such matching services as Garage.com have both business angels and venture capitalists as members.

### A New Breed: Silicon Valley Angels

The success of technology and software firms over the last two decades has given rise to a staggering number of young and wealthy entrepreneurs who have fully or partially cashed out of their ventures and are looking for new and exciting opportunities for their money and know-how. This has empowered a wide range of individuals to act on their angelic impulses. This new breed of "Silicon Valley angels" are setting up their own private angel investment funds to invest in the next generation of innovation, while some among them are investing together in syndicates. In fact, 10 percent of the CEOs in a 1998 ranking of the fastest-growing firms in the United States (the Inc. 100) consider themselves to be angels (Gruner, 1998). Just some of the better-known players (and their erstwhile corporate affiliations) who have also taken this step include Paul Allen (Microsoft), H. Ross Perot, John Sculley (Apple Computer), Jim Barksdale (Netscape), Ben Rosen (chairman of Compaq Computer), Chong-Moon Lee (founder of Diamond Multimedia), Leonard Riggio (chairman and chief executive of Barnes and Noble), Roger Sippl (founder of Informix Software), Ron Conway (cofounder of Altos Computer Systems), and Sandy Robertson (founder and CEO of the investment bank Robertson Stevens), to name a few prominent individuals. Although just a minority of angels in the United States, this class is conducting far larger deals than those of the average investor, and certainly on a more professional level. They conduct more due diligence than the average business angel and demand to see the prospect of higher returns and potential exit routes before they invest. Of particular note, the investment behavior of business angel and Microsoft cofounder Allen resembles that of a venture capital firm more than of an angel. Through his private business angel fund, Vulcan Ventures, he currently holds a portfolio of fifty-eight innovative ventures (with a majority ownership in only three), including such well-known firms as Beyond.com, Dreamworks SKG, Egghead Software, and Go2Net. Though Allen's business angel investments (with most in the hundreds of millions of dollars each) are clearly in a different league from most, it highlights that many of the most active entrepreneurs from the past appear to be some of the most active business angel investors in the making today.

### The Rise of Angel Syndicates

The last few years have also seen a dramatic increase in the number of angels who are investing as part of an investment syndicate, an approach that allows them to collectively make larger and more frequent investments (though these remain smaller than those funded by even small venture capital firms). Indeed, research has shown that more experienced investors tend to prefer such co-investment groups (Van Osnabrugge, 1999b). They usually meet regularly, and deal origination and outside access to the group is typically through one or more of its members. To retain members' anonymity, many of these syndicates (also called angel alliances) establish a storefront (or façade) for the general public. One syndicate of particular note is the Band of Angels in California; it is run by an ex–venture capitalist and its 120 members include Compaq Chairman Ben Rosen and former Hewlett-Packard CEO Dean Morton (Gordon and Grover, 1998). This group averages $600,000 per investment (about ten times the size of the average angel deal) and since January 1995 has invested $45 million in eighty-four companies. As these companies grew, they went on to raise an additional $200 million from venture capitalists and other investors. Another syndicate, Capital Investors, in Washington, D.C., includes the vice chairman of MCI WorldCom, John Sidgmore; a top AOL executive, Stephen Case; and the chief executive of Cybercash, William Melton (Mourkheiber, 1999). These investors are among a small group that each puts at least $100,000 into a pot for seed investments. Syndicates such as these have helped to legitimize this form of investing and appear to reside somewhere in the middle of the investment continuum, with business angels and venture capitalists on the poles (Mayfield, 1999), as Figure 3.2 illustrates.

From left to right, this continuum also suggests (1) the stage of investment preferred, from seed to later stages; (2) the amount of investment, from small to large; (3) the investor's investment experience, from little to great; (4) the formality of the investment process, from informal to formal; and (5) the risk averseness of the investors, from low to high.

**Figure 3.2.  The Venture Capital Continuum.**

| Informal | | Formal |
|---|---|---|
| Individual angels | Angel syndicates | Venture capital firms |

Angel syndicates offer investors clear advantages:

- Pooling money to invest in larger deals otherwise out of reach
- Diversification across multiple investments
- Leveraging and sharing of network contacts and investment expertise (such as screening, due diligence, and monitoring)
- The ability to add more investments to an existing portfolio (Kelly and Hay, 1999)
- The ability to add further follow-on rounds to existing investments

However, these syndicates also incur certain running costs and may not be appropriate for those investors who wish to have a large say and active involvement in their investments.

Even though single-deal syndicates are formed specifically for just one deal, multideal syndicates are ongoing and organized to make multiple deals over many years. Typically, a member of the group brings a particular investment opportunity to the attention of the syndicate, on the understanding that the member will invest in the deal. The deal is then evaluated by the group in a venture forum (Sohl, 1999). Each member can decide individually whether to participate in a particular deal that the syndicate decides to undertake and how much he or she wants to be involved in each investment they make. Once such a commitment is obtained, the participating angels have to supply the funds within thirty to sixty days, as needed. Larger and more complicated syndicates often look for opportunities with broader and deeper markets and higher minimum return requirements than simpler syndicates do (Mayfield and Bygrave, 1999). In most cases, one member of the syndicate acts as the lead angel, assuming a liaison role between the entrepreneur and the syndicate (Mayfield and Bygrave, 1999). In other cases, an outsider with no financial commitment to the group (known as an "archangel") is hired to perform this function. These individuals may be responsible for performing due diligence and coordinating the allotment of investment duties among members. Syndicate deals tend to be more professional than the average business angel deal.

In addition to the traditional equity gap, some have suggested that a second capital gap may be emerging in the United States for firms seeking capital in the $1–3 million range (Sohl, 1999). If this is indeed the case, the rise of angel syndicates, which can easily fund deals in this range, may alleviate this financing concern.

With a 1997 federal law allowing profits from financing start-up ventures to be tax-deferred if rolled over into new start-ups within sixty days, and with the increase of angel syndicates, there has been growth in the number of angels (and amount of invested funds) participating in early-stage deals. However, business angels still do not seed as many early-stage investments as is potentially possible because of a number of inefficiencies in the informal venture capital market; thus the equity gap still remains.

### Business Angel Market Inefficiencies

Unfortunately, as with the external equity market in general, the informal venture capital market of business angel finance is quite inefficient (Wetzel, 1987; Harrison and Mason, 1991b), thanks to the fragmented nature of the market, imperfect channels of communication, and the invisibility of business angels (their preference for anonymity) (Harrison and Mason, 1992a; Freear, Sohl, and Wetzel, 1994a). Indeed, if it becomes widely known that an individual has money to invest, then he or she may be besieged with hundreds of proposals per year, when his or her desire may be only for three or four. Alternative explanations have suggested that there is a mismatch of investment preferences and available investment opportunities (Mason and Rogers, 1996), unfamiliarity with successful investment techniques on the part of both investors and entrepreneurs (Wetzel, 1987), and the misconception of many entrepreneurs that business angel funding is financing of the last resort (Mason and Harrison, 1990). Clearly, nothing could be further from the truth.

These inefficiencies impose high search costs on both investors and entrepreneurs (Mason and Rogers, 1996; Wetzel, 1987). In the informal market, therefore, entrepreneurs can find only limited guidance in locating business angel funding, and the majority of business angels tend to rely on random discovery of potential investment opportunities. Even though somewhere there is a business angel willing to put money into almost any investment opportunity, matching business angels and entrepreneurs is a real concern. Consequently, the financing potential of business angels is not being fully used, and many business angels in the United States (and abroad) complain that they have sizable uncommitted funds available for investment—sometimes up to three times the amount of their current investment portfolio— but they cannot locate suitable investment opportunities (Wetzel and Freear, 1994; Mason and Harrison, 1996b; Landstrom, 1993). In California alone, the state Research Bureau estimates that young companies need an additional $18 billion to $97.5 billion in angel funds (Chan, 1999)!

### The Role of Matching Services

Government policy schemes have not been very successful, but one of the most promising approaches to easing business angel market inefficiencies and lessening the equity gap in general may be the emergence of matching services. These organizations afford a means of cost-effective communication between entrepreneurs seeking finance and business angels seeking investment opportunities by way of computer matching, venture forums, breakfast meetings, or some kind of publication. They enhance the business angel market efficiency of finance by making both investors and entrepreneurs visible, improving deal flow, and enlarging the pool of business angel funding by increasing the number of active angels in the market (Mason, 1993). It is guesstimated that maybe 5–10 percent of all business angel investment goes through matching services; despite their advantages, they may be just the tip of a potentially sizable iceberg and so have only limited impact. Yet they are still one of the best means for potential individual investors and entrepreneurs to find each other, especially for those less-experienced angel investors. Because we feel that matching services offer many benefits, we have dedicated Appendix One to listing more than seventy of these firms (and angel alliances) in the United States in great detail. Until now, few data were collected on these organizations beyond their names and addresses.

## Venture Capitalists

Once a small but fast-growing firm has evolved into a medium or large-sized venture, its funding needs may grow beyond the means of individual business angel investors; it is usually at this stage that formal external finance networks become available.

Venture capital firms may be the most likely source of external equity funding for those few entrepreneurial firms with high enough growth potential to meet the restrictive investment criteria of the venture capitalists. Traditionally, venture capital was described as investment in long-term, risky equity finance where the primary reward for the providers is an eventual gain, rather than interest income or dividend yield. However, as we will see, recent shifts in the investment preferences of the industry appear to have changed these objectives somewhat.

Over the last two decades, venture capitalists have helped to create such well-known corporations as 3Com, Apple Computer, Cienna, Cisco Systems, Digital Equipment Corporation, Federal Express, Genentech, Hotmail, Intel, iVillage.com, Lotus, Microsoft, Oracle, Vitesse Semiconductor, and Yahoo! among others. Success stories abound to make venture capital an often-talked-about and "sexy" source of financing. Of particular note, venture capitalists invested $3.5 million in Apple Computer in 1978 and 1979 for a 19 percent stake, which was worth $271 million in December 1980 when the company had its $1.4 billion IPO. More recently, on February 7, 1997, Cienna, a manufacturer of fiber optic communications equipment, became the most successful venture capital–funded IPO ever, achieving a $3.4 billion valuation on its first day. The three venture capitalists who invested a combined $3.5 million for a 61 percent stake less than three years before now held an investment worth almost $2.1 billion (Wasserman, 1999).

Of course, Internet companies have also had their fair share of successes. Venture capitalists invested $2 million in Yahoo! when it was still in its earliest stages. Today, that stake is worth $4.4 billion, a twenty-two-hundredfold return on investment ("Start-up Firms . . .," 1999). Likewise, a venture capital fund invested $1.5 million in eBay in June 1997 to help finance the online auction firm. When the firm went public nineteen months later, their share of stock was worth $2.4 billion—a return of 160,000 percent in just under two years (Wilmsen, 1999a)! Of course, there is no need to remind you that such success stories are very rare.

In general, venture capitalists tend to fund high-growth ventures, some in their earlier stages (although still later in stage than most business angel deals) and with little track record, that do not yet have access to the quoted securities markets and are still too risky for bank lending (Zacharakis and Meyer, 1995). In supporting nonestablished investments, venture capitalists use their own business skills (though not as actively as business angels), while they may also fund second-round and development capital for later-stage firms that usually need less assistance.

## The Venture Capitalists' Investment Shift

Although in the early 1980s the venture capital industry invested modestly in early-stage firms, after the 1987 stock crash the industry in this country shifted its investment focus away from start-ups and early-stage firms, in favor of mature ventures (that is, development finance) and leveraged buyouts and buyins (Freear, Sohl, and Wetzel, 1993, 1995a; Mason, 1996a). This was clearly an unfortunate shift away from classic venture capital (meaning, provision of new equity), which involves forming, building, and harvesting new firms with a long-term focus, toward greater emphasis on "merchant" venture capital (provision of replacement equity), which emphasizes transaction crafting and closing, fee generation, financial engineering know-how, and short-term gains (Bygrave and Timmons, 1992; Sweeting, 1991). Regrettably, this blurred the division between venture capital and merchant banking. Although the U.S. share of venture capital investments in early-stage investments dropped below 25 percent, it has reemerged somewhat since the early 1990s; many venture capitalists are now more willing to invest in early-stage deals, especially those that are technology-related, which is where the largest returns have recently been attained. However, in 1998, still only 28 percent of all venture capital was invested in just 1,122 early-stage firms (compared to 20,000–60,000 firms by business angels), although twice this amount went to mature firms in need of expansion funds, most of which are existing portfolio companies (NVCA, 1998). Even more surprising, venture capital investments in "start-up" firms number fewer than three hundred annually (Sohl, 1999). This shift toward expansion financing is shown in Figure 3.3.

Unfortunately, start-up and early-stage deals are much rarer in the UK and Europe (Brouwer and Hendrix, 1998). In the UK, such investments accounted for 27 percent of the full amount

**Figure 3.3. Venture Capital Invested by Stage from 1980 to 1998.**

% of Total Amount Invested

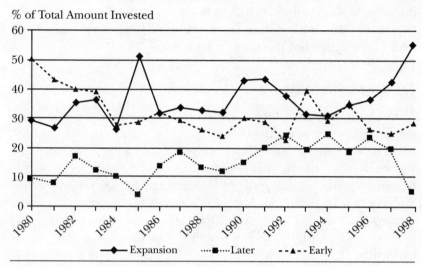

─◆─ Expansion  ·····■···· Later  ─ ─▲─ ─ Early

*Source:* adapted from NVCA (1999, p. 22).

invested by the venture capital industry in 1984, with this percentage falling to 10 percent by 1988 and just 4 percent in 1995 (BVCA; 1995). However, during the same period (1984–1995), buyin finance and management buyouts (leveraged buyouts, in U.S. terms) increased from 21 percent to 73 percent of the total amount invested annually by the venture capital industry (BVCA, 1995). Happily, early-stage deals may now be gaining some popularity again.

For structural reasons, it is quite understandable why later-stage and larger firms may be more attractive for venture capitalists than small and early-stage ventures, particularly given venture capital's high overhead costs, high evaluation and monitoring costs relative to the size of the investment, long payback period, and inherently high risks when investing in an early-stage venture. Table 3.2 lists further explanations for why venture capitalists might be reluctant to invest in early-stage firms.

Since many venture capitalists prefer to invest in entrepreneurial firms that are no longer in their start-up and early stages, middle-aged ventures (which business angels sometimes nursed as

**Table 3.2. Reasons Venture Capitalists Might Prefer
Later-Stage and Expansion Investments.**

| *Later-Stage and Expansion Investment Characteristics* | *Start-up and Early-Stage Investment Characteristics* |
| --- | --- |
| Established business | An idea |
| Predictable cash flow | No income, only uncertain costs |
| Customer and competitors known | Customers and competitors unclear |
| Often low-tech | Commonly high-tech |
| Market often domestic | Market necessarily international |
| Experienced management team | One person and a "vision" |
| Due diligence possible | Due diligence almost impossible |
| Pricing possible | Pricing very difficult |
| "Hands off" venture capital style | "Hands-on" style critical |
| Potential liquidity | Illiquidity |
| Low ratio of research and monitoring costs to deal size | High ratio of research and monitoring costs to deal size |
| Historically favorable rates of return | Historically poor rates of return |
| Fewer investments needed to spread fund risk | More investments needed to spread fund risk |
| Larger deal sizes, so fewer investments needed to invest total VC fund | Smaller deal sizes, so more investments needed to invest total VC fund |
| Short-term investment horizon | Long-term investment horizon |
| Outright failure rare | Outright failure frequent |

*Source:* partially adapted from Murray (1992), as cited in Mason and Harrison (1992).

start-ups) are clearly their funding preference. Venture capital is seldom the most suitable source of funding for start-ups firms, despite what the media hype about a select few venture capital–funded Internet start-ups may imply. It is important to remember that of the nearly one million firms that are started each year in the United States, only one to two thousand actually receive venture capital financing (Podolny and Feldman, 1997), leaving a huge imbalance between supply and demand. The growth rates demanded by venture capitalists are normally way beyond what most businesses can realistically achieve. Venture capitalists only support the cream of the crop, the lucky few. As this book shows, for most entrepreneurs business angels are a much more suitable and realistic initial funding option.

## Banks

Banks rarely take risky investments of a venture capitalist nature, preferring to limit their risk by lending to firms that offer some form of collateral (Alvarez and others, 1997). This appears to make sense; even if a bank has a successful investment repaid it makes only 4–6 percent, but when it loses the money it can lose it all, in addition to attorney's fees (Posner, 1993). Although banks are generally the most important source of external funding for small firms once they are established and creditworthy, they are relatively unimportant for those small firms in their start-up or early stages, which have high-growth potential and thus high risks (Roberts, 1991; Murray, 1994). In general, because early-stage small firms lack a track record or reliable information on the entrepreneurs, are illiquid, and have volatile profit and cash flow measures, banks often restrict lending to these firms since it is difficult and costly to evaluate the risks (Alvarez and others, 1997; Binks and Ennew, 1997). One venture capitalist interviewed for this book summed up the difference between banks and venture capitalists: "Banks are interested in minimizing risk; venture capitalists are interested in minimizing the positive correlation between risk and return. What we want to do is get off the curve and find deals where we are getting a higher return for a lower risk. Banks just don't want risk." Unfortunately, one myth is particularly difficult to kill: that commercial banks make loans to start-up firms (Posner, 1993).

In a 1994 study of start-up firms in the high-tech industry, more than two-thirds of ventures considered banks as a potential source of funds—even though this source failed to materialize for the majority, as Table 3.3 shows.

A new study in New England found that about 70 percent of start-ups seek bank financing but that perhaps half of these are eventually successful (Lange, Warhuus, and Levie, 1999). Unfortunately, high-tech firms may find even greater obstacles on account of their high risks and technically savvy nature. A recent U.S. study found that of those who were denied a bank loan, the reason for denial in 36 percent of the cases was that the banker did not understand the business, in 31 percent that the firm had too much debt outstanding, and in 29 percent of cases that acceptable collateral was lacking (Alvarez and others, 1997). Almost as a rule, since most early-stage firms do not have positive cash flow, profitability, or solvency, banks rarely lend to them without a personal guarantee or collateral (Alvarez and others, 1997; Brophy and Shulman, 1992). In fact, the level of collateral required by banks tends to be around two and a half times the value of the borrowing, although valuation, depreciation, and revaluation costs possibly associated with taking collateral may further restrict the

**Table 3.3.  Considered and Actual Sources of Finance for High-Tech Start-ups.**

| Source of Finance | Percentage of Firms Considering Source | Percentage of Firms Actually Securing Source |
|---|---|---|
| Founder's savings | 69 | 49 |
| Bank loans | 69 | 7 |
| Money from family or friends | 12 | 9 |
| Money from government agencies | 48 | 9 |
| Venture capital (business angel and VC) | 45 | 10 |
| University endowments | 5 | 6 |
| Strategic partners | 29 | 6 |

*Source:* Moore (1994).

lending practices of banks. Those entrepreneurs without sufficient collateral may fall into a debt gap.

Unfortunately, the restrictive lending situation for small firms
has become worse in recent years, especially during the last recession, as banks experienced substantial losses from Third World
debt, international property debt, and domestic corporate and
small-business failures (Harrison and Mason, 1996a; Eglin, 1994).
Thanks to these losses, banks in the United States (and abroad)
sought to rebuild their asset bases by reappraising and changing
lending practices, which further restricted the availability of debt
finance to small (especially early-stage) firms. As a result of these
changes, banks have tightened their lending criteria (Alvarez and
others, 1997; Harrison and Mason, 1996a), now requiring more
collateral, placing more emphasis on the level of gearing, limiting
access to overdraft facilities (which frequently substituted for equity rather than working capital), using more risk-sensitive pricing
systems, and placing more reliance on the borrower's cash flow
and business plans, to make the lending decision. The end result:
bank managers have a strong lending preference for bigger firms
rather than smaller ones. Regrettably, it has been said that a bank
usually only lends money to small firms once it can prove that they
do not need it!

Though perhaps not formally a credit crunch for small firms,
there are undoubtedly increasing mismatches between what the
banks are prepared to supply, and under what conditions, and
what small businesses demand (Harrison and Mason, 1996a). Unfortunately, fast-growth entrepreneurial firms, which are indirectly the focus of this book, may in particular be adversely
affected by the lending practices of banks, entailing even greater
reliance on business angels and venture capital financing. Luckily,
receiving some sort of venture finance in the early stages can also
ease the bank-lending process at a later stage. As Table 3.4 shows,
commercial banks become an important source of finance for
those mature firms raising a second round of funding.

Small firms that have raised finance from external investors
are attractive propositions for banks since they are likely to have
strong balance sheets, which can support borrowings, and are
likely to be growth-oriented so as to attract outside investors in the
first place (Mason and Harrison, 1996b). Indeed, with such out-

**Table 3.4.  Main Sources of Funds for Entrepreneurial Firms over Progressive Rounds of Financing.**

| Source | First Round | Second Round | Third Round |
|---|---|---|---|
| Entrepreneur's personal savings | 74% | 7% | 13% |
| Family and friends | 5 | 4 | 0 |
| Business angels | 7 | 34 | 29 |
| Venture capitalists | 5 | 13 | 6 |
| Nonfinancial corporations | 6 | 15 | 16 |
| Commercial banks | 0 | 15 | 10 |
| Public stock issues | 3 | 10 | 26 |

*Source:* adapted from Roberts (1991).

side equity support often coming from a strong equity investor, a firm's gearing ratio (the ratio of debt to equity) may improve to reduce the lending risks for banks (or others) at a later time (Campbell, 1999).

## Nonfinancial Corporations

Increasing in popularity in the 1980s, many large manufacturing firms provided venture capital funds to young technology firms developing complementary technology. Such corporate venturing was adopted by many Fortune 500 businesses and was seen as strategic investment in new ideas (Roberts, 1991). Though corporate venturing has not been a hot topic in recent years, nonfinancial firms are now often seen by entrepreneurs as an exit opportunity rather than a source of growth funds. Although very successful firms have traditionally preferred to realize gains by taking themselves public in an IPO (see the next section), in light of the recent variability of the IPO market many have instead opted to be sold to large corporations. This allows these buyers to use acquisitions of small firms to complement their product or service offerings, and small firms to use this new influx of strategic funding to further expand operations. Using their strong share prices, many large bureaucratic corporations are able to purchase small firms with new and exciting innovations by handing over some of their stock, rather than cash ("Start-up Firms . . .," 1999).

As well as an effective way of coopting promising technological developments, such corporate venturing prevents these small firms from allying with the competitors or from competing directly against these buyers (Wasserman, 1999). As a result, ever more entrepreneurs today are starting ventures with the sole objective of being bought out by larger nonfinancial corporations, and receiving unfathomable wealth in the process ("Start-up Firms . . .," 1999). Microsoft's acquisition of Hotmail and WebTV (for $425 million and $400 million respectively) are two perfect examples. Venture capitalists seem to like this too; the number of privately owned venture capital–backed firms acquired in this way increased from 162 in 1997 (totaling $3.3 billion) to 184 in 1998 (totaling $7.9 billion), of which more than 40 percent were computer-related ventures (NVCA, 1999).

As recently noted in the *Economist* ("Start-up Firms . . .," 1999), though, this change in exit strategy may be starting to affect the nature of innovation itself, with new technology ventures shunning development of the "transformational technologies" that dramatically altered their fields, and instead electing to pursue niche markets. The objective of many high-tech entrepreneurs today is to obtain quick returns, rather than have a dramatic and innovative impact. Yet this trend may not be necessarily all negative. Since many entrepreneurial successes in the past originated from technologies developed in large corporations as a by-product of federally funded R&D, the decline in federal scientific research funds over the last two decades and the insufficient level of private R&D funding has increased the importance of funding start-ups by means of venture capital and by larger nonfinancial corporations (Wasserman, 1999).

## IPOs and the Equity Markets

Once a firm emerges from the high-risk early stages of development, where it was primarily dependent on funds from the entrepreneur, family and friends, business angels, and sometimes venture capitalists and bank financing, the next step may be to list the firm's shares on a publicly traded financial market. Although only a small minority of entrepreneurial firms eventually have an IPO, there are a number of advantages to doing so:

- A stock market listing attracts further external capital that can be used to fund the firm's growth.
- A market listing permits investors who funded the firm in the early stages to realize their locked-in investments for a financial gain, which can then be reinvested elsewhere.
- Naturally, entrepreneurs are also rewarded for their adventurous endeavors.
- Rendering to entrepreneurs the opportunity to possibly repurchase shares of stock at a later date, and so regain control of their ventures, may make them more willing to seek external equity capital in the early stages of their ventures.

To satisfy the rigorous listing requirements and pay the high listing costs of an exchange, a venture must be very successful, have maintained healthy growth rates, and be beyond the early stages of its development. Interestingly, at the IPO stage, providing finance for the firm's growth is usually not the major motivation; rather, procuring exit routes and share liquidity is primary. In addition, a public stock offering may also seem attractive because it does not directly involve soliciting the types of finance provider possibly exhausted in earlier rounds of financing (Freear, Sohl, and Wetzel, 1991). However, IPOs can be quite complicated on account of the resulting management changes, refinancings, regulatory requirements, reevaluations, and so on (Bygrave and others, 1999).

Few firms are fortunate enough to reach this, the traditionally most profitable, stage of exit for entrepreneurial investors. In the United States, it is estimated that only 1 percent of corporations are publicly traded and only 0.25 percent are listed on an organized exchange (Wetzel, 1986a). The SBA estimates that fewer than one in a thousand new ventures actually have an IPO ("Startup Firms . . .," 1999). This means that much less than 1 percent of corporate start-up ventures are eventually able to develop a market for their shares on an exchange (Wetzel, 1996), which may be partly because an IPO has to be in the $20–50 million range to

create a market for a firm ("The Financing of . . .," 1996). As we
have seen, many high-growth ventures in the high-tech sector
have recently elected to explore trade sales to larger corporations
instead.

Nevertheless, entrepreneurs tend to be more optimistic about
getting a listing than these statistics suggest they actually should
be. A whopping 73 percent of the new technology-based firms in
a 1991 study actually believed that a public stock offering was
"highly likely" or "probable" (Freear, Sohl, and Wetzel, 1991). In
addition, venture capital–funded firms were more optimistic than
angel-funded firms about this funding option (Freear, Sohl, and
Wetzel, 1991), probably because the former are in a later development stage and larger in size; indeed, having venture capital
funds and accompanying guidance do dramatically increase the
odds of ever reaching the IPO stage.

Interestingly, around 26–33 percent of all IPOs in the United
States are venture capital–funded firms (Sahlman, 1990; Carter
and Van Auken, 1994), while in the UK, for instance, this appears
to be the case for 48 percent of IPOs (Murray, 1995a). Considering the low percentage of firms funded by venture capitalists,
these seem to have a disproportionally higher probability of going
public. In certain industries, such as software and biotechnology,
the percentage is even higher (Wasserman, 1999). Although the
IPO market for venture capital–backed firms was particularly
healthy from 1991 to 1996 (raising more than $12.2 billion for
280 firms in 1996 alone), only $5 billion and $3.8 billion were
raised in 1997 and 1998 respectively (NVCA, 1999). Regardless, it
is important to remember that IPOs give firms only a small fraction of the overall capital supplied by venture capitalists, and especially business angels (Gaston, 1989; Mason and Harrison,
1991). Yet, the IPO and equity markets have an important influence over the flows of venture capital within an economy (Bygrave
and Shulman, 1988).

Despite their economic influence and benefits, IPOs may not
enable investors to immediately sell their stake holdings in entirety (thanks to vesting requirements), and the companies may
not be able to choose their funding partner (and possibly subject
it to an unfriendly takeover). This, and the variable IPO market of
the last two years, have also helped make trade sales a common

# Figure 3.4. A Financial Chronology of Amazon.com (1994–1999).

| Price/Share | Time Line | Sources of Funds |
|---|---|---|
| $.001 | **1994**<br>July '94–<br>November '94 | **Founder**<br>Jeff Bezos starts Amazon.com;<br>he invests $10,000 and borrows $44,000. |
| $.1717 | **1995**<br>February '95–<br>July '95 | **Family**<br>Founder's father and mother invest a combined $245,500. |
| $.1287–<br>.3333 | August '95–<br>December '95 | **Business Angels**<br>Two angels invest a total of $54,408. |
| $.3333 | **1996**<br>December '95–<br>May '96 | **Angel Syndicate**<br>Twenty angels invest $46,850 each on average,<br>for a total of $937,000. |
| $.3333 | May '96 | **Family**<br>Founder's siblings invest $20,000. |
| $2.3417 | June '96 | **Venture Capitalists**<br>Two venture capital funds<br>invest $8 million. |
| $18 | **1997**<br>May '97 | **Initial Public Offering (IPO)**<br>Three million shares are offered on the equity market,<br>raising $49.1 million. |
| $52.11<br>(exercise price on<br>loan warrants) | **1998**<br>Dec '97–<br>May '98 | **Loan and Bond Issue**<br>$326 million bond issue is used to retire<br>$75 million in loan debt and to finance operations. |

$1,327.50 (in April 1999, adjusted for two stock splits)

*Source:* data partially adapted from Smith and Kiholm (forthcoming).

exit route for venture capital–funded firms. The equity markets are clearly a funding option that only few entrepreneurial firms are able to use, but their presence, and the promise of eventual liquidity, stimulates many investors (both business angels and venture capitalists) to fund in the entrepreneurial arena.

The financial history of Amazon.com (Figure 3.4) is a good example of some of the financial sources that high-growth entrepreneurial firms can use throughout their evolution.

# Part Two

# The Two Main Sources of Funding

Business Angels and
Venture Capitalists

*Chapter Four*

# The Value of Business Angels and Venture Capitalists

We have already argued that the business angel market is critical to the survival and growth of young entrepreneurial firms. Chapter Four shows that the size and untapped potential of this market dwarfs that of all others. Even compared to the formal venture capital market, the angel market is the oldest and biggest market for venture capital finance in the United States. Unfortunately, business angels' know-how and capital are two of this country's least understood and underused economic resources, and the business angel market in the United States (and other countries) is operating far below its potential (Wetzel, 1993).

## The Nature of Business Angel Investments

Business angels are individual investors with varied backgrounds, so generalizing about them as a whole is overly simplistic; nevertheless, they do have unique characteristics and advantages that are noteworthy (Figure 4.1).

We suggest that angels enjoy at least ten advantages:

1. *Business angels prefer smaller-size investments than venture capitalists.* The funding amounts fall within the equity gap—the range of funding sought below $100,000–500,000 that is normally too small to entice institutional investors to participate, primarily because of those investors' sizable due diligence and monitoring costs (Mason and Harrison, 1993a; Freear, Sohl,

**Figure 4.1.  The Pros and Cons of Business Angel Investments.**

| Angels' Characteristics | Investment Characteristics | Added Bonuses |
|---|---|---|
| Value-adding | Seek smaller deals | Leveraging effect |
| Geographically dispersed | Prefer start-up and early-stage | Give loan guarantees |
| More permissive investors | Invest in all industry sectors | No high fees |
| | Like high-tech firms | |

*Advantages*

**Business Angels**

*Disadvantages*

| Little follow-on money | Want a say in firm | Could turn out to be "devils" | No national reputation to leverage |
|---|---|---|---|

and Wetzel, 1996; Harrison and Mason, 1992a). However, few firms can raise $5 million until they have raised up to $500,000 for their early growth and development. This presents a sort of catch-22 for entrepreneurial firms and makes the advent of business angels, and their preference for small investments (often less than $100,000 per angel, as Chapter Nine shows), a necessary blessing.

2. *Business angels usually invest in start-ups and early-stage ventures,* the ones having the most difficulty obtaining outside funds (Mason and Harrison, 1993a, 1995; Freear, Sohl, and Wetzel, 1996). Even Stanley E. Pratt, the former publisher of *Pratt's Guide to Venture Capital Sources,* the bible for the venture capital community, admitted to the suitability of business angels in his advice for entrepreneurs: "Unless you're highly unusual, I wouldn't waste my time with venture capitalists . . . I'd look for individual [investors]" (Posner, 1993, p. 55). Studies show that business angels make up a whopping 44 percent of all external equity investors supporting firms with revenues less than

$3 million, 26 percent of those funding firms with revenues of $3–10 million, and only 4 percent of all external investors funding ventures with revenues above $10 million (Posner, 1993).

3. *Business angels make investments in virtually all industry sectors* (Mason and Harrison, 1995). The range of investments they fund is unlimited. We have come across angels who have funded bathing suit companies, prototypes of sailboats, and even a syndicate in Nebraska that funded a new hockey arena for a semiprofessional hockey team. Sector aside, however, it should be noted that what most attracts angels to an investment is high growth potential (as opposed to lifestyle or mom-and-pop operations).

4. *Business angels are more flexible in their financial decisions than venture capitalists* and tend to have different investment criteria, longer investment horizons ("patient money"), shorter investment processes, and lower targeted rates of return (Freear, Sohl, and Wetzel, 1996; Harrison and Mason, 1991a, 1992a; Deakins, 1996).

5. *Raising funds from business angels does not involve the high fees* incurred when raising funding from financial institutions (Harrison and Mason, 1991a).

6. *Most business angels are value-added investors* in that they contribute their personal business skills to furthering young businesses (Mason and Harrison, 1996b) and therefore may elect to invest locally to facilitate involvement (Wetzel, 1983; Mason, Harrison, and Allen, 1995). This free assistance and advice from an investor who, quite often, is a seasoned veteran of the business world is priceless for young entrepreneurs starting out and would not normally be affordable by other means. Since angels prefer to invest locally, their sector experiences and preferences often align strongly with many of the new firms in the area. An obvious example are the many wealthy high-tech entrepreneurs in Silicon Valley who are now investing their own funds in the next generation of local high-tech firms.

7. *The business angel financing market is more geographically dispersed* than the formal venture capital market; business angels can be found everywhere, not just in major financial centers. This is

particularly important for regional development since many angels elect to invest in a firm within a few hours' drive of their homes, thereby helping to retain and recirculate wealth within geographic areas (Mason and Harrison, 1995, 1996b). Indeed, angel investing tends to be very regional in nature. Angel funds are particularly plentiful in areas such as California and Massachusetts, but other places emerging as particularly influential areas are North Carolina, Colorado, the Pacific Northwest, Austin (Texas), and central Utah (Sohl, 1999). In certain other regions, the supply of finance is slightly scarcer, leading some states to set up high-tech venture funds with state money to seed early-stage firms. These funds are capitalized annually to the tune of $50 million in Pennsylvania, $50 million in Virginia, and $87 million in North Carolina and $19 million in Illinois, but they have only limited effect ("Helping High-Tech Firms . . .," 1999). Angels now already provide substantial sums in these areas, and with proper incentives their funding power could be vastly increased. One such interesting initiative has been undertaken by the government of Singapore to boost local entrepreneurship ("15 High-Tech Startups . . .," 1999). A $10 million Business Angel Fund (BAF) has been set up to stimulate investments by angels (including foreign angels) in start-up firms in Singapore, matching investments made by these or institutional investors in high-tech start-ups. The success of such schemes remains to be seen.

8. *Obtaining money from a business angel has a leveraging effect* in that it makes the investee firm more attractive to other sources of possible finance (Mason and Harrison, 1996b; Mason, Harrison, and Allen, 1995). Angel investments certainly heighten venture capital interest in such ventures.

9. *Business angels are also instrumental thanks to the loan guarantees they offer* their investee firms, in addition to the money they personally invest. The angel who helped Apple Computer get off the ground in 1977 invested $91,000 and guaranteed another $250,000 in credit lines.

10. *Angels are not averse to funding technology companies,* which inherently come with high risks. In fact, U.S. angels fund 60 percent of all young technology firms looking for $1 million or less in start-up funds (Chan, 1999). In Silicon Valley alone, business angels bankrolled 786 start-up companies in 1998, in-

vesting a combined $4.55 billion (Talton, 1999). We found that 64 percent of U.S. matching services believe that their angels prefer high-tech investments, 21 percent claim their investors are indifferent, and only 15 percent believe high-tech opportunities are not preferred.

Business angels also have a few disadvantages, and we call attention to four in particular:

1. Business angels are less likely to make follow-on investments in the same firm (Mason and Harrison, 1995). Conversely, venture capitalists spend around two-thirds of their funds on expansion funding of their existing portfolio firms.
2. Business angels prefer to have a say in the running of the firm, which may force the entrepreneur to give up some degree of control (Mason and Harrison, 1995). Some business angels may have limited expertise in running the particular type of investee firm they fund, making their contribution less value-added and more meddlesome.
3. A small minority of business angels may turn out to be "devils" who have self-serving motives for investment (Mason and Harrison, 1995), rather than promoting the good of the firm.
4. Unlike many venture capital firms, business angels do not have the national reputation and prestige of a big-name institution, which can be crucial if the firm is successful enough to seek assistance from an investment bank for a private placement or IPO (Spragins, 1991).

Fortunately, it is widely agreed that the advantages of business angels generally outweigh their disadvantages; this has prompted some to conclude that an active informal venture capital market is a prerequisite for a vigorous enterprise economy (Mason, 1996a).

## Overall Size of the Business Angel and Venture Capital Markets

Although business angels can be hard to find, their "lack of visibility does not imply . . . lack of importance in the supply of equity capital" (Wetzel and Freear, 1994, p. 4). It is well documented in both the United States and the UK that the business angel market is the largest source of risk financing for entrepreneurial firms, vastly exceeding the institutional venture capital industry (Mason, Harrison, and Allen, 1995; Mason and Harrison, 1993a, 1996a; Benjamin and Margulis, 1996; Wetzel, 1987). Gaston (1989) even suggests that the amount of business angel investment in the United States almost exceeds that of the combined total of all other financing sources of external equity for start-up and early-stage growth firms, while Benjamin and Margulis (1996) believe that business angels represent some 61 percent of new venture funding.

Obtaining accurate numbers for the size of this market, however, is very difficult. On account of the anonymity of business angels, estimating their market size involves inducing measurements from small samples; this has yielded a variety of assessments from the academic sector. These back-of-the-envelope figures should therefore be considered only as rough estimates rather than definitive (Mason, 1996b). But regardless of the diversity of the findings, it is universally agreed that the business angel market is enormous.

In the early 1990s, it was estimated that there were around two million business angels in the United States, each with a net worth of more than $1 million excluding their primary residence (Freear, Sohl, and Wetzel, 1996; Ou, 1987) and holding anywhere from $100 billion to $300 billion (Ou, 1987; Wetzel and Freear, 1994) in equity investment portfolios. About three hundred thousand of these U.S. business angels (or one-eighth of the angel population) (Wetzel and Freear, 1994) invested $10–30 billion annually (Wetzel and Freear, 1994; Freear, Sohl, and Wetzel, 1995a; Gaston, 1989) in about twenty thousand to sixty thousand small firms (Wetzel, 1987, 1993, 1996; Freear, Sohl, and Wetzel, 1992b), even though about one hundred thousand start-ups annually met the minimum funding requirements of business angels (Wetzel and Freear, 1994). More recently, however, it has been estimated that angels invest $50–60 billion annually in U.S. firms, of which $15 billion goes into sixty thousand high-risk, early-stage firms (Benjamin and Margulis, 1996). Meanwhile, the National Venture Capital Association (NVCA) has suggested that angels may actually invest around $100 billion annually (Cullen, 1998). It has even been estimated that business angel investments account for 0.15 percent of the U.S. gross domestic product, or GDP (KPMG, 1992). Interestingly, many of the estimates from the early 1990s are already a number of years old and some were collected during economic times less expansionary than those we have had over the last few years. Thanks to recent prosperity, we believe that many of these amounts may be significantly greater today; a quite conservative estimate is probably around the $50–60 billion mark annually. Yet even some of the conservative numbers given here still highlight the incredible size of the angel market.

In contrast to the U.S. angel market (see Figure 4.2), the U.S. venture capital industry holds a portfolio of around $50 billion; in 1998 it invested $4.8 billion in 1,122 early-stage firms, while about twice this amount ($10.1 billion) was spent on supplementary (follow-on) investments to existing portfolio companies (NVCA, 1999). This disparity between the business angel and venture capital markets suggests that business angels fund to entrepreneurial firms three to five times more annually than the venture-capital industry does (Freear, Sohl, and Wetzel, 1996; Mason and Harrison, 1993b)! Since business angel investments are, on average, of a much smaller size, academic estimates claim that business angels in the United States fund between thirty and forty times the number of entrepreneurial firms financed by the formal venture capital industry (Wetzel and Freear, 1994; Gaston, 1989).

**Figure 4.2. The Comparative Size of Angel Versus Venture Capital Investment Activity.**

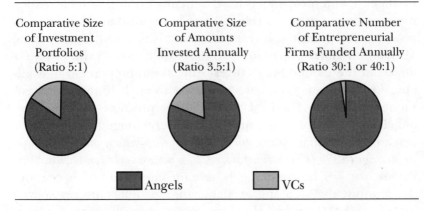

| Comparative Size of Investment Portfolios (Ratio 5:1) | Comparative Size of Amounts Invested Annually (Ratio 3.5:1) | Comparative Number of Entrepreneurial Firms Funded Annually (Ratio 30:1 or 40:1) |

Similarly, in the UK, where the business angel market is slightly less developed than its counterpart in the United States, it has still grown substantially over the last ten to fifteen years (ACOST, 1990; Mason and Harrison, 1996b). It is estimated that in the UK there are thirty thousand to fifty thousand business angels (Bowden, 1994; Mason and Harrison, 1993b), who have invested more than three times as much in small entrepreneurial firms as the formal venture capital market (with investments around £4 billion and £1.25 billion respectively; Van Osnabrugge, 1998; Stevenson and Coveney, 1994; Mason, Harrison, and Allen, 1995). The number of firms that business angels fund in the UK may also be thirty to forty times greater than the number supported by venture capitalists (Van Osnabrugge, 1998). In Canada, angels are also an important economic force, investing between $500 million and $1 billion each year in entrepreneurial firms (Gordon, 1999).

## The Vast Untapped Potential of the Business Angel Market

Despite its significant size, the potential scale of the business angel market is significantly greater than the current figures suggest (Mason, Harrison, and Allen, 1995; Mason and Harrison, 1993a, 1993b). The size of the business angel market could *potentially* become *ten to twenty* times larger than it is today (Freear, Sohl, and Wetzel, 1996; Reitan and Sorheim, 1999).

There are a number of reasons for this. First, the market is inefficient, and most angels have difficulty finding suitable investment opportunities; therefore they have substantial funds still available for potential investment (Harrison and Mason, 1996a; Mason and Harrison, 1996b). KPMG (1992) found that business angels in the United States invest only about 80 percent of available funds (those they have allocated to such high-risk investments). However, other U.S. evidence indicates that business angels may be investing a much lower percentage than this. Our research shows that *individual angels may each have around $312,000 on average ($225,000 median) reserved for more angel investments.* Similarly in the UK, business angels have the equivalent of three times the amount invested still available for possible entrepreneurial investments (Mason and Harrison, 1993a), and 70 percent of business angels in a 1994 study cited the lack of suitable business proposals as the most common reason for not investing more (Stevenson and Coveney, 1994). We found that 80 percent of U.S. matching services believed that their angels would have made more investments over the last three years if there had been more suitable investment proposals. However, we uncovered a number of additional reasons for this curtailed investment activity:

## Main Reasons Angels Do Not Make More Investments

- Lack of business proposals matching their investment criteria
- Lack of quality business proposals
- Lack of trust in the entrepreneur or management team
- Lack of experience in pricing deals
- Lack of experience in due diligence and monitoring
- Lack of available funds

Matching services may slightly ease this inefficiency in both the United States and abroad, but only a small proportion of business angels use them. It is clear that current matching services can at best play a secondary, or support, role to personal and business contacts as the primary information sources for investment proposals, although they are still very important.

Second, entrepreneurs often reject funding offers from business angels. One study found that four times as many offers are made as are accepted (Mason and Harrison, 1996a; Mason, Harrison, and Allen, 1995). If this is truly the case, it reinforces the need for both entrepreneurs and private investors to be educated about the feasibility and realism of funding offers, and particularly on how to effectively negotiate such proposals to a mutually satisfactory outcome.

Third, the business angel market is underdeveloped and still has scope for expansion. In the United States alone, one in every twenty households has a net worth of at least $1 million (Cruz, 1999). In fact, the United States has four million households worth more than $1 million; 275,000 of these are worth $10 million or more (E. N. Wolff, quoted in De Bare, 1999). Since this 5 percent of (millionaire) households holds 68 percent of the net worth in this country, there are many more potential angels out there who may be enticed to invest. In particular, the active business angels in the market are significantly outnumbered by "virgin angels"—high-net-worth individuals with entrepreneurial backgrounds who wish to make their first entrepreneurial investment but have not yet done so (Freear, Sohl, and Wetzel, 1994a; Wetzel and Freear, 1994). Matching services tell us that 20–30 percent of their subscribers are virgin angels. U.S. studies have shown that there may be ten to twenty times as many virgin as active angels (Wetzel and Freear, 1993; Riding and Short, 1987). Motivating these potential investors to take the step of investing may be difficult, especially since in recent years the stock market offered generous returns of 20–30 percent annually and much lower risk than that inherent in business angel deals. Virgin angels may be most influenced to invest by assistance in investment monitoring, opportunities to participate with other business angel investors, and possibly a reduction in the capital gains tax (Freear, Sohl, and Wetzel, 1992a). Our research shows that there are a number of factors motivating angels to invest:

*Factors That Most Motivate Angel Investors to Invest*

- Good trust in the venture's entrepreneur and management team
- Opportunities to co-invest with other more experienced investors
- Opportunities to learn from successful business angels
- Corporate finance advice about making and structuring investments
- Better tax incentives or tax relief

In particular, more knowledge sharing about certain aspects of the investment process results in first-time investors' taking the plunge, as the next list shows. This book details each of these activities in great detail.

*Investment Processes That Could Enable
More Angels to Invest Wisely*

- Initial screening of investment opportunities
- Finding investment opportunities
- Due diligence

- Pricing and structuring deals
- Negotiating deals
- Monitoring the investment
- Exiting the deal

It has been suggested that with the right combination of enticements it is possible to entice over half of the virgin angels to become active business angels (Mason and Harrison, 1993b). Clearly, there is a need to convince virgin angels that investing only a fraction of their investment portfolio in the form of unquoted investments makes sense (Mason and Harrison, 1993b).

Business angel finance is clearly smart money since most business angels are value-adding investors whose experience and investment behaviors can be of great benefit to entrepreneurs. However, this market is clearly not reaching its funding potential, which may certainly restrict its ability to further curtail the equity gap. As the investment criteria of other investors in the market become more conservative, individual sources of venture capital (from business angels) seem likely to become even more significant in financing entrepreneurial companies in the near future.

## Tapping the Billions of Dollars in Unused Angel Funds

The vast size and power of the business angel market in the United States is not well understood but is of incredible importance to our entrepreneurial sector and, indirectly, to maintaining our economic growth and standard of living. On a macro level, it is important for our nation to encourage informal venture capital investment so that more of the business angel market's potential can be realized. There are a number of ways, some more practical than others, in which we could promote investments.

### Awareness

First, awareness needs to be raised among both entrepreneurs and investors of the business angel funding option and the feasibility and benefits of matching services. With the greater efficiency, lower search costs, and improved deal flow that these services generate, it is hoped that investors will be more apt to find those investment opportunities having suitable characteristics. Crude estimates say that probably only 5–10 percent of all business angels use matching services, and a majority of the deals of even those investors may be sourced through other means. This is partly due to the limited number of ventures these services can offer and their resource limitations. To correct these problems, government initiatives are needed to support and promote matching services so that these low-profit or nonprofit services can expand in size and number to reach more participants. In addition, matching services may be able to make a significant difference in facilitating and promoting investment activity in those U.S. regions such as Alaska where such activities are currently limited.

## Education

Second, business angels and entrepreneurs must receive greater education about the ins and outs of business angel investing. This is imperative to obtain alignment of realistic expectations. All too often, entrepreneurs have unrealistic expectations about how to secure external funds, how the types of financier vary, how much of their firm's equity they need to surrender for funds, and what else they can demand from investors. Exposure to the views of both parties, advice on how to prepare effective business plans and contracts, and a closer look at the characteristics that generally make deals suitable for both parties leave fewer surprises for these practitioners. This book certainly aims to aid in many of these crucial aspects, but it is clearly only a small step in the overall effort required. In addition, exposure to success stories involving business angel deals has been shown to dramatically increase interest in, and motivation for, such deals.

## Inducements

Third, more inducements are needed to motivate investment by virgin angels and "latent angels" (those who have not made an angel investment within the last three years but have done so in the past). In particular, making available guidance on conducting deals (such as offered in this book) and better tax incentives may raise their willingness to support entrepreneurial firms. The existence of co-investment syndicates that they can join may also give them the incentive to start investing, but with the added bonus of shared-expertise, guidance, and diversification. In addition, if stock market returns decline in the near future, these individuals may be more willing to pursue the business angel funding alternatives in attempting to maintain high returns on their investment dollars.

## Role Models

Fourth, with the growth and success of the high-tech sector over the last two decades, a whole new class of business angels has evolved out of young and middle-aged high-tech entrepreneurs who successfully cashed out of the high-tech firms they founded. Such investors have grown in number (as has the average amount of their available funding), and although some invest in the funding realm of small venture capital firms most act as traditional business angels. Many of these investors are now supporting the next generation of high-tech products and producing a number of angel success stories. Hopefully, they will act as role models for others who have struck it rich and are now looking for a fun way to invest their entrepreneurial abilities and funds.

## Promotion by Other Financiers

Fifth, it is clear that the health of the business angel market has many beneficial implications for a wide range of other practitioners and intermediaries in the market. This is why it is crucial that banks and venture capital firms, especially, aid promoting the business angel marketplace, indirectly helping themselves in the long run as those firms that angels supported in their early stages come to them for secured loans or development equity finance. Banks certainly have the infrastructure to disseminate information to their customers, and venture capitalists often have access to quality deals, which are too small for them to consider but which they could pass on to business angels and matching services for assistance. Similarly, the federal SBA, though already an excellent source of free information for entrepreneurs, can easily distribute more business angel–specific information to all those who may find it beneficial.

## Business Angel Mutual Funds

Lastly, as we discuss in Chapter Fifteen we believe that mutual funds may be established within the next decade, each ready to make business angel–like investments in hundreds, if not thousands, of young entrepreneurial firms. Although one large U.S. mutual fund family has already started considering the practical feasibility of such investor funds, their formation will probably have a significant effect in motivating transfer of large amounts of unallocated high-risk money to young entrepreneurial firms. In particular, such funds offer many advantages that, we hope, will propel a minority of the ten-to-twenty million virgin angels in the United States (as well as other kinds of investor) to finally invest a small proportion of their portfolio in a diversified fund of un-quoted entrepreneurial ventures.

## Conclusion

Despite its inefficiencies and underused potential, the business angel market today already offers many benefits and much financial power that the venture capital market can only dream of having. Increasing this market's efficiency has only positive implications for the many other complementary practitioners in the entrepreneurial realm. Although this chapter has chronicled the vast size of the market, and ways to potentially increase it, the next chapter has more direct application for entrepreneurs since it shows them how to personally capture some of this market's funding power for their growing ventures.

# Chapter Five

# Harnessing the Power of Business Angels and Venture Capitalists

The search for business angel funds is often difficult, requiring confidence and persistence on the part of the entrepreneur. Without a guide for this search process, such as the one offered in this chapter, an entrepreneur's effort may not be readily rewarded. Just identifying business angels is troublesome (Haar, Starr, and MacMillan, 1988; Mason, 1996a; Gaston, 1989), primarily because:

- There are no directories of business angels
- Business angels prefer anonymity, to avoid being deluged with investment proposals
- The subject matter of business angel investments is often private and personal
- Business angels come from a diverse and dispersed population of wealthy individuals
- There are no public records of their investment transactions (Freear, Sohl, and Wetzel, 1996; Mason and Rogers, 1996)

## Ten Ways to Find Business Angels

Entrepreneurs, and anyone else interested in reaching private investors, may wish to follow any of a number of techniques to increase the odds of finding a suitable angel. We propose ten ways to do so (Figure 5.1).

## Figure 5.1. Finding Business Angels.

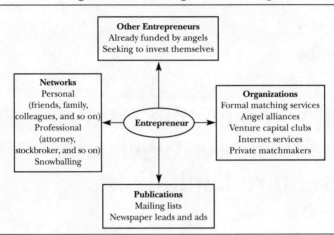

## Personal Networks

Entrepreneurs should tell their former colleagues and friends about their business opportunity, since many people know at least one person who may have the means and inclination to make an investment. Using your own network of personal contacts is essential since it is perhaps the easiest way to generate some interest, and it is hardly a one-sided effort. Business angels, like venture capitalists, are also actively looking for ventures; finding an angel who believes that your particular venture meets all of his or her investment criteria may offer a challenge, but it is a challenge that may be just a temporary situation to be overcome. We actually met one entrepreneur recently who had received all of his $250,000 business angel money from former colleagues and a number of his college professors. These investors required little selling since they were already familiar with his work ethic and potential to make the venture a success.

## Professional Networks

Entrepreneurs should contact their attorneys, accountants, stockbrokers, and other professionals they employ to see if they know or have worked for any wealthy individuals who sometimes make entrepreneurial investments and who may be interested in the entrepreneur's investment opportunity. Most business angel deals are conceived through professional and personal network contacts; probably more are solicited and developed on the golf course or at social gatherings than one could count. Two years ago, one of this book's authors was involved with an Internet start-up that (through a lucky turn of events) received an initial $100,000 investment from the father of one of the firm's lawyers—a business angel living temporarily in the Far East. The lawyer was so enthusiastic about the firm's idea that he actually convinced his father to invest. Since that investment, another business angel (residing much more locally) has invested $300,000, and the firm is now in the process of raising at least $5 million in venture capital. Other, more formal, professional organizations such as local chambers of commerce, boards of trade, and similar business associations may also be able to suggest leads in locating potential angel investors.

## Snowballing

It is important to remember that since businesses have their own personal networks identifying one business angel who buys the opportunity can snowball into locating several others (Neiswander, 1985; Short and Riding, 1989; Postma and Sullivan, 1990). One caveat: quality, not quantity, is the overriding criterion. Finding just one good business angel is all you need to get the ball rolling; for every venture, no matter how unusual, there is a business angel out there willing to fund it. We have even seen cases where one business angel likes an investment opportunity so much that he or she invites business angel friends to get in on the deal to spread the risks, and also to leverage as much business expertise as possible.

## Formal Matching Services

Business angels registered with formal matching services can be reached by joining one of these introduction services and attending their venture forums (Stevenson and Coveney, 1994; Mason, Harrison, and Allen, 1995; Mason, 1993). Although this may involve a fixed rate for membership, these costs may well recoup themselves many times over once angel financing is found. These organizations are often not-for-profit or university affiliated and offer entrepreneurs access to angel investors, while maintaining the anonymity of the potential investors. They also organize venture forums where entrepreneurs and investors can meet face-to-face. About 10–15 percent of entrepreneurs using these services, and around 40 percent of those presenting at venture forums, receive equity financing (Sohl, 1999). These networks may each have upwards of two hundred investor and entrepreneur members (Sohl, 1999). Investors associated with matching services may also be wealthier and potentially more active in their search for investee firms than many think. See Appendix One for a list of these services.

## Angel Alliances

Less formal angel alliances have also been created within the last few years by angels themselves, to cater to their own investment needs. Many such angels are very successful high-tech entrepreneurs with sizable funds available to invest, usually far exceeding those of the average U.S. business angel. Compared to individual angels, these alliances may be able to offer larger sums of money and expertise by pooling resources and know-how, but their participants tend to be more professional and so may have higher standards and be more formal when it comes to the investment negotiations and contract. When these angel syndicates meet, it is usually to discuss the merits of an investment opportunity already screened and championed by one of the angels in the group, rather than as a means of identifying new opportunities. Some of these syndicates are very small, while others may have in excess of one hundred angel investors. To protect the anonymity of their members, some even have storefronts to attract attention and deals (Sohl, 1999). The emergence of these loosely organized angel groups is certainly very encouraging and will have an important impact on the overall size and power of the business angel market in the years to come. See Appendix One for a list of these angel groups as well.

## Venture Capital Clubs

Offering a variety of services to their members, venture capital clubs or forums usually meet regularly as a means for investors and entrepreneurs to come together and share educational opportunities (Sohl, 1999). Some clubs have a small number of angels who invest together, while others act more as a resource for entrepreneurs to sharpen their business plans and presentation skills. These clubs are less professional, elite, and close-knit than the angel alliances, and they tend to use the venture forum (that is, the meeting) as a screening process to listen to various entrepreneurs rather than to discuss the merits of an opportunity that one of the members has found and is verbally backing, as is typical in an angel alliance. A number of these organizations are featured in Appendix One.

## The Internet

The Internet has a number of electronic matching networks specializing in finding start-up funds for suitable entrepreneurs and investment opportunities for private investors (and often small venture capital firms too). Around thirty are currently operating on the World Wide Web. If you have access to the Internet, you may want to start with some of the networks listed here (Nittka, 1999), although many of the formal matching services listed in Appendix One also have Web links.

*Electronic Matching Services on the World Wide Web*

United States:
| | |
|---|---|
| ACE-Net | http://ace-net.sr.unh.edu/ |
| American Venture Capital Exchange | http://www.avce.com |
| America's Business Funding Directory | http://www.businessfinance.com/ |
| Capital Connection | http://www.capital-connection.com/ |
| Capital Matchmaker | http://www.matchmaker.org/capital/ |
| Commercial Finance Online | http://www.cfol.com/ |
| Finance Hub | http://financehub.com/ |
| Garage.com | http://www.garage.com/ |
| Investors Network | http://www.investorsnet.com/venture/index.html |
| Money Hunter | http://www.moneyhunter.com/ |

Canada:

| | |
|---|---|
| Investment Exchange | http://www.tinvex.com/ |

United Kingdom:

| | |
|---|---|
| Development Capital Exchange | http://www.equity-invest.com/ |
| Equity Link | http://www.equitylink.co.uk |
| Local Investment Networking Company | http://www.linc.co.uk |
| Oxfordshire Investment Opportunities Network | http://www.oxtrust.org.uk/oion/ |
| Startup Group | http://suf1.com |
| Venture Capital Report | http://www.vcrl978.com |
| Venture Site | http://www.venturesite.co.uk |
| Xénos | http://www.xenos.co.uk |

Germany:

| | |
|---|---|
| Business Angels Network Germany | http://www.exchange.de/band/ *and* http://www.business-angels.de |
| German Equity Forum | http://www.exchange.de/ekforum/ |
| Deutsche Internet Beteiligungsbörse | http://www.netit.de/dib/ |

France:

| | |
|---|---|
| Club Business Angels | http://www.clubbusinessangels.com/ |
| Réseau des Entrepreneurs | http://www.business-angels.com/ |

*Source:* partially adapted from Nittka (1999).

The U.S. government has even established a website called Angel Capital Electronic Network, or ACE-NET (the first entry in the list), which promotes angel matches and investments by providing links to its many member matching services (in more than thirty-five states) and extending some interesting data and links to entrepreneurs and investors. These electronic networks have up to now only had limited success and were responsible for less than 1 percent of the equity capital raised in 1997 (Sohl, 1999). According to Sohl (1999), this may be due in part to the face-to-face nature of angel investing, the failure of these networks to fully address the regional geographic nature of the finance market, and the value-added component of angel investments that may be lacking through this matching medium. Even so, these services are still evolving and should certainly not be overlooked. Also, the SBA's website (www.sba.gov/) and Appendix Two of this book list many valuable online resources for investors and entrepreneurs.

## Matchmakers

Checking the *Wall Street Journal* almost certainly leads to ads for matchmakers who specialize in introducing entrepreneurs and business angels to one another (Gruner, 1998). But be sure to check the track record of such an intermediary for raising money, ask for references from individuals for whom he or she has raised money in the past, and make sure that you do not pay the matchmaker's fee until the money has actually come in. A success fee of 5–10 percent raised is reasonable (Spragins, 1991).

For more academic and research-oriented readers, we also offer two additional methods:

## Mailing Lists and Publications

Large-scale sample surveys of high-net-income individuals can be undertaken from purchased mailing lists in the hope that some of them may have engaged in business angel investments (Haar, Starr, and MacMillan, 1988; Postma and Sullivan, 1990).

## Investee Firms

Business angels can be contacted through their investee firms, who can act as intermediaries for the introduction (Aram, 1989; Gaston, 1989). However, this involves finding firms that have received business angel funding and are willing to contact their investors on your behalf. Also, many angels are currently successful business owners, so meeting as many local business owners as possible can lead to an angel contact (Riding, 1998).

For researchers in the business angel field, practical reasons restrict the feasibility of random samples, and therefore most academics rely on convenience samples. Because of the invisibility of business angels, Harrison and Mason (1992a) conclude that a group of randomly selected business angels would not necessarily be more representative than one collected with a convenience sample (Mason and Rogers, 1996). Even as we contacted investors for our research, it was clear that business angels preferred anonymity, especially in comparison to venture capitalists. In setting up our interviews with countless business angels, often extensive explanation was required as to the purpose of our inquiry and how we found them, whereas only minimal explanation was required by most venture capitalists. A number of business angels refused to participate in the interviews, without giving a reason, while only a few venture capitalists declined.

Since we, as researchers from a reputable business school, experienced some roadblocks in our attempts to conduct anonymous interviews, most entrepreneurs in search of substantial financial investments are likely to discover similar problems. This is the reality of the business angel market, despite what others may tell you. The good news is that the advice in this chapter makes the road much less bumpy; besides, entrepreneurs usually need the investment of only one business angel to end the search process and to continue the growth of their venture.

## Types of Business Angels

Although business angels have many common traits, the heterogeneity of their population has been recognized for some time. Researchers and practitioners have suggested quite a range in the number of business angel types: two (Kelly and Hay, 1996; Van Osnabrugge, 1999b), three (Postma and Sullivan, 1990), five (Evanson, 1998), six (Coveney, 1996), nine (Benjamin and Margulis, 1996), and even ten (Gaston, 1989)! We believe that some of these general categorizations (and their various degrees of overlap) are helpful in comprehending the divergence within the business angel population, but they should not be considered definitive. In our research, we found that many of the angels we have met over the years do not fit neatly into any one of the many categories suggested. But for fun and insight, here are some of the angel classifications that have been suggested over the years (Table 5.1).

## Table 5.1. Types of Angels According to Several Researchers.

*Evanson (1998): five types*

| | |
|---|---|
| Corporate angels | These private investors use their severance or early-retirement pay from former senior management positions at Fortune 1000 corporations to make entrepreneurial investments. Typically, they seek a new senior management job in the investment, want to be involved in one investment at a time, have about $1 million in cash, and make investments in the $200,000 range. |
| Entrepreneurial angels | The most active of the angel investors, they invest the largest amounts, generally $200,000–500,000. They tend to have been successful entrepreneurs themselves, now looking for ways to diversify their portfolio or expand their current business, rather than looking for a new job. |
| Enthusiast angels | Less professional than their entrepreneurial counterparts, these angels invest in firms more as a hobby now that they are in their later years. They tend to invest smaller amounts (from ten thousand to a few hundred thousand dollars) across a number of companies in the hope that one will have an IPO, but they do not actively participate in their investments. |
| Micromanagement angels | These angels prefer great control over their investments, often micromanaging them from a seat on the company board rather than through active participation. They may invest in as many as four companies at a time, adding value as well as money to each. |
| Professional angels | As investors from backgrounds in professional careers (doctors, lawyers, accountants), these angels prefer to invest in firms that offer a product or service with which they have experience, frequently offering their sector expertise to the investee firm, although they're usually not too actively involved. Generally investing in a number of firms simultaneously, they tend to invest from $25,000 to $200,000 each and prefer to co-invest with their peers. |

*(continued)*

**Table 5.1.** (*continued*)

*Benjamin and Margulis (1996): nine types*

| | |
|---|---|
| Value-added investors | As very experienced investors (often former bankers or professional venture capitalists), these angels take an active role in the multiple investments they make. They prefer to invest in firms close to home and concentrate on industry sectors in which they have experience. They normally invest $50,000 to $250,000 per deal. |
| Deep-pocket investors | These angels tend to be successful entrepreneurs who have sold their firms and want to invest in industry sectors they know. They prefer a high degree of control over their investee firms and often contribute some assistance. Investing $50,000 to $250,000 per deal, they prefer a rate of return around 50 percent annually in each of the one to three investments they make annually. |
| Consortium of individual investors | This is a loose group of perhaps three to six unrelated business angels with significant entrepreneurial experience who make their own decisions (and so may not always invest as a team). Investing $50,000 to $500,000 per deal, they seek firms with a competitive advantage in which they can be passively involved. |
| Partner investors | Having a high desire for control, these angels invest in a particular young firm with the hidden intention of taking it over someday. They believe this is the best way to gain control of their own firm since the $250,000 to $1 million they are able to invest would normally not be enough to acquire an already established firm. |
| Family of investors | This group of family members pool their money so that one of their most trusted and business-skilled members can invest it in a venture on their behalf. To aid their investment, they actively contribute their experience, as well as $100,000 to $1 million. This is a particularly common angel type among Asian investors. |

## Table 5.1. (*continued*)

*Benjamin and Margulis (1996): nine types*

| | |
|---|---|
| Barter investors | As active hands-on investors, these angels have a preference for early-stage firms in which they invest capital, as well as some sort of infrastructure contribution (such as a warehouse site for the firm), in exchange for their equity stake. They normally invest up to $250,000 and prefer firms with a capacity to grow to $10 million in three to five years. |
| Socially responsible private investors | These angels prefer to invest in entrepreneurs with high moral values and ventures addressing major social issues. They provide handholding support, rather than business acumen, and tend to have inherited (rather than earned) wealth. |
| Unaccredited private investors | Generally less experienced and less wealthy than the other angel types, these investors prefer early-stage ventures in which they can get a relatively swift return on their investment dollars (three to five years). To the tune of $10,000–25,000 per deal, they invest (with the spouse's consent) in multiple firms, usually close to home. |
| Manager-investors | As wealthy former entrepreneurs or senior executives, these angels seek one last investment to which they can contribute actively for a lengthy period. Less experienced as investors, they are risk-averse, preferring conduct of extensive due diligence, ventures that are developed, and a staging of their $100,000 to $200,000 investment. |

*Gaston (1989): ten types in the United States*

| | |
|---|---|
| Business devils | These investors, often having a lower income level and educational achievement, invest in a firm with the aim of eventually gaining absolute majority control. Though difficult to detect initially as devils, they prefer to invest in small firms close to home in which they can be very actively involved. Their investment equity structure also tends to be quite complex. |

*(continued)*

**Table 5.1.** (*continued*)

---

*Gaston (1989): ten types in the United States*

---

| | |
|---|---|
| The godfather | This is the name given to business angels who have been successful in business, are often semiretired, and are looking for a young firm to mentor, usually as a part-time job. They tend to be wealthy individuals with high incomes who are a bit older and more business savvy than the average angel. They rarely seek majority control, give larger loans or guarantees than usual, and may constitute 25 percent of all angels. These investor-entrepreneur relationships have one of the highest satisfaction rates (83 percent) of all angel groups. |
| Peers | As already successful entrepreneurs, peers simultaneously assume the role of business angel, usually investing in small local firms. As one of the largest groups of angels, they tend to be young, unlikely to seek majority control, patient as investors, and sensitive to entrepreneurs' concerns. Lack of management talent is their number one deal killer. |
| Cousin Randy | These angels invest only in their own families' businesses and so are not a funding option for unrelated entrepreneurs. They represent possibly 10 percent of all angels, are young and experienced males who invest for a minority position, have low ROI expectations, and usually become active in running the family business. |
| Dr. Kildare | These investors are from traditional professions (medicine, accounting, law) and rely on their friends—as opposed to business associates—for information about investment opportunities. Constituting about 9 percent of angels, they generally have average business angel characteristics, except that they have less business and entrepreneurial experience, pay a high price for investment equity, offer a low level of assistance in their investee firms, expect low ROI, and have low satisfaction levels. |

## Table 5.1. (*continued*)

*Gaston (1989): ten types in the United States*

| | |
|---|---|
| Corporate achievers | As successful business executives from large corporations in the past, these investors now wish to be entrepreneurial in a top management slot. Possibly 13 percent of angels, these corporate managers desire to run the show and, in the midst of a career change, often take control of their investee firms from the entrepreneurs. They may not differ too much from business devils. |
| Daddy Warbucks | These are the wealthiest of all angels, responsible for 39 percent of all angel deals and investing 68 percent of all angel funds. They represent around a third of angels and, unlike some other types, are all millionaires. Though they make no more than an average investment per deal, they provide four times the amount of loans and guarantees. In general, they tend to own their own businesses; use business associates to find deals; take minority equity stakes; and prefer the finance, insurance, and real estate sectors. The level of success tends to be unusually high, as does their benevolence. |
| High-tech angels | These investors are only interested in funding companies that manufacture high-technology products, partly because their wealth originates from entrepreneurial success in this sector. They tend to be wealthier than the average angel, are experienced as businesspeople, and have a preference for co-investing in small angel groups. They are very active in their investee firms, rarely obtain voting control, accept a low ownership stake for the size of their investment, and are patient investors. |
| The stockholder | Least active in their investee firms, these investors may be less suited to entrepreneurs seeking outside assistance. They read the firm's reports and vote at shareholder meetings, but they play no other role in company operations. These inactive investors might |

*(continued)*

**Table 5.1.** (*continued*)

| *Gaston (1989): ten types in the United States* | |
| --- | --- |
| | make up 11 percent of all angels, and compared to most they tend to have less entrepreneurial experience, prefer to co-invest with others, are indifferent about investing in firms that are not local, invest infrequently, and invest amounts (and receive equity stakes) that tend to be small. |
| Very hungry angels | These investors not only want to invest more than opportunity dictates but also hope to double their level of business angel investment. These eager investors, possibly 15 percent of all angels, tend to make smaller-than-average investments, have high expectations for rate of return, have limited business experience, rely on friends to find them deals, and (although they aggressively seek majority control) have no more than average success—partly because they prefer larger-sized firms. |

Clearly, the number of angel types and names suggested over the years are plentiful, but they should only be used as a rough guide for the wide variety of private investors one can encounter. Being aware of this diversity can certainly help in deciding the type of investor most worthwhile for your business and the capacity in which you would like that investor to contribute. However, though most of these angel types pertain to individual investors, the number and amount of investments conducted through syndicates of multiple business angels investing together as a group is increasing. Entrepreneurs may encounter not only single investors but also groups of multiple investors, each with at least one lead investor who represents the group's interests.

## Searching for Venture Capitalists

For those experienced entrepreneurs seeking financial backing of firms that are established and have high potential growth, venture capital may well be an option to consider. Luckily, finding a list of venture capital firms is not terribly difficult. A search in any local library for *Pratt's Guide to Venture Capital* sources (see Appendix Two)—or for those abroad, *Venture Capital Report's Guide to Venture Capital in the U.K. and Europe*—answers your search needs. However, this may only be of limited help. As we discuss in detail in Chapter Eight, approaching a venture capital firm with no prior contact or connections (that is, a cold call) only rarely results in a funding offer. These professional investors normally find investments through a broad web of network contacts and referrers, people whose endorsements justify analyzing those investment opportunities further. The implication for entrepreneurs is that if they wish to seek venture capital backing, they must use any professional contacts they may have. Further complicating this search, venture capitalists in general have shifted their investment focus over the last decade to larger and more established firms, and in particular to providing further rounds of finance to companies in which they already have an equity stake—with the exception of early-stage Internet firms, which remain popular.

## Types of Venture Capitalists

As with business angels, venture capital firms are not all the same and can be easily classified based on asset size, sector focus, the level of the firm's independence from its fund providers, and, of course, preferences for investment stage. Even though the majority of venture capital firms now focus primarily on expansion capital, a minority consider seed and early-stage investments, particularly in Internet and technology fields. These seed venture capital firms tend to be much smaller in size and act as a hybrid between business angels and the average venture capital firm. Most venture capitalists require, as a minimum, that your firm has a product with high potential that is somewhat proven, a skilled management team, a market with a high growth rate, a competitive advantage, and financials that project multimillion dollar company revenue streams within a matter of years; but the investment criteria of seed venture capital firms tend to be slightly more relaxed. Pursuing such companies may be the best option for those growing firms that want to raise amounts in excess of what business angels are willing to provide, but below what would interest most venture capital firms—roughly the $500,000 to $4 million range.

## Search Advice for Entrepreneurs and Investors

With guesstimates suggesting that probably more than $50 billion in business angel funds is made available each year in the United States for some of the youngest and riskiest fast-growing firms, the aim of entrepreneurs should be to effectively secure a slice of this financial pie. Unfortunately, as we have already seen, the business angel marketplace is inefficient, and business angels are difficult to locate. These circumstances have implications for both entrepreneurs (breaking through the invisibility barrier of business angels) and angel investors (to prepare for effective investing).

---

### Search Tips for Entrepreneurs

1. Entrepreneurs should try to personally finance and bootstrap their firms as long as possible, until the need for external growth finance becomes evident and unavoidable.

2. Entrepreneurs should carefully weigh the pros and cons of business angels *before* they initiate the search for, and discussions with, private investors.

3. If business angel finance is deemed appropriate, entrepreneurs should form realistic expectations of roughly how much money they need and how much equity they are willing to surrender.

4. Entrepreneurs should try to learn as much as they can about business angels and how they behave; they should decide what type of business angel they prefer in their firm and what role they want the investor to assume. For example, some young ventures in need of accounting and finance assistance often try to find a business angel with such skills to contribute, in addition to money.

5. Entrepreneurs must sharpen their business plans with the latest information, realistic financial projections, and rough potential valuations—topics dealt with in depth in Chapters Twelve, Thirteen, and Appendix Three. All too

often, investors see poor business plans that do not explicitly show that the entrepreneur has fully thought out possible scenarios. Realistic financial projections show the competence and care of the entrepreneur.

6. Entrepreneurs should try to follow any of the ten methods listed in this chapter for finding business angel investors. In particular, they should wisely exploit their contacts and networks to the fullest so that they are heard.

7. Finally, entrepreneurs must learn to discriminate between investor types and not just take the first offer, but rather the one most appropriate for the good of the firm. Entrepreneurs should also carry out due diligence of their own on potential investors; it certainly is a two-way street. Once a worthy investor has been found, entrepreneurs should learn how to hold their own in the negotiations stage. Chapter Thirteen is dedicated to this very important skill.

## Search Tips for Business Angels

1. Investors must truly decide whether they want and are able to assume the high risks of business angel investing. They should realize that allocating only a small portion of their investment portfolio (say, 5–15 percent) may be the best way to get started in the entrepreneurial investment arena. Setting a rough investment limit controls initial risk exposure and frees up some money for additional expansion funds if investments are successful. Staging investment over time is one way to reduce the risks of business angel investing. Many angels call the funds they invest "casino money" since if they lose them or make a small return, it will not affect their standard of living—but they might hit the jackpot.

2. Investors should determine in which industry sectors they feel most comfortable. Many business angels prefer to invest in sectors in which they have experience since it allows them to contribute assistance to the firm and judge the risks of the investment well. Throughout our research, we have

(continued)

seen many cases in which investors chose areas they just did not understand (such as high-tech), only to lose their investment within a short period—often to their complete surprise.

3. Decide whether you would feel more comfortable investing alone or in a syndicate with other angels or personal acquaintances. As discussed, many angels are motivated to invest in part by the opportunity to share investment risk and expertise with others. Others prefer to give active hands-on assistance to their investments and may prefer to invest alone (or with one other person) so that they have more control and potentially fewer differing opinions (and egos) to deal with.

4. Investors should determine how they are best able (and most prefer) to assist a potential investee firm. Being up front in responding to an entrepreneur's wishes and needs allows both parties to form realistic expectations and accommodate one another's desires. All too often, we see investors and entrepreneurs signing a deal oblivious to a stark mismatch between the level of hands-on investor assistance offered and that desired. This may lead to much tension that could be avoided if intentions are made clear from the start.

5. Investors should be familiar with the investment criteria and practices of their peers (such as those offered in the next few chapters) so that they can judge an investment opportunity's merits on unbiased grounds, rather than getting swept up by their emotions and gut feeling. In fact, one of the most common postinvestment complaints we hear from business angels is that they should have analyzed their investee firms much more closely before investing. We cannot stress too strongly the need for careful due diligence.

6. Investors in search of entrepreneurial opportunities should employ their network contacts to locate firms worthy of consideration. We occasionally encounter business angels who approach small firms they admire, to offer a cash infusion without solicitation from the firm.

*Chapter Six*

# Understanding the Investors' Structural and Personal Differences

To fully understand the investment behavior of business angels and venture capitalists, it is important to first look at their structural and personal differences, and the environment in which they operate. This allows us to understand exactly *why* business angels and venture capitalists behave in a certain way, rather than just learning *how* they behave.

## Separation of Ownership and Control

When business angels or venture capitalists invest money in an entrepreneurial company in exchange for a portion of its equity, a separation of ownership and control is created since the investors own part of the firm but the entrepreneur still largely controls its daily operations. In such an arrangement, one party (the "principal") delegates work and responsibilities to another (the "agent"), who performs that work on the principal's behalf (Jensen and Meckling, 1976). Such agency relationships can take many forms, but here we use them to analyze the dynamics between investors and those individuals whose businesses they invest in.

Investors monitor the entrepreneurs, who in turn are obliged to use the money invested to further the best interests of the firm (and thus those of the investors), rather than their own personal interests. Human nature almost inevitably dictates that whenever an investor places any amount of money with an entrepreneur (whom the investor usually does not know very well), there is some concern that the entrepreneur may not use that money in the manner intended. But checking up on this may be difficult because of *information asymmetries*—that is, situations where the entrepreneur knows much more about the intricate operations of the firm and its money requirements than the investor does. This complicates the entrepreneur's attempt to raise outside equity finance from potential investors who have to assure themselves (through screening and due diligence) that the entrepreneur is a worthy risk.

Clearly, this is why we use *contracts* when investing, to align the interests of both parties so that they engage in cooperative effort, to relieve the worries of the investors, and to allow each party to protect its own interests. Contracts specify the rights of the entrepreneur, performance criteria on which the entrepreneur is evaluated, and the payoff functions both parties face (Fama and Jensen, 1983). Because of the potentially divergent interests and concerns of investors, entrepreneurs, and managers, any organization is therefore a "nexus of contracts" (Jensen and Meckling, 1976; Hart, 1995).

Although contracts reduce the potential for agency costs in the firm, unfortunately they cannot eliminate them, and it can be costly to write and enforce contracts (Fama and Jensen, 1983). This means that the problems associated with asymmetries of information cannot be fully contracted away; in addition to using contracts, investors usually screen entrepreneurs and firms actively before investing and monitor them after investment to limit the potential for abuse.

## Uncertainty and Limited Control over Entrepreneurial Outcomes

In addition to different levels of information and the potential for high agency costs, small start-up firms operate in a high-risk environment in which there is usually a long time lag between an investment and the very uncertain result. Fried and Hisrich (1989) say that "venture capital portfolios, even of highly successful partnerships, have historically shown low or even negative returns in their first two or three years ('the lemons come home early' is an industry cliché). As a result, the performance of a partnership is very hard to measure until most of its investments have been liquidated, often six to eight years after the partnership was created" (p. 264).

Many new ventures are launched despite these numerous and often consequential uncertainties, which can only be resolved by going forward. However, since most start-up firms have only limited resources, unexpected snags can quickly exhaust available funding and lead to bankruptcy (Gorman and Sahlman, 1989).

## The Complex Structure of Venture Capital

The structural difference between business angels and venture capitalists is the difference in their investor bases. Business angels are accountable only to themselves because they invest in entrepreneurial ventures with their own money. Venture capitalists raise financing from outside providers (such as pension funds and other institutional investors) on a competitive basis and then invest those funds in entrepreneurial ventures. Since most venture capital funds are organized as partnerships, these fund providers are referred to as limited partners (LPS). In 1998, 60 percent of new capital extended by all LPS came from pension funds, 12 percent from corporations, 11 percent from individuals and families, 10 percent from financial and insurance firms, 6 percent from endowments and foundations, and 1 percent from foreign investors (NVCA, 1999). Venture capitalists prefer to raise large funds (for economies of scale). Since LPS invest in venture capital funds for purely financial reasons, the venture capitalist's primary aim is to gain financial returns from their investment portfolio so they can repay the original sum to their fund providers and take a percentage of the profit for their own income. In fact, in addition to their original investment, fund providers receive 80 percent of the capital gains earned by the venture capital fund, while venture capitalists earn the balance of the capital gains (the "carry" is usually 20 percent) plus their 2–3 percent annual management fee (Bygrave and Shulman, 1988). Venture capitalists do not get their share of the carry until the LPS have been reimbursed for the capital invested. Figure 6.1 clarifies this arrangement.

Venture capitalists clearly have an additional level of the agency relationship to deal with that business angels do not: that of the fund providers (see Figure 6.2). This has ignited an academic

## Figure 6.1. The Flows of Venture Capital.

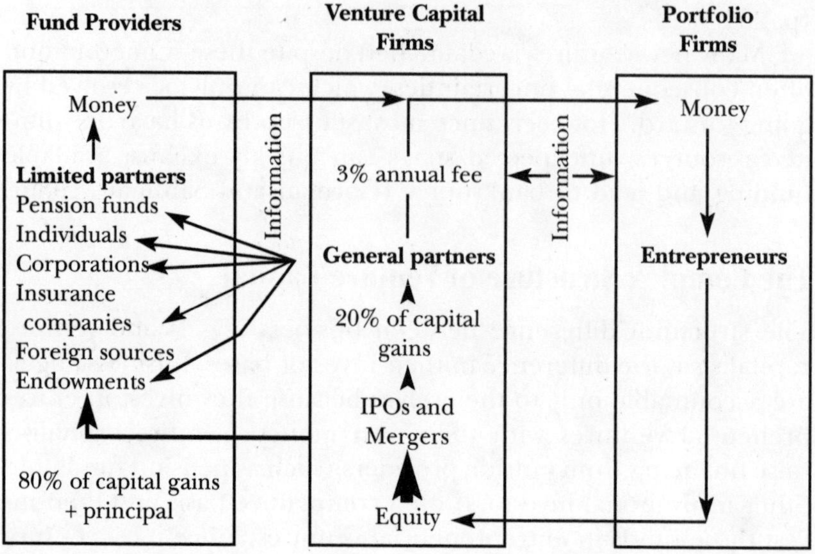

| Fund Providers | Venture Capital Firms | Portfolio Firms |
|---|---|---|

Money → ↗ Money

**Limited partners**
Pension funds
Individuals
Corporations
Insurance
 companies
Foreign sources
Endowments

Information

3% annual fee

**General partners**

20% of capital
gains

IPOs and
Mergers

Equity ←

80% of capital gains
+ principal

Information

Money

**Entrepreneurs**

*Source:* Bygrave and Shulman (1988).

argument of sorts (Murray, 1991). Some believe that the venture capital firm's customers are actually the fund providers who provide the money that is invested in entrepreneurial firms. They feel that the investee firms are "raw material" and claim that venture capitalists must demonstrate to the fund providers the ability to add value to the funds invested. Others believe that the customers are those entrepreneurial firms in which the investments are made, and the fund providers are seen as suppliers of the raw material (Duggins, 1993). Although we will not pick sides, we lean toward the former approach as a means of explaining the difference between business angels and venture capitalists in their investment approaches.

The venture capitalist's relationship with fund providers (the LPS) and investee firms therefore forces the venture capitalist to wear two hats and contend with both the supplier and the user of finance in the volatile environment of entrepreneurial investing. In a sense, our focus in the next few chapters is on ascertaining

**Figure 6.2.  Comparison of Business Angel and
Venture Capitalist Agency Relationships.**

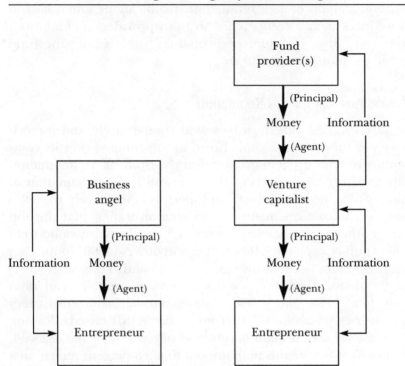

how this additional agency relationship for the venture capitalist firm (with its fund providers) forces the venture capitalist to choose different investment practices from those of the less-restricted (and less-accountable) business angel.

## How Venture Capitalists Reduce Risk for Their Fund Providers

Unlike business angels, venture capitalists face pressures to demonstrate competent investment behavior as a means of reducing their fund providers' concerns about potential agency risk. Because it takes time to realize performance results, the number of ways in which venture capitalists signal competence is increasing, while the need for such prudent behavior is also becoming more important. In particular, venture capitalists hope that ensuring the impeccability of their reputation, qualifications, and rules and procedures signals competence to fund providers and acts as a good indication of future performance (while easing the fund providers' monitoring duties).

## The Venture Capitalist's Reputation

Venture capital funds must be raised competitively, and the primary way for a venture capital firm to win funding over its competitors is to have a better reputation (Norton, 1995). Reputation depends on many aspects of the firm and is the culmination of small procedures, conduct, and performance levels that the venture capital firm maintains. By demonstrating that the top U.S. venture capitalists were perceived to add more value than other venture capitalists, Rosenstein and others (1990) found that reputation and performance go hand in hand. Thus, with a better reputation than competitors, a venture capitalist can raise more total funds and so earn higher annual management fees (which average around 3 percent of the funds raised). Raising more money is important because, as one venture capitalist said, "It doesn't take a genius to figure out that a 5 percent return on a $100 million is better than 20 percent on $10 million" (Sapienza, Manigart, and Vermeir, 1996, p. 467). The size of a particular venture capital firm is therefore often a function of its past investment success and reputation (Gupta and Sapienza, 1988; Zacharakis and Meyer, 1995).

But building a reputation as a venture capitalist by investing in early-stage ventures is difficult and risky. Even if they are successful, these investments do not realize a return for seven to ten years. Although returns are less impressive in financing later-stage deals, this is less risky and allows venture capitalists to show good returns, and so build up their reputation and attract more funds. Hence, venture capitalists face a trade-off between a high-risk, high-return strategy with a long-term horizon on the one hand and a low-risk, low-return strategy with a short-term horizon on the other (Norton, 1995). It is not surprising that young venture capital firms tend to take companies public earlier than older venture capital firms do, to establish a reputation and successfully raise capital for new funds (Gompers, 1996).

But even if a venture capitalist has a good reputation, easing up on the rules and procedures that initially earned that strong reputation is unwise. Since the venture capital community is small and networked, reputations echo loudly and can be easily damaged—possibly inviting potential replacements into the market (Sapienza and Korsgaard, 1996; Cable and Shane, 1997). Though often overlooked, a venture capitalist's reputation is also among the most important criteria influencing an entrepreneur's decision to accept a funding offer, especially among older and more experienced entrepreneurs (Smith, 1999).

## The Venture Capitalist's Qualifications

Another way for venture capitalists to signal competence is to hire individuals for the team who have excellent qualifications and experience in the industry. This may explain why the prospectus of a venture capital fund usually lists the education levels and industry experience of all the venture capitalists. It is surely no coincidence that so many of them have M.B.A.s from top schools. In fact, fund providers almost always want to see the qualifications of the general partners of the venture capitalist firm before they invest (Fried and Hisrich, 1989). Good qualifications are yet another performance substitute that venture capitalists (and other firms) use to reduce the uncertainty and perceived agency concerns for their fund providers.

## Up-Front Rules and Investment Procedures Followed

Since portfolio returns are not realized by the venture capitalist for as long as ten years, and observation of outcomes by fund providers thus cannot be effectively employed as a means of reducing agency concerns, the agreement between the venture capitalist and the fund providers is highly complex. To reduce any investment hesitations and gain financing from fund providers, venture capitalists may establish up-front rules they agree to follow in managing the fund providers' money, and they may even advertise these rules in their publicity material. One manager of a matching service interviewed summed it up this way: "Venture capitalists invest someone else's money, so they have to work to criteria they've promised their subscribers they're going to work to." A venture capitalist also told us that the rules are vital: "Venture capitalists are investing money on behalf of pension funds; we get our money by raising funds. They don't want us goofing off and having fun. We're not here to enjoy ourselves or satisfy our egos; we're here to make capital gains to benefit pension funds. That sort of constrains what we do." To further signal that they behave competently, venture capitalists meticulously document decisions to show that they take every care in picking the best investments.

In a pioneering study, Sahlman (1990) identified a number of procedural mechanisms that venture capitalists and fund providers employ to reduce concern about agency costs:

- Specifically prohibiting certain acts by the venture capital firm that would cause conflict of interest (for example, receiving payment separately from the company being invested in)
- Employing mechanisms to ensure gains are distributed to investors
- Using resources to monitor the venture capital firm
- Having the venture capital firm regularly furnish specific information to the fund providers

Following such careful procedures in picking investments also aims to limit a venture capitalist's accountability, should the investment fail to realize an adequate return. Figure 6.3 clarifies the complex signals and relationships so crucial to a venture capitalist firm.

## Increasing Power of Fund Providers

In recent years it has become highly important for venture capitalists to reduce asymmetries of information for their fund providers as the marketplace in which venture capitalists try to raise money has become more competitive in the United States and abroad, with more competitors vying for funds (Robbie, Wright, and Chiplin, 1997, 1998; Murray, 1995a; Sapienza, 1992). This has made it even more imperative for venture capitalists to market

## Figure 6.3.  Information Signals and Agency Pressures in a Venture Capitalist's Early Investment Process.

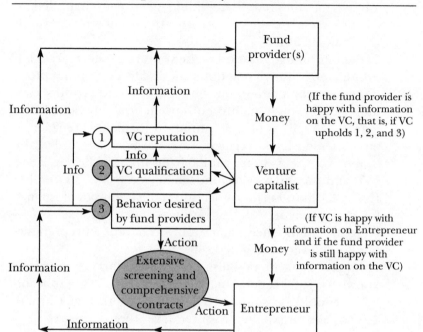

themselves favorably to suppliers of finance by using qualified employees, up-front rules, and thorough procedures in the investment process so that fund providers can easily monitor them and they can signal their high level of competence.

A number of factors contribute to this increased power of the fund providers and force them to monitor their venture capitalists more closely:

- Increased transparency of returns has accentuated the ability to benchmark the performance of venture capital firms, offering fund providers a much more informed picture than ever before. (Robbie, Wright, and Chiplin, 1997). The venture capital industry is being driven by the requirements of institutional fund managers who are under growing pressure to achieve better-than-average short-term results. Since these fund managers often only have a three-to-four-year job horizon, they may prefer liquid investments in traded securities to early-stage venture investments in ten-year funds (Murray, 1995b).

- Rapid internationalization of the venture capital market has brought an influx of new domestic and foreign competitors, increasing competition for the supply of fund provider capital and for high-quality entrepreneurial investments in markets already at or past saturation (Sapienza, 1992; Sapienza, Manigart, and Vermeir, 1996). From 1988 to 1998, the number of U.S. venture capital firms increased from 358 to 547, and the number of funds managed from 776 to 1,108 (NVCA, 1998). Furthermore, alternative sources of finance for entrepreneurs (such as business angels and business alliances) and the increasing sophistication of entrepreneurs has eroded venture capital returns.
- Fund providers are now also being advised by organizations known as "gatekeepers" that determine which venture capitalists should be supplied (Robbie, Wright, and Chiplin, 1997), thus raising the pressure on venture capitalists.
- There is an increasing trend toward making a smaller number of investments involving larger amounts. This allows fund providers to focus on fewer relationships; since they are now also less diversified, it increases fund providers' need to monitor (Robbie, Wright, and Chiplin, 1997).
- Fund providers now need, and ask for, more nonstandard information from venture capitalists.

Venture capitalists have responded to these rising pressures in a number of ways:

- They have increased information flows to the fund providers by enhancing their communication and reporting approaches. Currently, venture capital firms offer four to six packets of information (annual, semiannual, or quarterly reports; semiannual portfolio evaluations; annual presentations or visits) to fund providers each year.

- As bargaining power moves to the fund providers, the management fees of the venture capitalist come under pressure at a time when investee companies also expect a greater level of service from their venture capitalist investors (Murray, 1995a). Front-end fees (up to 2–3 percent of committed funds) are sometimes eliminated.
- Venture capitalists are placing greater emphasis on quicker exits and therefore increasing their investments in later-stage and more mature firms.
- More venture capitalists are incorporating preset performance targets and stipulating minimum returns to their investors. Some also require capital repayment from entrepreneurs upon realization of individual investments.
- Venture capitalists are promoting an image of awareness and responsiveness to the needs of fund providers, aiming to market themselves and differentiate their services in the marketplace (Murray, 1995a; Robbie, Wright, and Chiplin, 1997).

This is clearly a volatile situation, but in the last few years the funding situation has improved, and we have started to see a shift again. More investment funds are now willing to fund venture capitalists, especially those supporting Internet firms, in the hope of realizing the sizable rewards already seen in this sector. In fact, a record $25.3 billion was raised by the U.S. venture capital industry in 1998, thanks in part to the healthy distributions the venture capital industry has returned to its limited partners over the last few years, and to the rebalancing of fund providers' stock portfolios in response to stock market growth into areas such as private equity (NVCA, 1999).

The relationship between venture capitalists and their limited partners is clearly a complex dance that continues to evolve. This is clearly evident in the tectonic shift in the relationship that we have witnessed at the time of writing.

Now that we have taken a long and detailed look at the structural differences and pressures between venture capitalists and business angels, it should be clear that behaving competently when investing is vital for venture capitalists, though only a matter of personal discretion for business angels.

## Personal Differences Among Investors

To better understand the investment behavior of business angels and venture capitalists, we now take a closer look at how their personal characteristics differ.

### Age and Education

Looking at the types of business angel in the last chapter, we can generalize and say that these investors on average tend to be in their late forties, which is significantly older than most venture capitalists. In the United States, business angels are predominantly male (around 97 percent) and have an average age of forty-eight to fifty (Wetzel and Freear, 1994, Freear, Sohl, and Wetzel, 1991, 1994a), while their counterparts in the UK and Europe tend to be slightly older because of the influence of higher taxes on the rate of capital and wealth accumulation (Harrison and Mason, 1992a; Mason, Harrison, and Chaloner, 1991a).

Since venture capitalists do not invest their own accumulated wealth and are typically recruited directly out of college, their age is typically around the early to mid-forties. Senior managers in venture capital firms tend to be more involved in the postfunding process, while midlevel (and younger) managers are generally more involved in the prefunding process (Gorman and Sahlman, 1989).

Overall, most business angels are well educated. Depending on the geographical regions sampled, studies have found that anywhere from 80 percent (Aram, 1989) to 94 percent (Wetzel and Seymour, 1981) of business angels have college degrees, of which 42 percent (Aram, 1989) to 56 percent (Haar, Starr, and MacMillan, 1988; Freear and Wetzel, 1991) have a graduate education. Canadian and Finnish business angels also have high education levels (Duxbury, Haines, and Riding, 1996; Short and Riding, 1989; Lumme, Mason, and Suomi, 1996), while in the UK business angels appear to have a slightly lower level of formal education. One study found that 40 percent had public school as their final education level (Van Osnabrugge, 1998), while another found that 74 percent held a college degree (Harrison and Mason,

1992a). One interesting finding is that active business angels in the UK have statistically lower education levels than those business angels who are less active investors (Coveney, 1996).

As one would expect, venture capitalists tend to be highly educated. Many have M.B.A.s and other postgraduate degrees from top schools. Similar to what is found in the United States, a recent British study shows that all venture capitalists surveyed had a college degree, while 60 percent had postgraduate degrees, and 13 percent had Ph.D.s.

## Business Backgrounds

Having backgrounds in entrepreneurship themselves (more often than not), business angels tend to have significantly more small business experience than venture capitalists. In the United States, around 87 percent of business angel investors have moderate to substantial general business experience (Freear and Wetzel, 1991). Contrary to popular belief, relatively few lawyers, doctors, and other professionals are currently functioning as business angels. Similarly in the UK, 92 percent of business angels have small-business experience, and even in Sweden, 69 percent of business angels have been business managers of small or medium-size firms (Landstrom, 1993). A Finnish study, though, claims that this experience may not actually be that advantageous. Lumme, Mason, and Suomi (1996) found that successful business angel investors tend to spend more time working in top and middle-management positions in large and medium-sized companies, while unsuccessful investors usually originate from top management positions in small companies.

This may be good news for venture capitalists because they typically have little experience in small business and instead are often recruited straight from a top U.S. graduate school in their late twenties and then trained as investors rather than as business managers (Rea, 1989; Bygrave and Timmons, 1986). Indeed, a UK study found that only about half (52 percent) of venture capitalists have small-business experience; the majority were actually accountants in the past. Similarly in the United States, Rosenstein, Bruno, Bygrave, and Taylor found that the entrepreneurs' high expectations of their venture capitalists were at times met with disappointment: "Venture capital board members have great credentials . . . but have no operating experience. . . . A typical venture capitalist has zero operating experience. Only 40 percent of their time is [spent in] working with their portfolio companies once or twice a month. That is not enough time to understand the workings and intricacies of a start-up business" (1990, p. 245).

Often past entrepreneurs themselves, business angels clearly tend to be more experienced than venture capitalists in managing small firms.

## Entrepreneurial Experience

Business angels are significantly more entrepreneurial than venture capitalists, with anywhere from 75 to 83 percent having such start-up experience, compared to about a third of venture capitalists (Wetzel and Seymour, 1981; Gaston and Bell, 1988; Van Osnabrugge, 1998). These numbers are similar to those found in the UK, where 75–80 percent of business angels have started at least one firm and around half are multiple founders. Surprisingly, these percentages are even higher in Finland (Lumme, Mason, and Suomi, 1996) and Sweden (Landstrom, 1993). Conversely, only 38 percent of venture capitalists are past entrepreneurs and only 27 percent multiple founders (Van Osnabrugge, 1998; Mason and Harrison, 1991).

Interestingly, around 75 percent of business angels claim that their principal source of wealth is their own past business, while the remaining 25 percent earned it from quoted investments. This is also evident in the substantial number of business angels who told us that they had started and sold successful firms before investing in an unquoted firm to be involved in the entrepreneurial process again. One wealthy business angel stated his reason for making angel investments: "Because I've started a number of businesses myself and have never worked for anyone else, I'm completely unemployable. So I can understand what's involved in starting a small company since I've done it so many times."

This experience of starting, managing, and harvesting a successful entrepreneurial firm—"street smarts" (Freear, Sohl, and

Wetzel, 1992a, p. 379)—may give business angels empathy for a fellow entrepreneur starting a firm (Freear, Sohl, and Wetzel, 1992a; Sullivan, 1991). It may also explain why those with entrepreneurial experience prefer investing in very early-stage ventures (Aram, 1989) and why virgin angels tend to have significantly less entrepreneurial experience (Coveney, 1996). Interestingly, studies have shown that entrepreneurs in general perceive their downside risk to be less than other investors do and are more likely to support start-up firms (rather than established firms) as investors (Sullivan, 1991).

Our knowledge of the entrepreneurial backgrounds of venture capitalists is somewhat scarce, but Sapienza, Manigart, and Vermeir (1996) further support the proposition that venture capitalists for the most part have little entrepreneurial experience: "Anecdotal evidence suggests that if venture capitalist's greater experience is as a financier of new ventures rather than as a practitioner in the venture's industry, the danger of resentment on the part of the CEO is great (Sapienza and Timmons, 1989). Indeed, we heard complaints in interviews with both venture capitalists and entrepreneurs about venture capitalists who were 'financial MBA-types' or who 'never started any business of their own'" (p. 448).

## Investment Experience

As professionals investing in unquoted firms for a career, venture capitalists naturally make significantly more such investments than business angels do. Although there is some diversity among business angels as to the frequency and number of their investments, researchers from a number of countries agree that business angels generally lack investment experience and on average invest infrequently (Mason, Harrison, and Allen, 1995; Wetzel, 1987). In the United States, one New England study found that the average number of entrepreneurial investments made over the last five years by business angels is 2.45 (Freear and Wetzel, 1991), while two West coast studies claim that business angels typically make two or three investments every three years (Aram, 1989; Gaston, 1989). By comparison, business angels in the UK make a total of about four investments in their careers on average, with more than 65 percent of angels making two or more (Van Osnabrugge, 1998); another study found that when business angels are active as investors, they fund on average 2.4 firms every three years.

Unfortunately, little is known about the number of unquoted investments made by individual venture capitalists in the United States for their venture capital firms. Since many of the venture capital firms in the UK are U.S. subsidiaries and all operate on the same U.S. model, it is interesting that venture capitalists there have each made around twenty-three investments on average, with the median twenty (Van Osnabrugge, 1998). In fact, whereas only 3 percent of the venture capitalists had made three or fewer investments, 55 percent of business angels had. Furthermore, the average number of years of venture capital experience for venture capitalists in the United States ranges from six to eleven (Gorman and Sahlman, 1989; MacMillan, Kulow, and Khoylian, 1988). With so many years of experience on average, it is no surprise that venture capitalists are able to invest many more times than business angels. Studies also clearly show that with more experience and expertise, venture capitalists make much better investment decisions (Shepherd, Zacharakis, and Baron, 1998).

## Main Differences Between Angels and Venture Capitalists

After reviewing the personal characteristics of these two investor types, we are left with the overriding impression that business angels tend to be entrepreneurial-manager types, whereas venture capitalists tend to be financial-investor types. Though not completely unexpected, this insight is useful to entrepreneurs who might wish to initiate discussion with either type of financier, and it also offers valuable background as we examine the differences throughout their investment processes in the next few chapters. Table 6.1 shows some of important investor differences that we explore in this book.

The next few chapters are invaluable reading for any entrepreneur hoping to court one of these investors—and also for investors hoping to develop, or improve, their investment strategies.

**Table 6.1.  Main Differences Between Business Angels
and Venture Capitalists.**

| Main Differences | Business Angels | Venture  Capitalists |
|---|---|---|
| Personal | Entrepreneurs | Investors |
| Firms funded | Small, early-stage | Large, mature |
| Due diligence done | Minimal | Extensive |
| Location of investment | Of concern | Not important |
| Contract used | Simple | Comprehensive |
| Monitoring after investment | Active, hands-on | Strategic |
| Exiting the firm | Of lesser concern | Highly important |
| Rate of return | Of lesser concern | Highly important |

# Business Angel and Venture Capitalist Differences Throughout the Investment Process

# Chapter Seven

# Investors' Motivations and Investment Criteria

For entrepreneurs positioning their firms for the funding process, understanding what motivates business angels and venture capitalists to invest is vital. Investors too can learn from other investors about which characteristics to look for in their search for a sound investment opportunity.

## Stages in the Investment Process

An investor's full investment process, from searching for a deal to final exit, is a lengthy and complicated array of distinct stages. This chapter focuses on investment motivations and criteria, with Chapters Eight through Eleven documenting the rest of the stages illustrated in Figure 7.1. This framework can apply to both business angels and venture capitalists; it therefore serves as a good structure for comparison of the two investor types.

## Investment Motivation for the Business Angel

Since an investor's motivation for investing in entrepreneurial firms influences his or her particular criteria, understanding these motivations is crucial. As might be expected, for the venture capitalist financial profitability is the primary concern, while for the business angel the reasons vary (though fitting neatly into three main categories: opportunity for financial gain, playing a role in the entrepreneurial process, and other nonfinancial factors).

Here is how business angels generally rank them, in decreasing order of importance:

*Business Angels' Primary Motivation for Investment*

- Expectation of high financial reward
- Playing a role in the entrepreneurial process
- Fun and satisfaction of being involved in an entrepreneurial firm
- Creating a job for oneself, and possibly some income
- Sense of social responsibility

## Financial Reward

It is undeniable that most business angels, regardless of region, are motivated first and foremost by the opportunity for high financial reward. Most angels hope to quintuple their money in

**Figure 7.1.  Stages in the Investment Process.**

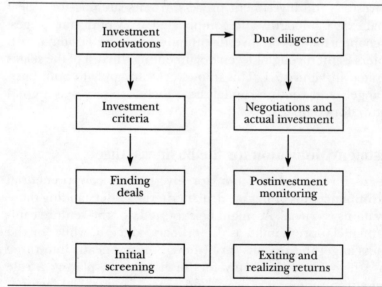

five years, although only a few actually do. Some business angels realize such rewards by structuring an income stream into their investment contract (getting paid as if they were an employee), while most hope to sell the investment in the future through a trade sale or stock listing to obtain a large financial return.

Although the second word in the term *business angel* gives the impression that altruism is a major investment motivation, altruism is rarely the primary investment motivation for angels. Understandably, a number of the business angels we have spoken to over the years believed the term to be a bit of a misnomer, and some even resented its use. One business angel complained: "It's not a term that I particularly like. *Angel* implies that someone floats along and bestows money on people and wanders off and disappears into the sunset." Another stated: "We are not all pure and good and don't wear a halo; the trouble is that we may be perceived as a divine person coming along to create miracles when all other avenues are lost, rather as if you were parting the Red Sea."

It is therefore important for the entrepreneur not to confuse the *angel* moniker with any altruistic or charitable impulse (see nonfinancial motivations below); the angel investment is primarily—as well as contractually and legally—a financial transaction.

## Playing a Role in the Entrepreneurial Process

The second most influential motivation is to play a role in the entrepreneurial process. Many business angels invest in early-stage firms more for the fun than primarily for possible financial reward. Being involved in the process is often something they have done successfully as entrepreneurs themselves, and now that they have more free time and money, they want to do it again. One business angel told us: "I'm an experienced uncle that the entrepreneurs can trust; I'm not in it for a fast buck. Besides, it's cheaper and more fun than buying a yacht." Another confided: "I enjoy investing in companies and getting involved; it's a real buzz. I enjoy the pleasure of building companies; when it becomes too administrative and established, I get out." Although investing is a part-time activity for most, for others getting involved is the best alternative to retirement. A common complaint is that retirement is too boring and unstimulating; this motivates many angels to put their years of business experience to good use. One successful business angel, who bought into a glass trading company, summed it up well:

> I invested because I wanted something to do, because I found my-self walking around the streets looking at potholes and thinking of complaining to the city council about them, and that sort of nonsense. It just gets yourself into such a state if you have been very active, and all of a sudden you don't have anything to do. It's extremely hard to start up again from zero. I'm just interested in business; it's the thing that turns me on. My hobby is getting up in the morning and coming to work; I absolutely love it. I was un-happy when I was retired. I'm a worker and I happen to have some cash. I like to help other people and get a tremendous buzz with this firm.

Enjoying involvement in the entrepreneurial process is a common element among many business angels and something that excites them greatly. One business angel summed up quite well this enthusiastic attitude to investing: "I feel this is a fantastically exciting sport: seeing the potential new start-ups, and get-ups, at a time of their development when they've made their plans and brought themselves to presentations. Some laugh at the idea of calling it a sport, but to me it seems like the gladiators in the Coliseum fighting for favors with their working lives, against heavy odds, for colossal rewards—and we can even join in."

## Nonfinancial Motivations

A minority of business angels are motivated primarily by non-financial factors. Altruism, in particular, is the key for some of those business angels who have been successful in business and would now like to pass their skills on to the next generation of entrepreneurs. Some of these business angels are especially altruistic in their investment decisions (that is, they do not invest primarily for the highest financial return—if any) because they wish to stimulate entrepreneurship (and thus jobs and economic prosperity) in their geographical region. This is common among business angels living in rural and sparsely populated areas.

## What Matters Most to Investors at Each Investment Stage?

Research indicates that criteria weigh more or less heavily at various stages of the investment process (Riding and others, 1993; Mason and Rogers, 1996). The entrepreneur and the management team are usually of primary importance overall, as we will see, but studies on business angels have shown that in the initial screening stages of the investment process (when investors look at many deals for a few that catch the eye), the market and product are the most important considerations, followed by the entrepreneur and management team and then financial considerations (Mason and Rogers, 1996; Riding and others, 1993). Although the financial projections of an investment opportunity are of only secondary importance initially, for business angels they are increasingly important in subsequent stages.

For venture capitalists, some studies have shown that the management team, like the financials, may not be of primary importance initially but critical later (Sweeting, 1991; Hall and Hofer, 1993; Zacharakis and Meyer, 1995). However, the entrepreneur remains the most important decision factor overall (MacMillan, Siegel, and Subbanarasimha 1985; MacMillan, Zemann, and Subbanarasimha, 1987), and the initial impressions of the venture's feasibility certainly influence a venture capitalist's subsequent evaluation of the entrepreneur (Sandberg, Schweiger, and Hofer, 1987).

## Ranking Investors' Investment Criteria

Investment criteria are the actual characteristics of investment opportunities that attract investors to invest. It is these factors of attraction (such as the entrepreneur's expertise, or the growth potential of a market) that initially tempt the investor and that are later verified in the due-diligence stage. Once verified, these criteria are reviewed again to render a possible investment decision. Of course, each investor is influenced according to personal criteria and investment characteristics, as are business angels in contrast to venture capitalists.

Overall, both business angels and venture capitalists believe that the entrepreneur and the management team constitute the criterion that most attracts them to the investment opportunities they actually fund (Van Osnabrugge, 1998, MacMillan, Zemann, and Subbanarasimha, 1987). After all, the quality of the management team indicates the potential upside of a venture, as well as the extent to which the downside risk may be reduced. This is usually followed in importance by the product and market, and then by the financial factors, although they are less critical to business angels than to venture capitalists (MacMillan, Siegel, and Subbanarasimha, 1985; Hall and Hofer, 1993; Mason, Harrison, and Allen, 1995). Although most past studies have used vague and general criteria—such as the quality of management (Sandberg, Schweiger, and Hofer, 1987)—we have broken these down here into various subcategories (as suggested by the investors we spoke to) and had hundreds of investors rank the criteria in importance to them for the last actual deal they made. Table 7.1 shows a selection of the most important investment criteria for business angels and venture capitalists.

However, in recent years both angels and venture capitalists have aggressively invested more in technology-related entrepreneurial firms. Let's take a look (Table 7.2) at how these investment criteria differed for those investors that we contacted who backed technology-intensive ventures, such as Internet start-ups and software firms (Van Osnabrugge, 1998).

Research has shown that generally those investing in technology firms tend to emphasize the growth potential of the firm's market, the overall and patent protection of the products, and the sales potential of the product. These rankings should not be considered as etched in stone, but they do give a rough indication of the preferences of investors. It is also clear that one factor usually does not commit an investor to an investment; rather, it is a combination of many. In fact, one business angel told us, "I had enough check marks in my mental list of what a company should look like, so I invested."

**Table 7.1.  Investors' Investment Criteria (in Rough Order of Importance) for All Investors.**

| Selected Investment Criteria (Among Twenty-Seven Overall) | Ranking by Business Angels | Ranking by Venture Capitalists |
|---|---|---|
| Enthusiasm of the entrepreneur(s) | 1 | 3 |
| Trustworthiness of the entrepreneur(s) | 2 | 1 |
| Sales potential of the product | 3 | 5 |
| Expertise of the entrepreneur(s) | 4 | 2 |
| Investor liked entrepreneur(s) upon meeting | 5 | 9 |
| Growth potential of the market | 6 | 6 |
| Quality of product | 7 | 10 |
| Perceived financial rewards (for investor) | 8 | 4 |
| Niche market | 9 | 13 |
| Track record of the entrepreneur(s) | 10 | 8 |
| Investor's strengths filling gaps in the business | 14 | 26 |
| Overall competitive protection | 21 | 11 |
| Local venture (geographically close) | 23 | 27 |
| Investor's understanding of the business or industry | 24 | 17 |
| Potential exit routes (liquidity) | 24 | 12 |
| Presence of (potential) co-investors | 26 | 25 |
| Formal competitive protection of product (patents) | 27 | 20 |

## Factors Attracting Investors

Although it may be accurate to state that similarities exist between business angels and venture capitalists for the *general* criterion groupings, this is not the case for many of the *specific* criteria. One venture capitalist actually emphasized these differences to us: "Institutional investors are much more rigorous and our criteria are tougher because we are doing the investment for only one reason: that is, to deliver returns to outside investors whose funds we manage. We should not be making investments because we like

**Table 7.2. Investors' Investment Criteria
(in Rough Order of Importance) for Technology Investors.**

| Selected Investment Criteria (Among Twenty-Seven Overall) | Ranking by Technology Business Angels | Ranking by Technology Venture Capitalists |
|---|---|---|
| Enthusiasm of the entrepreneur(s) | 1 | 1 |
| Trustworthiness of the entrepreneur(s) | 2 | 2 |
| Sales potential of the product | 3 | 6 |
| Expertise of the entrepreneur(s) | 4 | 5 |
| Investor liked entrepreneur(s) upon meeting | 5 | 7 |
| Growth potential of the market | 6 | 3 |
| Quality of product | 7 | 10 |
| Perceived financial rewards (for investor) | 8 | 4 |
| Niche market | 9 | 16 |
| Track record of the entrepreneur(s) | 10 | 11 |
| Product's informal competitive protection (know-how) | 11 | 12 |
| Overall competitive protection | 15 | 9 |
| Presence of (potential) co-investors | 18 | 20 |
| Investor's strengths filling gaps in the business | 20 | 24 |
| Potential exit routes (liquidity) | 24 | 13 |
| Formal competitive protection of product (patents) | 25 | 18 |
| Local venture (geographically close) | 26 | 27 |
| Investor's understanding of the business or industry | 27 | 17 |

working with or in a business. Angel investors are entitled to invest their own money and they probably make investments based on very soft financial criteria."

## The Entrepreneurs and the Management Team

For the majority of business angels, the entrepreneur is the greatest attraction to an investment. Many plan to work with the entrepreneur for a number of years in the firm and so want to make sure that he or she is compatible and qualified. Business angels invest in people, more so than in sectors or other factors. It is all about people, and if the people are wrong then business angels usually do not invest. But in addition to choosing a qualified entrepreneur to increase the chances of success, choosing one wisely to decrease potential agency worries (that the entrepreneur might not use the investor's money for the firm's best interests) is also paramount. One business angel told us: "You need to have total confidence in the people. After all, what are you doing? You are taking money out of your bank account and putting it in theirs, and we all know that there are plenty of people around who would run off with the money and profess this and that, and it becomes an expensive legal mess to unwrangle it. It probably would not be economically viable, and there would be a lot of heartache and wasted time and effort. You are really dealing with people."

Although business angels feel that investing in the right entrepreneur is important, they also realize that it is often impossible for firms at such an early stage of business formation (the ones that business angels prefer) to have a well-balanced management team. Instead, the angels intend to use their own skills to help balance the team. Conversely, a venture capitalist does not look upon a firm so favorably if it lacks a management team.

For venture capitalists, the quality of the entrepreneur and the management team are also paramount. Yet venture capitalists are also very attracted to the concept or idea or vision of the venture. This certainly does not mean that management quality is not always foremost; it just may not always be the main motivating factor. This depends on the sector of the investment, and the importance of the particular entrepreneurs to the sustainability and growth of the firm. One venture capitalist put it this way: "When we invest in technology-based businesses, it's more about the company having a unique proprietary position in what it's doing, a good-size market opportunity with good growth prospects, less competition, and a very strong management team. The idea and competitive position are of primary interest."

Some venture capitalists told us that this is because there are not always enough well-qualified entrepreneurs to fund and therefore they sometimes have to place more emphasis on the ideas in a venture. Because of this management gap, venture capitalists may recruit new or additional people to improve the quality of a management team (Ehrlich, Noble, Moore, and Weaver, 1994; Harrison and Mason, 1992b; Freear, Sohl, and Wetzel, 1996; MacMillan, Siegel, and Subbanarasimha, 1985). Even though business angels often prefer balancing a management team through their own input, especially as the firm increases in size, investment negotiations with venture capitalists have shown more success when the entrepreneur agrees to recruit talent to fill gaps (Rea, 1989). One venture capitalist even told us that he recently invested in an inventor's new idea and then recruited some people he knew and introduced them as the management of the company. But in general, before approaching a venture capitalist, entrepreneurs should make sure that they have the *right* people on their team, not just many to fill various positions. Depending on the sector, a good CEO, CFO, marketing manager, and chief engineer should be hired to span all areas with skilled people. Technical firms may also have an advisory board, preferably filled with seasoned industry veterans and experts.

These considerations notwithstanding, what Georges Doriot said in the 1940s still holds true today: "Always consider investing in a grade A man with a grade B idea. Never invest in a grade B man with a grade A idea" (Bygrave and Timmons, 1992, p. 104). Only when venture capitalists cannot find ventures with high-quality entrepreneurs should they place less emphasis on the entrepreneur and more on recruiting a balanced management team. Here is how one venture capitalist expressed the importance of the entrepreneur to us: "What we would say is the key criteria— whether we stick to it is another matter—is the quality of the management, that is, the person. You could produce any numbers, but unless you have someone to carry it out, it's not too worthwhile."

   The great importance of management is also eloquently supported in the literature by MacMillan, Siegel, and Subbanarasimha, who note in their study that "five of the top ten most important criteria had to do with the entrepreneur's experience and personality. There is no question that irrespective of the horse (product), horse races (market), or odds (financial criteria), it is the jockey (entrepreneur) who fundamentally determines whether the venture capitalists will place a bet at all" (1985, p. 119). Five of the top ten criteria for the business angels and venture capitalists that we identified in the previous table also concern the entrepreneur. Table 7.3 shows roughly how they rank in our research.

## The Entrepreneur's Characteristics

Let's take a closer look at some of the variables of interest to investors. An entrepreneur's enthusiasm is certainly critical for business angels since it is often a good indication of an entrepreneur's drive and willingness to work hard; angels hope that this also demonstrates dedication to the venture. Research has shown that lack of trust in many entrepreneurs whom business angels meet radically curtails the level of their investment activity (Coveney, 1996). The trust that investors have in the entrepreneur is also particularly important for venture capitalists. The credibility and integrity of a management team must be flawless if investors are

**Table 7.3.  Importance of the Entrepreneur's Characteristics in Attracting an Investor.**

| Entrepreneur's Characteristics | Ranking by Business Angels | Ranking by Venture Capitalists |
|---|---|---|
| Enthusiasm | 1 | 3 |
| Trust | 2 | 1 |
| Expertise | 3 | 2 |
| Liked upon meeting | 4 | 4 |
| Track record | 5 | 5 |

going to place trust in the firm and part with their funds (Harrison, Dibben, and Mason, 1997). Although the technical expertise of the entrepreneur in the field is seen as a basic necessity, many business angels also consider an entrepreneur's commercial expertise important. Indeed, being a salesman is essential, and a number of investors complained that entrepreneurs often are not.

Conversely, venture capitalists are interested in whether an entrepreneur has founded a venture before and whether they have amassed the necessary management experience to run and market a firm in the relevant industry sector. Somewhat surprisingly, an entrepreneur's track record is not necessarily the primary criterion, although naturally there appears to be a general preference among investors for seasoned entrepreneurs. Lastly, the degree to which investors like an entrepreneur after the initial meeting gives an impression of how easy he or she is to work with. This is especially important for business angels who prefer hands-on involvement in their investments. The chemistry must feel right for angels to be willing to invest. This is somewhat less important for venture capitalists (MacMillan, Siegel, and Subbanarasimha, 1985), although it is still of concern (Sapienza and Timmons, 1989; Cable and Shane, 1997).

The characteristics of the entrepreneur, of course, have been found to be vital to the survival of new firms. In a study comparing high-potential start-up firms featured in *Inc.* magazine in 1991, those that survived and prospered differ from their fallen comrades by the fact that they are more likely to have entrepreneurs who

- Are willing and able to learn on the job throughout the start-up stage
- Devote much time and effort to working with suppliers and contractors
- Closely examine new entrants and potential competitors
- Get the firm's positioning right from the beginning
- Have ready access to the capital they need
- Specialize in customized products and services designed and made to order
- Operate within a growth industry (Gartner, Starr, and Bhat, 1998)

The entrepreneur's prior industry experience turned out, in this study, not to be a significant predictor of a firm's success.

## The Entrepreneur's Own Investment in the Firm

Many investors also prefer entrepreneurs who have put some of their own savings into the venture, to show that they are committed and have sacrificed to build the firm. This may also teach an entrepreneur the value of money and instill the ability to get the most out of every penny invested, rather than spending it freely and carelessly. To better align interests between parties, potential investors often want to see the entrepreneur personally commit (depending on the business and industry) up to 5–10 percent of the total amount he or she hopes to raise. Of course, an entrepreneur's sweat equity and forgone opportunity costs are also important. Still, the older the person and the more successful the entrepreneur (and management team) has been in past endeavors, the more investors expect some sort of personal financial commitment.

## The Product and Market

For business angels, one of the primary requirements is that a product be unique and lie in a profitable niche market. It has to be something that no one else is doing, not a me-too product. "Theme" restaurants, for example, were not of particular interest to most business angel investors we surveyed. Many business angels claim that the niche market does not have to be large to make a profit, but they prefer markets with growth potential. This is how one business angel described the market he invested in: "It is a fragmented market that is growing; as we say, 'Get rich on the niche.'"

What may give hope to many entrepreneurs is that business angels often care little about the proprietary nature of the specific product or the importance of the industry sector, which also often appears to be secondary. One business angel said, "The actual product doesn't matter too much; you can always learn about it," further underlining that business angels fund anything they take a liking to. They are indeed very open-minded investors.

Like business angels, venture capitalists also prefer ventures operating in a true market niche. But one venture capitalist cautioned: "What often happens [is] a product gets invented and it is looking for a niche, but it doesn't quite do it." Venture capitalists demand much higher growth rates from their investments than business angels do. This means that they are not interested in lifestyle firms that have "subcritical mass," but ones with huge potential. Venture capitalists focus on new industries with lots of room for growth: software, communications, and biotech or medical. Over the last few years, Internet and e-commerce ventures have been favorites. Mature and dying industries are of little interest. One venture capitalist summed up this general sentiment: "I'm only interested in funding businesses which operate globally, not parochial ones; they aren't worth the effort. We wouldn't invest in anything that will not conceivably be worth $50 million within five years."

Many academic studies have also shown that venture capitalists prefer product markets with growth potential (Sahlman and Stevenson, 1985; Robinson, 1987; Riquelme and Rickards, 1992; Rea, 1989; Wright and Robbie, 1996). In fact, studies reveal that a market offering unconstrained opportunity for rapid growth is significantly more important for successful negotiation with a venture capitalist than having a complete management team, a credible business plan, rapid return on investment, or favorable contractual terms (Rea, 1989). In short, entrepreneurs should not even consider approaching a venture capitalist if their venture is not part of a rapidly growing market or cannot create a new market with unconstrained growth.

Market and product potential are definitely vital to the venture capitalist's evaluation, and finding a growth market not yet saturated is of great importance since "early birds are not always winners in product markets, but late comers are almost always losers" (Sahlman and Stevenson, 1985, p. 97). A market's growth potential is also important for business angels (Mason, Harrison, and Chaloner, 1991a), but a 1991 study by Freear, Sohl, and Wetzel found that despite funding firms that have a similar market share in their respective industries, venture capitalists finance firms that are forecast to grow much faster than those that are angel-funded.

To grow fast, however, some sort of competitive isolation is also important. Compared to venture capitalists, business angels tend to be less concerned about knowing the industry in which the firm competes and less concerned about competitive isolation or the degree to which the entrepreneur has identified competition (Haar, Starr, and MacMillan, 1988). Table 7.4 ranks the way various aspects of a proposal appeal to the two types of investors. Business angels may be willing to take a risk with a start-up that has not yet proved its competitive standing, but most venture capitalists prefer opportunities that have been proven but are still under-capitalized. This decreases their risk, naturally, and allows them to concentrate on building the product, rather than proving its worth first. One venture capitalist even described his last investment to us as "such a good opportunity, it was like selling wheelbarrows at a gold mine."

Patents are not necessarily always the great investment attraction we imagine. Because of the time and legal complexities involved in applying for patents, entrepreneurs may be discouraged from entering that lengthy process (Deakins, 1996). This minefield of regulation does not always appeal to venture capitalists

**Table 7.4. Product or Market Characteristics That Attract Investors.**

| Product and Market Characteristics | Ranking by Business Angels | Ranking by Venture Capitalists |
|---|---|---|
| Sales potential of product | 1 | 1 |
| Growth potential of the market | 2 | 2 |
| Quality of product | 3 | 3 |
| Niche market | 4 | 5 |
| Informal competitive protection of product (know-how) | 5 | 6 |
| Nature of competition in the industry | 6 | 7 |
| Overall competitive protection of product | 7 | 4 |
| Formal competitive protection of product (patents) | 8 | 8 |

either, and a few even believe that public disclosure of the product design in the patent application actually leads to more competitive entry rather than less (Tyebjee and Bruno, 1984).

## The Financials

Realizing high financial return is the primary investment motivation for both business angels and venture capitalists, but this does not necessarily imply that investors view healthy financial projections as the best indicator of future success. Though the financial criteria are rarely stated explicitly as one of the major attractions (Mason, Harrison, and Allen, 1995; Hall and Hofer, 1993), they are often hinted at as the investor emphasizes the niche and growth potential of the market and the entrepreneur's capabilities. In general, business angels place less weight on how much financial projection and calculation entrepreneurs present them with. Rather, many seem to have a gut feeling that if the investment succeeds, it will succeed very well. Talking about his last investment, one business angel told us, "The financial considerations weren't paramount; I think I was bored at the time and I just wanted to do it." But that does not mean that entrepreneurs should avoid doing financial projections, or treat them carelessly. Like venture capitalists, business angels still want them present in the business plan, if only to show that the idea has been well thought out by the entrepreneur. This is certainly important for venture capitalists, who place more weight on the financials than business angels do (Freear, Sohl, and Wetzel, 1995a). This is partly because entrepreneurs and financial projections are linked; it is definitely not wise to consider the financials without keeping in mind who formulated them. One venture capitalist told us that "once you start separating the financial analysis from the people, you're in trouble. The numbers are only as good as the people who write them."

We now take a closer look at two categories of financial variables: those used to screen for potential gains, and those that are more important in actually running the firm actively and hands-on.

### *Financials Used to Screen Potential Gains*

The variables that investors often use to screen for profitable investment opportunities (projected financial rewards, return on investment [ROI], and high profit margins) are much more important to venture capitalists than to business angels. Many business angels are not too concerned with calculating financial projections and place little reliance on projected figures. Their investment decisions tend to be very subjective, relying on the impression the entrepreneur makes and believing in the person. One reason business angels do not always place so much emphasis on financial projections is that the investment opportunities they usually consider are vastly smaller in size and younger in stage than those favored by venture capitalists. Many of these firms are just unproven ideas; putting financial figures to the hoped-for success of these firms is speculative at best.

By contrast, venture capitalists emphasize financial projections that screen for potential financial returns (Muzyka, Birley, and Leleux, 1995; Wright and Robbie, 1996). ROI and net present value (NPV) calculations are common, if not standard practice. One declared reason for this concern is the financially driven nature of the fund providers (the limited partners). Most venture capitalists are return-driven because their LPs are return-driven: those who invest in venture capital firms look at return of investment as a measure of performance. Most of the firms that venture capitalists are interested in are already established, with credible revenue streams and profits, so return-based calculations are possible. Entrepreneurs hoping to approach a venture capitalist should ensure that they have detailed historical income statements, cash flows, and balance sheets, as well as comprehensive projections for the last few years. The assumptions should be clearly explained and cash flow forecasts—an important indication of the projected health of the firm—should be included since it is important to remember that "sales are vanity, profit is sanity, and cash is king."

### Financials Used as Cost Concerns to Be Monitored

In most of the firms typically funded by the business angels, one great weakness of the young start-ups is lack of financial controls and accurate accounts. This is understandable, but it also causes a major preinvestment hesitation for the business angels who must then handle this deficiency through their own input to the firm, often using their business experience to help with the accounting system. However, the angels' concern for the day-to-day financial controls may also stem from their lack of trust in the financial abilities of the (young and unseasoned) entrepreneurs they fund. One business angel told us: "I've always found that there's never enough money available for a small company, the entrepreneurs have never planned ahead for a cash-flow crisis. When it comes, they always try to fudge the figures to avoid the crisis, at least on paper, but if I keep a close eye on the financials, I can see the crisis coming and help."

It is common for business angels to scrutinize the firm's operating financials as they rationalize their active involvement: "If an entrepreneur gets money easily, he'll spend it lavishly. If he gets it the hard way, he'll spend it more wisely." The firms that venture capitalists finance typically have extensive financial controls, though they are not always perfect. Rather than solving this themselves, venture capitalists recruit new employees to handle the operating financials. One venture capitalist stated: "One of our concerns was that the entrepreneur wasn't that experienced in running a small business, so we put our man, a financial controller, in there, as well as our involvement." Table 7.5 shows the importance of some of the financial operating variables for business angels and venture capitalists we surveyed.

Overall, business angels are more concerned than venture capitalists with the financial variables that are important in day-to-day operations (Van Osnabrugge, 1998; Mason and others, 1994). This may be because business angels tend to be personally and actively involved, which is wise since they have fewer reserves to

Table 7.5.  **Importance of Financial Cost Concerns.**

| Financial Characteristics (Used as Cost Concerns to Be Monitored) | Ranking by Business Angels | Ranking by Venture Capitalists |
|---|---|---|
| Low overheads | 1 | 2 |
| Ability to break even without further funding | 2 | 1 |
| Low initial capital expenses needed (on assets) | 3 | 5 |
| Size of the investment (desired) | 4 | 4 |
| Low cost to test the market initially | 5 | 3 |

invest should the firm need it. If such a need arises, it forces the business angel to surrender more equity to attract further funding. For business angels, the size of the investment often influences how active or passive they are in the firm. The amount of the investment has to be right; otherwise angels are just not interested. Such funding requirements tend to be relatively unimportant for venture capitalists since they have large funds to invest (Robinson, 1987). In a recent survey, the size of investment sought by an entrepreneur was "very important" or "important" to 55 percent of business angels, while this was the case for only 26 percent of venture capitalists (Van Osnabrugge, 1998).

It appears that venture capitalists are concerned about financial variables used for potential screening of profits (before investment), while business angels are interested in the financial variables important in running a firm (after investment). This further confirms that business angels typically desire active involvement in the running of their firms.

## The Business Plan

Most entrepreneurs are under the impression that if they have a comprehensive and seamless business plan, they are sure to receive financing. As we discuss in Appendix Three, this is certainly important for securing funds, but the business plan itself (as opposed to the idea) is not always primary. The presentation of the business plan acts as a reflection of the entrepreneur, showing that he or she has really thought things through. Business plans are seen by business angels as necessary—a recent study found that more than three-quarters of business angels require seeing a business plan before investing (Mason and Harrison, 1996b)—but their importance in the investment decision is sometimes limited. One business angel told us: "I like to see professional business plans; the more professional [they are], the more likely I am to invest. If I get a business plan with lots of spelling errors or pages missing, or if the typing doesn't follow through, I'll just throw it away. Because if they can't present a business plan, then I don't think that they can run a business properly. Raising money is one of the most important things they'll be doing, and if they can't do that right grammatically, I don't bother."

On the other hand, a few angels we spoke to believe business plans are useless because the projections are usually unrealistic and undeliverable. One angel stated his frustration: "I don't have a lot of time for business plans. They're a bit like banks, asking us for cash-flow forecasts—they're all dreams. Everyone is optimistic when they write it out—a waste of effort." Some of the angels we encountered had even invested in ventures without developed business plans and actually helped their entrepreneurs formulate one so that they would be prepared for future rounds of financing.

Conversely, venture capitalists rely much more on a good business plan that is straightforward, honest, and realistic. Because venture capitalists evaluate business plans for a living, any deception in a plan is probably caught right away and greatly lessens a company's chances of receiving funding. Entrepreneurs should be truthful and complete. Venture capitalists prefer clarity of vision and a proposition that is a little different from the usual, especially in untried start-up firms. It is important for entrepreneurs to reach a balance between presenting how they are going to maximize the business opportunity, and giving sensible financial information.

In short, the business plan should be clear (Hall and Hofer, 1993; Zacharakis and Meyer, 1995), professional (Hall and Hofer, 1993), realistic (Keeley, Roure, and Loo, 1991), and well balanced (Keeley, Roure, and Loo, 1991). But more important, it should be short and concise, getting straight to the point, as briefly as possible summarizing the product, credentials of the management team, the financing sought and reasons why, the achievements of the venture to date, expected milestones, and exit strategies. As a remarkable illustration, the complete original business plan of Sun Microsystems was only twelve pages long (Nance-Nash, 1999).

## Other Attributes of the Business

In addition to the four main categories of investment criteria (entrepreneurs, product and market, financials, and business plan), there are a number of other important criteria. They are harder to categorize but still important in the investment decision. A number of them are listed in Table 7.6, in rough order of importance for the investors.

### Table 7.6.  Importance of Miscellaneous Criteria in Attracting Investors.

| Other Business Attributes | Ranking by Business Angels | Ranking by Venture Capitalists |
|---|---|---|
| Investor involvement possible | 1 | 3 |
| Investor's strengths filling gaps in business | 2 | 5 |
| Local venture (geographically close) | 3 | 6 |
| Potential exit routes (liquidity) | 4 | 1 |
| Investor's understanding of business or industry | 4 | 2 |
| Presence of (potential) co-investors | 6 | 4 |

## Possibility of Investor's Involvement

As we have already seen, business angels generally prefer to invest in entrepreneurial firms in which they can actively participate themselves, offering their years of business experience to help further their investments. This certainly explains why, among all the criteria, "investor's involvement possible," "investor's strengths filling gaps in business," and "local venture (geographically close)" are the top three for business angels. Such involvement by business angels can certainly make the difference between success and failure for their investee firms (Wetzel and Freear, 1994). In fact, 94 percent of U.S. matching services told us that their angels consider the location of the investment to be very important. This is less of an investment attraction for venture capitalists.

## Realistic Exit Strategies

For venture capitalists, investments offering potential exit routes and in business sectors they understand are attractive. After all, since (unlike business angels) venture capitalists must show competence to their fund providers, placing priority on investments that they fully understand and that have almost certain exit routes is a responsible way to invest. Entrepreneurs approaching a venture capitalist should develop a number of possible exit strategies.

## Opportunity to Co-Invest

There has been some confusion as to whether or not business angels prefer to co-invest. The recent dramatic rise in the popularity of angel syndicates and alliances and the proactive initiatives taken by matching services to arrange group angel deals indicate that business angels like investing in groups, but we must caution that this is not always the case. Even though the potential presence of co-investors is for many business angels a motivating investment factor (they feel more comfortable going in with others), many of these business angels actually prefer to co-invest only with people they know personally. Investing with people they do not know often limits their ability to exercise a degree of control over the firm through active involvement. One business angel echoes this point: "Co-investors attract if I'm in it purely for the investment; if it's an investment where I have a hands-on role it doesn't attract—otherwise you have too many egos involved, and it leads to conflict."

Since most business angels in the United States and the UK do not invest through a matching service, they often receive investment referrals from friends with whom they then co-invest. This may explain why in the United States we see anywhere from 60 to 92 percent of business angels preferring to co-invest (Freear, Sohl, and Wetzel, 1994a; Wetzel, 1983, 1986b; Haar, Starr, and MacMillan, 1988; Aram, 1989; Gaston, 1989; Kelly and Hay, 1996). In the UK, by contrast, this appears to be lower, around 29–44 percent (Mason and Harrison, 1993b, 1995). However, U.S. matching services that we sampled claim that possibly 80 percent of their angels do prefer to co-invest, with an average of four to six angels per deal.

For business angels, the opportunity to co-invest is often more important than for venture capitalists, but syndication among venture capital firms has a number of advantages (Wasserman, 1999). First, syndication spreads the costs of and responsibility for due diligence and gives investors a second opinion on their decisions. Second, co-investment allows venture capitalists to diversify their investment risks across a larger array of firms. Third, having investment partners makes it easier to raise funds for additional rounds of funding within the group, or to use the syndicate's contacts to court new investors. Fourth, syndication increases the ties that a venture capital firm has with its peers, aligning interests and building extensive contact networks. But syndication also has its problems, such as sharing the investment profits; internal transaction costs; and the costs to the lead venture capitalists, who must spend considerably more time running the deal—up to ten times the number of hours usually spent on a typical late-stage investment (Gorman and Sahlman, 1989). Actually, with the dramatic rise in recent years of venture capitalists competing to find and back the hottest new Internet start-ups, some of the most complex negotiations we have heard about have not been between venture capitalists and entrepreneurs, but between co-investing venture capitalists concerning who can assume the lead investor role.

Now that we have reviewed some of the investment criteria used by business angels and venture capitalists, Table 7.7 takes a closer look at how the business angels and venture capitalists we contacted roughly ranked all the criteria.

### Table 7.7. Summary of Investment Criteria (in Rough Order of Importance).

| Selected Investment Criteria | Ranking Overall by Business Angels | Ranking Overall by Venture Capitalists |
|---|---|---|
| **People or entrepreneur** | | |
| Enthusiasm of the entrepreneur(s) | 1 | 3 |
| Trustworthiness of the entrepreneur(s) | 2 | 1 |
| Expertise of the entrepreneur(s) | 4 | 2 |
| Investor liked entrepreneur(s) upon meeting | 5 | 9 |
| Track record of the entrepreneur(s) | 10 | 8 |
| **Market or product** | | |
| Sales potential of the product | 3 | 5 |
| Growth potential of the market | 6 | 6 |
| Quality of product | 7 | 10 |
| Niche market | 9 | 13 |
| Informal competitive protection of the product (know-how) | 12 | 14 |

*(continued)*

## Table 7.7. (*continued*)

| Selected Investment Criteria | Ranking Overall by Business Angels | Ranking Overall by Venture Capitalists |
|---|---|---|
| **Market or product** | | |
| Nature of competition in the industry | 17 | 16 |
| Overall competitive protection of the product | 21 | 11 |
| Formal competitive protection of the product (patents) | 27 | 20 |
| **Financials used to screen for potential gains** | | |
| Perceived financial rewards (for the investor) | 8 | 4 |
| Expected rate of return | 11 | 7 |
| High margins of the business | 15 | 15 |
| **Financials to monitor the operating firm** | | |
| Low overheads | 16 | 21 |
| Ability to break even without further funding | 18 | 19 |
| Low initial capital expenditures needed (on assets) | 19 | 24 |
| Size of the investment | 20 | 23 |
| Low cost to test the market initially | 22 | 22 |
| **Other business attributes (vital to hands-on role)** | | |
| Investor's involvement possible (contribute skills) | 13 | 18 |
| Investor's strengths filling gaps in business | 14 | 26 |
| Local venture | 23 | 27 |
| **Other business attributes (miscellaneous)** | | |
| Potential exit routes (liquidity) | 24 | 12 |
| Investor's understanding of the business or industry | 24 | 17 |
| Presence of (potential) co-investors | 26 | 25 |

## Factors Clinching the Deal

We asked business angels to identify one variable that distinguished the last investment they had actually made from other opportunities that they did not fund but seriously considered. In other words, when it comes down to making an investment decision, what aspect of an investment opportunity sways the vote in favor of doing it? Interestingly, angels most often chose one investment over another primarily according to the opportunity to get actively involved in the investee firm. Since involvement means working with the firm's founder, characteristics of the entrepreneur such as his or her perceived trustworthiness are also important criteria in swinging the vote among multiple investment opportunities (Table 7.8).

Similarly, a recent large-scale survey of more than two hundred investors asked business angels and venture capitalists to state what aspect of an investment opportunity that they had recently looked at very seriously convinced them finally *not* to invest

**Table 7.8.   Investment Criteria That Swing the Vote for Angels if Present in a Deal.**

| *Ten Most Important Factors in Swinging Angel's Vote for a Deal* | *Five Least Important Factors in Swinging Angel's Vote for a Deal* |
| --- | --- |
| 1. Investor's strengths filling gaps | 1. Growth potential of market |
| 2. Investor's involvement possible | 2. Venture is local |
| 3. Trustworthiness of entrepreneur | 3. Ability to break even without further funding |
| 4. Quality of product | |
| 5. Low initial capital costs | 4. Formal competitive protection of product (patents) |
| 6. Investor liked entrepreneur upon meeting | 5. Overall competitive protection of product |
| 7. Niche market | |
| 8. Low cost to test market initially | |
| 9. Track record of entrepreneur | |
| 10. Sales potential of product | |

(Van Osnabrugge, 1998). Interestingly, the character of a venture's entrepreneur and management team often makes the crucial difference (Figure 7.2).

This finding is well summarized by MacMillan, Zemann, and Subbanarasimha (1987), who found that each type of successful investment has an unsuccessful "twin" for which "the major difference between the winner and loser is some difficult-to-define venture team characteristic" (p. 129).

## Investors' Preinvestment Hesitations

A recent study asked investors what their most significant preinvestment hesitation was for a firm that in the end they actually funded (Van Osnabrugge, 1998). For business angels, financials of the firm were the biggest hesitation (for 28 percent of respondents), followed by the product or market (25 percent), the entrepreneur(s) (22 percent), and other business attributes

**Figure 7.2. Aspects Leading to Rejecting a Seriously Considered Investment Opportunity.**

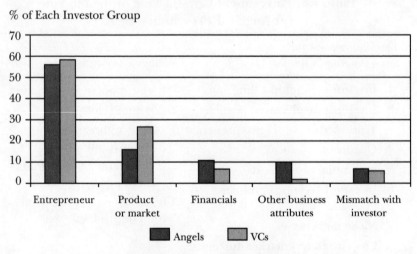

% of Each Investor Group

Subpar Factor of Seriously Considered Investment Opportunity that Made Investor Finally Not Invest

(15 percent). This seems to support our earlier assertion that business angels are often concerned about the state of a firm's financial controls and typically improve them by taking action themselves. Interestingly, the entrepreneur was the main hesitation for more than half of the investments seriously considered but not funded, while it was the main hesitation for less than a quarter of the investments made.

For venture capitalists, the product or market was the most significant hesitation (for 38 percent of respondents), followed by the entrepreneur(s) (33 percent), other business attributes (21 percent), and the financials (7 percent), as Figure 7.3 shows.

It should be noted that in Figure 7.3 the investor groups are considered quite independently. Thus, if more venture capitalists than business angels rate the entrepreneur as their main hesitation, it does not necessarily mean that venture capitalists have more reservations about the entrepreneur than do the business angels. This is important since the majority of business angels we spoke to had significant hesitations, while most venture capitalists

**Figure 7.3. Aspects Causing Investor to Hesitate.**

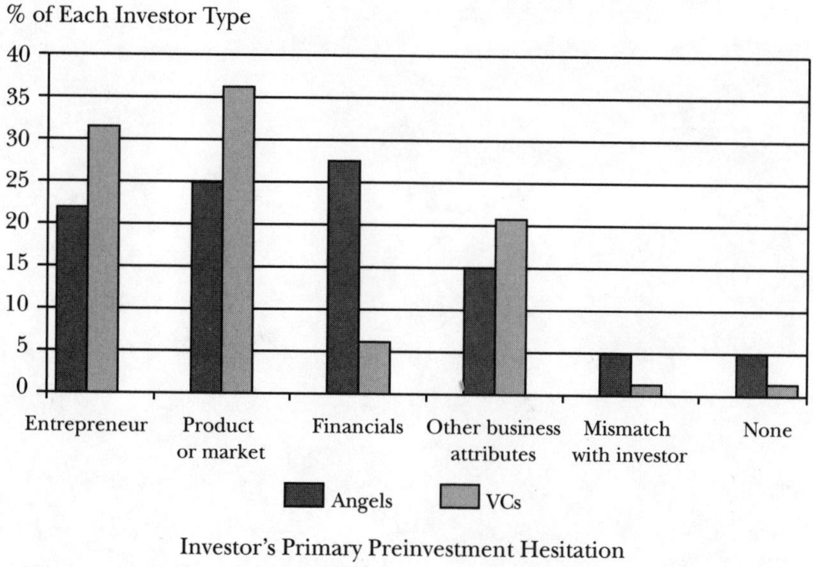

% of Each Investor Type

Investor's Primary Preinvestment Hesitation

appeared to have few, if any. Of course, as in any diverse group, there was also a minority of business angels who had few, if any, hesitations. One business angel even joked: "My greatest hesitation was investing in a horse-racing equipment company, because if the investment starts working, I might start betting some on the horses; that worries me—there goes the investment!"

Now that we have seen what investors look for in investments and what their greatest hesitations are, the next chapter shows how investors go about finding and securing such deals.

# Chapter Eight

# Screening the Deal and Conducting Due Diligence

To find one or two potential investment opportunities that are feasible and that match their investment criteria, investors must screen a myriad of potential opportunities. In particular, investors wishing to fund young entrepreneurial firms face a number of problems at the initial screening stage. First, unlike publicly traded companies, privately held firms do not have any historic data, such as dividend level and price movements, that aid in assessment. Second, investors do not have firm-specific knowledge to fully evaluate the opportunity. Third, it seems that attempts to fix investee firms after the investment has been made rarely work, thus making it important to fund top-quality firms from the start (Busenitz, Moesel, and Fiet, 1997).

To protect their limited financial resources, therefore, investors have to make sure that their "filtering" process only let through deals that closely match their investment criteria and have a good chance of reaching completion. This is why, in addition to finding deals and initial screening, it is crucial for investors to conduct thorough due diligence on the opportunity they are considering before parting with their hard-earned funds.

This chapter is dedicated to documenting how business angels and venture capitalists complete this trying process; it also presents the tools needed to do so successfully. Locating good deals to consider can be challenging, and selecting even one entrepreneurial opportunity to fund can be a lengthy and tricky affair— like panning for gold: "You have to sift through a lot of dirt before you find a nugget" (Cullen, 1998).

Although this chapter emphasizes the questions of screening and due diligence from the perspective of the likely investor, we want to make quite clear that this process should be a two-way street. Entrepreneurs should engage in due diligence on likely investors, to make sure they have a solid reputation, that they see the business plan (especially the exit; see Chapter Eleven) as the entrepreneur does, and that they are the kind of partner the young enterprise really needs. Not all money is equally attractive, depending on the characteristics of its owner; we discuss this fully in the next chapter.

## How Investors Find and Screen Deals

Business angels tend to look for investment opportunities in an ad hoc, unscientific manner, rather than adopting a proactive search, as we have already seen in Chapter Five (Mason and Harrison, 1992, 1993a; Atkin and Esiri, 1993). One explanation may be that business angels invest only on a part-time basis (Mason and Harrison, 1994). There is clearly much serendipity in business angel investments (Mason and Harrison, 1993a, 1996a), resembling a "giant game of hide-and-seek with everyone blindfolded" (Gaston, 1989, p. 4). Consequently, studies have found that business angels usually learn of investment opportunities through a network of friends and family, business associates, accountants, and lawyers as referrals, or directly from entrepreneurs; only a small number proactively use matching services preferring instead to use friends and business associates (Freear and Wetzel, 1991). It is the informal networks of friends and business associates that tend to be the most effective source (Wetzel, 1983; Freear and Wetzel, 1989, 1991; Haar, Starr, and MacMillan, 1988; Mason and Harrison, 1994; Landstrom, 1993). Bill Wetzel, one of the pioneering researchers in the business angel field, believes that such ad hoc reliance on friends makes the market mechanism for business angel financing "really very inefficient and random: who knows whom, who mentioned something on the golf course, who talked to his or her accountant lately, and who's looking for money. This makes the marketplace horribly time-consuming. Next to capital, time is the scarcest resource entrepreneurs have" (Mason, 1996a, p. 27).

In contrast to business angels, venture capitalists have extensive networks of referrers, yielding extensive investment deal flow (Fiet, 1991). They consist of their portfolio companies, their investors, and other venture capital firms, especially those with whom they are interconnected by co-investments (Bygrave and Timmons, 1986). In the past, some may have waited passively for deal proposals to be put to them (Sweeting, 1991), but recently venture capitalists have become proactive in their search for deals, especially for those wildly popular Internet opportunities. Indeed, in today's climate, almost all viable Internet firms are being captured in the venture capital net and offered attractive investment terms.

Because the venture capital communities in the United States are highly inbred, this may give many entrepreneurs the impression that there is substantially less competition between suppliers of capital than is indicated by the number of funds in the market (Tyebjee and Bruno, 1984). Compared to the superior information networks venture capitalists enjoy, there is considerable inefficiency in the flow, which restricts the amount and quality of the proposals that business angels receive. Perhaps because of this, business angels tend to scan investment opportunities until they find one of interest, conducting little serious ongoing comparison with other deals still coming in. In fact, a number of business angels told us that the investment proposal they eventually funded was the first one they seriously considered. Since venture capitalists have a greater investment deal flow than business angels, they have the option to conduct such comparisons, and they do so extensively. Their years of day-to-day experience also enable them to easily identify a suitable new opportunity when it crosses the desk. Of course, venture capitalists are full-time employees, and it is their job to make perhaps three to six investments per year; therefore they are expected to look at several deals at once.

## The Attrition Rate of Investment Opportunities

Regardless of the efficiency of investment networks and the number of deals flowing in, only a limited number can be carried through. Both business angels and venture capitalists experience

a significant rate of opportunity attrition—rejected opportunities
—as they try to find one suitable venture that matches their investment criteria.

Even though the attrition rate varies with the type of business
angel, most invest in only a fraction of the investment opportunities they see. In the United States, angels invest in around 22 percent of the deals they seriously consider (Gaston, 1989). However,
not all angels have a similar rate of acceptance. Entrepreneurs will
find hope in knowing that almost a quarter of business angels report acceptances in the 60–100 percent range (Gaston, 1989).
One UK study found that business angels typically receive thirty-
six investment proposals per year, become interested in about
eight of those, and offer to invest in two (Coveney, 1996). For most
angel investors, the acceptance rate appears to be higher for those
deals referred to them through their personal networks of trusted
friends, rather than through a matching service. From an entrepreneur's perspective, these high acceptance rates make business
angels an especially attractive and viable financing option to
pursue.

In contrast, venture capitalists invest in only about 1–3 percent of proposals received. One study found that more than
77 percent of proposals are rejected at the initial screening stage,
with a further 20 percent rejected during the due-diligence process, leaving fewer than 3 percent of the proposals to receive funding (Hall, 1988). This is certainly a more severe initial screening
process than that conducted by business angels. One venture capitalist even told us: "We got 300 approaches last year, 150 of those
in writing; we met with about 15, then about 10 for a second meeting, and of those we only did one or two." It is important for entrepreneurs to remember that although venture capitalists (and
other investors to a certain degree) may give positive feedback at
the various stages of negotiation, they should not get their hopes
up until the investment contract is signed. It is unfortunate, but
entrepreneurs are sometimes strung along unrealistically as potential investors enthusiastically say yes at each stage, only to have
their hopes dashed by a final no. Certainly, investors want to keep
entrepreneurs enthusiastic up to the moment when it becomes
clear they no longer want to invest in the venture. For entrepreneurs it is important to persist in the search for funds, especially

in light of the various funding sources available to those with a good investment opportunity. One venture capitalist noted: "Most people that complain about lack of venture funds have marginal ideas; and pretty often, are financially naïve. There is plenty of money for quality deals. And generally, good deals combined with open minded prospecting will end up in favorable financing positions" (Fiet, 1996, p. 18). However, as Appendix Three explains, entrepreneurs should not follow a shotgun approach to gain the attention of venture capitalists. Since venture capitalists have extensive networks, they find out which business plans have been previously rejected by other firms. Each rejection further reduces an entrepreneur's chances of getting funds. A rifle-shot approach of approaching investors selectively seems more appropriate than a shotgun approach (Wasserman, 1999).

## How Referrers Influence Investors

Business angel and venture capitalist investors face poorly defined investment environments, and the typical ventures they seek are often too small to be readily identifiable. For this reason, intermediaries play an important role in matching investors with ventures seeking funds, with the referral source significantly influencing the business angel's and venture capitalist's impression of an investment opportunity (Mason and Rogers, 1996; Hall and Hofer, 1993) and thus affecting the rates of deal acceptance and funding. For business angels, the rejection rate at the initial screening stage is associated with the referral source (Riding and others, 1993), implying that the closer the referee is to the referrer, the more likely it is that the investor will pursue the deal (Haar, Starr, and MacMillan, 1988). As noted in Table 8.1, friends, business associates, and lead investors are the three most productive sources for business angels, while attorneys, accountants, bankers, and gatekeepers are the least productive (Freear, Sohl, and Wetzel, 1992a; Freear and Wetzel, 1991; Harrison and Mason, 1991b).

In fact, it is not uncommon for business angels to meet other angels through deals and to choose to co-invest with them on subsequent investments. However, despite their benefits, these social networks also tend to be inefficient in nature (Mason and Harrison, 1993a); 32 percent of angels cite lack of reliable information

**Table 8.1.  Most- and Least-Trusted Referrers of Deals.**

| *Most Trusted Deal Referrers for Angels* | *Least Trusted Deal Referrers for Angels* |
| --- | --- |
| Friends | Attorneys |
| Business associates | Accountants |
| Lead investors in a syndicate | Bankers and gatekeepers |

flow as restricting their investment activity (Coveney, 1996). Yet the minority of very wealthy and very experienced business angels tend to have less trouble finding deals, thanks to their extensive personal networks of contacts and sources of deal flow. In fact, these investors believe that the best-quality deal flow comes from those sources and contacts they have developed after completing a number of deals: syndicate investor partners, entrepreneurs they have backed before, and tips from venture capitalists (Kelly and Hay, 1999).

Similarly, venture capitalists place much more weight on referrals from people they know and trust, and they also tend to invest in proposals passed on by those referrers (Wilson, 1985; Tyebjee and Bruno, 1984; Norton, 1995). Proposals from anonymous referrers (cold calls) are rarely even considered, and almost never funded. Most of these are ignored from the start, which helps to explain the high attrition rate (typically only 1–3 percent succeed) of proposals suggested for funding. For most venture capitalists, referrals from other venture capital firms and accountants are the primary sources (Fiet, 1996; Tyebjee and Bruno, 1984; Murray, 1995a). But business associates, other entrepreneurs, and their extensive networks of contacts also generate and further review deals for venture capitalists. One venture capitalist emphasized that the referral source is clearly a means of self-selection: "Obviously, when someone who you've known for quite a while and you respect their judgment refers something to you, you tend to put more credibility on that than some business plan that just arrived from a law firm which probably can't understand the business anyway." Not surprisingly, the networks that venture capitalists employ are much more efficient and formal than those used by business angels. Clearly, if entrepreneurs want to gain the attention of a venture capitalist, they should find a mutually known referrer to make the introduction.

## Sector Specialization of Investors

In addition to using referral networks, another way investors screen proposals is by specializing in a limited number of areas and screening opportunities in only those areas. This reduces the amount of initial screening necessary.

Business angels are usually quite open-minded about the industry sectors in which they consider investment, but their main requirement appears to be that they understand the generic business, rather than the sector. This understanding allows them to assess how they might add their own general business knowledge and experience to the firm. Interestingly, unlike in many other countries, business angels in the United States and Canada often prefer investing in high-technology and manufacturing ventures (Freear, Sohl, and Wetzel, 1995b; Mason, Harrison, and Allen, 1995) even though as a whole their preferences remain diverse. Compared to more diversified investors those angels who work on a specialization strategy tend to receive fewer investment proposals, accept a higher percentage of those proposals, and rely less on evaluation of the entrepreneur than on evaluation of the firm's market and technology (Landstrom, 1993).

Conversely, the majority of venture capitalists specialize according to geographical area, industry, and financing stage (Norton and Tenenbaum, 1993; Norton, 1995; Tyebjee and Bruno, 1984); their portfolios tend to be narrowly focused rather than diversified (Bygrave, 1987; Norton and Tenenbaum, 1993; Busenitz, Moesel, and Fiet, 1997). Venture capitalists are often interested in investing in only one or two areas, and many are constrained as to what sectors they can invest in by what is prescribed by their fund. These specialization strategies allow them to assess proposals with a better information base for the particular industry. In addition, most referrals from colleagues are for opportunities in their field(s) of specialization. As one venture capitalist told us: "Because we're specialists within the market, we have strong prejudices about where we should and shouldn't be putting money, and because we have points of view, it's like magnetism, because people know we have a certain point of view. Very few biotech firms call us up. We get almost nothing here that is not on target in principle—99.9 percent of things that come across our desk are within [our] scope. To me that shows how specialization works well."

Unfortunately, one study found that a possible consequence of employing a strategy of specialization and less diversification in early-stage financing of small firms is a lower level of performance (Gupta and Sapienza, 1988). Inability to diversify the risks of small high-risk firms across a well-balanced portfolio is the obvious reason. However, in practice venture capitalists do not always attempt to actively diversify their portfolios. For example, 83 percent of a UK sample of venture capitalists evaluated the risk of a new project in isolation, rather than in terms of the effect on portfolio risk (Hall, 1988). Yet by building themselves a stronger knowledge base upon which to evaluate the viability of investment proposals, venture capitalists can use a specialization strategy as a way of easing the initial screening process to select higher-quality proposals for the subsequent due-diligence process.

## Turning the Tables on Venture Capitalists

Interestingly, studies have also found that for the minority of entrepreneurs with ventures perceived as superb investment opportunities (often unique Internet-based firms, in today's market), the search for venture capital funds is a less rigorous process. In a recent study of entrepreneurs who have received venture capital funds, 71 percent received more than one offer to invest—and 54 percent received three or more, giving them the rare option to choose among venture capital firms (Smith, 1999). To do so, they spent forty hours on average gathering information about venture capitalists, with 29 percent spending more than one hundred hours. These entrepreneurs relied heavily on other entrepreneurs, on venture capitalists, and on their own experience to collect insights—three sources that present a rather limited picture. Surprisingly, more independent sources, such as accountants, consultants, lawyers, and the Internet, were used much less. But less surprisingly, these entrepreneurs typically do not stop soliciting interest from venture capitalists after receiving one offer; rather, they try to form a market for their firm's shares. To actually choose a venture capitalist to join the firm, entrepreneurs consider four main criteria in evaluating an offer: valuation, value-added services, the venture capitalist's reputation, and the attributes of the venture capitalist. Of these, a number of attributes are most important in selecting which investor's offer to accept:

*Characteristics of Venture Capital Firms Most Important to Entrepreneurs with Multiple Venture Capital Offers*

- Reputation for investing in successful companies
- Serving as a sounding board for the entrepreneurial team
- Personality compatible with the culture of the company
- Valuation
- Reputation for following through with staged investments
- Industry specialization of the venture capitalist
- Investment-stage specialization of the venture capitalist

---

*Source:* partially adapted from Smith (1999).

Although valuation is important, those entrepreneurs who select a venture capitalist based on reputation tend to have higher levels of satisfaction with the relationship than those who select based on price.

## The Due-Diligence Process

Absolutely vital to making a sound investment, due diligence verifies any business opportunities that survive the initial screening stage. This verification process consists of checking the accuracy of business plans, audited accounts, and management accounts; getting replies to warranty and other standard questionnaires; patent searches; and technical studies. Of course, unpublished accounting information and subjective information are important; these data are collected by calling customers, suppliers, lawyers, and bankers, and by checking trade journals. Due diligence emphasizes understanding and quantifying the *risk* of the proposed deal, rather than the upside.

*Some Factors Analyzed and Verified During Due Diligence*

- Track record of the management team
- Size and growth potential of the market
- Demand for product among target customers
- Ability to deliver product on time and at agreed price
- Competitive advantage of product
- Competitors
- Marketing and distribution plans
- Soundness of financial projections
- Assessment of assumptions used
- Assessment of intellectual property rights, if any
- Existing or possible legal contingencies
- Valuation for the venture

The due-diligence process is intended to be tough on invest-ment proposals. For venture capital investments, as few as 10–15 percent of proposals make it past the initial screening stage to the full due-diligence process, and only 10 percent of those receive funding. Indeed, the whole point of this process is to discover po-tential problems and to eliminate unsuitable proposals from fur-ther contention. This may be especially important in a start-up situation, where the venture has no track record or asset base and the market opportunity and competitive advantage of a product or service need to be verified. In large transactions of established firms, an external third party (such as an accounting firm) might be used to prepare a due-diligence report. Such a report would be underwritten by the accountant's professional indemnity insur-ance, which is an important mitigation of risk for a potential in-vestor who is accountable to others, as with a venture capitalist (Rigby, 1997). But venture capitalists primarily use these accoun-tants' reports to verify and validate information in their own due-diligence reports (Wright and Robbie, 1996).

It is important to realize that conducting thorough due dili-gence can be a long and difficult process for investors and should be undertaken only if they are very serious about a proposal. One business angel summed up this troublesome nature: "It's fair to say that the due-diligence process is the hardest thing that you have to do, to actually check out everything they say is true, that the market is there, that they have the necessary skills and background to do what they say they're going to do; that's the hardest bit, and that's general, regardless of what you invest in." Before incurring any expenses, venture capital firms usually negotiate an exclusivity period (sometimes called a "lockup") with an entrepreneur, guaranteeing that only they can conduct due diligence on the firm and allowing them to settle on definitive terms (Wasserman, 1999).

Despite such difficulties, when it comes to achieving an attractive rate of return on investment avoiding bad ones is still more important than hitting home runs (Benjamin and Margulis, 1996). We cannot overemphasize the importance of the due-diligence process for any investor. Venture capital is a bit like a marriage. You can do as much as you can beforehand to try to minimize the risk, but obviously you cannot eliminate all risk. But if you are fairly sure that you are not going to get along with someone, it would be silly to go on, because it will be very difficult to leave and get your money back. Therefore, investors should build certain due-diligence considerations into their investment processes:

- The stage of typical investments
- Investors' sector experience
- Sector research conducted by investors
- Extent of preinvestment contact with the entrepreneur
- Taking independent references on the entrepreneur
- Analysis of financial projections
- Demanding a comprehensive business plan before investment
- Research costs
- Size of investor's decision-making group
- Time and length of investment process

## Stages of a Typical Investment

Investment opportunities in their early stages have many inherent risks that the due-diligence process must expose. For instance, these ventures are not likely to have established relationships with buyers, distributors, suppliers, and other business associates. They may operate with skeleton staffs, positions unfilled, and responsibilities undefined, and the CEOs (entrepreneurs) may still be untested in the industry (Sapienza, 1992). Investigating early-stage investment opportunities can be challenging.

One way to ease the due-diligence process and partially reduce uncertainty is to invest in less-risky ventures whose characteristics are more easily verifiable. Funding later-stage entrepreneurial firms with greater total capitalization values is one strategy that can be employed. However, for business angels especially, funding mature firms is often not viable since the equity of such ventures is too expensive.

Indeed, one of the most valuable contributions of business angels is that they *prefer* investing in seed, start-up, and early-stage ventures (Freear and Wetzel, 1989; Mason and Harrison, 1996a). In fact, for business angels willing to invest at this stage of financing is often a very important nonfinancial consideration (Freear, Sohl, and Wetzel, 1994a); business angels become less likely to pursue investment in a firm as its size (sales and employees) increases (Wetzel and Wilson, 1985). In the United States, 55–72 percent of business angels invest in start-up or other early-stage ventures (Freear, Sohl, and Wetzel, 1995a; Freear and Wetzel, 1989, 1991; Haar, Starr, and MacMillan, 1988; Aram, 1989); similarly in the UK, 50–65 percent of business angels do so (Van Osnabrugge, 1998; Mason and Sackett, 1996; Mason and Harrison, 1996a). Only in Sweden do business angels prefer to finance more established firms (Landstrom, 1993). Although many business angels prefer early-stage firms because it is really the only stage in which they can get a piece of the action before being priced out of the market, others prefer start-ups and early-stage firms because they are more of a gamble.

Compared to business angels, venture capitalists have a lower propensity to finance nonestablished firms (Wetzel, 1996; Ehrlich, Noble, Moore, and Weaver, 1994; Freear, Sohl, and Wetzel, 1995a) and appear to have a shorter exit horizon and more risk aversion than business angels (Freear and Wetzel, 1990). The share of early-stage investments in the U.S. venture capital industry exhibits a wavelike pattern that is positively related to the number of IPOs in the market and the number of venture capital firms. Overall, in the United States the share of early-stage investments fluctuates around a trend line of 28 percent (Brouwer and Hendrix, 1998). But, even when venture capitalists do invest in early stage firms, these firms are often much larger than those favored by business angels, up to eleven times larger on average in one recent study (Van Osnabrugge, 1998).

Interestingly, the stage that venture capital firms prefer to invest in often depends on the life cycle of the investment fund. If their fund has been established for some years and its windup is not too far away, they may prefer not to invest in too many early-stage firms. In the early years of a new fund, venture capitalists may consider many more early-stage investments. Understandably, early-stage deals may be unattractive to venture capitalists for a number of other reasons, including their disproportionately large appraisal costs, difficult profit-generating opportunities, poor track records, smaller size relative to larger funds, heavy reliance on one person (entrepreneur), and sometimes the venture capitalists' inexperience with this type of investment.

## Complementarity of Business Angels and Venture Capitalists

Business angels and venture capitalists clearly tend to serve different stages of firms and contrasting size categories of growth firms (Wetzel and Wilson, 1985). In fact, with respect to total company revenue, 32 percent of venture capital–funded firms in the United States estimate revenues of $5–20 million, as opposed to only 16 percent of business angel–funded firms (Freear, Sohl, and Wetzel, 1991). Furthermore, the average corporate value of their early-stage deals still overwhelms that of business angels. This discrepancy increases when more of the established ventures that venture capitalists usually fund are considered. Most experts believe that business angel and venture capital investors play complementary roles in funding entrepreneurial firms, where business angels fund the start-up ventures that venture capitalists eventually finance when they are more established, needing funds more in the $2–3 million range (Freear, Sohl, and Wetzel, 1995a). This was also echoed with some frustration by one of the business angels we interviewed: "Venture capitalists will stand at the edge of the swimming pool with you, let you and some other private investors jump in first to test the waters, and then once we are all swimming comfortably, the venture capitalists will come in with one heck of a splash!"

## Investor's Sector Experience

The experience of investors in the industry sector in which they invest influences how strong an information base they have upon which to conduct due diligence. Business angels prefer to invest in fields with which they are familiar; they generally have worked in ventures similar to the ones in which they invest (Wetzel, 1983, Freear, Sohl, and Wetzel, 1995a; Aram, 1989). This experience is one of their most important investment contributions. But for many business angels, this means investing in a firm if they understand just the generic business problem, rather than the specific sector area. One business angel told us: "Although I've invested in widely differing markets, the companies all seem to have similar problems. I don't necessarily need experience in the [sector], as long as I think that I can add value." In Sweden, business angels' investment decisions also relate highly to their familiarity with the sector (Landstrom, 1995), while in Canada about two-thirds of business angels who were entrepreneurs themselves invest in the same industry in which they founded a company (MacDonald, 1991). However, in the UK studies have shown that business angels possess industry sector experience in only about 30–41 percent of their investments (Van Osnabrugge, 1998; Mason and Rogers, 1996; Stevenson and Coveney, 1994). In particular, 41 percent of business angels and 89 percent of venture capitalists have "some" or "extensive" sector experience, while 36 percent and 14 percent respectively admit to no sector experience at all (Van Osnabrugge, 1998).

Venture capitalists indubitably have even more experience in the sectors in which they invest (Ehrlich, Noble, Moore, and Weaver, 1994; Van Osnabrugge, 1999b; Haar, Starr, and MacMillan, 1988). This may be due to the high level of venture capitalist specialization as the technology of the investee firms becomes more complex (Bygrave and Timmons, 1986), or due to allowing venture capitalists to add more value to their investee firms

(Sapienza, Manigart, and Vermeir, 1996). However, Norton (1995) believes it might also be for reasons of reputation: "By examining only those deals related to the general partner's expertise, efforts are better focused on uncovering and examining deals in which the general partner has an information and skill advantage. Venture capitalists increase their reputation capital in the venture community by their expertise in certain technologies and industries" (p. 21). With a higher level of experience than business angels in the industry sector of the investee firms, venture capitalists have a better knowledge base from which to conduct thorough due diligence.

## Sector Research Conducted by Investors

The amount of research an investor carries out in the industry sector of the firm being funded is a good indicator of the total due diligence engaged in. In general, business angels conduct much less sector research than venture capitalists. Although angels in the United States are more professional than in the UK and in many other countries, they still tend to act independently, are confident in their own ability to make good decisions, and rely more on instincts and character than on hard research (Mason and Harrison, 1995). They rarely use professional advisors for research, electing instead to trust a few close referees (Haar, Starr, and MacMillan, 1988; Freear and Wetzel, 1991). Unfortunately, this laid-back attitude toward sector due diligence can lead to many regrets after the investment has been made. Many of the business angels who admitted to us that they did very little research greatly regretted not doing more. Instead, angels too often rely blindly on the projections that the entrepreneur puts in front of them. Reflecting on his past experience, one angel told us: "I let the entrepreneur do the research for us. I probably didn't do enough research into the potential sales figures because I was led on by the fact that I thoroughly enjoyed the subject matter and wanted to go into the market anyway. I just went on a feeling. I sadly regard it now as a learning curve; this spoiled investment turned out to be a rather expensive training course." Luckily, research has found that more-experienced business angels tend to learn from their mistakes—in general, "serial angels" conduct extensive evaluations of their investment opportunities (Van Osnabrugge, 1998).

In contrast, venture capitalists detail their sector research efforts extensively and many even share this responsibility with other venture capital firms with whom they co-invest. Venture capitalists have many contacts across a number of industries with whom they check before making an investment. A past venture capitalist told us: "Venture capitalists get on the phone and they then talk through the infrastructure and gather lots of different information. They sit at the center of these networks, and they swap and gather these bits of information. What they pick up is not what you can rationally put together, and they pick up all these little bits, and this helps them to gain a feel for the business."

Indeed, venture capitalists are well qualified to do this since they actually employ people who are used to digging up this type of information. Practically everyone at venture capital firms making nonestablished venture deals is an ex-consultant or ex-M.B.A. used to looking at markets and competitors, and specifically recruited for that purpose. In fact, in a recent study it was confirmed that venture capitalists conduct significantly more sector research than business angels, with 48 percent of venture capitalists and only 15 percent of angels doing "extensive" research (Van Osnabrugge, 1998). In total 89 percent of venture capitalists and 50 percent of angels perform "some" or "extensive" research, while 2 percent and 20 percent respectively admit to no research at all. This difference is especially meaningful if we consider that venture capitalists have significantly more experience in the sectors in which they invest.

## Extent of Preinvestment Contact with Entrepreneurs

Due diligence is intimidating to many since it involves getting and analyzing detailed and complex information about a firm's market, competition, and financials. But it also involves such simple things as meeting with the entrepreneur on frequent occasions to get a feel for his or her personality and taking simple third-party references on that person. There is little information on how many times business angels and entrepreneurs typically meet before a deal is made, we do know that angels meet less often than venture capitalists before making an investment offer. One recent study found that only 32 percent of business angels (versus 64 percent of venture capitalists) meet with entrepreneurs more than five times.

One reason venture capitalists have significantly more preinvestment contact with their investee firms may be that the venture capitalists have a longer, extensive investment process (Freear, Sohl, and Wetzel, 1991, 1995a). Interestingly, business angels usually only meet an entrepreneur if they are considering an investment opportunity seriously, while for venture capitalists this may not mean serious consideration but just an early stage in the vetting process. Although it is unusual, one business angel even admitted to us that "I never met the entrepreneur; I talked to him on the phone twice." In stark contrast to this, one venture capitalist stated: "We worked with them [the investee firm] for six months before we invested. We usually split up the people [entrepreneurs] so that we can talk to them one-to-one because ultimately we try to evaluate the people and how they work, and sometimes they don't say the same thing when they're in front of a co-entrepreneur."

## Accepting Independent References of Entrepreneurs

To assess the personal credibility of the entrepreneur, every investor must take independent references on the entrepreneur during the due-diligence process. Unfortunately, many business angels rely just on informal and intuitive judgments about the entrepreneur, rather than on detailed investigation (Mason, Harrison, and Allen, 1995). In fact, 54–66 percent of angels take no independent references on the entrepreneur at all (Mason and Harrison, 1996a; Van Osnabrugge, 1998), relying on themselves for information (Fiet, 1991; Mason and Harrison, 1995) and actually trusting networks much less than venture capitalists do as a means of getting information (Fiet, 1991). Meeting the entrepreneur only a few times and just going on gut feeling rather than getting independent references is a common regret for business angels. One angel told us: "I took a few references, but they weren't very formalized. And I have to say that this was one of my regrets, actually. In one of my investments, if I had checked out the individual, we would never have made the investment." Others, however, do not feel the need to take references since the entrepreneur has been referred by someone they trust or the entrepreneur has already been backed by co-investors.

Conversely, venture capitalists are usually meticulous in getting their references. Some told us that they never get fewer than six since most references passed on by the entrepreneur are usually glowing. Many prefer to inquire about companies that failed and ask people about the entrepreneur's biggest weakness rather than his or her assets. This is certainly much more enlightening. Additionally, a recent study found that 71 percent of venture capitalists, but only 8 percent of business angels, take three or more references, with the two groups averaging around four and one respectively (Van Osnabrugge, 1998). However, with so much information asymmetry in funding small ventures, it is also important for entrepreneurs to take independent references on investors (Wetzel, 1996). After all, they should know exactly who they are selling a piece of their firm to. Entrepreneurs may be afraid of scaring away a prospective business angel investor, but they should still make a tactful effort to find out just who they are courting.

## Analyzing a Venture's Financial Projections

Business angels tend to invest opportunistically rather than scientifically; rely heavily on gut feeling; and not calculate IRRs (internal rate of return), payback, and the like (Timmons, 1990; Baty, 1991; Mason and Harrison, 1996a). Only 30 percent of the business angels in a recent study claimed to have calculated expected rates of return for their last early-stage investment, and many had not and were unable to give return estimates (Van Osnabrugge, 1998).

### Investors' Use of Financial Projections

Relying on their years of business and entrepreneurial experience, business angels too often fall into the trap of not even remotely basing their investment decision on financial projections. One business angel who did not use return percentages rationalized his approach: "In a situation where it's almost a new business, you can't possibly know what the returns will be or anything you put down on paper. I think it's a mistake to get wrapped up in projections which are new, because with thirty kinds of independent data, none of which you can be confident are accurate, the number of possibilities you have are millions. It is different with leveraged buyouts of established businesses with track records."

On the other hand, almost all venture capitalists make return calculations; the financial measurements most often used are IRRs, discounted cash flows, and sometimes NPVs. In fact, Hall (1988) found that 93 percent of venture capitalists evaluate investment proposals in terms of IRRs, and others also use sensitivity analyses (Hall, 1988; Wright and Robbie, 1996). Most venture capitalists deny that they base their decision on gut feeling, rather than on rational evaluation of the entrepreneur and the business concepts of the investment. Although some venture capitalists may be skeptical of the validity of many financial projections, almost all conduct financial analysis. In fact, many venture capitalists almost always ignore the entrepreneur's financials and do their own. This may be a prudent move, especially with early-stage investments.

## Realism of Entrepreneurs' Projections

The lack of realism in the financial projections of many entrepreneurs often troubles both business angel and venture capitalist investors. They tend to complain about unrealistic entrepreneurs overinflating their firm's projections. However, even if the business angel does not place much weight on these financial projections, they should be present in the business plan, if only to show that the entrepreneur has thought about the business. Cash-flow projections may never even be approached in reality, but they do indicate what the potential might be and point out the possible problem areas. For entrepreneurs, there is certainly a thin line between presenting their ventures in the best light and going beyond the point of realism.

Venture capitalists may also view many of the entrepreneurs' projections with a skeptical eye, but they seem to place more emphasis on these calculations (especially the projected cash flows) than business angels do. Venture capitalists feel that they must make the most of the available information to best formulate a decision as to investing, even given the understanding that what is projected is unlikely to become reality. Although eventual conditions could turn out better than the projections, unfortunately they usually turn out worse. Yet investors have to accept a basis for going forward, and financial projections help greatly in this respect.

## Relying on Gut Feeling

Since business angels rely very little on financial projections and view them with severe suspicion, they commonly follow gut feeling to make the investment decision. One business angel told us that "it's about 70 percent just gut feeling and 30 percent financial analysis," while another angel claimed that because he usually invested on gut feeling, it was like "putting your finger in the air and hoping that the wind's blowing in the right direction." Many such business angels rationalize their emphasis on gut feel because of their many years of experience in, and empathy with, the entrepreneurial field.

Conversely, many venture capitalists told us that gut feeling should not enter into the investment decision since this is really a dangerous temptation to follow one's own ego. Instead, venture capitalists' decisions are almost completely based on comprehensive due diligence. Indeed, basing decisions on hard and verifiable facts shows investment competence to their fund providers, so venture capitalists cannot rely on gut feeling alone—everything has to be examined. If something does not seem true, venture capitalists have checks and balances in their organizations to ensure that the deal doesn't happen. This is probably the big difference from the business angel, since no one person in a venture capital firm can make the decision to invest, whereas a business angel can proceed entirely on his or her own. It may also be possible that venture capitalists rely less on gut feel for their investment decisions because compared to business angels they often do not have the entrepreneurial background with which to make such intuitive judgments.

## Investors' Demand for Comprehensive Business Plan

Since entrepreneurial ventures are usually at an early stage of development, it is unlikely that all the relevant factors that need discussion in a business plan can be thoroughly and convincingly addressed. This is of lesser concern for business angels than for venture capitalists since angels usually do not require so thorough a business plan as venture capitalists do (Haar, Starr, and MacMillan, 1988; Landstrom, 1993), although they do prefer a detailed business plan that is fully worked out (Mason and Harrison, 1994). As business angels make more investments, they tend to demand more detailed business plans (Aram, 1989). But in general, most business angels are usually not turned off by business plans that fail to be comprehensive and do not always put a stringent requirement on the entrepreneur to fully work out the incomplete factors before investment. Some business angels have even been known to invest without a business plan, although any entrepreneur serious about getting funding should definitely develop the best plan he or she can.

As one might expect, venture capitalists want the entrepreneur to fully address all the uncertainties and work them out as well as possible before funding. They rely heavily on a detailed business plan as a valuable source of information. In fact, it is not uncommon for some venture capitalists to work with the entrepreneur to improve the business plan before investing. This requirement for a meticulous business plan also demonstrates to the fund providers that the venture capitalist is taking every care in selecting an investment. Thorough business plans and their projections can also be used as a means of monitoring the entrepreneur's subsequent progress in growing the venture.

## Research Costs of Investing

To conduct thorough due diligence, research costs must be incurred. These consist of time and effort, as well as money. For venture capitalists, the costs may be large (tens of thousands of dollars for a single large investment) and require formal budgeting in addition to the normal staff and office expenses. The high cost of research certainly highlights why it is often not cost-effective for venture capitalists to invest in small firms.

For business angels, though, the size of the investment usually does not make it economical to conduct extensive research, and the cost of outside assistance can be prohibitive. Therefore, angel deals tend to be simple, with a minimum of due diligence, which means low-cost deals. One business angel reinforced this:

> What puts people off from these types of investments is the active due diligence that is needed—how do you check these people out? —and the cost of doing it. Most business angels can't afford to do it themselves, and the little company they are investing in doesn't want to finance it either. You have to decide about your own personal due diligence; am I prepared to put my money in and go with my gut feeling? Because that's ultimately what it is. There are a lot of lawyers and accountants on the circuit now. They're always saying, "You should use a professional accountant," "You should use a lawyer to do your due diligence." But nobody does; there are too many; we can't afford to pay for them all. It's really a do-it-yourself thing.

But of course, this does not mean that important corners should be cut. Hopefully, the information in this book gives business angels the insight needed to improve their due-diligence process. Unfortunately, in a recent study more than 80 percent of angels claimed they incurred no costs on their last deal (Van Osnabrugge, 1998).

## Size of Investors' Decision-Making Groups

Another measure of how thoroughly investors verify the viability of an investment proposal is the number of other people they consult before investing in a venture. In a business angel's case, this includes the spouse, family members, friends, accountants, and lawyers. For the venture capitalist it includes all the people on the venture capital firm's investment committee plus a number of other people in the venture capital firm, as well as referrers and industry associates who may also appraise the investment opportunity.

In general, business angels are pretty independent-minded investors. In the United States, around 84 percent rely solely on their own investment evaluations to make a deal (Freear and Wetzel, 1991). In the UK, more than two-thirds of angels usually, or always, make investment decisions independently, and just under two-thirds state that they are rarely or never influenced by recommendations from others (Harrison and Mason, 1992a). Specifically, business angels consult with far fewer people than venture capitalists do on average. One business angel summed this up: "I sometimes show my accountant, but you pay accountants to be pessimistic, not optimistic—to keep you in line."

Indeed, it may be hypothesized that the investment deliberation process is shorter for business angels than for venture capitalists because angels have a smaller number of people involved in the decision process (Freear, Sohl, and Wetzel, 1995a). Yet the increasing popularity of co-investment syndicates of angels that we have seen in recent years may signal the emergence of less-independent-minded angel investors, as well as the benefits of more consultation.

With an obligation to invest prudently, venture capitalists cannot make decisions without having them approved by an investment committee, which every venture capital firm has. This committee may comprise four to seven investment professionals, some of whom are from outside the firm (Gorman and Sahlman, 1989; Murray, 1995a). Of course, such a committee may also be a means of spreading the accountability for a particular investment decision. One venture capitalist described the structure of an investment committee this way: "Once the deal is accepted for due diligence, we appoint an approval committee, consisting of three senior directors of the firm, who meet two or three times during the due-diligence process. Then the director supporting the proposal argues for it, and another committee, the investment committee, which has an external chairman, has the final say—a final sanity check before the investment."

## Length of a Typical Investment Deal

Since entrepreneurs are often in a hurry to receive the funds they need to put their ventures on a path of growth, the length of the average investment process is of great importance to them in deciding to seek a financial suitor. This may make business angels appealing since, in general, they reach an investment decision more quickly than venture capitalists do, primarily because of their less thorough evaluation of potential investments and fewer constraints related to investor protocol (Timmons, 1990; Baty, 1991; Mason and Harrison, 1994, 1996a). In the United States, the average time from first meeting the entrepreneur to the actual investment (that is, from first seeing the investment opportunity to signing the check) is 2.5 and 4.5 months respectively for business angels and venture capitalists. It takes longer for entrepreneurs to have that important initial first meeting with a managing partner of a venture capital firm (1.75 months) than with a business angel (1 month; Wetzel and Freear, 1994). Thus in addition to the almost two months it takes to meet a venture capitalist—if you are lucky enough to do so—the actual time from the initial presentation to the venture capitalist's decision to invest in the firm may be nine weeks or so on average (Carter and Van Auken, 1994).

Some business angels waste no time investing in a good opportunity. From first meeting the entrepreneur to deciding (in principle) to invest, around 50 percent of business angels take less than a month, while more than 80 percent take less than three months.

The speed with which business angels typically make investments is often a function of their attitude that time is of the essence and therefore only so much due diligence can be done. It is all too common to hear angels ask (as one asked us), "Why waste time getting more information when you can be following your gut feeling and actually making the investment and running the firm?" Another angel echoed this: "There's no substitute for saying, 'I've got 80 percent of the data that I need; I'll have to trust the other 20 percent since it will take another two years to get the other 20 percent.' By then the window will have closed on the opportunity. If you want to feel that you have suspenders on everything you do, then you should not be in these kind of operations; you should work for the government or something."

Could this be a sound investment philosophy to follow? Venture capitalists generally do not think so. They feel that drawing out the investment process when funding early stage firms with no track record is in some cases wise. One venture capitalist reasoned:

Early-stage investments usually take longer because there's no track record—there are many things to check and subcontract. To an extent, the process is deliberately strung out; we want to sit beside these guys [the entrepreneurs] to see how they behave when things get stressful. Just get comfortable with them, because once you invest, you are stuck with it for four or five years. Chances are you are going to be on the board of the thing and it won't go like the business plan and chances are we are going to fall off somewhere along the line, so you have to be comfortable with these guys.

As one might guess, a common criticism of venture capitalists is the amount of time they take to finalize details and funding.

---

## Intellectual Property Due Diligence

Two sentences are appearing more and more often in business plans and private placement memoranda: "The company's technology is new and relatively untested. . . ." and "The company's success and ability to compete is dependent in part upon its proprietary technology."

That's fair warning, but isn't intellectual property also the basic source of value in most high-tech, early-stage companies?

How do the most astute and successful investors cope with intellectual-property risks? There are two methods that work. The first can be called the "George Soros technique." Several years ago, the international financier visited a small Seattle biotechnology company as the final step in his investment decision. Staff due diligence was complete, and Soros had concluded his meetings with management, but he still needed to know whether the company's "new and relatively untested" technology was likely to work. His approach was to interview the chief scientist and engineer. He sat with them in the lab, questioned them thoroughly, listened carefully, and decided to invest then and there. Not every investment has worked wonderfully for Soros, but that one did.

But what if the investor isn't as skilled as Soros? Should the investor just walk away? No; there is a second method, which can be called the "Arch technique." It's named after

(continued)

Arch Venture Partners. They invest in early-stage companies with novel, unproven, and exciting technologies. They ask world-class scientists to interview the company's chief scientist or engineer. Together, they judge whether the company's new and relatively untested technology is likely to work. The result has been some great scientific collaborations and some wonderful investments for Arch. Business angels often use the same technique by finding industry experts or by bringing in other, more experienced investors with technical knowledge.

Intellectual property is inherently tricky. Increasingly complex legal and financial solutions are being developed to cope with the problem, but, as in many investment decisions, the issue comes down to people. Just as quality management is most likely to build a successful company, quality scientific and engineering teams are most likely to develop technology that works. Use the George Soros technique or the Arch technique to get to know the technology and the scientific or engineering team.

Steven Loyd is an affiliate professor of finance at the University of Washington School of Business. His courses on financing early-stage ventures is part of the well-regarded U of W Program in Entrepreneurship and Innovation. He is a member of the Washington State Bar and chairman of the Northwest Capital Network (NCN), a nonprofit organization providing educational programs and forums for introductions between entrepreneurs and business angels. He is also a principal in a Seattle investment bank.

## Due Diligence in a Nutshell

In this chapter we have seen that for each of the dozen variables one can use to assess the due-diligence processes of business angels and venture capitalists, venture capitalists conduct significantly more due diligence than do their less-professional counterparts. Particularly, compared to business angels, venture capitalists invest in larger firms, have more sector experience, conduct more sector research, meet the entrepreneur more often before investing, take more independent references on the entrepreneur, analyze the financials more thoroughly, demand a more comprehensive business plan from the entrepreneur, incur more research costs (as a percentage of invested amount), consult more people before investment, and take longer to invest.

Although we might assume that the entire professional career of a business angel has prepared the person to conduct due diligence (Freear, Sohl, and Wetzel, 1992a), angels in general tend to be less sophisticated and more ad hoc in their due-diligence activities than venture capitalists are. Yet American business angels tend to be slightly more professional than those in other countries. Even so, they are not accountable to others for their investment decisions, and unlike venture capitalists they can invest on a gut feeling rather than on comprehensive research. Though there is probably more diversity within the business angel population as to the professionalism of the investment approach taken than within the venture capital population, it is important to remember that on average business angels are less rigorous investors.

One additional explanation for this difference in due-diligence procedures is warranted: some venture capitalists told us that individually they sometimes conduct extensive due diligence to protect themselves from blame in case an investment turns sour. One told us off the record that venture capitalists may overdo due diligence to cover their backsides and to sanitize the investment decision. He mentioned that one of his past investments on which he had done the most due diligence actually didn't turn out that well, and this was related to a number of factors that could not be covered by due diligence. Obviously, due diligence cannot assess all the possible risks, but it is the best that one can do with what is presented.

Conversely, business angels make little attempt to reduce the negative correlation of risk and return in the same manner that venture capitalists do. This laissez faire approach unfortunately often has negative consequences. Many business angels confessed to us that they had been naïve concerning the due-diligence process, particularly in their first angel investment. A common pattern can be seen, whereby angels take too many things at face value when they first become an angel, which usually results in a steep learning curve as they attack their second investment with more skill and professionalism. Yet the regrets of not conducting more research and taking a more realistic look at the investment risks before entering the deal remain all too common.

Most business angels are less experienced investors than venture capitalists and do not feel the same pressure as venture capitalists do to place themselves high on the learning curve of due diligence. It is important that angels be careful not to follow just their gut feelings and emotions when making an investment. One angel captured this difference between investor types in saying: "My investment decision is made in more of an upside-down fashion to that used by the venture capital industry. I rely less on the numbers, but more on the subjective impression of the entrepreneur—it has to feel right and I have to believe in it. I don't have to be analytical; I can go on instinct, unlike the venture capitalist. I don't have to rationalize my investment decision to a boss at the end of the day."

## The Change Now Being Witnessed

Within the last few years, angels entering the fray have been increasingly more professional, a minority who have gained experience themselves at the other end of the deal—as technology entrepreneurs. These high-tech angels are behaving like their venture capital counterparts and hopefully will act as positive role models for the majority of their fellow angels. Greater syndication of angel deals also allows more sharing of due-diligence tasks and expertise.

Hopefully, some of this chapter's insights will help entrepreneurs be successful in deciding which investor type to court and in their initial contact and negotiation processes. For business angels, this chapter has highlighted ways of improving their due diligence—one of the most important steps an investor has to take to avoid losing the funds invested and to be well positioned to reap the eventual rewards of entrepreneurial investments.

# Chapter Nine

# Negotiating and Forming the Legal Contract

Once an investor completes due diligence on a particular investment opportunity—and assuming he or she retains a degree of enthusiasm for a deal—it is time to negotiate valuation of the venture with the entrepreneur to render a fair equity stake in exchange for the funding. But regardless of the size of the stake, the real challenge for a small-firm investor often lies in managing the risk. One way is to gain some degree of contractual control through sound negotiations and contract formulation, as we show in this chapter (and again in Chapter Thirteen). Another way, as the next chapter discusses, may be to monitor the firm closely after the investment is made.

## How Investors Negotiate Deals

The negotiations process can be lengthy and difficult, a time where deals arrive at the extremes of greed for all parties. A deal is often struck between equally hesitant buyers and sellers. Negotiations involve bickering over the fair market value of the venture, which in an efficient market is the price at which assets should be exchanged between a willing buyer and willing seller when neither is acting under compulsion and both have equal access to all relevant information (Benjamin and Margulis, 1996). However, in the inefficient market for venture capital, the negotiation process is crucial because the market price is typically difficult to determine. Much reliance is therefore placed on the business plan and market projections to ascertain the worth of the venture; venture capitalists, especially, may use their own due-diligence reports for this purpose (Wright and Robbie, 1996).

## The Rigor of Negotiations

Even though both business angels and venture capitalists believe that the negotiated contract should be equally fair to both parties, "fairness" may differ in meaning somewhat between the two. Business angels usually negotiate less and are more easily satisfied than venture capitalists. Actually, in some cases there is no negotiation at all. One angel told us, "In my case, there was no deal to negotiate; the entrepreneur had a deal lying on the table—'Here are the terms, take it or leave it.'" This lesser degree of preparation for negotiations may leave many angels at a disadvantage in dealing with an entrepreneur. One recent study found that 78 percent of entrepreneurs seek professional advice from lawyers and accountants in drawing up investment agreements and reviewing deals, whereas only 38 percent of business angels use such assistance (Mason, Harrison, and Allen, 1995). The same study also found that concerning the intensity of the negotiations, 44 percent of entrepreneurs and only 38 percent of angels were able to identify issues that were difficult to agree on.

As is to be expected, many angels often do not negotiate hard over terms and conditions and equity share. In fact, a major difference between business angels and venture capitalists at the negotiation stage is the former's restraint in pushing the entrepreneur too much for a better deal, since this might affect the subsequent working relationship. Business angels typically want the deal evenly balanced to retain the chemistry between the angel and the entrepreneur. After all, at the end of the day, any business is a partnership, especially if it is a working partnership and chemistry has to be there to some degree. One angel told us: "I don't believe in negotiating hard. I think if the man makes a fair offer, you don't scream for the last penny. Because if you do that, it just causes a vicious circle, he'll then try to come back in some other way. If you put the cards on the table and are honest with each other, then it will pay for both parties."

To maintain favorable relationships, some first-time business angels may give the entrepreneur a better deal. As one angel stated: "One of the tricks of the game is not to do anything clever, because at the end of the day the business is the people. We actually wanted the entrepreneur to have a better deal." Conversely, angels should try to not give away *too* much to entrepreneurs. One first-time angel told us: "In my first deal, I was overgenerous to the entrepreneur. I allowed him to have a lot of options that I want to have, like he had the option to buy my shares after three years, even if I don't want him to. I would also have liked to change more of the investment terms, to give us more voting rights and the right to charge interest. My subsequent deals were fair to both parties."

Since venture capitalists invest other people's money for a living and do so with a professional obligation to those people, they are willing to negotiate with entrepreneurs and use comprehensive legal agreements. Venture capitalists are tough and experienced negotiators who rely heavily on the credibility of the business plan and management team to reach agreement (Rea, 1989). Although deals tend to be tailored to the circumstances of the projects involved and venture capital deals are typically the result of private negotiation without regulatory intervention or requirements, a growing set of identifiable principles and practices have come to be associated with the structuring and pricing of new venture financing (Brophy, 1992).

## The Length of Negotiations

Business angels spend less time negotiating than venture capitalists (Freear, Sohl, and Wetzel, 1995a; Mason and Harrison, 1996a). We know that venture capitalists often spend a median of four weeks (or just over seven weeks on average) in on-and-off negotiations; though many angels spend less than a week completing their negotiations, others spend longer (Mason, Harrison, and Allen, 1995; Van Osnabrugge, 1998). But because of the relaxed nature of business angel investments, much of the negotiation is conducted in casual discussion at informal moments throughout the investment process, whereas for venture capitalists it appears that negotiations (about valuation) are held at distinct stages of the process.

Business angels place little emphasis on drawing out negotiations. One angel told us "Negotiations were about ten minutes long. I liked it, and just went ahead with it," while others said that negotiations lasted for one evening or a week at most. One reason for this speed may be the angels' limited concern for legalities. "The negotiations were not too time consuming," one angel told us, "since we were happy with what was being offered; it was just that it got a bit tedious on the legals. It's what the entrepreneur wanted. I found them really a bit unnecessary since you're looking ahead into the future for something you can't know. The legals were disproportionate for the size of the investment."

Another reason business angels often negotiate and invest quickly is the entrepreneur's haste in getting the deal done to get the cash he or she so urgently needs. One angel complained that "I let the entrepreneur push me along too quickly and therefore didn't do as much due diligence as I might have done; I regret that."

As we would expect, venture capitalists spend more time actually negotiating to reach thorough agreements. Since entrepreneurs have to give up some of their equity, submit to the venture capitalists' restrictive covenants, and negotiate, this clearly takes some time. The legal process often takes anywhere from two or three weeks to two months, with many days of meetings in which documents are redrafted between rounds of discussion. Venture capitalists often speak to the entrepreneur every day during this process. These negotiations can be especially time consuming with early-stage ventures since they tend to be risky (Rea, 1989). In addition, when venture capitalists co-invest with other venture capital firms, this often entails negotiating both with them as well as the entrepreneur to reach a satisfactory agreement. This can make the negotiations process even longer. Conversely, if business angels prefer to invest with co-investors whom they know personally, the negotiation process can be less time consuming since the angels are more likely to agree on what they each want. The terms then need be negotiated only with the entrepreneur.

## The Terms of the Investment Contract

Reaching agreement on investing funds in a risky entrepreneurial firm naturally involves many factors on which both the investor and the entrepreneur must give and take to make the deal work. To protect each party, these issues are usually stipulated in an investment contract, including such basics as the size of the investment and each party's equity stake.

For many business angels, determining particular contractual structures or equity allocations is not the main investment concern; rather, they worry about whether the venture is too risky and whether it will succeed at all. This is naturally a function of the very young stage of the firms angels typically fund. The attitude often taken is that the quality of the investment contract can only be as good as the business, so even a very sound contract may be worthless if the business cannot support it. One angel told us: "People are so obsessed with equity. The number of people that fall out over 49 percent or 51 percent is pathetic. The reality is that equity is not important. 35 percent or 50 percent of nothing means nothing. Sophisticated financial structures are worthless. They don't reduce the risk of the firm; you have to make it first!"

Business angels evince concern for the viability of their investments, hoping that with luck their firm may break even and eventually grow profitable. Acting like the seasoned professionals they are, venture capitalists seem to take the success of their investment with a greater degree of certainty and confidence. Business angels often use relatively simple investment contracts, agreeing primarily on the number of shares for the invested amount and the salary of the entrepreneur. Indeed, angel investments commonly involve just a straight equity percentage exchange, without any standard investment formula (Norton, 1995; Short and Riding, 1989). Unfortunately, angels tend to formulate less-comprehensive investment contracts than venture capitalists do (Norton, 1995, Van Osnabrugge, 1998), in part because angels tend to be less sophisticated, often relying on "ad hockery" to price investments (Mason, Harrison, and Allen, 1995).

This often results in angels' providing funds on more liberal terms than do venture capitalists (Wetzel, 1986b; Norton, 1995), which has the effect of keeping the costs down for the entrepreneur (Mason and Harrison, 1995). Business angels also tend to include less specific terms in their contracts than venture capitalists, involving such things as exit routes or complex financial arrangements beyond the money invested for an equity exchange. In fact, only 47 percent of angels in the United States provide for liquidation in their investment contracts (Wetzel, 1986a). In the UK, only

70 percent of angels draw up formal investment agreements (Mason, Harrison, and Allen, 1995) and only 16 percent of investments involved instruments more complex than ordinary shares, allowing the angel to adjust his or her shareholding in light of investment performance (Mason and Harrison, 1996a). Only 29 percent of U.S. matching services told us that their angels like to use standard pro forma legal deal agreements, while 43 percent claimed their angels do not and 28 percent believed they are indifferent. The figures are similar in the UK (Coveney, 1996).

Business angels sometimes rationalize this attitude toward contracts by saying that they want something simple that people can understand. A venture capitalist commented on the angels' generally lesser emphasis on contractual agreements: "I think that, in general, angels may be confused over pricing and may pay more for a job than they should." We must emphasize here that it is important for business angels to form comprehensive contracts, rather than rely on just a handshake when making a deal. Even with the best intentions, things can go wrong and parties can fall out of favor with one another. Good contracts are among the best ways to protect the financial rewards as the venture ultimately becomes successful, and also to avoid friction later down the road. A poor attempt at an investment contract can later impede the investor's ability to control major decisions. Said one angel, "If I had to do anything differently, I would have liked to have taken more control over my investment."

As might be expected, venture capitalists often invest only if they can get agreement to their comprehensive investment contracts, which gives them a certain degree of control. Their investment contracts typically have three main characteristics (Gifford, 1997): staging the committed capital and preserving the option to abandon, a compensation system directly linked to value creation, and retaining means to force management to distribute the proceeds of the investment. Venture capitalists typically devise deal structures designed to control the risks of the venture capitalist–entrepreneur relationship by structuring the investment terms to shift risk to the entrepreneurs (Sapienza, Manigart, and Vermeir, 1996). This affords downside risk protection for the venture capitalist while preserving the upside risk potential (Norton, 1995).

The security of choice for venture capitalists is therefore preferred stock (Sahlman, 1988; Norton and Tenenbaum, 1992, Carter and Van Auken, 1994), which usually includes a conversion provision so that venture capitalists can share in the firm's success, and redeemable and puttable provisions that may allow him or her to exercise control over the firm (Norton, 1995). In addition to gaining the rights to limit certain capital expenditures and management salaries, these provisions or covenants "also establish the basis under which the venture capitalist can take control of the board, force a change in management or liquidate the investment by forcing a buy-back merger, acquisition or public offering, even though the venture capitalist holds a *minority* position" (Tyebjee and Bruno, 1984, p. 1053).

Let's take a look at some of the contractual clauses that venture capitalists have been known to include in their contracts. Not all such provisions are included in every investment contract, but many are favorites. Of course, venture capitalists realize that including all or too many provisions may be unrealistic and too aggressive, resulting in adverse selection whereby only poor and marginal firms agree to their terms (Amit, Glosten, and Muller, 1990). Following Wasserman's suggestion (1999), we segregate these contractual provisions into three categories of use: aligning incentives, controlling decision making, and protecting the financial downside.

## Provisions to Align the Entrepreneur's Incentives

To ensure that an entrepreneur behaves in the best interests of the enterprise, venture capitalists often insist that *stock options* and *stock grants* be a significant portion of the entrepreneur's compensation. This means that the entrepreneur's equity stake increases only if the venture capitalist's stake also grows (Wasserman, 1999). To guarantee that the entrepreneurs stick around, venture capitalists insist that the former adhere to *vesting schedules* for stock grants and options, to earn their stakes over a number of years. To allow them to participate in the upside, venture capitalists take a slice of the firm's equity, while also taking debt to protect their downside. Debt is ideal because debt holders get paid before equity holders in case the firm fails. So the perfect security is a mix of debt and warrants to purchase common stock (Wasserman, 1999). Even more common is convertible debt, where venture capitalists have the option to hold debt or equity, often holding debt when the firm has not yet proven itself and switching to equity in the case of an IPO or trade sale of the firm. Such convertibles drive up the valuation for early investors. To further align the entrepreneur, venture capitalists may include *performance and forfeiture provisions* that protect them in case the firm fails to hit milestones or financial targets, by forcing the entrepreneur to surrender some of his or her equity (Wasserman, 1999). This gives entrepreneurs an incentive to forward realistic financial projections.

## Provisions to Control Decision Making

To reduce the entrepreneur's ability to take unnecessary risks, venture capitalists often insist on controlling much of a firm's strategic decision making. Through their *board rights,* venture capitalists have a seat on the board so that they can voice their views. If the entrepreneur holds a majority of a firm's equity, investors may have little ability to influence important decisions. *Supermajority rights* separate control from rights to residual value, protecting the minority ownership (Wasserman, 1999). If, for instance, the firm's fortunes decline dramatically, the venture capitalist may be able to take control of the board. Other actions that can be harmful to the venture capitalist investors (such as transfer of control in case of a merger, company sale, or change in strategic direction) can also be controlled by venture capitalists to some extent through use of *covenants* and *restrictions.* To aid running the firm, the venture capitalists may oblige the entrepreneur to accept the *addition of managers* to improve the team. Similarly, the entrepreneur's *employment contract* may specify under which circumstances the board can fire the entrepreneur or the entrepreneur can elect to quit. Such contracts may also include *buyback provisions,* which mandate that the firm purchase the departing entrepreneur's stock at a preset price, and *noncompete clauses,* which prohibit the entrepreneur from competing with the firm for a certain length of time (Wasserman, 1999).

## Provisions to Protect the Financial Downside

As we discuss in the next section, *staging capital infusions* gives venture capitalists the option to abandon the investment if they learn adverse information about the firm (Wasserman, 1999). In addition to taking convertible debt to avoid dilution of the equity stake, as already discussed, venture capitalists usually receive *put rights,* mandating that the firm repurchase any or all of the venture capitalist's equity at appraised market value within a specified number of years. Buyback provisions similarly allow mandatory redemption of the venture capitalist's shares, while entrepreneurs may insist on having call rights on the firm.

Entrepreneurs usually prefer to have common stock, while venture capitalists prefer that the equity stake take a more senior position (preferred stock) to keep the entrepreneur from, say, liquidating the firm right after investment and taking a percentage of the funds. Additionally, to allow venture capitalists to maintain a constant share of a firm's equity in light of subsequent equity issues, they often have *antidilution provisions,* which give them preemptive rights to purchase new stock at the offering price. Similarly, venture capitalists use provisions regulating whether the entrepreneur can call stock splits and special dividends or issue new equity.

To prevent the entrepreneur from issuing stock at a price lower than that at which venture capitalists can convert their investment into common stock, they may want their conversion rights to include an antidilution adjustment (*ratchet*). Ratchets reduce the price at which venture capitalists can convert their debt into preferred stock, which effectively increases their percentage of equity (Wasserman, 1999). Interestingly, such antidilution is viewed unfavorably by potential acquirers of the firm, which in fact gives venture capitalists added negotiating leverage.

Lastly, since venture capitalists are under great pressure to realize returns for their limited partners, they want to have some control to force the entrepreneur to do things that allow them to exit the investment. Those firms with the potential to go public are tailored to an IPO, while others are designed for a trade sale to a larger firm. In an IPO or merger situation, says Wasserman (1999), venture capitalists may be able to extract additional value.

First, they can demand a cash payment at the time of the merger, which deters potential acquirers and effectively gives the venture capitalists additional negotiating leverage. Second, investment banks usually refuse to underwrite an equity offering if venture capitalists maintain a higher-priority claim than the stock the bank is underwriting, giving the venture capitalist additional power. An entrepreneur can mitigate such risk by including an *automatic conversion* in the shareholder agreement. Furthermore, since registering shares for an IPO is an expense venture capitalists themselves wish to avoid, they may employ *piggyback rights* to include their shares if the firm is filing a registration statement, or use *demand rights* to force the firm to file such a registration statement. For poorly performing firms, venture capitalists can exercise their *liquidation preferences* even against the wishes of management.

Since they are investing other people's money, often in early-stage and risky entrepreneurial ventures, having such contractual conditions is a necessary requirement for venture capitalists. One told us of his tough investment requirements: "We usually take a 33 percent equity stake, plus we have preference shares that compound annually at 44 percent." Faced with such investment options, entrepreneurs should be careful and well prepared before they tread into this financial arena. One business angel told us that the company in which he had invested deliberately decided to seek $1.5 million from several angels to avoid the danger of having too many restrictive controls imposed by a venture capitalist. For other entrepreneurs, though, a venture capitalist investor may be the best form of finance to rapidly grow the venture and receive valuable input to position the firm for a future IPO or trade sale.

## Staging the Investment

Regardless of the amount of contractual control an investor has or the amount he or she invests, more control is available by staging the investment over time, or in accordance with performance quotas reached. Providing the investment amount in increments renders the important option to revalue, abandon, or expand commitment to the investment (Sahlman, 1988; Norton, 1995). This also reduces any agency worries that the investors might have by helping them monitor their investments as entrepreneurs reach important predetermined milestones (Norton, 1995; Cable and Shane, 1997). Such staging of investments dependent on predetermined milestones or performance targets is a way for venture capitalists to limit their risk exposures in certain potentially risky deals (Ruhnka and Young, 1991). Since this increases the risk for the venture, entrepreneurs (especially older and more experienced ones) hold highly a venture capital firm's reputation for following through with staged investments as they decide whether to accept a funding offer (Smith, 1999). Certainly, if a venture capital firm abandons an investment or decides not to invest in the firm in a later round, this sends negative signals about the firm to other finance providers. One study showed that firms being denied follow-on funds by their venture capital investors find their chances of obtaining new venture capital funds reduced by 74 percent (Bygrave, 1987).

## The Size of Investments

Since venture capitalists often have large funds, accumulate high overhead costs, and are obliged to commit the full amount of their funds, they make much larger investments per deal compared to business angels. In contrast, thanks to limitations on their financial resources and risk preferences, angels usually prefer smaller amounts, investing only as much as they can comfortably lose. Because they invest only a small proportion of their wealth (Table 9.1), the amount an angel has for investing is relatively small compared to what a venture capital firm has. Losing the money may not affect their lifestyle, but it affects their pride.

Although business angels in the United States invest more than their foreign counterparts (Harrison and Mason, 1991b), U.S. studies show a high degree of variation. Two 1989 studies found that the investment size averaged $48,000–60,000 (Aram, 1989; Gaston, 1989), while two more recent studies suggest that this amount may range from $100,000 to $300,000 (Ehrlich, Noble, Moore, and Weaver, 1994; Freear and Wetzel, 1990). Our new research indicates that U.S. angels may each invest almost $145,000 per deal on average (median: $75,000), although the range of deals was anywhere from $25,000 to $500,000. Regardless of these variations, it is still clear that business angels invest significantly smaller amounts than venture capitalists (Ehrlich, Noble,

### Table 9.1. Maximum Percentage of Angels' Total Wealth Allocated to Angel Investments.

| Percentage of Maximum Wealth Allocation | Percentage of Angels in Category |
|---|---|
| 0–4 | 8 |
| 5–9 | 18 |
| 10–14 | 25 |
| 15–24 | 21 |
| 25–50 | 19 |
| More than 50 | 9 |

*Source:* Freear, Sohl, and Wetzel (1994a).

Moore, and Weaver, 1994; Freear, Sohl, and Wetzel, 1995a). Even when angels invest in syndicates, the size of start-up deals is usually only in the $100,000 to $1 million range ($600,000 on average in our study), raised from six to eight angel investors (Sohl, 1999). However, one aspect easily overlooked is that in addition to the money they invest, angels also regularly extend guarantees and loans to further help their investee firms. In Canada, the average angel investment is slightly more than $100,000, which is in part explained by the high costs of compliance in Canada making smaller investments uneconomical (Riding, 1998). In the UK, angels invest £50,000 on average, with a median of £30,000 (Mason, Harrison, and Allen, 1995; Van Osnabrugge, 1998), although some other studies claim that it may be higher (Stevenson and Coveney, 1994).

Conversely, the average size of a U.S. venture capital investment is considerably greater, nearly doubling in the last seven years to almost $6 million today; for Internet-related firms the average is $7.5 million (NVCA, 1999). The total amount of venture capital funds that individual start-up firms raise (in seed money plus primary and secondary financings) in the course of their growth has increased from an average of $9.5 million seven years ago to around $24 million today ("Start-up Firms . . .," 1999).

# Valuation: How Much Equity Do Investors Receive?

Trying to determine with an entrepreneur how much ownership an investor should receive for a given investment can be a very difficult process. Valuation is not an exact science with young speculative firms, but more of a creative exercise. To do it well, the tools of valuation must be used, as we explain in Chapter Twelve. Yet investors often believe that entrepreneurs are unrealistic about the amount of equity an investor should receive in exchange for an investment. One business angel told us: "An entrepreneur has an unrealistically high belief that his or her firm will succeed and therefore is often only willing to give a small amount away. Giving half the business to make it four times bigger makes the entrepreneur twice better off. It is crucial to see that an entrepreneur shows that he has thought deeply about this. It is crucial to a strong relationship with the angel and will avoid any possible resentment that the entrepreneur might have now or later concerning the percentage of equity surrendered."

There is some variation among business angels as to their preferred level of ownership, but in general they prefer minority shareholding (Ehrlich, Noble, Moore, and Weaver, 1994; Mason and Harrison, 1995, 1996a) and do not favor voting control in the firms they fund (Mason and Harrison, 1996b; Freear and Wetzel, 1991). In only 16 percent of cases did U.S. matching services that we surveyed believe that their angels preferred majority shareholding. One East Coast study from 1988 found that a significant proportion of business angels prefer less than 10 percent ownership (Haar, Starr, and MacMillan, 1988). Our research found that U.S. angels usually receive about 20 percent of the company equity on average, and when investing as a syndicate they receive around 32 percent on average. Similarly in the UK, business angels tend to have a 23–35 percent shareholding on average in their investee firms (Van Osnabrugge, 1998; Coveney, 1996).

Similarly, venture capitalists usually own less than 50 percent of the shares. In the United States, the average equity stake is 25 percent (Carter and Van Auken, 1994), while in the UK most venture capitalists also take a 10–30 percent equity stake in their investment (Cary, 1995). Taking one-third of a start-up company for a few hundred thousand in funds has given some venture capitalists the often-undeserved tag "vulture capitalists." On the contrary, venture capitalists usually do not wish to demotivate the entrepreneurs by taking a controlling interest, although they may have a degree of control through use of voting rights and ratchets. Though valuation is extremely important in an entrepreneur's decision to accept venture capital funds, it is not the most important factor for selection; more than 37 percent of entrepreneurial firms do not take the highest valuation offer presented to them (Smith, 1999). Entrepreneurs are often more concerned about the venture capitalist's reputation for investing in successful companies, whether it is compatible with the culture of the venture, and the investor's value-added service as a sounding board for the entrepreneurial team.

## Valuation: How Much Equity Do Entrepreneurs Surrender?

As champions of their own ventures that they have built with sweat equity and many forgone opportunity costs, entrepreneurs are naturally hesitant about giving up some of their equity control to an outside investor. But more often than not, this is a necessary move made in the best interests of the growing firm. Entrepreneurs contemplating this for the first time are understandably interested in how much equity others have given up in the past. We could give some examples, but the amount surrendered varies with the case and depends on the size of the investor's contribution, the firm's growth rate, and the features of the venture, among many other things. Unfortunately, there is no set formula for deciding how much an entrepreneur should surrender. But as Chapter Thirteen shows, using effective negotiation techniques can certainly make a degree of difference. What *is* apparent across all cases is that there is a definite relationship between the age of the company and the ownership percentage of the entrepreneur. In younger firms, entrepreneurs have usually been through only one round of finance and so have not yet had to give up majority ownership for additional rounds of financing. But entrepreneurs usually need a second round of financing—even though they may say they never will.

Unfortunately, our knowledge of how much entrepreneurs typically retain is scant for those funded by business angels. A recent study noted that 55 percent of angel-financed entrepreneurs of early-stage firms still had control of the equity stakes, while 50 percent of the venture capital–funded entrepreneurs did so. On average, the former had 52 percent of the firm's equity, while the latter had 48 percent (Van Osnabrugge, 1998). Similarly, in another study, venture capital–funded entrepreneurs had on average a 45.1 percent equity stake, while giving up an average of 31.5 percent of the equity in the first round, 19.7 percent in the second, and 10 percent more in the third round of venture capital financing (Bruno and Tyebjee, 1985). Figure 9.1 shows the average percentage of company equity entrepreneurs can expect to relinquish to venture capital investors over a number of financing rounds.

If he or she is concerned about dilution, then the later the entrepreneur waits to raise venture capital, the better. Of course, this depends on the venture capital climate, the enterprise, and the industry in question. Yet, it remains a safe assumption that business angel–funded entrepreneurs generally retain slightly more equity than venture capital–funded entrepreneurs since angel financing tends to be less expensive and more lenient than venture capital financing (Freear, Sohl, and Wetzel, 1995a). However, angels invest when the equity is still very cheap and so only

**Figure 9.1.  Average Equity Relinquished
to Venture Capital Investors.**

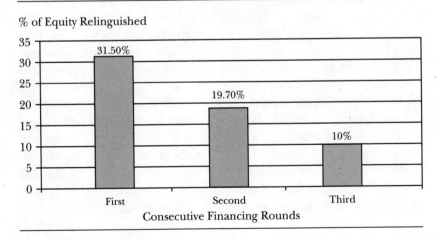

% of Equity Relinguished

provide a fraction of the financing per firm that venture capitalists typically invest.

## Is the Entrepreneur Replaceable?

In addition to giving up the rights to some of the unripened fruits of the growing firm, the entrepreneur is also concerned about possibly losing control of his or her creation and being replaced by a more experienced management team. Removal of the founders in such firms as Intel and Apple, to name just two seen in recent years, makes headline news. The relationship is usually not adversarial between the entrepreneur and investor, but the ability to replace an entrepreneur is usually related to the investors' contractual control. Initially most entrepreneurs cannot be replaced, but this becomes more feasible after a couple of rounds of financing.

As we have already seen, business angels are prone to getting personally involved as a means of rectifying problems in their investments, rather than replacing existing management with new recruits. Consequently, angels replace existing management infrequently and therefore emphasize finding a competent entrepreneur in the initial appraisal of the investment (Mason and Harrison, 1994).

Although the quality of the entrepreneur is important to both types of investor, venture capitalists are more proactive than business angels in replacing existing entrepreneurs if the venture is not running as well as expected; this is an option they try not to follow too frequently (Sweeting, 1991; Rosenstein, Bruno, Bygrave, and Taylor, 1989, 1990; Gorman and Sahlman, 1989; Bruton, Fried, and Hisrich, 1994; MacMillan, Kulow, and Khoylian, 1988). It is more common with the top venture capital firms in the industry (Rosenstein, Bruno, Bygrave, and Taylor, 1990; Ehrlich, Noble, Moore, and Weaver, 1994), but CEOs are more often dismissed for failure in strategic areas than operational ones (Bruton, Fried, and Hisrich, 1998). In the United States, Carter and Van Auken (1994) found that 29 percent of venture capital investments required a change of management, while in the UK Hall (1988) found that 73 percent of the venture capitalists interviewed replaced management when necessary.

This degree of venture capitalist control over investments is further supported by the findings of another U.S. study: "The venture capitalist, acting through the board of directors, typically gains the power to fire senior management in the initial negotiation. We asked venture capitalists how often they resorted to this final privilege. The answer is, 'Frequently.' The mean (in the statistical sense) venture capitalist has initiated the firing of three CEO/Presidents, or one CEO/President per 2.4 years of venture investing experience" (Gorman and Sahlman, 1989, p. 241). In a recent UK study, venture capitalists had replaced entrepreneurs in 5.7 unquoted investments on average (median: 3.0), while business angels had done so in only 0.45 deals (Van Osnabrugge, 1998). However, when compared more accurately as a proportion of the total number of private investments done, venture capitalists still have a greater tendency to replace entrepreneurs than business angels do, each having done so on average in 17 percent and 7 percent of their investments respectively. Yet such actions may make sense in certain conditions, since replacing a CEO typically has a strong positive effect on the firm's performance (no significant differences have been found between internal or external replacements; Bruton, Fried, and Hisrich, 1998).

What is important for entrepreneurs to remember from this chapter is that venture capitalists conduct more rigorous, lengthier negotiations than business angels and gain more authority by way of their thorough contract-formulation processes with the entrepreneur, as Table 9.2 shows.

**Table 9.2. Main Differences in Negotiation Behavior Between Angels and Venture Capitalists.**

| Negotiation Differences | Business Angels | Venture Capitalists |
| --- | --- | --- |
| Rigor of negotiations | Informal | Formal |
| Length of negotiations | Short | Medium to long-term |
| Terms of contract | Minimal | Extensive and detailed |
| Equity stake in venture | 20–30 percent (average) | 20–30 percent (average) |
| Exit provisions | Rare | Mandatory |

*Chapter Ten*

# Monitoring the Investment

After making an investment, many investors elect to actively monitor their new ventures. This may be in part to ensure that the entrepreneur uses the new funds competently, but it is also to offer their managerial assistance.

Business angels generally prefer more personal and active involvement in their investments than venture capitalists. This may be partly due to the angels' need to feel that they can protect their investment in these early-stage and high-risk ventures by influencing how their money is being used (Duxbury, Haines, and Riding, 1996). One angel told us: "I couldn't just be an investor in the venture and sit back and look at the results in each quarter; I wouldn't trust anyone that far. I get twitchy; I want to be involved." Yet angels also help for the sheer joy of involvement, often opting to babysit their entrepreneurs through the difficult stages of growing a venture. Not every business angel is involved hands-on, although active involvement is common across geographical regions and countries (Mason and Harrison, 1996a; Freear, Sohl, and Wetzel, 1995a).

Venture capitalists, however, usually do not take such an active approach as business angels. Rather, they prefer to monitor from afar and take on a more administrative role, instead of one that requires active involvement. Their duties at the venture capital firm tend to prohibit the level of active involvement that many angels are free to follow, although as with the angels, venture capitalist involvement varies across the scale. One venture capitalist appraised this common view: "It's not our business to get involved in the day-to-day running. Why would I want to do that? If you have the right people in there, you don't have to be there every day; that's not our business. We're more strategic. It's our business to make sure that we get the right people in there to run it." Yet understandably, many venture capitalists tend to be more involved with their few early-stage investments than with the more established ventures they usually fund.

Because the role that venture capitalists usually play in their investments is not so hands-on (but more strategic), there has been much debate in the United States and abroad over the amount of value-added by venture capitalists beyond provision of funding (Gorman and Sahlman, 1989), with some acknowledging that venture capitalists add value (Sapienza, Manigart, and Herron, 1992; Tyebjee and Bruno, 1981; Gupta and Sapienza, 1988; Landstrom, 1990) and others believing they add little beyond their funding (Busenitz, Moesel, and Fiet, 1997; MacMillan, Zemann, and Subbanarasimha, 1987). In truth, much of the value added is often intangible though still quite important to the progress of the investee firms. Indeed, venture capitalists may add value to their investee firms by using their networks of contacts to broker alliances, mergers, and acquisitions; recruiting key employees; providing access to consultants, investment bankers, and lawyers; helping analyze new market opportunities and high-level decisions; and bringing in key investors, among other things (Wasserman, 1999).

Yet confusion persists as to whether business angels or venture capitalists are more actively involved in the ventures they finance. In the only two studies to ever compare the postinvestment involvement of these two investor types (by analyzing responses from their investee firms), a U.S. study concluded that differences between angels and venture capitalists are minimal (Ehrlich, Noble, Moore, and Weaver, 1994); a UK study concluded that angels may be more active and play a more hands-on role in their investments than venture capitalists (Harrison and Mason, 1992b), although they acknowledged that the main difference between the two investor types may be qualitative rather than quantitative (Harrison and Mason, 1992b).

Given this disagreement, let's take a close look at the levels of possible involvement (from passive to hands-on) investors can follow, using the amount of time personally spent in being involved with an investee firm as a primary categorizing variable. Although classical finance theory may argue that an investor on the board of directors of a quoted firm is actively involved, it is clear when looking at entrepreneurial firms that investors on the board of such companies tend to be more passively involved compared to those who actually work in investee firms daily or weekly.

## Passive Monitoring Options for Investors

Passive options of investment monitoring include monitoring financial statements, advising on business strategy, and involving the board of directors. These methods are generally preferred and employed by venture capitalists rather than by business angels since the latter are more hands-on (MacMillan, Zemann, and Subbanarasimha, 1987; Harrison and Mason, 1992b). Most venture capitalists sit on a few boards but spend most of their time investing money rather than constantly looking over an entrepreneur's shoulder—they are usually involved in a nonexecutive capacity. Since most companies they fund have a full management team, venture capitalists are there primarily for strategy and guidance. One venture capitalists noted: "I see myself more as a financier, really. I want to be a friend to the entrepreneur. You may be policing the agreement, but having put your cash in, you are not looking to manage their business. So you make sure that they know that and they can talk to you openly and can open up with you. The entrepreneurs are now much more comfortable with our input because they are 100 percent sure that we don't want to run their business." Some venture capitalists may try to minimize their personal contact with entrepreneurs in favor of low-contact, fast-payoff investments (Cable and Shane, 1997), despite the value-adding potential of frequent interactions (Sapienza, 1992), especially for those entrepreneurs who are younger and less experienced (Smith, 1999).

Another explanation for venture capitalists' more passive approach to venture monitoring is their propensity to recruit new employees, especially industry and finance experts, to balance the management team of their investee firms and to ensure that the firm is run properly. One venture capitalist told us: "We are not averse to putting in our people to balance the management team.

The people we put in are outsiders, that is, not from the venture capital firm. Quite often we like to choose the person to come in to help run our investment. We often send proposals to people that specialize in the sector and often ask for their assistance." Filling the venture's management team with their own recruits may give venture capitalists confidence in the day-to-day running of the business, allowing them to adopt an administrative monitoring stance. Although both business angels and venture capitalists realize that a well-balanced management team is not always present in early-stage investments, many angels prefer to use their own input and skills to fill management gaps. This is actually something that attracts many angel investors. However, angels must recognized the limitations of their own involvement. As one told us: "We add to the management team to make it well balanced. If without our involvement it's not well balanced, then we wouldn't go near it."

As we just said, there are three main methods of monitoring an investment passively:

1. Financial statement monitoring
2. Business strategy advice and involvement
3. Involvement of board of directors

Venture capitalists often guarantee these monitoring rights in the investment contract with the entrepreneur (Wasserman, 1999).

## Monitoring the Financial Statements

To monitor the progress of an investment, venture capitalists rely on monthly financial reports; compared to business angels, they tend to monitor financial performance more (Rosenstein, Bruno, Bygrave, and Taylor, 1989; MacMillan, Kulow, and Khoylian, 1988), set higher performance targets for entrepreneurs to meet (Ehrlich, Noble, Moore, and Weaver, 1994), and give more frequent and detailed feedback if the venture is not achieving the financial targets that have been set (Ehrlich, Noble, Moore, and Weaver, 1994). Angels place less stringent financial controls on their investee firms, which allows entrepreneurs flexibility since less time needs to be spent on frequent generation of financial reports and more time can be devoted to pertinent activities in the venture (Ehrlich, Noble, Moore, and Weaver, 1994). It is important to remember that although business angels are interested in financial monitoring, they are likely to monitor and manage the *venture* rather than the *investment in the venture,* as a venture capitalist might (Harrison and Mason, 1992b).

## Giving Business Strategy Advice

Business strategy advice is investor input regarding the overall direction of the entire firm (Barney, Busenitz, Fiet, and Moesel, 1994). Both business angels and venture capitalists are active in this manner, but venture capitalists believe it is of greater importance. In fact, venture capitalists always expect to contribute some (if not most) of the venture's business strategy and resource utilization strategy (Busenitz, Moesel, and Fiet, 1997; Rosenstein, Bruno, Bygrave, and Taylor, 1989). Conversely, since business angels are generally more actively hands-on and may believe that they can influence the firm's strategy through their involvement, they often feel less pressure to give overtly strategic advice. In fact, one study found that venture capitalists considered offering financial and business advice and functioning as a sounding board as important roles (Sapienza, Manigart, and Vermeir, 1996), although there are some indications that entrepreneurs in more established firms and those pursuing technical innovations may be less receptive to venture capitalists' strategic advice (Barney, Busenitz, Fiet, and Moesel, 1994). Yet overall, a venture capitalist's value-added service as a sounding board to the entrepreneurial team is a very important factor in any decision to accept a venture capitalist's funding offer (Smith, 1999).

## Involving Board of Directors

One of the best ways for a venture capitalist to passively monitor the performance of the firm and influence strategy without being actively involved in its operations may be to take a seat on the board of directors. Compared to business angels, in general venture capitalists greatly prefer board involvement, with most venture capitalists insisting that it is a necessity. One venture capitalist emphasized the effectiveness of this hands-off monitoring option: "Part of having someone on the board as a director is that they're receiving and considering management information. But rather than being passive and just receiving information, we find that the best way to monitor is actually to be a director so that you still have some control over the company."

There remains much ambiguity in the United States as to the level of business angel involvement on a board. Three studies found only 15–37 percent of business angels on boards (Postma and Sullivan, 1990; Gaston and Bell, 1988; Freear and Wetzel, 1989), but another study found that 71 percent of angels and more than 90 percent of venture capitalists in their sample had a seat on the investee firm's board (Freear, Sohl, and Wetzel, 1990). Similarly in the UK, 60 percent of business angels take a seat on the board of directors, although in 20 percent of investments the venture is not a limited company and so has no board of directors (Mason, Harrison, and Allen, 1995; Mason and Harrison, 1996a). In Canada, a much lower percentage is witnessed, with 37 percent of business angels having a board seat (Short and Riding, 1989).

In contrast, there is ample evidence of the extensive level of board involvement by venture capitalists; it is not a major cause of concern for most companies ("Venture Capital in the United Kingdom," 1990). In the United States, it is widely acknowledged that venture capitalists are active and influential members on the board of early-stage ventures, playing a vital role in shaping the strategy of the firm, exploiting their enhanced networks for the firm's benefit, and monitoring financial performance (Rosenstein, Bruno, Bygrave, and Taylor, 1989; MacMillan and others, 1988; Ehrlich, Noble, Moore, and Weaver, 1994; Bygrave and Timmons, 1992; Gorman and Sahlman, 1989). Although we know that venture capitalists often dominate boards of entrepreneurial firms (Rosenstein, Bruno, Bygrave, and Taylor, 1989), in those firms financed by any of the top twenty venture capital firms in the United States "the board is significantly more likely to be structured to give venture capitalists outright majority control of board seats" (Rosenstein, Bruno, Bygrave, and Taylor, 1990, p. 247).

## Hands-on Involvement and Monitoring Options for Investors

Not all monitoring options are passive. Depending on their interest and available time, investors may opt for a more active role.

### How Actively Involved Do Investors Want to Be?

The possibility of involvement is an important attraction for business angels (Wetzel and Freear, 1994; Freear, Sohl, and Wetzel, 1993). One angel echoed: "I wanted to get involved again in business, rather than sitting on a beach. I get really bored. You think that life is passing you by, and it is. I want to be in the driver's seat; I don't want my investment diminished by someone else's decisions. You really need 'eyeball contact' on the job. You have to go in and talk to people and see them."

In a U.S. sample of business angel investors, 84 percent expected to play an active role in their investments (Wetzel and Seymour, 1981), while in the UK the possibility of investment involvement was "very important" for 35 percent of angels and for only half that percentage of venture capitalists, who often do not state this as an investment attraction (Murray, 1995a). Angels might want to fill gaps in the management team, although this is a lesser concern for venture capitalists. In a recent study, 64 percent of angels thought this was a "very important" or "important" attraction, compared to only 25 percent of venture capitalists (Van Osnabrugge, 1998).

An additional measure of the investor's preference for involvement is the importance of geographical proximity to the investor. As previously noted, locality is significantly more important to business angels than to venture capitalists. In fact, most business angels in the United States (Wetzel and Freear, 1994; Aram, 1989; Postma and Sullivan, 1990), the UK (Mason 1996a), Sweden (Landstrom, 1992), and Canada (Short and Riding, 1989) prefer an investment within a few hours' drive of home, partly because they prefer close working contact with their investment (Wetzel, 1983; Mason and Harrison, 1996b).

For venture capitalists, the location of the venture is of less concern (Sapienza, Manigart, and Herron, 1992; Sapienza, Manigart, and Vermeir, 1996; Sapienza and Timmons, 1989; Muzyka and others, 1993), although lead investors in venture capital deals with other venture capital firms do prefer to be close to aid the investment (Sapienza, Manigart, and Herron, 1992). Additionally, Sapienza, Manigart, and Vermeir (1996) found a new phenomenon: raising venture capital funds for investment in foreign markets, even though greater geographic distance reduces face-to-face contact. One venture capitalist told us: "Location is important insofar as it affects the business, rather than . . . how far we are prepared to travel. In general, location is not very important to us. We also have quite a lot of investments overseas, wherever the big market is."

## How Actively Involved Are Investors?

In the United States, 23–39 percent of angels work full-time or part-time in their investments (Postma and Sullivan, 1990; Freear and Wetzel, 1989, 1991; Freear, Sohl, and Wetzel, 1990, 1995a), while about half the angels sampled in the UK spent at least one day per week in the investee firm and more than 75 percent claimed to play a hands-on role (Mason and Harrison, 1996a, Stevenson and Coveney, 1994). Even in Sweden, 13 percent of angels have daily contact with their investments (Landstrom, 1992). However, in all these markets a substantial minority of angels (14 percent in the UK, for instance) prefer to monitor their investments passively, electing just to receive periodic financials and reports (Harrison and Mason, 1992b). This is similar to Japan, where 14 percent of wealthy people have angel experience and a third are interested in becoming angels, but active angels are reluctant to get involved in their investments (Tashiro, 1998). In the United States, 75 percent of investee firms find their relationship with angel investors to be very productive or moderately productive in receiving benefit above and beyond provision of finance (Freear and Wetzel, 1991). Unfortunately, in the UK 60–75 percent of ventures reported no such positive helpful contribution from angels (Harrison and Mason, 1992b), leading Landstrom (1993) to conclude that angels in the UK may actually be more passive than those in the United States. But even in the UK, angels are still quite active, especially compared to venture capitalists. On average, business angels visit 3.2 times per month, venture capitalists half as frequently.

For venture capitalists, though monitoring is an important way to increase return potential and reduce risk (Timmons and Bygrave, 1986; Norton, 1995; Busenitz, Moesel, and Fiet, 1997), it does appear to occur on a lower level of face-to-face involvement than for business angels. In the United States, one study found that venture capital firms on average visit their investments only nineteen times per year and spend one hundred hours in direct contact with them (Sahlman, 1990). In addition, a typical early-stage investment gets only about two hours per week from a lead venture capital investor (Gorman and Sahlman, 1989). Generally, the venture capitalist's face-to-face interaction with the entrepreneur may be strongly related to the amount of value added to the firm (Sapienza, Manigart, and Vermeir, 1996).

Although the majority of both investor types do not actively work daily on site with the firm (Ehrlich, Noble, Moore, and Weaver, 1994), both tend to be more involved in ventures if the investment is early-stage (Sapienza and Timmons, 1989), is in difficulty (Mason and Harrison, 1996a), or has a gap in the management team (Gorman and Sahlman, 1989); when the investor has a large equity stake (Sapienza and Timmons, 1989); and when the funder is the lead investor (Gorman and Sahlman, 1989). In a U.S. sample, venture capitalists monitored nine investee firms each on average (median: eight; range: four to twenty), and sat on five boards (Gorman and Sahlman, 1989), while venture capitalists in the UK personally monitor 10.3 firms each on average (median: 6; mean including outliers: 12.2; Van Osnabrugge, 1998), as Figure 10.1 shows.

Observing such a high level of monitoring commitment, Robinson (1987) found that the amount of time venture capitalists in the United States allocate to managerial assistance (that is, monitoring) is 35 percent of total staff time available during a given year. In addition, the average capital per firm and per professional have actually increased 87 percent and 85 percent respectively over the last ten years, leaving barely enough time to cover basic oversight responsibilities (NVCA, 1999). Capital under management per venture capital firm principal is now $27.9 million, almost 35 percent over the 1997 level, while the size of the average fund has almost doubled since 1993 to $76 million today

**Figure 10.1. Number of Investee Firms That Venture Capitalists
Personally Monitor.**

Cumulative % of VCs

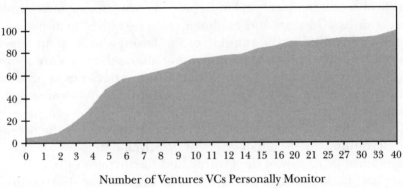

Number of Ventures VCs Personally Monitor

(NVCA, 1999). This may be particularly troublesome for high-tech start-ups, which are labor-intensive to monitor. One venture capitalist that we spoke to told us: "If you calculate it out, a director of a venture capital firm has on average six investments, and there are twenty working days in a month; then it will be difficult for him to even spend two full days on that investment, and he also has to invest in other businesses and exit from his businesses."

Because of such constraints, monitoring efficiency is clearly very important to venture capitalists (Sapienza, Manigart, and Vermeir, 1996). Some have even suggested that venture capital firms limit their involvement in investee firms to prevent the individual venture capitalist from "going native" and becoming too biased toward the venture, thereby compromising obligations to the fund providers (Sweeting, 1991), and also to keep entrepreneurs from becoming resentful about excessive intrusion (Sapienza, 1992).

## Monitoring in a Nutshell

Business angels are more involved hands-on in their investee firms than venture capitalists. Such active involvement in the operations of the investment may not be an option open to venture capitalists because of their time constraints (Freear and Wetzel, 1991; Tyeb-jee and Bruno, 1984). This limits venture capitalists to involve-ment through passive methods (such as strategic advice and board involvement) in a hands-off monitoring function—not unlike the role of senior managers in large companies overseeing many busi-ness units (Gorman and Sahlman, 1989)—rather than actually getting involved in the running of the business units as an angel would. However, it must be noted that although angels are more actively involved than venture capitalists, this does not imply that the majority are involved daily (that is, full-time) in running their investee firms.

The level of contractual control may have some influence in determining the level of investor involvement; however, geo-graphical proximity of the venture and the investor's preferences appear to be very important. Since angels have less control through their investment contracts, they often add value through active hands-on involvement in geographically close firms. Angel investors tend to be less concerned with seeking voting control and in many cases work full-time or part-time with the ventures after the investment is made (Freear and Wetzel, 1991).

Such hands-on involvement is not seen as vital for venture capitalists, since Sapienza, Manigart, and Vermeir (1996) claim that venture capitalists adequately handle these concerns contractu-ally. However, it should not be overlooked that another reason for their less hands-on approach is that venture capitalists recruit new employees to the investee firm. Therefore, active hands-on moni-toring may be less essential, assuming that they can trust the man-agement and monitoring abilities of their recruits.

*Chapter Eleven*

# Exiting the Investment and Realizing Returns

The main reason for making investments is, of course, to realize returns—preferably sizable returns. But at the time of investment, exit opportunities and ways of realizing returns are just some of the many variables that an investor considers in assessing the risk-reward ratio. Because an exit will probably not take place for at least five to ten years (in a potentially very different economic climate), investors might not fully consider exit opportunities until a later time. But as ventures grow and mature and investors wish to realize some (or all) of the financial gains on their investments, it becomes a serious concern to consider exit opportunities. In this chapter we examine exit preferences, intended investment time, and the rate of return for business angel and venture capitalist investors.

## Exit Routes Preferred by Investors

Freear, Sohl, and Wetzel's finding that in the United States "private individuals were more inclined to leave the method of liquidation undefined at the time of investment than were venture capital funds" (1990, p. 227) still rings true. Even in the UK, a recent study found that 91 percent of venture capitalists believed that potential exit routes were at least "of concern" (if not "important"), while this was the case with only 65 percent of business angels (Van Osnabrugge, 1998).

Unfortunately, the average business angel in the United States gives little thought to future exit routes and appears to be more

concerned about making the investment successful than opti-
mistically speculating about the riches of its success (Freear, Sohl,
and Wetzel, 1990, 1991; Freear and Wetzel, 1991). The fact that
angels often do not have clear exit plans at the time of investment
is also seen in the UK (Harrison and Mason, 1992a; Mason and
Harrison, 1996a; Atkin and Esiri, 1993), Sweden (Landstrom,
1993), and Finland (Lumme, Mason, and Suomi, 1996). A manager of a matching service supported this: "I never get asked by angels about exits. But venture capitalists are different because that's
the basis of their business: get in, get out." In fact, many angels believe that as long as the investment is successful, exit routes should
not be a concern.

Of course, this lack of focus on exit routes may be partly explained by inadequate exit routes when firms are very young
(Landstrom, 1993; Mason and Harrison, 1996a). In one study,
nearly half of the angels said they would be encouraged to invest
more if suitable exit routes were made available (Stevenson and
Coveney, 1994). However, the typical ventures that angels fund
may be too young to even visualize a possible exit route a number of years down the road. This was echoed by one angel: "It's
the easiest thing in the world to invest X thousand dollars, but
how do you retrieve it if you need to get it out? It's much easier
to buy into a company than to sell it!" Yet even for those angel-
funded ventures that are mature, IPOs are rare, since such exits
tend to be restricted to only the cream of the crop (Bygrave and
Timmons, 1992) and organizing an IPO involves high fixed costs
that are not practical for smaller firms. Therefore, trade sales to
larger firms are the preferred way that business angels harvest
their investment, as Mason and Harrison's findings (1999) in
Table 11.1 show.

Indeed, it may be easier for an angel to find a larger firm that
will buy for strategic reasons, often at a generous price. An example of just such a trade sale happened recently in Massachusetts
with the Cambridge-based Conley Corporation, which was
founded by a young entrepreneur with just an undergraduate degree and a knowledge of software. With the help of thirty angel investors, the firm was acquired for $50 million in a trade sale by a
much larger firm, leaving the twenty-nine-year-old entrepreneur
and his investors a great deal wealthier (Blanton, 1998).

### Table 11.1. Most Common Exit Routes for Angel Investments That Are Not Write-offs.

| Exit Route | Frequency Used (Percentage) |
|---|---|
| Trade sale or acquisition | 43.1 |
| Sale of shares to other shareholders | 26.4 |
| Sale to third parties | 16.7 |
| Going public (IPO) | 12.6 |
| Liquidation of assets | 1.3 |

Source: Mason and Harrison (1999).

Conversely, venture capitalists place much more emphasis than business angels do on identifying potential exit routes (potential liquidity) prior to investment, primarily on account of the exit pressure venture capitalists receive from their fund providers (Robbie, Wright, and Chiplin, 1997; Cable and Shane, 1997; Murray, 1995a). Indeed, venture capitalists only invest in ventures with enough upside potential to eventually render high financial returns (Wetzel, 1983; MacMillan, Siegel, and Subbanarasimha, 1985). Even though a number of exit choices exist (trade sale, IPO, leverage buyout or buyin, merger with another company), trade sales also remain the most common means of exit for venture capital–funded entrepreneurial firms, although IPOs are also important for larger firms and certainly more profitable for investors, as we saw in Chapter Three (Sapienza, Manigart, and Vermeir, 1996; "Venture Capital in the United Kingdom," 1990; Berglof, 1994). For this reason, venture capital investment contracts with entrepreneurs often stipulate procedures for future IPOs (Berglof, 1994). One venture capitalist told us: "The thing we look for most is the exit. We try to identify the exit before we go in, or if we want a trade sale, we try to identify a company that will buy it." Another noted: "Exit routes are of concern right from the word *go*. In fact, we focus on it with the entrepreneur right from the very beginning. If you don't focus on exits right from the beginning, you'll cause problems for yourself later; at least you have to have an understanding of what will happen in the long term."

# The Intended Length of Investment

Investment in an entrepreneurial venture obviously requires more time to show profit than does an investment in an established venture. Yet this is not of great concern to business angels since they tend to be rather relaxed about timing, often leaving it open-ended depending on investment performance. If successful, they may exit within five years; otherwise they may hang on for up to ten years and try to turn things around. One angel told us, "If a company can't show me that it's a winner within its first four or five years, then it probably isn't." The average (and median) expected holding period for business angels is around five years (Short and Riding, 1989; Freear, Sohl, and Wetzel, 1995a; Freear and Wetzel, 1991), with a typical range of three to seven years.

Venture capitalists are generally more concerned about exiting earlier, partly because of the pressure on them to realize returns for the fund providers, who often tend to have a short time horizon. However, the length of a feasible time horizon also depends on the industry sector. A software business, for instance, can usually get well positioned in five years, a biotech business in five to eight years (twelve if you are unlucky), and a new materials business can take a very long time to get right. Bygrave and Timmons (1992) found in their U.S. study that the holding periods for venture capital funds vary with the performance of the deal. The median length of investment with satisfactory (IRR of 25–49 percent) and exceptional (IRR of 50 percent or more) returns was about four years, while break-even or loss-making investments often take just two years. The memorable industry adage that lemons ripen before plums is certainly accurate. Perhaps surprisingly, investments with low returns (IRR of 1–24 percent) have the longest holding period, usually around six years.

A caveat to this description of expected investment duration must be the recent hyperactive Internet market. Companies are being formed, funded, and sold in less than eighteen months. A recent Harvard Business School graduate, Stig Leschley, formed a secondhand textbook company (Exchange.com) and sold it to Amazon.com for around $200 million—just six months after graduating! Granted, these high-profile examples are *not* the norm, but the effect may be to distort a potential angel's (or, to an extent, venture capitalist's) view of what is normal.

A few venture capitalists admitted to us that the short-term approach they take may sometimes act to the detriment of the needs of the investee firm. One noted: "You often have a situation of the tail wagging the dog, where the time cycle of investors is completely out of sync with business needs. If you're in a position to take a very long-term view, I think that you have the opportunity to make a lot more money, but it's quite painful." Another venture capitalist claimed: "I'm not at all convinced that one wants venture capital money in start-ups anyway because it's the wrong type of capital, I think. Even a ten-year period is not the right type of mind-set, per se, for start-up money. Because a venture capitalist, by definition, wants an exit, the whole strategy of how that money gets a satisfactory exit and return on its capital, puts, in principle, inappropriate pressures on start-up businesses." Overall, business angels tend to have slightly longer investment horizons than venture capitalists, which is why their investment is often called patient capital.

## Investors' Returns

Regrettably, most evidence on venture capital investment returns reflects *expected* returns (rather than *actual*) since venture capital funds usually do not publicize information on their actual investment returns, and so evidence rests largely upon the few funds that are publicly quoted (Mason and Harrison, 1999). As a result, Bygrave and Timmons (1992) suggest that "the industry abounds with anecdotes and hearsay" (p. 150). In reviewing the U.S. literature on venture capital returns of fund portfolios, they suggest that "rather than the folklore figure of 30 percent to 50 percent, actual returns have most often been in the teens, with occasional periods in the 20 percent to 30 percent range and rare spikes above 30 percent" (p. 153). Even the National Venture Capital Association admits that "the overall return of the venture industry has been 15–20 percent since inception" (NVCA, 1999). Of course, significant variables include the age of the fund, the year in which it was founded, and the size and investment focus of the fund, while the health of the IPO market is generally the most central influence on the return of venture capital investment (Bygrave and Timmons, 1992).

The measure of performance most often used in the venture capital industry is the internal rate of return of a fund. IRR considers the cash-on-cash returns from the sale of shares and disbursements (such as dividends), as well as the share of the fund's residual holdings in cash and investments in portfolio firms that are not publicly traded (Bygrave and Timmons, 1992, Mason and Harrison, 1999). Since business angels do not invest in portfolios, comparing their return on individual investments with that of venture capital portfolios may be inappropriate. A deal-by-deal comparison would seem more useful, although venture capital firms do not normally release such information on individual investments (Mason and Harrison, 1999). Let's examine what has been discovered by researchers over the years.

## Returns Initially Expected

Surprisingly, business angels are often unable to supply the rate of return they initially *expected* when they made an investment. Angels often believe that return projections are not important since they are confident that if the investment does succeed, the return will be high. One angel echoed this: "We want a return—that's why we're doing it, but we're not so much saying, 'Can the investment give us 25 or 30 percent IRR?' That is not really the way we look at it. What we're saying is, 'Is this business likely to be highly successful?' And if it is, we're most likely to make a very substantial return on our money." To many angels, the rate of return is hypothetical; they just aim for something better than what they could get from a bank. Other more professional angels, especially in angel syndicates, may make efforts to guesstimate return.

In addition to any capital gains they might make on the investment, some business angels also receive monthly or quarterly payments for their active involvement in the firm, similar to what a consultant would receive. This may be another way in which angels attempt to reduce risk after the money has been invested, but these payments are often low because of the limited cash flow of early-stage firms. Regardless of whether an angel receives a consulting income, the amount of time he or she actively puts into the investee firm may help to increase the overall value of the firm, but it also decreases the realistic rate of return for the angel because of his or her time cost (opportunity costs). One angel told us: "I was hoping for a reasonable return, but that is if you count my time as nothing. But it's still fun." Clearly, most angels do not mind (and are able to) put in some of their time and effort to ensure that their investments will be successful and render them a return down the road.

On average, the expected rate of return for business angels investing in start-ups and early-stage entrepreneurial ventures is around 30 percent or more in the United States (Freear, Sohl, and Wetzel, 1995a), the UK (Mason and Harrison, 1994, 1995), and Canada (Short and Riding, 1989), and about 20 percent for investments in established ventures (Mason and Harrison, 1994). Variations naturally exist with the economic climate, stage of investment, and geographical region. For instance, angels in the UK appear to have the highest return expectation, followed by those in the United States and then angels in Sweden (Mason and Harrison, 1994; Landstrom, 1993). Whatever the expectation, in reality business angels can expect about 30 to 40 percent of their deals to go bust.

Unlike business angels, venture capitalists usually have a pretty good idea of the percentage returns they *anticipate* on their investment. Since venture capitalists conduct much due diligence before investing and usually invest in larger and later-stage firms that have fewer uncertainties, it is easier to make predictions. Because their fund providers are IRR-driven, so are venture capitalists. One venture capitalist told us: "We have to, as a fund, give about a 30 percent-plus return to our investors. So, since some fail, we usually aim for about 50 percent plus on each investment."

Studies in the United States (Robinson, 1987; Freear, Sohl, and Wetzel, 1995a) and in the UK ("Venture Capital in the United Kingdom," 1990; Wright and Robbie, 1996) show the median (and mean) expected rate of return for venture capital investing in early-stage firms is 30–40 percent, and slightly lower for established investments (Wright and Robbie, 1996). Although few direct comparisons have been conducted, studies in the United States (Freear, Sohl, and Wetzel, 1995a), the UK (Mason and Harrison, 1992; Coveney, 1996), and Canada (Short and Riding, 1989) indicate that the investment return expectation of venture capitalists is generally greater than that of business angels. A recent study asking UK investors to state the average rate of return they expected on their last investment found that 54 percent of angels and 96 percent of venture capitalists expected to receive a return of more than 20 percent (Van Osnabrugge, 1998). On average, angels expected 30 percent return (median: 25 percent), while venture capitalists expected 39.2 percent (median: 40 percent).

Since business angels in general invest in early-stage and riskier ventures, the difference in return expectation may seem counterintuitive since angels should demand more. Part of the explanation may lie with the nonfinancial returns (the "psychic income") that angels receive from investing (Freear, Sohl, and Wetzel, 1995a). This difference between angels and venture capitalists seems even more surprising if one considers that venture capitalists hold a more diversified portfolio than angels, which theoretically should make total investment risk (and required return) lower. But Gupta and Sapienza (1988) found that most venture capitalists in the United States do not attempt to actively diversify their portfolios, instead preferring specialization. Of course, one could also argue that even with a diversified portfolio the risk might still be quite high thanks to the nature of the entrepreneurial market. Alternatively, the high due-diligence, administrative, and salary costs that a venture capital firm incurs may also add to the rate of return they require.

## Actual Investment Returns

Little or no information is available on *actual* rates of return realized by business angels (Mason and Harrison, 1995; Mason, 1996b; Freear, Sohl, and Wetzel, 1996). As private investors in entrepreneurial firms, business angels tend to be just that—private—especially about their investment habits and returns. Of course, many success stories abound of U.S. and international angel deals leaving their investors extremely wealthy, as Table 11.2 shows.

In the United States, one study actually found that 42 percent of business angels believe theirs to be the most profitable form of investment (Haar, Starr, and MacMillan, 1988), while another suggested that 60–65 percent of angel investments either lose money or break even (Benjamin and Margulis, 1996). In Canada, performance met or exceeded expectations in almost 50 percent of angel investments (Short and Riding, 1989), while in Finland we know that over half of angel investors experienced partial or

**Table 11.2.  Sampling of Successful Business Angel Deals.**

| Company Name | Angel Investor | Business | Investment | Value at Exit | Return (Number of Times over Investment) |
|---|---|---|---|---|---|
| Apple Computer | (Name withheld) | Computer hardware | $91,000 | $154 million | 1,692 |
| Amazon.com | Thomas Alberg | Online bookshop | $100,000 | $26 million | 260 |
| Blue Rhino | Andrew Filipowski | Propane cylinder replacements | $500,000 | $24 million | 48 |
| Lifeminders.com | Frans Kok | Internet e-mail reminder service | $100,000 | $3 million | 30 |
| Body Shop | Ian McGlinn | Body care products | £4,000 | £42 million | 10,500 |
| ML Laboratories | Kevin Leech | Kidney medical treatment | £50,000 | £71 million | 1,420 |
| Matcon | Ivan Semenenko | Bulk containers | £15,000 | £2.5 million | 166 |

*Source:* partially adapted from unpublished data provided by Amis Ventures in 1999.

full loss on their investment (Lumme, Mason, and Suomi, 1996). Mason and Harrison (1999) analyzed 128 exited angel investments in the UK and found that returns were negatively skewed: 34 percent were a total loss, 13 percent were a partial loss or broke even in nominal terms, 23 percent showed a return of 50 percent or above, and only 10 percent of deals generated a return in excess of 100 percent. This clearly demonstrates that angels are capable of realizing extraordinary returns from their very best investments. But since they only make one or two investments, they are less able to absorb a loss than a venture capitalist is, since the latter has a portfolio of investments; so angels must invest wisely, avoiding bad investments rather than going for home runs (Benjamin and Margulis, 1996).

It is generally assumed that the investment return of the professional venture capital investor looks healthier. A number of U.S. academics have claimed that venture capital investments have a significantly higher success rate than new ventures in general and better than firms not backed by venture capital (Hall and Hofer, 1993; Timmons, 1994; Zacharakis and Meyer, 1995, 1998). The many golden deals of the past would certainly strengthen this conclusion: Apple (return of 235 times the amount invested), Lotus (63 times), Compaq (38 times), and more recently, eBay (1,600 times; Brouwer and Hendrix, 1998). Although there is volatility from year to year, the average survival rate for venture capital–funded enterprises is about 65 percent (Sahlman, 1990), with 20 percent of all ventures, and 35 percent of all early-stage ventures, turning into total or partial losses (Bygrave and Timmons, 1992). The return of venture capital deals tends also to be skewed. In truth, the presence of one or two successful deals can make a venture capital fund very profitable, while the absence of such performers can mean a poor overall return. It is certainly industry folklore that venture capitalists often follow the two-six-two rule, namely, that on average in a portfolio of ten investments, two are expected to fail, six survive but make little or no returns—called "the living dead"—and two are expected to be very successful, bringing in the majority of returns for the investment portfolio (Bygrave and Timmons, 1992). In fact, Bygrave and Timmons (1992) found that almost 50 percent of revenues are generated by only 6.8 percent of investments; that is, one investment in fifteen returns more than ten times the original funding, bringing in about half of the final value of the portfolio. This is perfectly demonstrated in an early U.S. study that found that the overall return for venture capital portfolios is 18.9 percent on average, although eliminating the top 10 percent of investments resulted in an average return per investment of only 0.28 percent (Huntsman and Hoban, 1980). Clearly, attaining a high return depends on the investment exit route used, as Bygrave and Timmons (1992) point out in Table 11.3.

For venture capital–backed firms, IPOs are traditionally the preferred exit route since the average return is 22.5 times first-round investment, 10 times for second-round, and 3.7 times for third-round deals (Bygrave and Timmons, 1992). But looking at such average returns for the whole venture capital industry may be misleading since a high rate of return may be largely attributable to the top twenty venture capital firms, who tend to enjoy high

**Table 11.3. Distribution of Venture Capitalist Exit Routes and Realized Gains.**

| Exit Route | Percentage of Firms | Average Gain |
|---|---|---|
| IPO | 30 | 2.95 |
| Acquisition | 23 | 1.40 |
| Company buyback | 6 | 1.37 |
| Secondary sale | 9 | 1.41 |
| Liquidation | 6 | −0.34 |
| Write-off | 26 | −0.37 |

*Source:* Bygrave and Timmons (1992, p. 167), based on Soja and Reyes (1990).

returns (Sapienza, 1992). Indeed, new research indicates that when evaluating venture capital investments at least six years after funding, the amount of productive resources (informational, human, and organizational capital) controlled by a venture capital firm is an effective predictor of profitable exit (Busenitz and Fiet, 1999). Even after IPO, venture-backed stocks in general have shown higher returns than the NASDAQ and the S&P 500 (NVCA, 1999).

Directly comparing the actual returns of business angels with those of early-stage venture capital funds, Mason and Harrison (1999) conclude in their new study that although angels have a higher proportion of investments that perform poorly or moderately, they have fewer investments that lose money and a similar proportion of high-performance investments. Table 11.4 details the actual returns that angels and venture capitalists received on their investments in this study.

For investors to fully realize a return on their investment through an exit, it is crucial that the venture grow large enough to be floated on a stock exchange (through an IPO) or, more realistically, bought as a suitable acquisition for another larger firm. Business angels should ensure that they retain a certain percentage of the equity to be fully compensated for the high risks they assumed, so extending just a straight loan or loan guarantee

### Table 11.4. Comparison of Actual Returns from Angel and Venture Capital Investments.

| IRR (Percentage) | Business Angel Investments (Percentage) | Venture Capital Fund Investments (Percentage) |
|---|---|---|
| Negative | 39.8 | 64.2 |
| 0–24 | 23.8 | 7.1 |
| 25–49 | 12.7 | 7.1 |
| 50–99 | 13.3 | 9.5 |
| 100+ | 10.2 | 12.0 |

*Source:* Mason and Harrison (1999).

(without an additional equity stake) may not be wise since it does not allow the angel to fully participate in the firm's increase in value. Also, if the venture fails (as many do), creditors have priority recourse to the firm's assets and little may be left. This is why savvy angels often invest using redeemable preference shares, which give investors an equity stake for their investment and also pay them back their invested funds in the form of a loan. But the important lesson here for angels is that they should only invest money they can afford to lose. As the investment returns seen here attest, private investors should think very carefully before they invest their golden handshake from a former employer in an entrepreneurial venture (Mason and Harrison, 1999), possible—but not probable—high returns notwithstanding.

## Investors' Postinvestment Regrets (Things They Would Have Done Differently)

A recent study asked a number of investors what they would have done differently in their latest early-stage investment if they could do it all over again. A number of business angels expressed significant regrets, and many referred to the costly learning curve they experienced, especially on their first angel investment. The most common regret among angels was that they should have conducted more due diligence and obtained more contractual

control over their investments. "I should have done more research," one said; "it never occurred to me that it was a difficult
area." Another stated that "If I had to do it again, I would have dug
deeper and not been in such a rush to put the money in." Conversely, venture capitalists had fewer regrets, and they tended to
be less specific.

As Figure 11.1 shows, business angels wished (more than venture capitalists did) that they had conducted more preinvestment
due diligence (36 percent versus 5 percent), had more contractual control (13 percent versus 9 percent), and had not invested
(8 percent versus 1 percent; Van Osnabrugge, 1998). Venture capitalists expressed greater desire to have invested more (12 percent
versus 8 percent) and to have recruited more employees sooner
(17 percent versus 6 percent).

These results may indicate that each investor type has the most
postinvestment regret about the stage in their investment process

**Figure 11.1.  What Investors Would Do Differently
with Their Investments.**

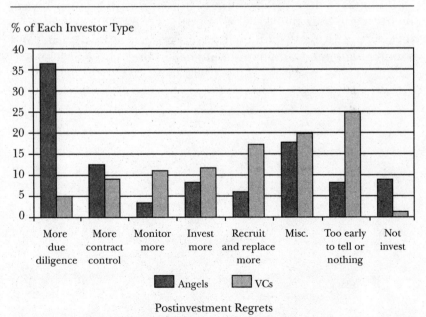

on which they concentrate least. Thus business angels tend to monitor after the investment has been made (a minor angel regret), while conducting less due diligence and gaining less control over the investment through comprehensive contracts (both major angel regrets). Similarly, venture capitalists appear to conduct extensive due diligence and write comprehensive contracts before making an investment (both minor venture capitalist regrets), while conducting little hands-on monitoring of their investments (more sizable venture capitalist regret). One additional factor may indicate that venture capitalists regret not conducting more monitoring of their investment: they would have recruited more new employees sooner for their investee firm.

The lessons here are clear for business angel investors in particular. To be a successful private investor in an entrepreneurial firm, it pays to be more like the professional venture capitalist by conducting thorough due diligence, forming a detailed investment contract, and lending a helping hand to the venture once a deal has been made. One would think that people investing their own hard-earned money would conduct more research into their investment possibilities. Surprisingly, this is usually not the case with angels. Yet countless success stories exist for angel investments made over the years. To join the ranks of these fortunate investors, active and potential angels must invest with care and sound judgment. Gambling should be left to casino visits.

# Part Four

# Attracting Business Angel Funds to Your Start-up Firm

# Chapter Twelve

# | **Valuing Your Firm**

Putting a value on a firm, particularly one in an early start-up phase, is more art than science. Valuation relies heavily on judgment, especially in relation to the methods, data, and assumptions used. Reaching a value for a quoted firm can be quite tricky, but it is even more difficult when assessing entrepreneurial firms, which are privately held and often still turbulent and unproven. In such instances, reaching an appropriate valuation greatly depends on the particular benchmarks used. Two investors presented with the same information are likely to arrive at contrasting valuations on account of conceptual differences and varying assumptions. One investor may elect to value the firm based on its present characteristics, the other on projected future performance. The choice of method stems from the circumstances; entrepreneurs and investors should be aware that judgments and assumptions affect the company value that is derived. But which methods are right? Which are wrong? Which are best?

In this chapter, we present a brief overview of the three main methods of valuing firms and their appropriateness, advantages, and disadvantages. Parts of this analysis are based on thorough work by Pesenti (1993) and Sahlman (1987). In the next chapter, we review negotiation tactics so that entrepreneurs can learn how to defend—or even better, increase—their valuation levels in the deal-making process. In the end, value calculations are often only a basis from which negotiations with investors start. More often than not, the final valuation is dependent on negotiation, presentation of the firm, and competition among interested investors.

## Valuation Methods

There are three principal valuation methods investors and entrepreneurs can use:

1. Ratios and multiples
2. Discounted cash flows
3. Net assets

None is best, but one may be more appropriate than the others depending on the situation. As we will see, the discounted cash
flows procedure suits valuation of high-growth, early-stage firms
with little or no income stream and few assets—those firms that
business angels and venture capitalists prefer. (Interested readers
should look at the venture capital method reviewed in the discounted cash flows section). Conversely, the ratios method—that
is, P/E (price to earnings) ratios and the like—is suited to established but profitable firms with few assets, while large firms with a
strong asset base may be estimated best through net asset valuation (Table 12.1).

## Ratios and Multiples

This common method is quite straightforward. The valuer (entrepreneur or investor) identifies one or more firms with some sort
of discernible market value that is "comparable" to the one being

**Table 12.1.  Most Appropriate Applications
of Valuation Methods.**

| Valuation Method | Most Appropriate Application |
| --- | --- |
| Ratios | Established and profitable firms with few assets |
| Discounted cash flow (DCF) | High-growth, early-stage firms with little or no income stream; the venture capital method is especially appropriate for young entrepreneurial ventures |
| Net assets | Large firms with strong asset bases |

*Source:* partially adapted from Pesenti (1993).

valued. Such firms, preferably in the same line of business, may be quoted on a stock market, or their worth may have been recently established in a private sale. Their value is then measured in a ratio of financial performance for the comparable firm, such as latest after-tax earnings. This ratio (or multiple) is then applied to the firm being valued to attain its valuation. For instance, if a retail firm with $1 million in after-tax earnings is comparable to two firms with price-to-earnings ratios of 9 and 11, then the value of this firm (9–11 times $1 million) may range from $9 million to $11 million. Though this approach may seem unsophisticated, it does make good use of existing market values.

### A Word of Caution

The strength of this method rests on how similar the comparable firms really are, in terms of their financials and also their business risk and growth opportunities. A valuer should consider relative levels of profitability, return on capital, growth rate, and debt capacity. If no suitable firm can be found for comparison, then a ratio for the industry sector could be used, assuming the firm's characteristics lie within the category. Of course, some firms may fit more than one sector. In today's market, valuing an electronic sporting equipment retail firm, for instance, on the P/E ratios of Internet firms, rather than on those of the sports retail industry, results in much higher valuation. Another worry is that using the ratios of publicly traded firms (which are liquid investments) for those of private firms (which are illiquid) may not be accurate. In such an event, a discount should be applied to the resulting valuation. Clearly, the ratios method is best for established businesses in which fewer uncertainties exist.

### Which Ratios to Use

There are a number of ratios valuers can use. The appropriate choice depends on the situation, but it may be best to compare the results of several approaches to ascertain a credible value.

### The P/E Ratio

Multiplied times after-tax earnings, the P/E ratio captures the value of equity, with earnings after taxes being the net sum that accrues to shareholders.

The P/E ratio is defined as:

$$\frac{\text{VALUE OF COMMON EQUITY}}{\text{PROFIT AFTER TAXES AND MINORITY INTERESTS}}$$

Of course, the value of the firm's outstanding debt must also be added to this amount to obtain the full value of the company. The P/E value is easily available, hence commonly applied, but it should be used only to compare a firm with others having similar (comparable) financial structures; accounting bases; and policies regarding depreciation, amortization, and capitalization of expenses. Earnings used must also reasonably reflect earnings to be attained in future years.

### Before-Tax Variation of the P/E Ratio

Alternatively, another form of the P/E ratio uses earnings *before* taxes and interest, since this may be a better measure of the income due to the business as a whole. By excluding taxes from the equation, the effects of financial structure (say, favorable tax treatment on debt interest) have less effect on the valuation. However, this method assumes that comparable companies have comparable tax rates.

### The Free Cash Flow Ratio

In this valuation method, it is assumed that a firm's ability to reward its investors is dependent on its free cash flow.

The free cash flow ratio is defined as:

$$\frac{\text{VALUE OF COMPANY}}{\substack{\text{FREE CASH FLOW AFTER TAX, BEFORE INTEREST} \\ \text{GENERATED BY OPERATIONS AND BEFORE} \\ \text{DISCRETIONARY EXPENDITURE}}}$$

An advantage of using this method of comparison is that earnings do not measure the reinvestment needed for future growth; free cash flow can be used for these purposes regardless of accounting convention. However, earnings ratios have the advantage of smoothing out short-term earning figures; in the free cash flow method it may be difficult to distinguish discretionary from necessary expenditures. Also, firms that do not have stable cash flows from period to period because of long investment cycles, strong cash demand for high-growth needs, or just the nature of their business may elect to avoid this valuation method.

### Historic Versus Future Ratios

Realized performance figures differ from projected future estimates, so care must be taken to compare likes when using ratios of comparable firms. Applying the *current* P/E for a comparable firm to *estimated* earnings is clearly faulty. Also, in some situations—such as high-growth ventures—using future ratios is more appropriate than using historical ones. Such valuation comparisons can certainly give an indication of how market value grows.

### Other Ratios

Additional ratios can be employed so long as they make conceptual sense and there is a reason for not using more accepted methods. For a young firm with high growth prospects but negative earnings, an appropriate ratio might be company value divided by sales, or any other ratio common in the particular industry.

## Discounted Cash Flows (DCFs)

In this method, the valuer forecasts the expected after-tax cash flows for a business for each future year and then uses an appropriate discount rate that captures the firm's risk to obtain the present value of the future income stream. This is the value of the firm.

Though this method avoids having to determine various discount rates (that is, cost of capital) for equity and debt, which are treated as one entity, it is quite complicated and can give valuers a false sense of precision should any of the assumptions be questionable. The accuracy of this method depends on the quality of forecasts attained, and the assumptions upon which they are based. (Assumptions can influence the end result, so a sensitivity analysis should be undertaken to gain better impression of the firm's value.) Determining the discount rate, for one, can be tricky. Traditionally traded firms may be able to use the *capital asset pricing model* (CAPM) to gain an indication of their discount rate, but private entrepreneurial firms should add a premium (penalty) since their shares are illiquid.

The DCF measure, however, only discounts future cash flows up to a certain future time. This means that the ongoing value of the business may not be fully appreciated in the valuation. Thus, a terminal value should also be computed since the ongoing business will have value. This can be done by applying a benchmark ratio to the final-year forecast, or a free cash flow perpetuity-type formula. One relatively simple terminal value formula is:

$$\text{TERMINAL VALUE} = S * m * (1-g/R) / (k-g)$$

where

S = sales for following year

m = after-tax earnings margin

g = long-term growth rate in annual sales

R = after-tax return on capital employed

k = rate of return on assets

The beauty of the DCF method is that it can give a reasonably illuminating company value even if the firm is going through some short-term changes.

### The Venture Capital Method

Many of the aforementioned methods may be of little use in valuing a start-up or early-stage venture. Such companies rarely have a positive level of earnings since their projections often follow a classic "hockey stick" shape: initial losses and a high rate of burning up cash, followed later by cash generation and profits. The value of these businesses depends not on what they have now but on what their future potential is. In its most basic form, the value of a start-up is essentially the terminal value of the future firm minus the cash needed to get it to that stage.

For example, a small early-stage venture may need an investment of $500,000 to generate annual earnings of $1 million five years hence. Suppose a syndicate of business angels approach the venture with an investment offer. These investors might assume that the future business can secure a P/E of 15 (compared to similar firms), and that their required rate of return on such a deal is 50 percent. How much is the firm worth now, and how much equity should the investors demand?

The value of the firm (including the new cash infusion) can be calculated as the price of the firm (that is, earnings times P/E ratio) divided by the investors' discount rate over the five-year period until the first earnings appear:

$$(\$1 \text{ MILLION} * 15)/(1 + 50 \text{ PERCENT})^5 = \$1.98 \text{ MILLION}$$

The equity stake that the business angel syndicate should demand equals:

$$\$0.5 \text{ MILLION}/\$1.98 \text{ MILLION} = 25 \text{ PERCENT}$$

Thus, the higher the investors' required rate of return, the lower the company valuation and the higher the investors' equity stake. Demanding a return of 50 percent or so may be quite reasonable for such a high-risk investment; venture capitalists may demand a discount rate of as much as 40 to 70 percent for start-up and early-stage ventures. Such a rate seems sensible to investors since a high discount rate may in part compensate for their hands-on postinvestment contributions, and also to bring realism to the usually optimistic financial forecasts that entrepreneurs present. Since a high proportion of early-stage ventures never make it, those seeking outside funds need to have the capacity for high potential rate of return to offset the more likely investment losses that investors may experience.

## Net Assets

The ratios and DCF are top-down methods, where expected future earnings are used to obtain an estimated value of the firm today by valuing the firm as a going concern into the future. Asset valuation is a bottom-up method, in that it directly assesses the current value of a firm's assets minus its liabilities, as if it were being wound up and sold. The strength of this approach depends on how closely the value of the separate parts resembles that of the whole. The firm's book value is always a good starting point in such a valuation process.

However, as valuers sift through a firm's balance sheet, care must be taken to remember that

- Book values and market values often differ
- Depreciation depends on the accounting method used
- Replacement cost may be a better value to use than depreciated historic cost on certain assets
- Some assets may be illiquid (cannot be sold)
- An accurate assessment of working capital needs to be made
- Borrowings may be best judged at their face value
- Certain debts and liabilities may be off-balance sheet and should not be forgotten
- The value of brand names and patents may be significant, although they will not show up on the balance sheet

In this sense, a firm's goodwill should be valued separately and added to its equity value from the balance sheet. Of course, a valuer should also consider whether the current assets of the business can reasonably sustain the projected growth rate, or whether a large cash infusion is needed. If so, this would certainly affect the valuation process adversely.

## Misconceptions

Each valuation method we have briefly reviewed has certain advantages and disadvantages, as outlined. Yet valuation methods are often viewed through an aura of precision. This is clearly a misconception. Regardless of method, there is always uncertainty about the value obtained. Entrepreneurs and investors should take care to fully understand the conceptual aspects of the method they employ, to ensure they do so sensibly. One way to verify the valuation obtained is to conduct the analysis using more than one method, assuming each is appropriate to the particular company. If two or more methods result in significantly different numbers, the valuer must ask why this is the case. The usual explanation is that unrealistic and incorrect assumptions (about the firm's current situation or future potential, or about the valuation model) have been used for at least one method. With care and understanding of the models used, robust valuations can be obtained, though they should always be viewed with some degree of skepticism.

## The Value of Valuations

Regardless of the amount of number-crunching an entrepreneur undertakes to obtain a reasonable monetary value for the business, the real value of the firm today is what someone else is willing to pay for it. Early-stage entrepreneurial firms are illiquid investments whose value depends on the interest of at least one willing buyer. Value is as much a matter of finding such a buyer and exciting him or her about the venture as anything else. The difficulty is that young firms encompass many intangibles, and placing value on such things as management expertise and entrepreneur sweat equity may be trying. Of course, the investor may also bring many benefits to the firm (such as credibility and industry knowledge) in addition to funds, which are likewise difficult to value. Since the final valuation price struck between entrepreneurs and investors is often highly influenced by the negotiating skills of the parties involved, the next chapter is dedicated to reviewing the critical negotiation process.

# Chapter Thirteen

# Negotiating the Funding Agreement

Possibly the most misunderstood aspect of the relationship between entrepreneurs and potential investors is negotiating that relationship. This is likely because in popular use the term is loaded with pejorative connotations of high-pressure, sleazy, unethical tactics. Many entrepreneurs and private investors view negotiating an agreement as one of the more distasteful aspects of the whole process and are glad to put it behind them.

This is a limited view of both the nature and value of negotiation. Lax and Sebenius define negotiation as "a process of potentially opportunistic interaction by which two or more parties, with some apparent conflict, seek to do better through jointly decided action than they could otherwise" (1986, p. 11). The key point is that the process of negotiation *allows* resolution of disputes, and creation of value. Nor should the negotiation be viewed as nasty medicine that will make one feel better at some unspecified future point in time: properly approached, negotiation over funding and other aspects of investor involvement in the firm can be a wonderful process of forging new alliances and discovering many benefits for both sides.

## A Quick Primer on Basic Negotiation Concepts

Negotiation is increasingly becoming a complex and theoretical academic field. Here is a quick outline of some important concepts; much of what is presented here is wholly drawn or otherwise adapted from Lax and Sebenius (1986), and Sebenius (1997).

## Interests

Your interests in a negotiation are *whatever you care about that is at stake in the interaction*. Put otherwise, your interests are a major part of the answer to "Why are you in this negotiation?"

### The Full *Set of Interests at Stake*

It is a naïve entrepreneur indeed who limits interests to the question of "How much money can I get?" Some interests are *tangible and objective*, such as funding level, profit, timing, quality level, and specifications. However, and perhaps just as important, interests may also be *intangible and subjective*. These include the relationship, the character of the negotiating process, the precedent it sets, fairness to both parties and their constituencies, sustainability, the effect on reputation and self-image, whether trust is enhanced or eroded, and the like. Inexperienced negotiators often err by letting "hard interests" (the economics of a deal) drive out crucial "soft interests" such as relationships, precedents, and fairness.

Further, you should not automatically read *selfish, short-term, and financial* in front of *interests*. You may care also about the welfare of your group, or organization, and you may have genuinely altruistic concerns in a negotiation; your concerns may be long-term, strategic, and reputational. But *whatever* you care about at a fundamental level, that which is potentially affected by the negotiation falls in the category of interests—the raw material for negotiation. Of course, just as you seek to advance the full set of your interests, the other side(s) will be doing exactly the same thing. The *full* set of *their* interests, as they see them, is central for you to assess in the negotiation.

### Interests, Issues, and Positions

To sharpen the concept of interests, we should distinguish among *interests, issues,* and *positions*. The *issues* in a negotiation are those items that are on the table for explicit agreement: amount to be invested, equity granted, terms of payback, and so on. *Positions* are your stands on the various issues. Interests, we have said, are the underlying concerns or deeper dimensions of value affected by resolving the issues under negotiation. Positions on issues obviously affect underlying interests but need not be identical to them. For example, in an equity negotiation an *issue* may be the amount to be invested, on which your *position* is a request for $150,000. Though your underlying interests as reflected in this request obviously include gaining liquidity, they may also involve internal organizational politics, external signals, and retention of control (Figure 13.1).

### Positional Versus Interest-Driven Negotiation

This distinction among interests, issues, and positions has an important implication for the character of negotiating. *Positional bargaining* envisions the process as a dance of positions that, if negotiation is successful, ultimately converge to an agreement—or not, in the case of an impasse. *Interest-driven bargaining* sees the process primarily as reconciliation of underlying interests and concerns. Although there is an important role for positional bargaining, a frequent way to move stalled negotiations forward is to *look behind conflicting positions to understand deeper interests.* For example, a venture capitalist and an entrepreneur may squabble over the amount of equity the venture capitalist should receive in exchange for investment, without realizing that the underlying interest is not percentage of equity per se for either side; for the entrepreneur it is a question of retention of control (which the venture capitalist may be happy to grant), and for the venture capitalist it is a question of ROI (which the entrepreneur is happy to grant as a legitimate concern).

## Alternatives and the Bargaining Range

An important factor in negotiations is the set of alternatives that each side has, relative to doing the deal in question. Your alternatives reflect the course of action you will take if the proposed deal

**Figure 13.1. Influential Factors in the Negotiation Process.**

is not possible. Depending on the situation, it may involve simply walking away and doing without any agreement, or going to another potential investor or investment prospect. If asked whether you should agree to a particular deal, assess your most realistic alternatives to sharpen the decision by asking, "As compared to what?"

• *Alternatives determine the existence of a possible bargaining range.* Critically, the value for you of your alternative sets the threshold—in terms of your interests—that any acceptable agreement must exceed. Doing "better" in terms of each party's interests than the alternatives of each is a necessary condition for an agreement. Alternatives imply the existence or absence of a possible bargaining range.

---

By way of example, imagine a simple situation in which the amount of equity to be invested has been decided (for argument's sake, imagine it is 25 percent). All that remains to be negotiated is the amount to be invested in exchange for this level of equity. Assume also that the entrepreneur has another investor who has agreed to pay $125,000 for this 25 percent equity, which the entrepreneur finds a low but acceptable alternative; this is the entrepreneur's alternative. Also, assume the investor has determined that he or she will not part with more than $175,000 for the 25 percent equity. A potentially profitable bargaining range exists—agreement can be better for each side than its fallback position, which is the value of its alternative—and the process determines whether, how, and where the parties end up within it.

| ENTREPRENEUR'S | BARGAINING | INVESTOR'S |
|---|---|---|
| MINIMUM . . . | RANGE | . . . MAXIMUM |
| $125,000 ———————————————————— $175,000 | | |

---

It is quite possible that no bargaining range exists: the entrepreneur already has a more attractive offer than the investor is willing to make. Sometimes the best deals are the ones you do *not* make. Of course, each side typically knows only its own alternatives and must continuously assess and reassess the other side's. (Many negotiators have only a hazy sense of their alternatives.)

   • *Alternatives are associated with negotiating leverage.* Alternatives define the minimum, necessary conditions for a deal to exist —that each side's interests must be served at least as well in a deal as by its alternative. The ability and willingness to walk away from the table is often associated with negotiating influence. The better *your* alternative appears both to you *and* to the other party, the more credible your threat generally is to walk away unless the deal is improved.

## Negotiation Strategies "At the Table" Versus Those "Away from the Table"

Most people think of negotiation primarily as tactical and interpersonal actions at the table. Entrepreneurial strategies *away from the table* also affect the core elements of the process (parties, interests, alternatives). If you face a tough negotiator and have not taken the time to develop alternatives, you are in a difficult position. Looking around for other potential investors, creating publicity for your firm and product, generating favorable valuation models, and so on, are all moves away from the table that can make the process at the table much easier and more pleasant.

## Application to the Entrepreneurial Financing Negotiation

The concepts discussed thus far are of particular relevance to the negotiation between entrepreneurs and their investors.

### Value Claiming Versus Value Creation

With these simple concepts in mind, we see how terribly tempting it is for negotiators to lock into positional bargaining, which is often equated with a "distributive" mind-set: How much of the pie do I get? Such a model is largely distributive (or value claiming) in nature.

Most negotiations, however, contain elements of both cooperation and competition; the parties can enlarge the pie as well as divide it. The tension between cooperative moves toward creating value and competitive moves toward claim is fundamental to negotiation and affects virtually all tactical and strategic choice. The key is to manage this tension constructively and craft valuable agreements that promise to be sustainable. Thus, an angel may be more interested in being seen as a valuable member of the team, but this may manifest as a desire for more equity than the entrepreneur is comfortable with. Being willing to explore creative options for the angel's involvement can grow the pie (create value) and make the equity question less central and fraught. A basic rule of thumb is to try to find issues that both sides can agree on first (which is value creating), before tackling the thornier (or value-dividing) questions, although in reality there is always a degree of simultaneity.

Certain issues are always basically distributive—the percentage of equity, for example. As one of the authors tells his students, "Equity negotiations are tough, because no matter what else happens, the total is always 100 percent." However, there are questions such as vesting, timing, and voting rights, relating to equity share, that are not necessarily distributive and that may help create value. Table 13.1 gives a rough idea of a subset of issues typically negotiated in an entrepreneurial investment, showing which general issues are distributive and which have value-creating potential.

**Table 13.1.  Value-Claiming Issues Versus Value-Creating Issues in Entrepreneurial Negotiations.**

| Distributive Issues (Value-Claiming) | Integrative Issues (Value-Creating) |
|---|---|
| Share of equity | Timing of investment and vesting schedule |
| Price per share | Debt seniority |
| Value of company | Voting versus nonvoting rights |
| Discount and interest rates | Investor involvement |
| Amount to be invested | Entrepreneurial team employment security |
| Performance milestones | Tax exposure (who bears it?) |

## Negotiating the Value of the Company

Another set of negotiation issues was raised in the previous chapter. Two parties of goodwill may simply disagree as to the value of the company. Even though examining assumptions and the like goes a long way toward opening up the basis of the disagreement, a fundamental difference of opinion might remain. As Mark Twain put it, "It is differences of opinion which make for horse races." In such a case, it may be possible to structure a *contingency agreement,* which allows reexamination of the investment contract after enough time has passed to reveal if one or the other side was right. Although it is important to avoid moral hazard—and many venture capital firms dislike complicated contingencies—angel investors may be receptive to well-structured, incentive-compatible contingency agreements.

Many entrepreneurs are intimidated about negotiating the valuation of their company, especially against venture capitalists with official-looking spreadsheets and reports. They should not be, although (as the previous chapter stressed) they must prepare their own figures carefully and realistically. In recent years, the amazing multiples at which Internet start-ups such as Amazon.com and eBay traded have further eroded traditional financial analysis. A venture capitalist told us that in the case of Internet start-ups "we don't try and bargain using traditional valuation models any more. Rather, we look at comparable firms, what they were funded for, and what percentage of equity the investors took, and we go from there."

## Summary and Prescriptions

Negotiation is a means of advancing the full set of your interests by jointly decided action. It is increasingly a way of life for effective entrepreneurs and managers, rather than a special skill mainly for important deals and disputes. Negotiation analysis involves ten steps that should be examined interactively to craft the most effective approach.

1. You should assess the relevant *context* (or situation): key elements of the setting that locate and shape the negotiation. Is this

an Internet deal? What else is going on in the industry space? What other comparable companies have been funded recently, and for what amount? Is this investor savvy regarding this industry sector?

2. Relentlessly focus on how each side sees its basic negotiation problem and how the solutions to these problems are interdependent. Venture capitalists may have concerns about the stage of your company relative to the age of their fund, or perhaps they are trying to establish a reputation for investing in a particular sector. Angel investors might have had a bad experience and want to understand how things will be different this time.

3. Each side constantly weighs its basic negotiation problem: the choice between perception of the available deal and the alternatives in terms of how its interests are served. Your job is to develop a superior alternative so that you are not unduly pressured at the table, and so that disaster does not result if the deal falls through.

4. Since agreement represents simultaneous solution of all sides' problems, solving *their* problem is part of solving *your* problem. This book has stressed again and again the issues facing investors, be they business angels or venture capitalists; the entrepreneur who focuses on those issues and tries to help the investor with these problems stands a far better chance of being funded. If you just want their money and don't care about their problem, you have dismal prospects for success.

5. A big negotiating challenge is to manage the tension between the cooperative and competitive aspects of the problem constructively. Although there are always some issues that are essentially distributive in nature, these should not consume the majority of effort and creativity in the deal-making process. Seek value-creating options as a means to escape the divide-the-pie mentality.

6. To understand the joint problem, assess the structure of a negotiation and the people involved. Remember that structure and people are mutually influential, not independent and separate sets of considerations.

7. Structural elements include the parties, interests, no-agreement alternatives, and the potential for a jointly beneficial agreement.

8. Assessing the *people* involved should focus both on *individual* and *social* aspects. Knowing, for example, that the person across from the desk is a first-year associate at a venture capital firm who is afraid of making mistakes affects the kind of information you stress and reassurances you give, relative to dealing with a senior and experienced partner in the same firm.

9. Assess the opportunities for creating and claiming sustainable value. Remember, this is a partnership. The desire to win at all costs is likely to spell disaster for the future relationship. This applies to both sides and should be raised as an issue if it is felt that the negotiation is becoming too distributive and competitive.

10. Use these assessments to craft a strategy for actions both at and away from the table.

# Part Five

# Becoming a Successful Business Angel Investor

*Chapter Fourteen*

# Steps in Effectively Making Your First Investment in an Entrepreneurial Firm

Almost anyone with money to spare can sign a check and instantly become a business angel. But doing so prudently—in a way that has a reasonable probability of investment success—has its challenges.

## Ten Investment Tips for Prospective Angels

Over the last few years, our conversations with angels, venture capitalists, and entrepreneurs (some successful, others not) have allowed us to formulate a list of some of the most common advice. Prospective angels should, for starters, consider these ten investment tips.

1. *Verify that you are truly angel material; not everyone qualifies for a halo.* Before making an angel investment, prospective investors should be certain that they have the personality, time, and skills to make unquoted investments. Set limits on how much money you can reasonably invest; you must make sure that you can truly live comfortably (without a significant change in lifestyle) if it takes several years—or much longer if things don't turn out as planned—to recover your investment. Angels often refer to such funds as casino money since they have to play the odds to win the big rewards. But in angel investments, the game is not stacked

against the players. Your efforts before and after the deal can help you improve the odds. If only this were true in Las Vegas!

2. *Invest only in industries in which you have sufficient knowledge.* An all too-common complaint from angels is that they invested in an industry sector with which they were unfamiliar; thus they did not fully comprehend the risks of the investment and were unable to contribute much hands-on expertise. The high-tech industry in particular offers potentially high returns, but it can be very difficult to understand, especially for those without specialized technical background or training. To minimize your risk and make the best use of your skills, invest in industries in which you feel most competent.

3. *Co-invest, depending upon your level of experience, funds, trust, and preference.* On the subject of whether or not to invest alone, we have heard and read many conflicting opinions. As with so many things, it all depends on the situation. For those investors with significant industry experience and a preference for being actively involved in their investments, investing alone may be appealing since peer guidance and sharing due diligence adds little extra value. Investing alone also gives those who want to be involved greater personal influence over the direction of their investment, free of possibly clashing with other investor egos. Of course, there are tradeoffs: it is more difficult to diversify across a number of investments, and some larger deals are out of financial reach. Conversely, for novice or first-time angels, or those with less experience and money to invest, joining an angel syndicate may be one of the best ways to learn the tricks of the trade and share the many costs that arise in the investment process. This sort of co-investing or syndication appears to be an increasingly popular and typical way for angels to approach the investment process.

4. *Invest in entrepreneurs who want your help, not just your money.* Most angels want to have some sort of say over the direction of their entrepreneurial investments. Such involvement is a good way to keep an eye on the investment and shape its evolution. Though angels do not necessarily want to make key decisions, they want their opinions to be heard. Investing in entrepreneurs who seek experienced advice and input, as well as funds, is one way to ensure that the investor's influence is taken se-

riously. Partly because of this concern, investors must weigh their level of personal chemistry with the entrepreneur before making an investment decision; it is important to invest in someone you can get along with and work with as a partner. Entrepreneurs and their angel investors should discuss and agree on the level of investor participation expected in the firm. Setting realistic expectations from the start makes the long ride smoother.

5. *Don't back a one-trick pony.* Whenever possible, try not to back an inflexible, one-product firm (Gordon, 1999). Investing in a firm that has a single product aimed at one market raises the risk involved, especially if the firm does not show some of the flexibility that allows repositioning in case the product is not well received. If you do support a specialized firm, make sure it has a realistic plan B, in case plan A does not work out.

6. *Reach a valuation that is fair to both sides; it's a relationship!* Valuation is naturally important to investors and entrepreneurs alike; both hope to reach the most advantageous deal for themselves, without driving the other party off. But short-term gains can lead to long-term losses. In our research, we have seen many cases in which lopsided investment deals led to resentment and disputes later on, in successful as well as unsuccessful ventures. To avoid such potential impediments, it is crucial that the investment deal be fair and pleasing—or at a minimum sustainable—for both sides.

7. *Don't skimp on due diligence or the legal details.* Unfortunately, as we have seen it is not uncommon for angels to invest hastily without conducting even minimal due diligence or employing tight legal contracts. Though doing so incurs additional costs, these may pale compared to the cost of losing most of the invested funds on a deal that probably should not have been made in the first place. In fact, not conducting more due diligence is one of the most common regrets voiced by angels (especially novice ones) who have made deals. Again, investing in an angel syndicate is an excellent way to spread the costs and experience necessary for sound due diligence and legal work.

8. *Predetermine your exit strategy.* There is no point in investing if you cannot get your money out again, but entrepreneurial investments are inherently illiquid. Although being overly specific

regarding exit several years hence may be optimistic speculation, entrepreneurs and investors should discuss and agree (in advance) on likely exit scenarios and how much each person will get paid in the event of these outcomes. It is important to first agree on the entrepreneur's annual salary; the investor may demand that any additional money made by the firm first go to repaying the investment, after which a more even allocation with the entrepreneur can be undertaken (Brodsky and Burlingham, 1997). The investor should also have the ability to force the entrepreneur to take money out of the firm; otherwise it may be difficult for the investor to realize any of the gains. All too often, inexperienced angel investors skip such arrangements, only to regret it later.

9. *Structure the deal to minimize your risk.* Since business angel investments inherently have above-average risk, investors should structure their deals to minimize risk. A number of ways to do this have already been discussed, such as undertaking due diligence, using legal contracts, and being able to force a payout from the firm. Another option that has been suggested is for the investor to initially take a majority stake in any new firm he or she funds (say, 51 percent). Then, when the initial investment has been paid back, the equity stake declines (to, say, 20 percent), giving the entrepreneur equity control again (Brodsky and Burlingham, 1997). This allows the investor to have strategic control over the venture when the investment is most at risk. However, in such a deal, the investor should only offer some advice, allowing the entrepreneur to exercise full decision control in daily running of the business. After all, it is the entrepreneur's firm, and he or she must remain committed to what is being built. Investors should only try to exercise equity control when the firm is in trouble and needs to be realigned. A final option for minimizing risk is for the investor to fully consider the potential liability that may be associated with taking a seat on the board (Cullen, 1998). Being aware of, and protecting against, such potential perils can make the angel investment process an enjoyable and rewarding experience.

10. *Do not put all your eggs in one basket.* Diversification is the heart of sound financial investment strategy, and there is certainly no exception with angel investments. First, they should constitute only a small proportion (5–15 percent, depending upon wealth and age) of an investor's total portfolio (stocks, bonds, mutual

funds, and so on). As the high-risk end of the portfolio, angel deals add diversity, but they should also be made in light of existing investments. Second, within the angel investment portion of the portfolio, as much diversity should be undertaken as is reasonable. Venture capital portfolios reveal that it is usually a minority of deals that account for most profits. One good way of diversifying is to invest small amounts in a number of deals with an angel syndicate or a few trusted co-investors. If this is not an attractive option, then rigorous due diligence, a sound investment contract, and active involvement in the investment may be good ways to protect your investment interests.

## Questions to Ask Yourself at Each Stage of the Investment Process

At each stage of the investment process, there are a number of questions that you should ask yourself as an angel investor. Many of these questions emanated from investor interviews, while others were drawn from Murray (1998) and Van Osnabrugge (1998).

### Deciding to Invest

An angel investment is a bold move that requires reflection. As a potential angel, you must be confident that you have the financial funds, temperament, experience, and skills to be a supporter of entrepreneurial firms. These questions may help you decide whether or not to take the angel leap:

- Am I able and willing to commit a significant amount of money and at least five to seven years of time to a speculative venture?
- If my investment sours and I lose the money, will it affect my lifestyle?
- What skills, experience, and contacts do I have to offer young entrepreneurial firms?
- Do I have the free time to commit to such an investment?
- Am I comfortable letting someone else spend my money and make the decisions central to the welfare of my investment?
- How active do I want to be in my investments?

## Setting Your Investment Criteria

Before starting the search process for a likely investment opportunity, you should have a good idea of what your investment criteria are, and then stick to what you are comfortable with. As a prospective angel, you may decide to concentrate only on those industry sectors in which you have experience, those you can understand, or those to which you are confident they can add value.

- Overall, how willing am I to invest in business angel deals?
- How many angel investments do I want to make in total? How much money am I willing to risk per deal?
- In what industry sector(s) am I most experienced and most comfortable investing?
- How far am I willing to travel to help my investment?
- Am I more comfortable investing with others, or by myself?
- Realistically, what potential returns am I looking for in an investment deal?
- What basic characteristics am I looking for in the entrepreneur? the product? the target market? the overall business plan?
- Which issues are most important to me, and which am I willing to compromise on?

## Starting Your Search

The search for investment opportunities can be undertaken in a number of ways, as Chapter Eight shows. Professional and personal contacts are the most common means of finding deals, although more formal matching services are also becoming a popular option. Through such informal and formal networks, you can find a myriad of potential deals.

- Which of my personal friends or business associates might have the network contacts to help me find some potentially attractive angel opportunities?
- Should I try to join an angel syndicate so that I can co-invest with others?
- Which matching services in my area offer high-quality opportunities?

- What do other investors in the area have to say about these services?
- What aspects of the search do I really need help and guidance with?
- Rather than waiting to find a suitable early-stage firm, are there any impressive young ventures in the area that I may want to approach with an unsolicited offer for funding?

## Screening Investment Opportunities

Once investment opportunities start flowing in—and they will—the initial screening process should remove all those that do not match your criteria. Research shows that angels have a steep learning curve and often commit numerous first-time mistakes and endure subsequent regrets. If you are a novice investor, you should be patient and careful to obtain advice and insight from seasoned investors before committing to a venture. Invest in haste, and you will regret at your leisure.

- Who referred this opportunity to me? Do I fully trust their recommendation?
- Do I understand and have experience in this industry sector?
- What makes this investment opportunity unique among all the others?
- What kind of investment return can I realistically expect to receive?
- How much money are the entrepreneurs looking for? How much equity are they willing to surrender in return?
- What are the most likely exit routes for this investment opportunity?
- Overall, does this investment opportunity fit well with my investment criteria?

## Evaluating the Business Plan

Of all the investment opportunities seen, only a very small proportion deserve rigorous evaluation of the business plan and initiation of talks with the entrepreneur.

- Is the business plan professional? Does it present credible, compelling, and comprehensive information?
- Have the entrepreneurs shown that they fully understand the market and the business?
- Does the firm have the necessary management team to bring the projections to reality? If not, how do they plan to fill the gaps?
- Does the product have a certain degree of competitive protection from current and potential competitors?
- Are the predictions of market growth rate credible? Does the firm have the resources and abilities to realistically capture the projected percentage of this market?
- If plan A doesn't work, what is their backup plan?
- How much money and sweat equity have the entrepreneur and management team committed to this venture?

## Meeting the Entrepreneur(s)

If the business plan holds up to your scrutiny, then an initial meeting with the entrepreneur and the management team may be the next logical step. In addition to being an opportunity to view the company's offices, you have a chance to assess the entrepreneur's personality and the potential chemistry for a working relationship. You can also review and verify the assumptions and projections in the business plan, and gain a tentative idea of the investment terms and valuation that the entrepreneur expects. About half of the prospects still alive die at this stage, and it is important that you not commit to anything just yet—go home, think it through, and talk about it with trusted advisors. Subsequent meetings involve detailed discussion about the specifics of valuation and the terms of investment.

- Is my first impression of the entrepreneur a good one?
- Do the members of the management team appear to be enthusiastic, work well together, and have genuine respect for each other's opinions?
- Does the management team inspire my confidence? Are the team members competent and worthy of my hard-earned dollars, and can I realistically envision myself working with them for the next few years?

- Does the entrepreneur really want the hands-on assistance of a business angel investor? Or is he or she just interested in obtaining funds, regardless of the source?
- How many other investors, if any, is the entrepreneur currently talking to? Am I the backup candidate?
- What kind of investment deal is he or she looking for? How much equity will the entrepreneur give up, and how much money is sought?
- What exactly is my investment going to be used for?

## Conducting Due Diligence

Enter this stage only if you are pretty confident that this is a deal for you. Due diligence is long and tedious, involving significant time and financial costs. Although angels often do not conduct it thoroughly, this stage is crucial for identifying potential pitfalls. Although you can easily undertake most due diligence yourself, for financial, legal, and market assessment outside advisors and industry contacts may be invaluable. Of course, these information-collecting tasks require cooperation from the company; if this is not forthcoming, then it may not be worth going any further. To avoid incurring frivolous due-diligence costs, some larger investors require the entrepreneur to sign a formal lockup agreement giving the investor an exclusivity period, for a number of weeks or at least until a deal is reached or abandoned. Of course, due diligence should be a two-way street—the entrepreneurs are sure to want to check your references too!

- Do I know enough about the market to justify *not* obtaining some independent third-party appraisals?
- What do independent references on the entrepreneurs tell me?
- What do the company's own employees say about the entrepreneurs?
- What do my contacts in the industry know about this firm and the market?
- What do their suppliers, competitors, and customers say about the firm?
- What does analysis of the audited financial statements tell me about the firm?

- What is the size of the potential market? What type of market share can the firm realistically achieve?
- Does the firm have well-defined strategic plans for marketing, sales, and distribution that will allow them to reach projected sales growth?
- What are the firm's plans to stay innovative and ahead of competition?
- Are there any legal claims or liabilities outstanding against the firm or the entrepreneurs?
- What do the firm's employment contracts promise concerning bonuses, pensions, and stock options?
- What tax issues are central to the firm and my investment?
- Are there potential exit routes to realize my gains? If so, how realistic are they? How long will I have to wait for them?

## Negotiating the Deal and the Legal Contract

If the due-diligence process has not raised too many red flags to deter your interest in investing, then negotiation with the entrepreneur is the next logical step. Negotiation can be quite difficult; buying a chunk of someone else's firm is a sensitive process, often determined more by personal chemistry than the cash offered (Murray, 1998). Yet the negotiation process is extremely important because the valuation agreement is likely to depend on your skills as a negotiator more than on the results of valuation models. If valuation and equity shares cannot be agreed on, then the deal is almost certain to fall through. Reaching an amicable settlement requires time, although too often we see angels hurrying through this stage—much to their later chagrin, as Chapter Nine has shown.

- Is the valuation reached by the entrepreneur realistic for the industry?
- Has more than one method been used to derive this valuation?
- Is the entrepreneur's valuation similar to the one I have calculated? If not, what explains the differences?
- Have I hired professional legal advice to write up a sound and enforceable investment contract?
- Are the responsibilities of my participatory role within the firm clearly outlined?

- What sort of fees, if any, will I receive for my assistance in the firm?
- Have we agreed on guidelines to allow me to monitor the firm's progress?
- Have we agreed on realistic performance targets for the firm to attain?
- Do I invest my funds all at once, or in stages based upon the performance targets?
- Are my exit options specified? Do I have the ability to force a payout?
- How will my equity position in the firm change, relative to those of the entrepreneurs, if more equity needs to be sold in a later round of fundraising?

Once the deal is signed and you hand over your check, your duties as an angel really start. You must monitor your investment so that you can help guide the firm to profitability and eventually seek an exit route to realize your return.

## Monitoring the Investment

Most business angels relish the opportunity to put their business experience to good use in their entrepreneurial investments. Like the vast majority, you can play an active role beyond providing funds; you can be an invaluable source of free advice for the entrepreneur.

- How can I best add value to this firm? Where is my expertise most needed?
- Do I want to be actively involved in daily operations, or stay on the strategic level? How active do the entrepreneurs want me to be?
- Will my input be taken seriously and be respected? How much influence can I exert without hurting my relationship with the entrepreneurs?
- Should I take a seat on the board?
- Do I really need or want some sort of monetary compensation for my active assistance?

## Exiting the Deal

The main point of investing is to eventually exit the deal with a handsome investment return. Although likely exit routes are often difficult to assess at the time of investment, you will see prospective routes as the investment progresses.

- How many years am I willing to commit to my investment in this venture?
- If I exit financially now, will it materially affect the health of the firm?
- How can I best exercise my contractual exit options?
- Have I fully considered the tax consequences of exiting the investment now? Should I roll over my capital gains to another opportunity to avoid capital gains taxes?
- What are my most likely and profitable exit possibilities: sale to existing shareholders or a third party? liquidation of the firm's assets? a trade sale? an IPO?
- Is there a chance of the firm going public or being bought up in a trade sale? If so, should I hold out for this possibility?

## Conclusion

Indications are that only about a quarter of all angel investments result in healthy gains, and only one in ten produce spectacular returns. The exit process is important, and has to be undertaken prudently to minimize your losses, or—if you are fortunate—to maximize your gains.

# Part Six

# The Future of the Business Angel Market

# The Business Angel Market in the New Millennium

In the fifteen years since the business angel market was first seriously examined, we have seen dramatic changes. Although already large, the market has grown tremendously in size and influence to fully secure its unrivaled and undisputed role as the most important source of outside funds for our nation's tens of thousands of entrepreneurial firms. All indications are that this course of growth will not change anytime soon. Over the next decade, we see four major trends continuing to have significant implications for our entrepreneurial and business angel marketplaces.

## Globalization

Thanks to technological advances, we have witnessed rapid globalization of financial markets and ideas over the last few decades. Certainly, globalization of the business angel market concept has not been left behind (Sohl, 1999). In the last few years, recognition and promotion of business angel investing has been seen across Europe, South America, Asia, the Middle East, and Australia—practically across the globe. Especially in Asia, angel investing is being heavily promoted as one of the best ways to resuscitate economies from recession. In the United States, such an entrepreneurial mind-set has already become ingrained in our society. The desire to own one's own home has been replaced by the desire to own one's own business (Sohl, 1999). Entrepreneurship is an accepted way of life, undertaken by an ever larger percentage of our population. Our country's entrepreneurial successes have been a source of inspiration to the next generation of entrepreneurs, here and abroad. Entrepreneurship is becoming common in foreign countries, as its traditional stigmas are being replaced with tolerance and acceptance. Where entrepreneurship flourishes, so does the business angel market.

*Implication: Business angels are becoming pervasive and influential in the U.S. economy especially, as well as abroad.*

## Technology

The dramatic technological advances of recent years have been extremely beneficial to our entrepreneurial economy. As well as enabling entrepreneurs (and established firms) to function effectively and competitively, technology itself has sparked creation and growth of countless entrepreneurial firms. In recent years, the Internet in particular has unleashed a torrent of entrepreneurial activity; thousands of firms have been created with the aim of eventually reaching multimillion-dollar quotations on our receptive and enthusiastic stock markets. With this increase in entrepreneurship, the demand for business angel funds has skyrocketed. Already the largest financiers of technology firms today, the population of potential business angels receptive to funding our next generation of innovative firms has grown with the dramatic increase in the number of entrepreneurs cashing out of high-tech firms with millions of dollars in their bank accounts. Indeed, the next generation of business angels will be younger, richer, and more entrepreneurial than those of the past.

Technology has also enabled greater sharing of information on entrepreneurial issues, such as finding business angel investors and locating quality entrepreneurial opportunities to fund. Although still undergoing some teething problems, technology has certainly aided the traditionally inefficient process of matching entrepreneurs and entrepreneurial funds. Over the next few years, as they find their niche, Internet matching services will have a growing impact in promoting entrepreneurship in new and innovative ways.

*Implication: Traditional barriers to entrepreneurship are being broken, and greater technological efficiency is improving the matching of a grow-*

*ing amount of wealth (searching for investment opportunities) with a greater number of entrepreneurial firms (seeking investment support).*

## The Structural Change in Our Economy

As already alluded to, the number of entrepreneurs successfully cashing out of entrepreneurial firms is at an all-time high. In today's receptive environment for entrepreneurship, more people are taking the plunge, and many are succeeding beyond their wildest dreams. Particularly in the technology sector, we are seeing young entrepreneurs walk away with millions (and on the rare occasion, billions) after only a few years of hard work and much good fortune. Left with such financial resources, and a well-developed entrepreneurial skill base, these individuals are joining the ranks of business angels, investing money in more firms than we have traditionally seen in the angel market.

But the very rich, and these "silicon millionaires," are not the only ones investing in start-up entrepreneurial firms. Individuals from the upper-middle class are a significant and growing proportion of the business angel population. Thanks to the impressive growth in our stock markets and our business economy as a whole, many ordinary Americans are finding themselves with increasing liquidity, and looking for places to invest it. Some of these individuals are investing a small proportion of their wealth in entrepreneurial ventures—often for the fun of being involved in the entrepreneurial arena, but primarily in the hope of someday being able to join the ranks of the high-tech nouveau riche constantly glamorized in the media.

*Implication:* The United States has a huge and growing number of potential angels, many of whom are in fact joining the ranks.

## Formalizing Angel Deals

With the proliferation of entrepreneurship and business angel investments in our society, we have started to witness a formalization of business angel investing. In the past, little was known about this form of financial support for our entrepreneurial economy, but the many success stories and the growing influence of the business angel sector have led others to hop on the bandwagon. As with any area that is hot, business angel deals are attracting attention. The angel funds so central to Amazon.com, and the angel hats now worn by such notable businessmen as Sculley, Allen, Perot, and Barksdale—all entrepreneurs who have had a significant impact on the world of technology—have greatly increased the profile of business angel investing. As in the financial sector, growing interest in a particular field leads to formal innovations catering to these needs. The business angel market has already seen a wave of formalization with the widespread and growing popularity of business angel syndicates in particular. Such groups of wealthy individuals invest together in a portfolio of entrepreneurial firms—a nice variation on the stock investment clubs of the past. These syndicates are now investing amounts far in excess of what we have seen angels invest in the past, and they have begun blurring the boundaries between angels and venture capitalists, with angels increasingly playing in a formalized investment game. This has led to more co-investment between these two investor types and continued strengthening of their relationship (Sohl, 1999). Venture capitalists are more aware than ever before of the important and synergistic role that private investors play; business angels fund the start-ups of today that will be the venture capital investments of tomorrow.

Over the next few years, we expect even more formalization of business angel deals as established financial organizations step into the sector, probably as brokers of new financial instruments packing angel deals into a single security. As in numerous financial sectors where banks and other institutions continually invent, package, and sell unusual and complex financial instruments (be they new derivatives, options, or options on options!), so too will the business angel market see its share of innovation. In the last few years alone, we have seen large banks and consulting firms move into the business angel field with educational initiatives, financial services, and even investment funds. This will only increase as the angel market continues to grow. In Chapter Four we mentioned the mutual fund family that is exploring a possible business angel fund, to operate similarly to a venture capital fund. Though still in conceptual infancy, implementing and promoting such innovative ideas and financial initiatives further diversifies the reach of the business angel market as we know it.

*Implication: Continued formalization of angel deals will create more, and increasingly diverse, possibilities for business angel investment.*

## The Angelic Road Ahead

As the largest and most influential group of financial supporters of entrepreneurial firms today, business angels will become an even more significant force in our economy over the coming years. Many powerful trends are working to bolster our entrepreneurial investment climate; initial projections suggest that the business angel market will at least double within the next decade. This nation's business angels are destined to be a central pillar for the entrepreneurial economy of the new millennium. The twenty-first century will indubitably bear witness to a new age of entrepreneurship in the United States and hopefully abroad. At the core of it—as has always been the case, but in increasingly large numbers—will be the business angel.

# Part Seven

# Putting the Wheels in Motion

# Appendix One:
# A Detailed List of More Than Seventy Matching Services in the United States

Matching good investment opportunities with the funds of private investors is not an easy task for either party. If personal and business networks—the most popular matching methods—do not provide any leads, then entrepreneurs and investors may want to consider using matching services to find each other, as discussed in Chapter Five. We believe that formal matching services are destined to play an important role in the future.

## Types of Matching Service

These organizations come in a number of forms:

- Formal matching services
- Groups of angel investors (angel alliances and syndicates)
- Breakfast and luncheon groups of casual investors (venture capital clubs and forums)
- Internet-based matching services
- Other varieties

As the first detailed list of its kind, this appendix documents more than seventy U.S. matching services, specifying the classification of each and its main matching methods. For good measure, we have also included a number of other types of beneficial service organization, such as a few small business incubation centers and some venture capital firms that do early-stage deals.

## How Our List Is Organized

To ease the search process, the matching services are categorized alphabetically by geographic region (the number of services for the region is given here in parentheses):

| | |
|---|---|
| Nationwide (2) | New England (13) |
| California, Nevada, | New Jersey and |
|   Arizona, Hawaii (8) |   New York (5) |
| Canada (1) | Northwest (7) |
| Great Lakes (9) | Southeast (11) |
| Mid-Atlantic (6) | Southwest (4) |
| Midwest (5) | Great Plains (4) |

To collect the information for our list, we contacted each organization on multiple occasions. More than three-fourths of the organizations we were able to find in the United States cooperated and are featured here; others preferred anonymity, for reasons unknown.

We must caution that the information comes directly from the firms (in most cases by postal reply, but in some instances from their website), and so we can not guarantee its accuracy. Success rates or other pieces of relevant information not revealed may be listed as *NA* (not available). Since we can only show what the matching services wanted us to reveal, this list should be used only as a good starting point for your search, rather than as a definitive source.

## New Insights into the Angel Market

During our data-collection process, we also decided to obtain some statistical data about the types of angel deals being conducted through these organizations; after all, these services take the pulse of the health of the larger business angel market. With the assistance of two of the leading angel experts in the United States, Jeff Sohl and Bill Wetzel from the University of New Hampshire, we developed a comprehensive questionnaire. To give you a taste of what you can expect from these services, here are some of our findings. Because of the great diversity of angel investment activities, we also include the median (that is, half of the data above, half below) and range data since they should be accurate indications of the market (Table App1.1).

Interestingly, 70 percent of the matching services organize some sort of venture forum so that investors and entrepreneurs can meet, 36 percent offer investor-specific matching services for individual members, 35 percent print a newsletter with opportunities, and 30 percent use the Internet as at least one of their matching tools. To find subscribers (entrepreneurs and investors), word-of-mouth is the most effective method of advertising. Fifty-eight percent of these services are not-for-profit and 42 percent are private, while 65 percent actively screen investment opportunities before featuring them. Fifty-three percent of the matching services believe that there have not been enough government initiatives to aid the business angel market. In particular, more tax initiatives and less government regulation were the preferred solutions.

We also asked the matching services to give us a better impression of their angel investors' views on a number of interesting issues (Table App1.2).

As you can see throughout the various findings, the heterogeneity of the angel-entrepreneur matching services in the United States is striking. (The next list gives you an even better indication of the matching services available in your region.) Their data and descriptions should enable you to determine which best serve your needs, whether you are an entrepreneur or an investor. But we urge readers to collect detailed brochure information from each service and talk to other practitioners before deciding to join a particular organization. Each has its own focus and set of offerings; you must decide which is best for you. This list and the set of resources in Appendix Two are intended simply to help those interested in entering the angel investment arena get off to a good start. A good review of securities and tax laws for making small-business investments is also recommended; you may want to check out such information on the ACE-Net website (http://ace-net.sr .unh.edu/pub/).

**Table App1.1. What the Matching Services Tell Us About U.S. Angels, Entrepreneurs, and Themselves.**

| | On Average | Median | Range |
|---|---|---|---|
| Characteristics of the Angel: | | | |
| Amount a typical angel investor has reserved for potential angel investments | $311,875 | $225,000 | $40,000 to $1 million |
| Amount invested per deal per angel | $144,687 | $75,000 | $25,000–500,000 |
| Equity investors typically receive in a deal | 21% | 20% | 1–50% |
| Service's members who have invested in last three years | 59% | 75% | 4–100% |
| Angels who are serial investors | 48% | 45% | 5–100% |
| Subscribers who have never made an angel investment | 32% | 20% | 0–95% |
| Average age of angel investors | 49 | 50 | 40–55 |
| Angels who prefer to co-invest | 77% | 80% | 20–100% |
| Deals in which there is co-investment | 72% | 75% | 20–100% |
| Number of investors in an average angel deal | 6 | 4 | 2–25 |
| Amount invested per deal by an angel syndicate | $601,315 | $300,000 | $50,000 to $3 million |
| Equity a co-investment syndicate typically receives per deal | 32% | 25% | 10–100% |

**Table App1.1.** (*continued*)

| | On Average | Median | Range |
|---|---|---|---|
| Entrepreneurs: | | | |
| Typical maximum sought by entrepreneurs | $3.77 million | $2.25 million | $50,000 to $20 million |
| Typical average sought by entrepreneurs | $750,000 | $1.14 million | $50,000 to $5 million |
| Typical minimum sought by entrepreneurs | $334,622 | $100,000 | $10,000 to $5 million |
| Per individual matching service: | | | |
| Number of investors per matching service | 95 | 53 | 6–853 |
| Number of firms seen by investors annually | 49 | 25 | 3–300 |
| Number of deals referred to investors over last three years per matching service | 98 | 33 | 2–500 |
| Firms featured that are at seed stage | 22% | 20% | 0–60% |
| Firms featured that are at start-up stage | 34% | 30% | 10–80% |
| Firms featured that are at early stage | 34% | 30% | 10–100% |
| Successes per matching service: | | | |
| Successful matches made through service since formation | 27 | 15 | 2–150 |
| Successful matches made through service in 1998 | 6 | 5 | 0–21 |
| Successful matches made through service in 1997 | 7 | 4 | 1–30 |

**Table App1.2. What Are Your Typical Angel Investors' Preferences on These Issues?**

| Matter of Preference | Percentage Answering Yes | Percentage Indifferent | Percentage Answering No |
|---|---|---|---|
| Do they prefer to invest in high-tech ventures? | 64 | 21 | 15 |
| Do they prefer a majority, rather than a minority, shareholding? | 16 | 35 | 48 |
| Do they like to use standard, pro forma, legal, deal agreements? | 29 | 28 | 43 |
| Do they consider the location of their deals to be very important? | 94 | 6 | 0 |
| Do they prefer to co-invest with other private investors? | 64 | 27 | 9 |
| Do they expect their investment activity to increase over the next five years? | 52 | 20 | 28 |
| Do they think they would have invested in more ventures over the last three years if there had been more suitable proposals? | 80 | 13 | 7 |

**ACE-Net Network**                          Region: Nationwide
The Access to Capital Electronic Network (ACE-Net), also known
as the Angel Capital Electronic Network, is a national listing service that allows investors to find small, growing ventures through a
secure database over the Internet. This network has affiliate offices
across the country. (On the Web: http://ace-net.sr.unh .edu/)

| | | | |
|---|---|---|---|
| CA | La Jolla | UCSD Connect | (858) 822-1830 |
| CA | Newark | Bay Area Regional Technology Alliance | (510) 354-3900 |
| CT | New Haven | Southern Connecticut State University | (203) 392-5633 |
| DC | Washington | Howard University Small Business Development Center | (202) 806-1550 |
| FL | Tallahassee | Jim Moran Institute | (850) 644-3372 |
| GA | Warner Robins | Advanced Technology Development Center | (912) 953-4028 |
| ID | Idaho Falls | Idaho Innovation Center | (208) 523-1026 |
| IL | Chicago | The Illinois Coalition | (312) 814-3482 |
| IN | Muncie | Midwest Entrepreneur Education Center | (765) 285-9002 |
| KS | Topeka | Kansas Technology Enterprise Corporation | (913) 296-5272 |
| MA | Cambridge | Technology Capital Network | (617) 253-2337 |
| MD | Largo | Prince George's County Economic Development Corp. | (301) 386-5600 |
| ME | Augusta | Maine Science and Technology Foundation | (207) 621-6350 |
| MI | Lansing | Small Business Association of Michigan | (800) 362-5461 |
| MN | Coon Rapids | Anoka County Economic Development Partnership | (612) 786-0869 |

| MN | Minneapolis | Minnesota Investment Network | (617) 672-3494 |
| MO | St. Louis | Center for Emerging Technologies | (314) 615-6908 |
| MT | Polson | The Montana Private Capital Network | (406) 883-3051 |
| NC | Raleigh | U.S. Investor Network | (919) 782-8559 |
| ND | Grand Forks | Center for Innovation | (701) 777-3134 |
| NJ | Newark | NJIT Enterprise Development Center | (973) 643-5740 |
| NM | Albuquerque | Technology Ventures Corporation | (505) 843-4018 |
| NV | Las Vegas | Business Advocacy + Development Alliance | (702) 486-4335 |
| OH | Cleveland | Enterprise Development | (216) 229-9445 (ext. 122) |
| PA | Philadelphia | Ben Franklin Partnership | (215) 972-6700 |
| PR | San Juan | Office of Entrepreneurial and International Support | (787) 250-0000 (ext. 2124) |
| TN | Oak Ridge | Technology 2020 | (423) 220-2020 |
| TX | Austin | The Capital Network | (512) 305-0826 |
| VA | Fairfax | George Mason University Entrepreneurship Center | (703) 277-7700 |
| WA | Seattle | Northwest Capital Network | (206) 441-3123 |
| WI | Madison | Wisconsin Department of Commerce | (608) 267-0313 |
| WV | Fairmont | West Virginia High Technology Consortium Foundation | (304) 366-2577 |

**MIT Enterprise Forum, Inc.**                    Region: Nationwide
With eighteen chapters worldwide, the MIT Enterprise Forum offers unique programs and network opportunities for both entrepreneurs and investors. This network has affiliate offices around the country and abroad. (On the Web: http://web.mit.edu/entforum/www/chapters/chapters.htm)

| | | | |
|---|---|---|---|
| CA | Pasadena | Caltech/MIT Enterprise Forum | (626) 395-4049 |
| CA | San Diego | MIT Enterprise Forum of San Diego | (760) 431-4891 |
| CA | San Francisco | MIT Enterprise Forum of the Bay Area | (650) 321-6332 |
| CA | Santa Barbara | Central Coast MIT Enterprise Forum | (805) 484-8855 |
| CN | New Haven | MIT Enterprise Forum of Connecticut | (860) 275-0294 |
| DC | Washington | MIT Enterprise Forum of Washington-Baltimore | (703) 528-5793 |
| MA | Cambridge | MIT Enterprise Forum of Cambridge | (617) 253-8240 |
| MA | Boston | Startup Group | (617) 482-5550 |
| NH | Manchester | MIT Enterprise Forum of New Hampshire | (603) 668-1400 |
| NY | New York City | MIT Enterprise Forum of New York City | (212) 681-1112 |
| OR | Portland | Oregon Entrepreneurs Forum | (503) 790-2555 |
| PA | Pittsburgh | MIT Enterprise Forum of Pittsburgh | (412) 967-9335 |
| TX | Dallas–Fort Worth | MIT Enterprise Forum of Dallas–Fort Worth | (972) 883-6364 |
| TX | Houston | MIT Enterprise Forum of Texas | (713) 659-5531 |
| WA | Seattle | MIT Enterprise Forum of the Northwest | (206) 233-7527 |
| Canada | Toronto | MIT/York Enterprise Forum | (905) 943-7160 |
| Israel | Jerusalem | MIT Enterprise Forum of Israel | 011-972-2-624-2442 |
| Mexico | Mexico City | MIT Enterprise Forum of Mexico | 011-525-662-1418 |
| Taiwan | Taipei | MIT Enterprise Forum of Taiwan | 011-886-2-719-1293 |

# Arizona Technology Incubator/Arizona Technology Venture Fund

## Region: California, Nevada, Arizona, and Hawaii

Mr. Tom Emerson
Arizona Technology Incubator/Arizona Technology
Venture Fund
1435 North Hayden Road
Scottsdale, AZ 85257-3773

tel: (602) 990-0400
fax: (602) 970-6355
e-mail: ati@getnet.com
http://www.asu.edu/ia/economic/ati/

| | |
|---|---|
| Classification of service: | Technology business incubators |
| Date of formation: | 1992 |
| Industry preferences: | High-tech |
| Stage of firms preferred: | Seed, start-up, early stage |
| Matching methods: | Internet and venture forums |
| Primary matching method: | Venture forums |
| No. of employees: Full-time: | 4 |
| Part-time: | 1 |
| Volunteer: | 150 |
| Organization type: | Private, not for profit, university affiliated |
| Firms featured by service: | 20% Seed, 40% Start-up, 40% Early |
| Additional services offered: | Regional operates for Arizona for ACE-Net |

| | |
|---|---|
| No. of investors participating: | 25 |
| No. of firms seen by investors/yr: | 10 |
| No. of venture forums/yr: | 1 |
| No. of firms using forum/yr: | 14 |
| $ range sought: Typical max: | $8 mil |
| Typical min: | $0.5 mil |
| Average: | $3 mil |
| Investors invested thru service: | 25 |
| Successful matches: 1997: | NA |
| 1998: | NA |
| Since formation: | Not tracked |
| Service actively screen firms?: | Yes |

**Company Literature** **(This information was obtained from the company's website without independent verification.)** Founded in 1992, ATI was initiated by Arizona State University President Lattie Coor and the Arizona Innovation Network (AIN). The vision was to create a vehicle to strengthen Arizona's economy by developing a true public/private partnership through which the university, government agencies, and private enterprise could share resources and network with technology-based businesses. ATI's mission is to ensure the formation and attraction of successful, fast growth technology-based companies within Arizona in order to achieve technology transfer, create jobs, and enhance economic development; doing all of the above while becoming financially self-sufficient by the year 2000. To be considered for ATI, an applicant must be a technology-based business with a novel product or manufacturing process. Consulting or wholesale businesses will not be considered for admission. Selection will be based on the ability of the candidate business to meet certain standards. Matching the investors through the internet and venture forums is also undertaken to help finance firms to grow. The Arizona Technology Incubator hosted the 1995 National Business Incubation Association (NBIA) Annual Conference.

# Cal Tech/MIT Enterprise Forum
## Region: California, Nevada, Arizona, and Hawaii

Mr. Nick Nichols
Cal Tech/MIT Enterprise Forum
Industrial Relations Center 1-90
Pasadena, CA 91125

tel: (626) 395-4041
fax: (626) 795-7174
e-mail: entforum@its.caltech.edu
http://www.caltech.edu/~entforum

| | |
|---|---|
| Classification of service: | Evening and morning meetings for investors, entrepreneurs and others |
| Date of formation: | 1984 |
| Industry preferences: | High tech |
| Stage of firms preferred: | Stage, start-up, early, and expansion stages |
| Matching methods: | Venture forums |
| Primary matching method: | Venture forums |
| No. of employees: Full-time: | 1 |
| Part-time: | |
| Volunteer: | |
| Organization type: | Not for profit and university affiliated |
| Firms featured by service: | 10% Seed, 50% Start-up, 30% Early, 10% Expansion |
| Additional services offered: | Small executive roundtables for start-up CEOs |

| | |
|---|---|
| No. of investors participating: | 5–10% 200 members |
| No. of firms seen by investors/yr: | 20–30 featured in programs |
| No. of venture forums/yr: | 9 |
| No. of firms using forum/yr: | Audience—900 (no formal networking contacts) |
| $ range sought: Typical max: | NA |
| Typical min: | NA |
| Average: | NA |
| Investors invested thru service: | NA |
| Successful matches: 1997: | NA |
| 1998: | NA |
| Since formation: | NA |
| Service actively screen firms?: | No |

**Company Literature** (This information was obtained from the company's website without independent verification.)

The forum grew out of a series of workshops conducted by the MIT Alumni Association in Cambridge and New York in 1971. Formed in 1984, the Forum is a joint venture of the Caltech Industrial Relations Center and the MIT Alumni Association. The mission of the Caltech/MIT Enterprise Forum is to encourage the growth and success of technology-based entrepreneurial ventures in Southern California. Through its monthly programs, the Forum provides advice, support, education, and networking opportunities to technology-based ventures in the Southern California area. Programs address a range of key entrepreneurial issues from financing, marketing, and business planning to executive leadership and staffing. Case presentations feature companies in emerging technology areas reviewing their business plans with expert panelists. Special sessions examine new entrepreneurial opportunities, such as Internet ventures. The Annual Workshops utilizes small interactive breakout sessions led by experts and successful entrepreneurs to provide detailed information on starting and growing new ventures.

**What Sets This Service Apart?** The contacts, reputation, outreach to organize and conduct quality and stimulating programs to educate entrepreneurs.

## Community Entrepreneurs

**Region: California, Nevada, Arizona, and Hawaii**

Dr. Richard Crandall  
Community Entrepreneurs Organization  
P.O. Box 37  
Corte Madera, CA 94976

tel: (415) 435-4461  
fax: (415) 435-4841  
e-mail: RPCrandall@aol.com

| | | | |
|---|---|---|---|
| Classification of service: | Breakfast luncheon | No. of investors participating: | 30 |
| Date of formation: | 1983 | No. of firms seen by investors/yr: | 50 |
| Industry preferences: | none | No. of venture forums/yr: | 6 |
| Stage of firms preferred: | Seed and start-up stage | No. of firms using forum/yr: | 50 |
| Matching methods: | Venture forums | $ range sought: Typical max: | $200K |
| Primary matching method: | Venture forums | Average: | $50K |
| No. of employees: Full-time: | 1 | Investors invested thru service: | 20 |
| Part-time: | | Successful matches: 1997: | 5 |
| Volunteer: | | 1998: | 6 |
| Organization type: | Not for profit | Since formation: | 40 |
| | | Service actively screen firms?: | No |

Firms featured by service: 50% Seed, 50% Start-up  
Additional services offered: Business information, education, free consulting, and referrals.

**Company Literature** (This information was provided by the company without independent verification.)
CEO is a volunteer entrepreneurial support group. Helping people raise money is only part of the group's goal. It acts as an informal sounding board, provides educational programs, brainstorming, and general encouragement. Like the world of angel investment, most money is raised through the group not through a formal "MIT" screening and presentation process, but through informal contacts and introductions made in person over time.

**What Sets This Service Apart?** Peer support and free volunteer consulting.

# Garage.com

**Region: California, Nevada, Arizona, and Hawaii**

Mr. Bill Reichert
Garage.com
420 Florence Avenue, Suite 300
Palo Alto, CA 94301

tel: (650) 470-0950
fax: (650) 470-0940
e-mail: service@garage.com
http://www.garage.com

| | |
|---|---|
| Classification of service: | A formal matching service |
| Date of formation: | 1997 |
| Industry preferences: | High-tech and life sciences |
| Stage of firms preferred: | Seed, start-up, and early stage |
| Matching methods: | Internet, newsletter/magazine, investor specified criteria, and venture forums. |
| Primary matching method: | Relationships |
| No. of employees: Full-time: | 10 |
| Part-time: | 2 |
| Volunteer: | |
| Organization type: | Private |
| Firms featured by service: | 40% Seed, 50% Start-up, 10% Early |
| Additional services offered: | Coaching, connections, and hands-on grooming. |

| | |
|---|---|
| No. of investors participating: | >100 |
| No. firms seen by investors/yr: | 50 |
| No. of venture forums/yr: | 15 |
| No. firms using forum/yr: | varies 15–100 |
| $ range sought: Typical max: | $2.5M |
| Typical min: | $500K |
| Average: | $2M |
| Investors invested thru service: | 75 |
| Successful matches: 1997: | |
| 1998: | |
| Since formation: | 12 |
| Service actively screen firms?: | Yes |

**Company Literature** (This information was obtained from the company's website without independent verification.)
Our tag line says it all: We start up startups. Garage.com is dedicated to helping entrepreneurs and investors build great high-technology companies. Our approach is simple: Find the most promising entrepreneurs and start-up companies and put them together with experienced high-tech investors. Along the way, we provide entrepreneurs and investors with advice, information, and research to ensure that garage.com start-ups have the best chance of succeeding. Garage.com focuses on companies that represent the most attractive investment opportunities for individual and professional high-tech investors. We only target startups in the information technology and life sciences industry segments. Generally, these companies are seeking $500,000 to $1,500,000 in seed funding, but this range may vary. Garage.com member entrepreneurs have their intelligence, drive, and vision to find strong partners, make good decisions, and build great companies. From thousands of business plans submitted, only those demonstrating the greatest potential will be selected for presentation to investors. Garage.com member investors are selected through an equally stringent set of criteria. To qualify, investors must have sufficient financial resources (net worth of at least $1,000,000), investment experience, and high-technology expertise to provide value to start-up companies. New offices will soon open in Boston and Seattle, with plans for further regional offices in entrepreneurial and high-tech centers around the U.S.

**What Sets This Service Apart?** Extensive screening of start-up companies, hands on grooming of start-up companies. Extensive network of quality investors and organization that can help start-up companies, broker dealer status, other proprietary info resources.

# Los Angeles Venture Association

**Region: California, Nevada, Arizona, and Hawaii**

Ms. Christine Buteyn
Los Angeles Venture Association
626 Santa Monica Boulevard, Suite 129
Santa Monica, CA 90401-1006

tel: (310) 450-9544
fax: (310) 393-0657
e-mail: LAVA4@aol.com
http://www.LAVA.org

| | |
|---|---|
| Classification of service: | Breakfast luncheon with presentations |
| Date of formation: | 1982 |
| Industry preferences: | None |
| Stage of firms preferred: | NA |
| Matching methods: | Venture forums |
| Primary matching method: | Venture Forums |
| No. of employees:  Full-time: | |
| Part-time: | X |
| Volunteer: | |
| Organization type: | Not for profit |

| | |
|---|---|
| No. of investors participating: | Not tracked |
| No. firms seen by investors/yr: | NA |
| No. of venture forums/yr: | 12 |
| No. firms using forum/yr: | NA |
| $ range sought:   Typical max: | NA |
| Typical min: | NA |
| Average: | NA |
| Investors invested thru service: | Not tracked |
| Successful matches:         1997: | NA |
| 1998: | NA |
| Since formation: | NA |
| Service actively screen firms?: | No |

Additional services offered:    Membership directory and special price to attend events

**Company Literature**    (This information was obtained from the company's website without independent verification.)

The Los Angeles Venture Association (LAVA) is a not-for-profit informal monthly forum that brings together venture capital investors and other money providers, entrepreneurs, business executives, academics, management candidates for new ventures, and providers of professional services needing new ventures. In short, LAVA has been designed as a networking vehicle for its members to share and exchange information about each others' interests and needs. Monthly breakfast meetings are the second Tuesday of every month with registration beginning at 7:00 A.M. and the program convening promptly at 7:30 A.M. Quarterly evening meetings have been scheduled, as well. In addition to meeting venture investors and entrepreneurs in a relaxed professional environment, LAVA members benefit from the monthly programs that feature speakers who are successful entrepreneurs and venture capitalists. There are also periodic business plan presentations which are evaluated by a distinguished panel of business professionals. Members also receive a quarterly newsletter which features helpful and informative articles that point the way with practical ideas. Last, but not least, all members are listed in a membership directory which is distributed annually to the membership and serves as a further networking tool. The LAVA Board of Directors is committed to making it a vibrant organization and a valuable resource for all of its members.

**What Sets This Service Apart?**    LAVA provides the arena for networking between entrepreneurs, capital providers and service providers.

# Orange Coast Venture Group

**Region: California, Nevada, Arizona, and Hawaii**

Mr. Atticus Wagner
Orange Coast Venture Group
23011 Moulton Parkway, F2
Laguna Hills, CA 92653

tel: (714) 859-3646
fax: (714) 859-1707
e-mail: OCVG1@aol.com
http://www.ocvg.org

| | | |
|---|---|---|
| Classification of service: | Breakfast/luncheon meeting | |
| Date of formation: | 1985 | |
| Industry preferences: | NA | |
| Stage of firms preferred: | Seed, start-up, and early stage | |
| Matching methods: | Monthly meetings | |
| Primary matching method: | Monthly meetings | |
| No. of employees: Full-time: | 3, administrative staff | |
| Part-time: | 0 | |
| Volunteer: | 0 | |
| Organization type: | Not for profit | |
| No. of investors participating: | | NA |
| No. firms seen by investors/yr: | | NA |
| No. of venture forums/yr: | | NA |
| No. firms using forum/yr: | | NA |
| $ range sought: Typical max: | | NA |
| Typical min: | | NA |
| Average: | | NA |
| Investors invested thru service: | | NA |
| Successful matches: 1997: | | NA |
| 1998: | | NA |
| Since formation: | | NA |

**Company Literature** (This information was obtained from the company's website without independent verification.)
The Orange Coast Venture Group is a nonprofit organization formed in 1985 to bring together the people in Orange County who are interested in new enterprise and the process of creating it. The Group is comprised of professionals involved in the entrepreneurial process—people with bright ideas and the practical skills required to implement those ideas. The Orange Coast Venture Group serves three primary interests groups: entrepreneurs (inventors or innovators with ideas for new ventures, individuals with business plans, executives of development stage companies, senior executives with more established high growth enterprises, and qualified individuals seeking to join venture companies), capital providers (members of venture capital firms, private individual investors, investment bankers, commercial bankers, small business investment corporations, and the venture arms of larger corporation), advisors (providers of professional services, including accountants, lawyers, management consultants, marketing communications professionals, members of the academic community and others serving entrepreneurial companies).

## Small Business Development Center

**Region: California, Nevada, Arizona, and Hawaii**

Mr. Jeff Johnson
Small Business Development Center
1706 Chester Avenue, Suite 200
Bakersfield, CA 93301

tel: (805) 322-5881
fax: (805) 322-5663
e-mail: Wolu@lightspeed.net
http://www.kccd.cc.ca.vs/sbdc

| | | |
|---|---|---|
| Classification of service: | Business consulting service (not an investor matching service) | |
| Date of formation: | 1990 | |
| Industry preferences: | | |
| Stage of firms preferred: | | |
| Matching methods: | | |
| Primary matching method: | | |
| No. of employees: Full-time: | 3 | |
| Part-time: | 1 | |
| Volunteer: | | |
| Organization type: | Subsidized by state and federal government, community college-based | |

| | |
|---|---|
| No. of investors participating: | NA |
| No. of firms seen by investors/yr: | NA |
| No. of venture forums/yr: | NA |
| No. of firms using forum/yr: | NA |
| $ range sought: Typical max: | NA |
| Typical min: | NA |
| Average: | NA |
| Investors invested thru service: | NA |
| Successful matches: 1997: | NA |
| 1998: | NA |
| Since formation: | NA |
| Service actively screen firms?: | NA |

272

# UCSD Connect

**Region: California, Nevada, Arizona, and Hawaii**

Dr. Bill Otterson, UCSD Connect
University of California, San Diego
Mail Code 0176F
La Jolla, CA 92093-0176

tel: (619) 552-0649
fax: (619) 552-0649
e-mail: botterson@ucsd.edu
http://www.connect.org

| | | | |
|---|---|---|---|
| Classification of service: | NA | No. of investors participating: | NA |
| Date of formation: | 1985 | No. firms seen by investors/yr: | NA |
| Industry preferences: | NA | No. of venture forums/yr: | NA |
| Stage of firms preferred: | NA | No. firms using forum/yr: | NA |
| Matching methods: | NA | $ range sought: Typical max: | NA |
| Primary matching method: | NA | Typical min: | NA |
| No. of employees: Full-time: | 14 | Average: | NA |
| Part-time: | 4 | Investors invested thru service: | NA |
| Volunteer: | 10 | Successful matches: 1997: | NA |
| | | 1998: | NA |
| Organization type: | Not for profit, university affiliated | Since formation: | NA |

**Company Literature** (**This information was obtained from the company's website without independent verification.**)
Founded in 1985 at the urging of the local business community, UCSD CONNECT was created to foster economic development in San Diego by nurturing high-tech and bio-science entrepreneurship, facilitating interaction between the University and the business community, and further developing San Diego's business infrastructure. CONNECT's goals are to link high-tech and biotech entrepreneurs with the resources they need for success: money, markets, management, partners, support services, and technology, as well as access to government officials. Often referred to as an incubator without walls, CONNECT has accomplished this throughout educational and networking programs, practical business seminars and technology transfer demonstrations, domestics and international strategic and financing forums. Practical rather than theoretical, CONNECT's programs have been credited with giving company executives a "mental picture" of what they can achieve, while providing access to the resources which help accomplish these goals. CONNECT's programs also serve business service providers, attorneys, accountants, bankers, investors and market specialists—by providing them with knowledge about emerging technologies and access to new business opportunities. The program functions as a catalyst for growth, providing a forum for the exchange of ideas and the opportunity to network with peers, and facilitates the ripple effect that the success of various high-tech industries has on the community which supports them. Entering its second decade, CONNECT has been instrumental in nurturing technology companies, including telecommunications, multimedia, high technology, biotechnology, biomedical and environmental concerns, that have become the leaders in their industries. CONNECT also provides an opportunity for the biotech and high-tech communities to learn about research taking place at the University, and for the University community to learn about research taking place in industry. CONNECT is entirely self-supporting and receives no finding from the University or the State of California. It is supported by membership dues, course fees, and corporate underwriting for specific programs.

# MIT/York Enterprise Forum, Inc.

**Region: Canada**

Mr. Eric Cole
MIT/York Enterprise Forum, Inc.
c/o EDC Business Strategies, Inc.
101 Withrow Avenue
Toronto, Ontario M4K 1C8

tel: (416) 466-0633
fax: (416) 466-0633
e-mail: edc@istar.ca

| | | |
|---|---|---|
| Classification of service: | Breakfast/luncheon meeting and business planning | |
| Date of formation: | 1989 | |
| Industry preferences: | NA | |
| Stage of firms preferred: | Expansion | |
| Matching methods: | Investor-specified criteria, venture forums, and planning | |
| Primary matching method: | Venture Forums | |
| No. of employees: Full-time: | 1 | |
| Part-time: | | |
| Volunteer: | | |
| Organization type: | Private and university affiliated | |
| Firms featured by service: | 25% Seed, 25% Start-up, 25% Early, 25% Expansion | |
| Additional services offered: | Expert consulting, panel advisory input. | |

| | |
|---|---|
| No. of investors participating: | 100 |
| No. of firms seen by investors/yr: | 15 |
| No. of venture forums/yr: | 7 |
| No. of firms using forum/yr: | 10 |
| $ range sought: Typical max: | $5M |
| Typical min: | $250K |
| Average: | $1M |
| Investors invested thru service: | NA |
| Successful matches: 1997: | 2 |
| 1998: | 10 |
| Since formation: | |
| Service actively screen firms?: | No |

**Company Literature** (This information was obtained from the company's website without independent verification.)
The Enterprise Forum is an organization which fosters entrepreneurship and provides networking and learning opportunities from entrepreneurs who innovate in their use of technology. This is done by hosting events which bring together entrepreneurs, investors, and other business professional for an evening idea exchange. Organized and operated by the alumni of the Massachusetts Institute of Technology (MIT), York University's Faculty of Administrative Studies and members of the business community, The Forum is a nonprofit, volunteer organization. It's format is based on the MIT Enterprise Forum which was founded in 1978 and operates in 18 cities in the USA, Europe and Mexico, as well as Toronto. The Toronto chapter has been active since 1988 and has hosted 2500 participants.

**What Sets This Service Apart?** Forums are unique to Canada due to expert consulting.

# Coral Ventures

**Region: California, Nevada, Arizona, and Hawaii**

Mark Headrick
Coral Ventures
60 South 6th St. Suite 3510
Minneapolis, MN 55402

tel: (612) 335-8666
fax: (612) 335-8668
e-mail: lboulger@ix.netcom.com
http://coralventures.com

| | | |
|---|---|---|
| Classification of service: | Institutional venture Capital firm (not a group of angel investors) | |
| No. of investors participating: | | 30 investors in our current fund |
| Date of formation: | 1983 | |
| Industry preferences: | Information tech, telecommunication, healthcare/medical | |
| No. firms seen by investors/yr: | | Not Applicable |
| No. of venture forums/yr: | | Not Applicable |
| No. firms using forum/yr: | | |
| $ range sought: Typical max: | | $20M |
| Typical min: | | $100K |
| Average: | | $5M |
| Stage of firms preferred: | Seed, start-up, early stage | |
| Investors invested thru service: | | NA |
| No. of employees: Full-time: | 8 | |
| Part-time: | 1 | |
| Organization type: | Private | |

**Company Literature** (This information was obtained from the company's website without independent verification.)
Coral Venture, a private venture capital firm specializing in the technology and healthcare industries, manages more than $300 million of capital in five funds and has invested in some 60 companies nationwide. We believe that outstanding, entrepreneurial management teams with energy and vision—backed by a venture capital firm supporting that vision with perseverance and long-term commitment—can develop companies that will become the market leaders to tomorrow. We take an active role in our portfolio companies. The Partners use their extensive experience as entrepreneurs, executives, and venture capitalists to found and build enterprises that create substantial market value and generate high financial returns for their investors. While we are primarily interested in emerging and early stage companies, we also invest selectively in larger stage opportunities. Our limited partners include corporate and private placement funds, universities, foundations, and individuals.

**What Sets This Service Apart?** Experienced investors with a track record, references from current and past portfolio companies regarding our value-added assistance, seed early/stage investing.

# Environmental Capital Network

**Region: Great Lakes**

Mr. Keith Raab
Environmental Capital Network
416 Longshore Drive
Ann Arbor, MI 48105

tel: (734) 996-8387
fax: (734) 996-8732
e-mail: kraab@recycle.com
http://bizserve.com/ecn/

| | |
|---|---|
| Classification of service: | A formal matching service |
| Date of formation: | Sept. 1994 |
| Industry preferences: | Companies commercializing environmental technologies, products, or services |
| Stage of firms preferred: | Seed, start-up, early, and expansion |
| Matching methods: | Newsletter, investor-specified criteria and forums |
| Primary matching method: | Venture Forums |
| No. of employees:   Full-time: | 4 |
| Part-time: | |
| Organization type: | Not for profit |
| Firms featured by service: | 10% Seed, 25% Start-up, 50% Early, 15% Expansion |
| Additional services offered: | Investor to investor networking. Business plan reviews for companies by investors. Raising capital training seminars for entrepreneurs. Annual Investors only conference. |

| | |
|---|---|
| No. of investors participating: | 200 |
| No. firms seen by investors/yr: | 150 |
| No. of venture forums/yr: | 2–3 |
| No. firms using forum/yr: | 45 |
| $ range sought:   Typical max: | $10M |
| Typical min: | $250K |
| Average: | $3M |
| Investors invested thru service: | NA |
| Successful matches:   1997: | NA |
| 1998: | NA |
| Since formation: | NA |
| Service actively screen firms?: | No |

**Company Literature**
The Environmental Capital Network is a not for profit organization offering specialized services that introduce individual, professional, and corporate investors to early and expansion stage companies and assist firms commercializing a wide range of industrial processes, energy, and environmental technologies, products, and services. Our goal is to be recognized as the environmental technology and service industry's most successful networking and capital sourcing service. To this end, our organization is working to become more proactive in matching promising companies with potential investors and service providers. The Environmental Capital Network creates value through its growing proprietary network of active investors specializing in this field, its highly regarded products, and its growing national and international recognition by environmental technology companies and service providers.

**What Sets This Service Apart?**   Environmental technology focus. Full service membership organization assisting companies at all stages of development. Our forums are the largest consolidation of investors interested in environmental technologies in the nation.

# Minnesota Investment Network Corporation (MIN-Corp.)

**Region: Great Lakes**

Mr. Steve Mercil
Minnesota Investment Network Corporation (MIN-Corp.)
111 Third Avenue South
Suite 420
Minneapolis, MN 55401

tel: (612) 672-3474
fax: (612) 339-5214
e-mail: mincorp@mincorp.org
http://www.mincorp.org

| | |
|---|---|
| Classification of service: | Other—Venture Capital |
| Date of formation: | 1998 |
| Industry preferences: | Manufacturing and high-tech |
| Stage of firms preferred: | Seed, start-up, early, and expansion stages |
| Matching methods: | Present deal floor for organized angels |
| Primary matching method: | Other, Present deal floor for organized angels |
| No. of employees: Full-time: | 4 |
| Part-time: | 1 Intern |
| Volunteer: | |
| Organization type: | Not for profit |

| | |
|---|---|
| No. of investors participating: | 20 |
| No. of firms seen by investors/yr: | 10 thus far |
| No. of venture forums/yr: | N/A |
| No. of firms using forum/yr: | 16 in group thus far |
| $ range sought: | 10% of fund |
| Typical max: | $50K |
| Typical min: | $250K |
| Average: | |
| Investors invested thru service: | 20 |
| Successful matches: 1997: | 6 |
| 1998: | 3 |
| Since formation: | 22 |
| Service actively screen firms?: | Yes |

Firms featured by service:  25% Seed, 25% Start-up, 25% Early, 25% Expansion

**Company Literature  (This information was obtained from the company's website without independent verification.)**
Minnesota Investment Network Cooperation (MIN-Corp.) is a not-for-profit venture fund with a purpose to promote community economic development by building the capacity for equity investment primarily in rural Minnesota's companies. An essential short fall in the equity investment infrastructure in rural Minnesota is the lack of local networks for angel investors committed to investing in companies that will build the local economy. Currently, MIN-Corp. is assisting in the formation of formal investment groups (Regional Angel Investor Network Organization Groups) set up as limited liability corporations. Previously, MIN-Corp. assisted in the organization and expansion of Lakes Venture Group, LLC in Alexandria, Minnesota. Based on this experience, MIN-Corp. has developed a template to foster the development of ten Regional Angel Investor Network Groups around rural Minnesota. This template (Regional Angel Investor Network Template) contains the ingredients and recipe necessary to brew a Regional Angel Investor Network Group. In an attempt to limit professional fees, MIN-Corp. provides all the ingredients or materials in paper and electronic format for easy and quick customization. MIN-Corp. will participate as a member contributing up to 10% of all other committed capital not to exceed $100,000 per group. To aid in limiting operating expenses MIN-Corp. will provide administrative assistance.

# National Business Incubation Association

**Region: Great Lakes**

Ms. Dinah Adkins
National Business Incubation Association
20 East Circle Drive, Suite 190
Athens, OH 45701

tel: (740) 593-4331
fax: (740) 593-1996
e-mail: dadkins@nbia.org
http://www.nbia.org

| | | | |
|---|---|---|---|
| Classification of service: | Our members work with angels and start-up and emerging companies | No. of investors participating: | Unknown |
| | | No. firms seen by investors/yr: | Unknown |
| Date of formation: | 1985 | No. of venture forums/yr: | NA |
| Industry preferences: | NA | No. firms using forum/yr: | NA |
| Stage of firms preferred: | Seed, start-up, and early stage | $ range sought:    Typical max: | NA |
| Matching methods: | | Typical min: | NA |
| Primary matching method: | NA | Average: | NA |
| No. of employees:    Full-time: | 7 | Investors invested thru service: | Unknown |
| Part-time: | 6 | Successful matches:    1997: | NA |
| Volunteer: | Many | 1998: | NA |
| Organization type: | Not for profit | Since formation: | NA |
| | | Service actively screen firms?: | No |
| Additional services offered: | Information on angels, how to contact angels, and how to prepare companies for equity investment. | | |

**Company Literature**   (This information was obtained from the company's website without independent verification.)
Business Incubation is a dynamic process of business enterprise development incubators nurture young firms, helping them to survive and grow during the start-up period when they are most vulnerable. Incubators provide hands-on management assistance, access to financing and orchestrated exposure to critical business or technical support services. They also offer entrepreneurial firms shared office services, access to equipment, flexible leases and expandable space—all under one roof. An incubation program's main goal is to produce successful graduates, businesses that are financially viable and freestanding when they leave the incubator, usually in two to three years. Thirty percent of incubator clients typically graduates each year. The National Business Incubation Association is a private, not-for-profit 501 (c) (3) membership organization with headquarters in Athens, Ohio. The Association is governed by an elected 15-member voting Board of Directors representing the nation's leading incubators.

**What Sets This Service Apart?**   Hands-on contact with entrepreneurs and investors.

# Private Investors Network

**Region: Great Lakes**

Mr. Dave Miller
Private Investors Network
Bloomington Small Business Development Center
216 W. Allen Street
Bloomington, IN 47403

tel: (812) 339-8937
fax: (812) 335-7352
http://www.thestarcenter.com

| | |
|---|---|
| Classification of service: | A grp. Of angel investors |
| Date of formation: | 1996 |
| Industry preferences: | Information tech and health care |
| Stage of firms preferred: | Start-up and early |
| Matching methods: | Venture forums and breakfast meetings and monthly mailing |
| Primary matching method: | Venture forums |
| No. of employees: Full-time: | 0 |
| Part-time: | 0 |
| Volunteer: | 6 |
| Organization type: | Not for profit |
| Firms featured by service: | 15% Seed, 40% Start-up, 30% Early, 15% Expansion |
| Additional services offered: | Access to Mid-Atlantic Venture Association activities; membership in Baltimore-Washington Venture Group. |

| | |
|---|---|
| No. of investors participating: | 126 dues paying members |
| No. firms seen by investors/yr: | 125 |
| No. of venture forums/yr: | Monthly breakfast meetings |
| No. firms using forum/yr: | 30 |
| $ range sought: Typical max: | 3 mil |
| Typical min: | 500K |
| Average: | 1 mil |
| Investors invested thru service: | 22+ |
| Successful matches: 1997: | 10 |
| 1998: | 12 |
| Since formation: | NA |
| Service actively screen firms?: | Yes (passively) |

**Company Literature**   (**This information was obtained from the company's website without independent verification.**) The Private Investors Network (PIN) is an angel network that brings together accredited investors and emerging growth companies in the Mid-Atlantic region (Maryland, Virginia and the District of Columbia). These angels are principals who invest in private equity transactions raising between $250,000 and $3 million. With background as cashed-out entrepreneurs, institutional investors, and individuals, PIN members can provide entrepreneurs with access to capital, management expertise, and other critical resources. The Mid-Atlantic Venture Association (MAVA) is PIN's parent organization. MAVA and PIN's affiliate, the Baltimore-Washington Venture Group, provide additional support for PIN.

**What Sets This Service Apart?**   Nonprofit "angel" investors. Only monthly meetings. Tied to a venture capital trade association.

# Southeastern Michigan Venture Group

**Region: Great Lakes**

Mr. Kevin J. Reitzloff
Southeastern Michigan Venture Group
P.O. Box 36452
Grosse Pointe, MI 48236

tel: (810) 772-0222
fax: (810) 772-4093
e-mail: BuckmAssoc@aol.com
http://www.semug.com

| | | |
|---|---|---|
| Classification of service: | Breakfast luncheon | |
| Date of formation: | 1985 | |
| Industry preferences: | No preferences | |
| Stage of firms preferred: | Start-up and early stage | |
| Matching methods: | Inernet and newsletter | |
| Primary matching method: | Meetings | |
| No. of employees: Full-time: | | |
| Part-time: | | |
| Volunteer: | 12 | |
| Organization type: | Not for profit | |
| | | |
| Firms featured by service: | 20% Seed, 30% Start-up, 30% Early, 20% Expansion | |

| | |
|---|---|
| No. of investors participating: | 30 |
| No. firms seen by investors/yr: | 50 |
| No. of venture forums/yr: | Not Applicable |
| No. firms using forum/yr: | Not Applicable |
| $ range sought: Typical max: | 3 mil |
| Typical min: | 250K |
| Average: | 1 mil |
| Investors invested thru service: | NA |
| Successful matches: 1997: | NA |
| 1998: | NA |
| Since formation: | NA |
| Service actively screen firms?: | Yes |

**Company Literature** (This information was obtained from the company's website without independent verification.)
The key to the Southeastern Michigan Venture Group (SEMVG) is networking. Meeting people that have complementary professional interests in an effort to form dynamic, productive relationships. We strive to be within the community for small and medium size businesses to meet and work with financing sources and providers of professional services to produce results. Our monthly meetings provide a forum for entrepreneurs to meet and explain their companies to potential investors. In addition, our members include a diverse mix of business professionals, such as attorneys, consultants, and accountants. They can provide valuable assistance in developing an entrepreneur's company.

**What Sets This Service Apart?** We offer a network of service providers, lenders, as well as investors. This provides entrepreneurs with a complete package of assistance.

**Region: Great Lakes**

Beth Dunham
The Collaborative
10 South 5th Street, Suite 415
Minneapolis, MN 55402-1004

tel: (612) 338-3828
fax: (612) 338-1876
e-mail: info@collaborative-online.com
http://www.collaborative-online.com

| | | | |
|---|---|---|---|
| Classification of service: | Full service, 750-member organization and publisher | No. of investors participating: | NA |
| | | No. of firms seen by investors/yr: | NA |
| | | No. of venture forums/yr: | NA |
| Date of formation: | 1987 | No. of firms using forum/yr: | NA |
| Industry preferences: | NA | $ range sought: Typical max: | NA |
| Stage of firms preferred: | NA | Typical min: | NA |
| Matching methods: | NA | Average: | NA |
| Primary matching method: | NA | | |
| No. of employees: Full-time: | 7 | Investors invested thru service: | NA |
| Part-time: | NA | Successful matches: 1997: | NA |
| Volunteer: | NA | 1998: | NA |
| | | Since formation: | NA |
| Organization type: | Private | | |

**Company Literature** (This information was obtained from the company's website without independent verification.)
The Collaborative assembles and distributes high-quality information from the real-life experiences of our network through programs and published materials and by facilitating communication among our members. We help provide solutions to problem all merging businesses face, with an unmatched resource of local expertise. With more than 750 members, The Collaborative is the largest membership organization in Minnesota serving growth-oriented, emerging market companies. Our mission is to simulate company growth through the collective knowledge and expertise of our members—entrepreneurs, managers, investors, and professionals. Founded in 1987 as the subscription-based publication, New Venture Review, we became The Collaborative in 1989 with the addition of meetings and workshops. We have since steadily expanded the services we provide, both in publications and innovative programs.

# Venture Club of Indiana, Inc.

**Region: Great Lakes**

Ms. Margo Jaqua
Venture Club of Indiana, Inc.
P.O. Box 40872
Indianapolis, IN 46240-0872

tel: (317) 253-1244
fax: (317) 253-1211
e-mail: mmjaqua@msn.com
http://www.ventureclub.org

| | | | |
|---|---|---|---|
| Classification of service: | Breakfast luncheon | No. of investors participating: | 287 members |
| Date of formation: | 1984 | No. of firms seen by investors/yr: | 24 |
| Industry preferences: | N/A | No. of venture forums/yr: | 12 |
| Stage of firms preferred: | Start-up, early, and expansion | No. of firms using forum/yr: | 24 |
| Matching methods: | Newsletter and venture forums | $ range sought: Typical max: | $2 mil |
| Primary matching method: | Venture Forums | Typical min: | $200K |
| No. of employees: Full-time: | | Average: | $1 mil |
| Part-time: | 1 | Investors invested thru service: | NA |
| Volunteer: | | Successful matches: 1997: | NA |
| | | 1998: | NA |
| Organization type: | Not for profit | Since formation: | NA |
| | | Service actively screen firms?: | Yes |
| Additional services offered: | Networking among the membership | | |

**Company Literature**  (This information was obtained from the company's website without independent verification.)

The Venture Club of Indiana is a not-for-profit organization founded in 1984 to act as a catalyst for capital flow and business assistance to emerging businesses. Current membership consists of 287 individuals from the investment and business formation community the Club meets monthly; at each meeting, two entrepreneurs are given the opportunity to present their business plans and to discuss their capital needs with the membership. This forum provides an opportunity for entrepreneurs to interact with diverse resources that would not otherwise be together in one place. Each monthly meeting also features a guest speaker of note who presents experiences and insights on topics relevant to entrepreneurs.

# Wisconsin Venture Network

**Region: Great Lakes**

Mr. James R. Lang
Wisconsin Venture Network
P.O. Box 51030
Milwaukee, WI 53202-0021

tel: (414) 224-7070
fax: (414) 271-4016
http://www.maxnetwork.com/wvn.

| | | |
|---|---|---|
| Classification of service: | A luncheon meeting | |
| Date of formation: | 1983 | |
| Industry preferences: | None | |
| Stage of firms preferred: | Early stage | |
| Matching methods: | Newsletter and venture forums | |
| Primary matching method: | Investor-specified criteria and venture forums | |
| No. of employees: Full-time: | | NA |
| Part-time: | | NA |
| Volunteer: | Board of directors | NA |
| Organization type: | Not for profit | |
| Firms featured by service: | 33% Seed, 33% Start-up, 33% Early | |
| Additional services offered: | Venture review panel—service which critiques presentation, business plan, and concept. | |

| | |
|---|---|
| No. of investors participating: | 12+ |
| No. firms seen by investors/yr: | 200+ |
| No. of venture forums/yr: | 2 |
| No. firms using forum/yr: | 150+ |
| $ range sought: Typical max: | $2 mil |
| Typical min: | $200K |
| Average: | $500–100K |
| Investors invested thru service: | NA |
| Successful matches: 1997: | NA |
| 1998: | NA |
| Since formation: | NA |
| Service actively screen firms?: | No |

**Company Literature** **(This information was obtained from the company's website without independent verification.)**
The Wisconsin Venture Network (WVN) came to life in late 1983. The WVN is a forum where entrepreneurs can routinely talk to investors and other resource people. It is a place where referrals to the right type of "help" can be made. The WVN is where encouragement and empathy can be expressed, and where real progress can be made in making a specific deal truly happen. The resources of the WVN are available to any individual or firm interested in funding or managing a business. The Network assists both start-ups and companies in the later stages of growth. To be part of the WVN, all you need is the entrepreneurial spirit.

**What Sets This Service Apart?** We offer a very broad forum for investors and entrepreneurs to make introduction to their plans and criteria.

# Baltimore Washington Venture Group

**Region: Mid-Atlantic**

Dr. Charles Heller, Baltimore Washington Venture Group
Dingman Center for Entrepreneurship
The University of Maryland Business School
College Park, MD 20742-1815

tel: (301) 405-2144
fax: (301) 314-9152
e-mail: dingman@mbs.umd.edu
http://www.mbs.umd.edu/dingman/

| | | | |
|---|---|---|---|
| Classification of service: | Group of angels, Breakfast/luncheon | No. of investors participating: | 125 |
| Date of formation: | 1982 | No. of firms seen by investors/yr: | 100 |
| Industry preferences: | Technology | No. of venture forums/yr: | 1 |
| Stage of firms preferred: | Seed, start-up, early stage | No. firms using forum/yr: | 100+ |
| Matching methods: | Newsletter, investor-specified criteria, venture forums | $ range sought:  Typical max: | $2 mil |
| | | Typical min: | $200K |
| Primary matching method: | Private investors network (deals presented | Average: | $500K |
| | monthly at investors meetings) | Investors invested thru service: | 25 |
| No. of employees:  Full-time: | 6 | Successful matches:  1997: | 3 |
| Part-time: | 9 | 1998: | 5 |
| Volunteer: | 20 | Since formation: | 15 |
| Organization type: | Private, not for profit, university affiliated | Service actively screen firms?: | Yes |
| Firms featured by service: | 30% Seed, 40% Start-up, 30% Early | | |
| Additional services offered: | Networking breakfast; presentations or circulation of selected deals to Garage.com; directory; quarterly newsletter; coaching; business plans reviews. | | |

**Company Literature  (This information was obtained from the company's website without independent verification.)**
The Dingman Center for Entrepreneurship is part of the Robert H. Smith School of Business at the University of Maryland, College Park. It was established in 1986, with the seed capital provided by Michael D. Dingman, chairman and CEO of Shipston Group Limited, and an alumnus of UMCP. In 1990, the Dingman Center new director, Dr. Charles O. Heller, set up a dual goal for the Dingman Center of: a) becoming the focal point for entrepreneurship in Maryland and the surrounding region by virtue of creating the major resouce center for entrepreneurship in the area, and b) becoming one of the top-tier academic centers for the entrepreneurship in the nation. Since that time, the Center has made tremendous progress, and it is well on its way to all its objectives. The keystone of the Dingman Center's outreach is its mentor program. Nearly 200 volunteer mentors—successful entrepreneurs, attorneys, accountants, executives, and faculty—have assisted more than 300 early stage companies in nearly every area of business and management. The Center's Baltimore-Washington Venture Group (in partnership with the Private Investors Network) is playing a vital role in facilitating private equity investments in, and loans to, emerging growth firms; more than $4 million has been invested in the region's companies in recent months through PIN. The Dingman Center's education and networking programs—seminars, roundtables, workshops, conferences, and short courses—have become the best-attended business-related programs in the region. It hosts special conferences, including its annual Venture Capital Forum and several events for woman entrepreneurs—for Maryland and Northern Virginia. The Dingman Center also serves as a "window" into the University's expertise for emerging growth firms and works closely with companies in the region's incubators. It has an active international program, with primary activities in The Bahamas and the Czech Republic.

**What Sets This Service Apart?**   We provide an opportunity for face-to-face meetings of investors and founders; we have 200 mentors who assist entrepreneurs.

# Ben Franklin Technology Center of Southeastern Pennsylvania

**Region: Mid-Atlantic**

Ms. Elizabeth Hofheinz      tel: (215) 382-0380
Ben Franklin Technology Center of Southeastern Pennsylvania    fax: (215) 387-6050
University City Science Center      http://www.benfranklin.org
3624 Market Street
Philadelphia, PA 19104-2615

| | | | |
|---|---|---|---|
| Classification of service: | Group of angel investors and electronic-only network | No. of investors participating: | NA |
| Date of formation: | 1983 | No. of firms seen by investors/yr: | NA |
| Industry preferences: | None | No. of venture forums/yr: | 1 |
| Stage of firms preferred: | NA | No. of firms using forum/yr: | 8 to 10 |
| Matching methods: | Venture forums and regular monthly meetings | $ range sought:   Typical max: | NA |
| Primary matching method: | Regular monthly meetings | Typical min: | NA |
| No. of employees:  Full-time: | 30 | Average: | NA |
| Part-time: | | Investors invested thru service: | NA |
| Volunteer: | | Successful matches:    1997: | NA |
| | | 1998: | NA |
| Organization type: | Not for profit and subsidized by state government | Since formation: | NA |
| | | Service actively screen firms?: | NA |

Additional services offered:   Programs that support the investing process, monthly membership meetings.

## The Dinner Club, LLC

**Region: Mid-Atlantic**

Mr. John May
The Dinner Club, LLC
402 Maple Ave. W.
Vienna, VA 22180

tel: (703) 255-4930
fax: (703) 255-4931
e-mail: john@thedinnerclub.com
http://www.thedinnerclub.com

| | |
|---|---|
| Classification of service: | A group of angel investors |
| Date of formation: | 1999 |
| Industry preferences: | High-tech |
| Stage of firms preferred: | |
| Matching methods: | Internet, newsletter, and venture forums |
| Primary matching method: | Venture forums |
| No. of employees: Full-time: | |
| Part-time: | 3 |
| Volunteer: | |
| Organization type: | Private |

| | |
|---|---|
| No. of investors participating: | 50 |
| No. firms seen by investors/yr: | 24 |
| No. of venture forums/yr: | 11 |
| No. firms using forum/yr: | 24 |
| $ range sought: Typical max: | $3 mil |
| Typical min: | $500K |
| Average: | $1.5 mil |
| Investors invested thru service: | NA |
| Successful matches: 1997: | Not Tracked |
| 1998: | Not Tracked |
| Since formation: | Not Tracked |
| Service actively screen firms?: | Yes |

**Company Literature** (This information was obtained from the company's website without independent verification.)
The Dinner Club is a group of regional angel investors who collectively make early-stage private equity investments into promising new ventures which have the prospect of achieving a high rate of return. The Club meets once a month for dinner and presentations by entrepreneurs, after which the Club votes on whether or not to make investments.

**What Sets This Service Apart?** Manager-led private investor investment club.

# Hampton Roads Private Investors Network

**Region: Mid-Atlantic**

Mr. Jim Carrol
Hampton Roads Private Investors Network
Small Business Development Center (SBDC)
400 Volvo Parkway
Chesapeake, VA 23320

tel: (757) 664-2592
fax: (757) 548-1835
e-mail: jcarrol@hrccva.com
http://www.hrccva.com

| | |
|---|---|
| Classification of service: | A group of angel investors |
| Date of formation: | N/A |
| Industry preferences: | Seed, start-up, early |
| Stage of firms preferred: | Newsletter and venture forums |
| Matching methods: | Investor-specified criteria |
| Primary matching method: | 1 |
| No. of employees: Full-time: | 1 |
| Part-time: | |
| Volunteer: | |
| Organization type: | Private, not for profit |

| | |
|---|---|
| No. of investors participating: | 25 |
| No. firms seen by investors/yr: | 10 |
| No. of venture forums/yr: | NA |
| No. firms using forum/yr: | NA |
| $ range sought: Typical max: | $500K |
| Typical min: | $10K |
| Average: | $200 |
| Investors invested thru service: | 4 |
| Successful matches: 1997: | 3 |
| 1998: | 1 |
| Since formation: | 4 |
| Service actively screen firms?: | No |

**Company Literature** (This information was obtained from the company's website without independent verification.)
The Hampton Roads Private Investors Network provides entrepreneurs with a cost-effective method for finding private sources of seed and start-up capital, and in turn, provides investors with a convenient, confidential, method for uncovering early-state or high-growth companies. Operating under the auspices of the Small Business Development Center of Hampton Roads, Inc., the Network is a not-for-profit service/educational organization, and charges only a flat fee for its services. The Network manages a confidential database containing names and information about investors and entrepreneurs. Investors complete an application indicating their investment criteria or preferences, and certifying they are a qualified investor. Entrepreneurs complete an executive summary and submit a profile of their venture to the Network. The information from the application is entered into the Network's computer matching system which searches the database for a match between investor requirements and the entrepreneur's need for capital. The Network then sends information about the business opportunity in a confidential format to the investors whose investment criteria matches the entrepreneurial profile. Investors may then require an introduction or make direct contact with the companies that are of interest to them, or match their profile. The Hampton Roads Private Investors Network matching process ends with the formal introduction.

**What Sets This Service Apart?** Local concentration on Hampton Roads businesses/ventures

## MIT Enterprise Forum of Pittsburgh, Inc.

**Region: Mid-Atlantic**

Mr. Phillip H. Smith
MIT Enterprise Forum of Pittsburgh, Inc.
Smith, Yuill & Company, Inc.
102 Haverford Road
Pittsburgh, PA 15238

tel: (412) 967-9335
fax: (412) 963-7910

| | | |
|---|---|---|
| Classification of service: | Evening Forums / Panel reviews / Q&A | |
| Date of formation: | 1973 | |
| Industry preferences: | High-tech | |
| Stage of firms preferred: | Early, expansion stage, and organizations in trouble who need help | |
| Matching methods: | Venture forums | |
| Primary matching method: | Just forums | |
| No. of employees:  Full-time: | 0 | |
| Part-time: | 0 | |
| Volunteer: | 16 | |
| Organization type: | Not for profit | |
| Additional services offered: | We match mentors to start-ups if they ask for them. | |

| | |
|---|---|
| No. of investors participating: | 5 to 6 |
| No. firms seen by investors/yr: | NA |
| No. of venture forums/yr: | 8 to 10 |
| No. firms using forum/yr: | NA |
| $ range sought:    Typical max: | NA |
| Typical min: | NA |
| Average: | NA |
| Investors invested thru service: | 60+ |
| Successful matches:    1997: | Not Tracked |
| 1998: | Not Tracked |
| Since formation: | Not Tracked |
| Service actively screen firms?: | Yes |

**What Sets This Service Apart?**    We operate on the same principles as the MIT Forum in Cambridge—help start-ups.

## Pennsylvania Private Investors Group

**Region: Mid-Atlantic**

Lennart Hagegard
Pennsylvania Private Investors Group
3625 Market Street, Suite 200
Philadelphia, PA 19104

tel: (800) 288-3302
fax: (215) 387-6050
http://www.ppig.com

| | |
|---|---|
| Classification of service: | Formal matching service |
| Date of formation: | |
| Industry preferences: | Tech |
| Stage of firms preferred: | Early stage |
| Matching methods: | Internet, newsletter, investor specified criteria, and venture forums |
| Primary matching method: | Investor-specified criteria |
| No. of employees:  Full-time: | 3 |
| Part-time: | 10 |
| Volunteer: | |
| Organization type: | Not for profit |
| | |
| Firms featured by service: | 5% Seed, 30% Start-up, 50% Early, 10% Expansion, 5% Other |
| Additional services offered: | Educational services |

| | |
|---|---|
| No. of investors participating: | 35 |
| No. firms seen by investors/yr: | 25 |
| No. of venture forums/yr: | 10–11 |
| No. firms using forum/yr: | 25–30 |
| $ range sought:  Typical max: | $2 mil |
| Typical min: | $250K |
| Average: | $1 mil |
| Investors invested thru service: | 30 |
| Successful matches:  1997: | 3 |
| 1998: | 2 |
| Since formation: | 10 |
| Service actively screen firms?: | Yes |

**Company Literature**  (This information was obtained from the company's website without independent verification.)

Pennsylvania Private Investors Group (PPIG) is dedicated to providing a forum for entrepreneurs to present their business plans to investors for the purpose of obtaining financing. The members of PPIG are sophisticated individuals and institutional investors who invest in small, privately held, early-stage companies. PPIG is not an investments pool. The members make their own investment decisions and negotiate terms of their investment directly with the companies. PPIG is administered by the Ben Franklin Technology Center of Southeastern Pennsylvania and the Wharton Small Business Development Center.

**What Sets This Service Apart?**  Professional screening, educational seminars.

# Indiana Business Modernization and Technology Corporation

**Region: Midwest**

Mr. Bill Glennon
Indiana Business Modernization
and Technology Corporation
1 N. Capitol Ave., Suite 925
Indianapolis, IN 46204

tel: (317) 635-3058
fax: (317) 231-7095
e-mail: bglennon@bmtadvantage.org
http://www.bmtadvantage.org

| | | | |
|---|---|---|---|
| Classification of service: | Make loans | No. of investors participating: | NA |
| Date of formation: | 1982 | No. of firms seen by investors/yr: | 40 |
| Industry preferences: | Manufacturing and software | No. of venture forums/yr: | 1 |
| Stage of firms preferred: | Seed, start-up, early, and expansion stage | No. firms using forum/yr: | 30 |
| Matching methods: | Venture forums and loans and | $ range sought: Typical max: | $10M |
| | technical assistance | Typical min: | $100K |
| Primary matching method: | Venture forums | Average: | $2M |
| | | Investors invested thru service: | NA |
| No. of employees: Full-time: | 40 | Successful matches: 1997: | 10 |
| Part-time: | 10 | 1998: | 10 |
| Volunteer: | Many | | |
| Organization type: | Not for profit and partially subsidized | Since formation: | |
| | by the state and federal government. | Service actively screen firms?: | NA |
| Firms featured by service: | 20% Seed, 20% Start-up, 40% Early, 20% Expansion | | |

**Company Literature** (This information was obtained from the company's website without independent verification.)
The Indiana Business Modernization and Technology Corporation (BMT) has developed specialized programs and services that focus on
the needs of our clients. Experienced professionals from BMT's direct and affiliated programs can offer the guidance you need to meet
the day-to-day challenges of running a business, tackle special technical and business issues, and help solve industry wide problems such
as workforce shortages. Through its wide array of programs, BMT has helped thousands of Indiana companies increase sales, improve
cash flow, reduce costs and access a world of business, technology, and financial resources.

# Kansas Technology Enterprise Corporation

## Region: Midwest

Mr. Richard A. Bendis
Kansas Technology Enterprise Corporation
214 SW 6th, First Floor
Topeka, KS 66603-3719

tel: (785) 296-5272
fax: (785) 296-1160
e-mail: Rbendis@ktec.com
http://www.ktec.com

| | | | |
|---|---|---|---|
| Classification of service: | Technology economic development investment holding company. | No. of investors participating: | 60 |
| | | No. firms seen by investors/yr: | 25 |
| Date of formation: | 1986 | No. of venture forums/yr: | 2 |
| Industry preferences: | Technology | No. firms using forum/yr: | 15 |
| Stage of firms preferred: | Seed, start-up, and early stage | $ range sought:   Typical max: | $2 mil |
| Matching methods: | Internet, newsletter, investor | Typical min: | $50K |
| | criteria, and forums | Average: | $500K |
| Primary matching method: | Internet | Investors invested thru service: | NA |
| No. of employees:  Full-time: | 17 | Successful matches:     1997: | 10 |
| Part-time: | | 1998: | 12 |
| Volunteer: | Many | Since formation: | NA |
| Organization type: | Not for profit | Service actively screen firms?: | Yes |
| Firms featured by service: | 60% Seed, 20% Start-up, 20% Early | | |

**Company Literature**  (This information was obtained from the company's website without independent verification.)
The Kansas Technology Enterprise Corporation (KTEC) is a Renaissance network. Whether it's through the science of technology research or the art of valuing a start-up company, KTEC is the architect of a comprehensive technology economic development network in Kansas. At KTEC, we have designed and built an integrated, statewide network to support researchers, inventors, and business through each phase of the technology life cycle; from a basic idea to a successful product. Our many programs and affiliate organizations' functional areas include research, investment, and business assistance. Whether you are a university researcher, a small company looking for financing, an entrepreneur writing a business plan, or an established company developing technology, we can help you realize your goals. The innovative structure of the KTEC network, and the quality and diversity of programs, has positioned Kansas as a model for other states. Kansas is recognized both nationally and internationally as a leader in using commercialization of technology as a foundation for economic development. Inventors and companies today must work quickly to develop technologies before the commercial window of opportunity closes. KTEC has the expertise and resources to help speed up the development process and turn innovative ideas into marketable products.

**What Sets This Service Apart?**  Diversified portfolio of other programs.

291

# Missouri Venture Forum

**Region: Midwest**

Mr. Tom W. Siegel
Missouri Venture Forum
917 Locust, 5th Floor
St. Louis, MO 63101

tel: (314) 241-2683
fax: (314) 621-2529

| | |
|---|---|
| Classification of service: | A breakfast luncheon |
| Date of formation: | 1985 |
| Industry preferences: | None |
| Stage of firms preferred: | Seed, start-up, early, and expansion |
| Matching methods: | Newsletter, investor-specified criteria and forums |
| Primary matching method: | Newsletter |
| No. of employees: Full-time: | 4 |
| Part-time: | |
| Volunteer: | 30+ |
| Organization type: | Not for profit |
| Firms featured by service: | 35% Seed, 30% Start-up, 30% Early, 5% Expansion, Other |

| | |
|---|---|
| No. of investors participating: | 50+ |
| No. firms seen by investors/yr: | 30 |
| No. of venture forums/yr: | 10+ 1 major conference |
| No. firms using forum/yr: | 3 |
| $ range sought: Typical max: | $5 mil |
| Typical min: | $25K |
| Average: | $250K |
| Investors invested thru service: | 20–30 |
| Successful matches: 1997: | 3 |
| 1998: | 3 |
| Since formation: | 15–20 |
| Service actively screen firms?: | Yes |

**Company Literature** (This information was obtained from the company's website without independent verification.)
Missouri Venture Forum is a not-for-profit organization formed in 1985 that serves as a catalyst bringing together the people genuinely interested in helping entrepreneurs. Entrepreneurial activity and access to capital is facilitated through: networking, education, and information exchange. Members are interested in helping businesses find the capital required to grow and prosper. Missouri Venture Forum's mission is to provide a means for investors and entrepreneurs to make mutually beneficial relationships, designed to drive new business formation and growth, through networking, education, and information exchange.

**What Sets This Service Apart?** The Missouri Venture Forum is a very dynamic, growing organization with arguably the best networking opportunity in the region. Each meeting also features a proven entrepreneur or financier as our main speaker.

# The Meyering Corporation

**Region: Midwest**

Mr. Carl Meyering
The Meyering Corporation
20630 Harper Ave. Suite 103
Harper Woods, Mi 48225

tel: (313) 886-2331
fax: (313) 886-5237
e-mail: cmeyering@ameritech.net

| | | | |
|---|---|---|---|
| Classification of service: | Group of Angels | No. of investors participating: | 24 |
| Date of formation: | 1967 | No. firms seen by investors/yr: | 12 |
| Industry preferences: | MFC tech. and new patents | No. of venture forums/yr: | Not Applicable |
| Stage of firms preferred: | Seed, start-ups, early, expansion | No. firms using forum/yr: | Not Applicable |
| | stage, and patents | $ range sought:     Typical max: | $1.5 mil |
| Matching methods: | Investor-specified criteria | Typical min: | $250K |
| Primary matching method: | Investor-specified criteria | Average: | $500K |
| No. of employees:   Full-time: | 4 | Investors invested thru service: | 50 |
| Part-time: | | Successful matches:    1997: | 4 |
| Volunteer: | | 1998: | 5 |
| Organization type: | Private | Since formation: | 67 |
| | | Service actively screen firms?: | Yes |
| Firms featured by service: | 10% Seed, 20% Start-up, 10% Early, 60% Expansion | | |
| Additional services offered: | Have contacts to match funds over our decrease limit | | |

**Company Literature**   (This information was obtained from the company's website without independent verification.)
The Meyering Corporation got into the funding angel industry because it was unable to find business deals and was turned down by the local banks. Carl Meyering approached a group of other young businesses to form an investing group to help each other. The group matured into the angel group as each man became successful. Our success attracted other angels who had the same funding problems and had the desire to assist others who have good ideas and no funding. Our approach is different for each deal as each deal is different from the other. We are very palpable in our inventing style. Funding should match cash flow needs and meet the financial emergencies that occur in every business. Over the years we have developed major contacts in every industry that we have an investment interest in. This gives us a leg-up on the competition. Fairness on both sides of a deal generally insures success.

**What Sets This Service Apart?**   We have all the contacts in all the industries we are interested in.

# Venture Network of Iowa

**Region: Midwest**

Mr. Brice Nelson
Venture Network of Iowa
Iowa Department of Economic Development
200 E. Grand Ave
Des Moines, IA 50309

tel: (800) 532-1216
fax: (515) 242-4776
e-mail: smallbiz@ided.state.ia.us
http://www.state.ia.us/sbro

| | |
|---|---|
| Classification of service: | A formal matching service |
| Date of formation: | 1993 |
| Industry preferences: | None |
| Stage of firms preferred: | All quality opportunities regardless of their stage of development |
| Matching methods: | Internet and venture forums |
| Primary matching method: | Venture forum |
| No. of employees: Full-time: | 1 |
| Part-time: | |
| Volunteer: | 25 |
| Organization type: | Subsidized by government |
| Firms featured by service: | 10% Seed, 10% Start-up, 50% Early, 30% Expansion |
| Additional services offered: | Networking services in a variety of ways including state program assistance, marketing, networking, establishing matching services. |

| | |
|---|---|
| No. of investors participating: | 100 |
| No. of firms seen by investors/yr: | 25–25 |
| No. of venture forums/yr: | 5 |
| No. of firms using forum/yr: | 4–5 |
| $ range sought: Typical max: | $5 mil |
| Typical min: | $100K |
| Average: | $400K |
| Investors invested thru service: | 25% |
| Successful matches: 1997: | 6 |
| 1998: | 7 |
| Since formation: | Not Tracked |
| Service actively screen firms?: | Yes |

**Company Literature** (This information was obtained from the company's website without independent verification.)
Venture Network of Iowa (VNI) is an excellent resource for the formation of new, viable businesses throughout Iowa. Every other month, VNI provides interactive networking sessions that are broadcast live via the state's fiber optic communications network to multiple locations statewide. Iowa inventors and entrepreneurs can interact with investors in the hope of forging profitable, long-term business relationships. VNI enhances Iowa's entrepreneurial climate and accelerates the rate of Iowa business formation and growth by providing a forum in which Iowa entrepreneurs are offered an outlet to present their products, services as corresponding capital needs to investors and venture capitalists.

**What Sets This Service Apart?**  We provide an opportunity to qualify entrepreneurs on a statewide basis via the Iowa Communications Network that covers over 300 cites in Iowa. VNI was just named 1998's state model of excellence for venture + seed capital development by the SBA.

## 128 Venture Capital Group

**Region: New England**

Mr. Michael Belanger
128 Venture Capital Group
Bedford Road
Lincoln, MA 01773

tel: (781) 259-8776
e-mail: vcg@erols.com
http://www.erols.com/vcg

| | |
|---|---|
| Classification of service: | A breakfast meeting for investors, entrepreneurs, and others |
| Date of formation: | 1982 |
| Industry preferences: | High-tech |
| Stage of firms preferred: | Seed and startup |
| Matching methods: | Venture forums |
| Primary matching method: | Venture forums |
| No. of employees: Full-time: | |
| Part-time: | |
| Volunteer: | X |
| Organization type: | Private |
| Firms featured by service: | 50% Seed, 50% Start-up |

| | |
|---|---|
| No. of investors participating: | 150 |
| No. of firms seen by investors/yr: | $400 |
| No. of venture forums/yr: | 12 |
| No. of firms using forum/yr: | 300 |
| $ range sought: Typical max: | $250K |
| Typical min: | $50K |
| Average: | $1M |
| Investors invested thru service: | NA |
| Successful matches: 1997: | NA |
| 1998: | NA |
| Since formation: | NA |
| Service actively screen firms?: | No |

**Company Literature** (This information was obtained from the company's website without independent verification.)
Established in 1982, the Venture Capital Group meets monthly, on the second Thursday at the Newton Marriot for networking between individual investors, emerging company representatives, bankers and professional venture capital investors interested in emreging technologies and markets. Meetings are open to all interested parties including new participants, such as Management Team Candidates and Professional Service Providers. All participants are invited to briefly introduce themselves and their situation to the entire group. A contact list of all of that meeting's participants is provided at the close of the meeting.

**What Sets This Service Apart?** Best networking in the area.

# Brown University Research Foundation/Brown Venture Forum
## Region: New England

Ms. Joann Tillman/William Jackson  
Brown University Research Foundation/Brown Venture Forum  
42 Charlesfield Street  
P.O. Box 1949  
Providence, RI 02912  

tel: (401) 863-3528  
fax: (401) 863-1836  
e-mail: Joann_Tillman@brown.edu  
http://www.brown.edu/Research/Research_Foundation/

| | | |
|---|---|---|
| Classification of service: | Evening open forums and daytime start-up clinics | |
| | No. of investors participating: | 6 |
| | No. firms seen by investors/yr: | 6 |
| Date of formation: | 1984 for Brown Venture Forum | |
| | No. of venture forums/yr: | 6 |
| Industry preferences: | High growth potential | |
| | No. firms using forum/yr: | NA |
| Stage of firms preferred: | Early and expansion stage | |
| $ range sought: | Typical max: | NA |
| Matching methods: | Venture forums | |
| | Typical min: | NA |
| Primary matching method: | Newsletter | |
| | Average: | NA |
| No. of employees: Full-time: | 2 | |
| Part-time: | Investors invested thru service: | NA |
| Volunteer: | Successful matches: 1997: | NA |
| | 1998: | NA |
| | Since formation: | NA |
| Organization type: | Not for profit and university affiliated | |
| | Service actively screen firms?: | No |

**Company Literature**  (This information was obtained from the company's website without independent verification.)
The forum was started in 1984 by local business representatives under the leadership of William Jackson, the President of the Brown University Research Foundation. The Forum was established to promote the creation and expansion of high-growth potential businesses in the region. The Forum regularly brings together entrepreneurs, venture capitalists, experienced business representatives, and others who share the goal of starting and expanding businesses. It provides an opportunity for individuals to access the region's business network. Free, open meetings are held once a month through the season from November through May. Some meetings focus on aspects of growing a successful business, that is, securing financing or marketing; and may address issues common to an industry segment. Others center on one or more growing companies from the region, where a representative from each company describes his company's business and may seek advice on specific questions. In an objective analysis, selected panelists comment on the problems and the promise of the company and offer advice on potential means to resolve issues of entrepreneurs. Early stage companies and groups just getting a business going have an opportunity to come before a diverse panel of experts to receive constructive criticism on their business plans and proposals. In a friendly, unbiased environment, a useful dialogue is established. Meetings are open only to the presenting company, forum sponsors, invited guests, and panelists.

# Connecticut Venture Group

## Region: New England

Mr. Mike Roer
Connecticut Venture Group
425 Katona Drive
Fayetteville, CT 06430

tel: (203) 333-3284
fax: (203) 256-9949
e-mail: mikeroer@snet.net
http://www.ct-ventrues.org

| | | | |
|---|---|---|---|
| Classification of service: | Breakfast luncheon | No. of investors participating: | 200 |
| Date of formation: | 1974 | No. of firms seen by investors/yr: | 300 |
| Industry preferences: | All | No. of venture forums/yr: | 1 annual, 12 |
| Stage of firms preferred: | Early and expansion stage | | monthly events |
| Matching methods: | Internet, newsletter, and venture forums | No. firms using forum/yr: | 50 |
| Primary matching method: | Venture forums | $ range sought: Typical max: | $5 mil |
| No. of employees: Full-time: | 2 | Typical min: | $250K |
| Part-time: | | Average: | $1 mil |
| Volunteer: | | Investors invested thru service: | Not Tracked |
| Organization type: | Private, not for profit | Successful matches: 1997: | 12 |
| | | 1998: | 12 |
| | | Since formation: | Not Tracked |
| | | Service actively screen firms?: | NA |

Firms featured by service: 0% Seed, 10% Start-up, 20% Early, 70% Expansion

**What Sets This Service Apart?** The first venture organization. Growing by 40% per year.

# Gould Financial Network

**Region: New England**

Mr. Neil Gould
Gould Financial Network
86 Front Street
Merrimack, NH 03054

tel: (603) 429-1631
e-mail: GouldNC@aol.com

| | |
|---|---|
| Classification of service: | A group of angel investors, a breakfast/luncheon meeting, member association for entrepreneurial growth |
| Date of formation: | 1987 |
| Industry preferences: | Manufacturing and high tech |
| Stage of firms preferred: | Stage, start-up, early, and expansion |
| Matching methods: | Newsletter, investor-specified criteria, and venture forums |
| Primary matching method: | Investor specified criteria |
| No. of employees: Full-time: | 6 |
| Part-time: | 3 |
| Volunteer: | 1 |
| Organization type: | Private |
| Firms featured by service: | 5% Seed, 10% Start-up, 40% Early, 30% Expansion, 15% Other |

| | |
|---|---|
| No. of investors participating: | 449 |
| No. firms seen by investors/yr: | 20–30 |
| No. of venture forums/yr: | 2 |
| No. firms using forum/yr: | Less than 5% |
| $ range sought: Typical max: | $2M |
| Typical min: | $250K |
| Average: | $750K |
| Investors invested thru service: | 185 |
| Successful matches: 1997: | 4 |
| 1998: | 1 |
| Since formation: | 65 |
| Service actively screen firms?: | Yes |

**What Sets This Service Apart?** We became actively involved in the project by working in unison with the principals.

# Maine Investment Exchange (MIX)

## Region: New England

Ward Graffan Jr.
Maine Investment Exchange (MIX)
120 Exchange Street
PO Box 7462
Portland, ME 04112-7462

tel: (207) 871-0234
fax: (207) 775-6716
e-mail: business@maineco.org
http://www.mixForum.org

| | | | |
|---|---|---|---|
| Classification of service: | Breakfast luncheon with presentations | No. of investors participating: | Varies |
| Date of formation: | 1996 | No. of firms seen by investors/yr: | 20 |
| Industry preferences: | None | No. of venture forums/yr: | 4 |
| Stage of firms preferred: | Early stage | No. of firms using forum/yr: | 20 |
| Matching methods: | Internet and venture forums | $ range sought: Typical max: | $1.5 mil |
| Primary matching method: | Venture forums | Typical min: | $50K |
| No. of employees: Full-time: | 0 | Average: | $300K |
| Part-time: | 0 | Investors invested thru service: | NA |
| Volunteer: | 8 | Successful matches: 1997: | NA |
| Organization type: | Not for profit | 1998: | NA |
| | | Since formation: | NA |

Firms featured by service:   Seed, 20% Start-up, 60% Early, 20% Expansion, Other

**Company Literature**   (This information was obtained from the company's website without independent verification.)
The Maine Investment Exchange (MIX) was created by Maine & Company in 1996 and is supported by private businesses throughout Maine. The organization was established to provide forums for qualified entrepreneurs seeking risk capital. Although MIX cannot guarantee that successful investments will be made, it does provide an opportunity for entrepreneurs to meet potential investors. Investors, professional advisors, and other interested parties register for each MIX forum event. If investors and entrepreneurs find a mutual attraction to one another they are free to negotiate as desired. MIX asks only that participants inform MIX of relationships that resulted from forum exposure. An entrepreneur registers by submitting an application, a copy of their business plan, and an executive summary. There is a $50 non-refundable application fee. The application will be screened and, if selected, the entrepreneur is invited to make a 15-minute presentation at the next MIX forum. If selected, presenters are required to pay an additional $200 fee.

**What Sets This Service Apart?**   Only service in Maine.

# New Hampshire Business Development Corp.

**Region: New England**

Mr. Jeffrey Pollock
New Hampshire Business Development Corp.
1001 Elm St.
Manchester, NH 03101

tel: (603) 623-5500
fax: (603) 623-3972
e-mail: JMPollock@NHBDC.com
http://www.nhbdc.com

| | | | |
|---|---|---|---|
| Classification of service: | Venture Capital Firm encouraging angel co-investment | No. of investors participating: | 12 |
| | | No. of firms seen by investors/yr: | 2–3 |
| Date of formation: | 1992 | No. of venture forums/yr: | 1 |
| Industry preferences: | Intellectual property | No. firms using forum/yr: | 6–8 |
| Stage of firms preferred: | Early and expansion stage | $ range sought: Typical max: | $1 mil |
| Matching methods: | Investor-specified criteria and venture forums | Typical min: | $300K |
| | | Average: | $500K |
| Primary matching method: | Investor specified criteria | Investors invested thru service: | 12 |
| No. of employees: Full-time: | 5 | Successful matches: 1997: | 2 |
| Part-time: | 2 | 1998: | NA |
| Volunteer: | 0 | Since formation: | NA |
| Organization type: | Private | Service actively screen firms?: | Yes |
| Firms featured by service: | 100% Early | | |

**Company Literature** (This information was obtained from the company's website without independent verification.)
New Hampshire Business Development Corporation is a unique, for-profit corporation, dedicated to fostering entrepreneurial growth within our state. Our company partners with the lending community to provide tailor-made solutions for non-bankable lending needs. We are a knowledge-based company with a strong record of success in restructuring loans that traditional banking methodologies might otherwise forego. Our lending team is dedicated to superior service to our customers and long-term relationships with our lending partners. As our lending partner, you are guaranteed direct access to our senior underwriters.

**What Sets This Service Apart?** We provide opportunities to co-invest.

# St. Paul Venture Capital

**Region: New England**

Mr. Rick Boswell
St. Paul Venture Capital
138 River Road
Andover, MA 01810

tel: (978) 837-3198
fax: (978) 837-3199
e-mail: rboswell@stpaulvc.com
http://www.stpaulvc.com

| | | | |
|---|---|---|---|
| Classification of service: | Early stage venture capital partnership | No. of investors participating: | NA |
| Date of formation: | 1988 | No. firms seen by investors/yr: | NA |
| Industry preferences: | Intro tech, consumer, health care | No. of venture forums/yr: | NA |
| Stage of firms preferred: | Seed, start-up, early, and expansion | No. firms using forum/yr: | NA |
| Matching methods: | NA | $ range sought: Typical max: | $5 mil |
| Primary matching method: | NA | Typical min: | $500K |
| No. of employees: Full-time: | 40 | Average: | $3 mil |
| Part-time: | 5 | Investors invested thru service: | NA |
| Volunteer: | | Successful matches: 1997: | NA |
| | | 1998: | NA |
| Organization type: | Private | Since formation: | NA |
| | | Service actively screen firms?: | NA |

Firms featured by service: 25% Seed, 50% Start-up, 15% Early, 10% Expansion

**Company Literature** (**This information was obtained from the company's website without independent verification.**)
St. Paul Venture Capital invests in emerging growth companies which have the potential to generate excellent performance, achieve leadership in the marketplace, and create significant shareholder value. With an annual investment placement that is among the top 20 venture capital firms in the United States, we have committed more than $750 million to venture capital investments since our founding in 1988. This includes direct investment in more than 80 companies and indirect investments in over 2000 companies through venture partnerships. Our direct investments in high-potential growth companies range from $1 million to $10 million over the course of our relationship. Although we invest at all stages of private equity, the majority of our investments are in early stage venture capital, with a focus on three major industry areas: Information technology, consumer-related, including education, and health care. We evaluate ourselves with the same rigor we apply to our investments, judging our performance on our success in creating shareholder value, providing market leadership through excellence, fostering innovation and creativity and building strong working relationships. The relevant time span for such evaluation is measured in decades and careers, not in the next few years.

# Technology Capital Network at MIT

**Region: New England**

Ms. Rosann Mejias, Office Manager
Technology Capital Network at MIT
P.O. Box 425936
Cambridge, MA 02412

tel: (617) 253-2337
fax: (617) 258-7395
e-mail: imfo@tenmit.org
http://www.tenmit.org

| | | | |
|---|---|---|---|
| Classification of service: | Formal matching service and a breakfast/luncheon | No. of investors participating: | Proprietary |
| | | No. firms seen by investors/yr: | 50–100 |
| Date of formation: | 1984/1991 | No. of venture forums/yr: | 6 |
| Industry preferences: | High-tech | No. firms using forum/yr: | 50+ |
| Stage of firms preferred: | Seed, start-up, and early stage | $ range sought: Typical max: | $5 mil |
| Matching methods: | Investor-specified criteria and venture forums | Typical min: | $500K |
| | | Average: | $2 mil |
| | | Investors invested thru service: | NA |
| Primary matching method: | Venture forums | Successful matches: 1997: | 15 |
| No. of employees: Full-time: | 1 | 1998: | 10 |
| Part-time: | 2 | | |
| Volunteer: | 2 + sponsors | Since formation: | Unknown |
| Organization type: | Not for profit/university affiliated | Service actively screen firms?: | Yes (only for high growth potential) |
| Firms featured by service: | 10% Seed, 20% Start-up, 60% Early, 10% Expansion | | |
| Additional services offered: | Educational programs—all geared to funding and growing a business. | | |

**Company Literature** (This information was obtained from the company's website without independent verification.)

The Technical Capital Network (TCN) is a not-for-profit organization which utilizes a proprietary, computerized matching process to provide introductions between entrepreneurs and private investors. TCN is the nation's longest established venture capital network. Our unique means of matching entrepreneurs with investors was started by Professor William Wetzel at the University of New Hampshire in 1984, as the Venture Capital Network. It was brought under the auspices of the MIT Enterprise Forum of Cambridge, Inc. in 1991 and renamed. TCN provides high-net-worth individuals with a convenient, confidential mechanism for examining opportunities to invest in entrepreneurial ventures. It also serves professional venture capital funds and corporate investors who are interested in early-stage, high-growth companies. TCN helps entrepreneurs whose companies have the potential for generating substantial capital gains search for sources of seed and start-up capital. TCN provides opportunities to be matched with individuals investors and others interested in early-stage private companies. Many of these investors (angels) have created their own successful ventures and have substantial ventures and have substantial experience to bring to the company, along with their investment. Other services provided by TCN include Venture Capital Forums, Investors Pooling meetings, an Entrepreneurs' Financing Roundtable series which meets monthly, and other educational activities. Investors and entrepreneurs can benefit from TCN's services by becoming a member of the TecNet Network. TCN charges low fees due to the generosity of sponsors.

**What Sets This Service Apart?** Our reputation, our longevity, our success.

# Startup Group

**Region: New England**

Mr. David Amis
Startup Group
123 South Street, 5th Floor
Boston, MA 02111

tel: (617) 482-5550
fax: (617) 482-5551
e-mail: David@suG1.com
http://www.suG1.com

| | | | |
|---|---|---|---|
| Classification of service: | Matching service and fund | No. of investors participating: | 50 |
| Date of formation: | Nov. 1997 | No. firms seen by investors/yr: | 50 |
| Industry preferences: | None | No. of venture forums/yr: | 12 |
| Stage of firms preferred: | Start-up and early stage | No. firms using forum/yr: | NA |
| Matching methods: | Internet, investment-specified criteria, | $ range sought:   Typical max: | $2 mil |
| | venture forums, and venture summary service | Typical min: | $200K |
| Primary matching method: | Investor-specified criteria | Average: | $400K |
| No. of employees:   Full-time: | 6 | Investors invested thru service: | NA |
| Part-time: | 2 | Successful matches:   1997: | NA |
| Volunteer: | | 1998: | NA |
| Organization type: | Private | Since formation: | NA |
| | | Service actively screen firms?: | Yes |
| Firms featured by service: | 10% Seed, 40% Start-up, 40% Early, 10% Expansion | | |
| Additional services offered: | Capital raising bootcamps, angel investors workshops. | | |

**Company Literature**   (This information was obtained from the company's website without independent verification.)
Startup Group is a matchmaker service whose primary objective is to bring together entrepreneurs and private investors to facilitate seed, start-up, and expansion capital investment deals. Startup Group screens entrepreneurs by reviewing business plans and by preparing unique and highly focused summaries that address the key business issues. Summaries are forwarded to subscribing private investors who are actively looking to invest in early stage businesses. After reviewing the summaries that interest them, investors contact the entrepreneur directly to initiate their own due diligence and investment process. By accessing a qualified network of investors who are actively looking to invest in seed, start-up, and expanding business, entrepreneurs reduce the transaction costs and time to raise capital. Entrepreneurs also increase their chances to find value-added investors to help their business grow. Both entrepreneurs and investors benefit from Startup Group's process of preparing for an investment transaction, as well as the management team's experience in the practical issues associated with raising capital and making early stage investments.

**What Sets This Service Apart?**   Experience as the previous manager of the world's oldest matchmaker (VCR), our fund which co-invests with angels, and our best practices website.

## The Breakfast Club

**Region: New England**

Mr. Dick Morley
The Breakfast Club
R. Morley Incorporated
586-3 Nashua Street, Suite 56
Milford, NH 03055

tel: (603) 878-4365
e-mail: morley@barn.org
http://www.barn.org

| | |
|---|---|
| Classification of service: | Breakfast luncheon |
| Date of formation: | 1978 |
| Industry preferences: | High-tech |
| Stage of firms preferred: | Seed stage |
| Matching methods: | None |
| Primary matching method: | Network |
| No. of employees:   Full-time: | |
|                             Part-time: | |
|                             Volunteer: | |
| Organization type: | Private |

| | |
|---|---|
| No. of investors participating: | 0–20 |
| No. of firms seen by investors/yr: | NA |
| No. of venture forums/yr: | 0 |
| No. of firms using forum/yr: | Not Applicable |
| $ range sought:   Typical max: | $500K |
|                         Typical min: | $50K |
|                         Average: | $100K |
| Investors invested thru service: | NA |
| Successful matches:       1997: | NA |
|                                   1998: | NA |
|                         Since formation: | 50+ |
| Service actively screen firms?: | NA |

Firms featured by service:     50% Seed, 40% Start-up, 10% Early

**Company Literature**   (**This information was obtained from the company's website without independent verification.**)
R. Morley Inc. (RMI) is a consulting firm that specializes in the application technologies that are at or beyond the leading edge to the manufacturing and computer systems industries. We also promote lectures and seminars facilitating that application of complexity science and agent based systems across a wide range of disciplines

**What Sets This Service Apart?**   We make quick decisions.

# The Northeast Recycling Investment Forum

## Region: New England

Ms. Mary Ann Remolador
The Northeast Recycling Investment Forum
The Northeast Recycling Council
139 Main Street, Suite 401
Brattleboro, VT 05301

tel: (802) 254-3636
fax: (802) 254-5870
e-mail: NERC@sover.net
http://www.NERC.org

| | | | |
|---|---|---|---|
| Classification of service: | Other, hold investment forums, annually | No. of investors participating: | 70–100 |
| Date of formation: | 1988 | No. firms seen by investors/yr: | 10 to 15 |
| Industry preferences: | Manufacturing | No. of venture forums/yr: | 1 |
| Stage of firms preferred: | Start-up | No. firms using forum/yr: | 10 to 15 |
| Matching methods: | Venture forums | $ range sought:  Typical max: | $5 mil |
| Primary matching method: | Venture Forums | Typical min: | $100K |
| No. of employees:  Full-time: | 4 | Average: | Not Tracked |
| Part-time: | 2 | Investors invested thru service: | at least 10 |
| Volunteer: | 0 | Successful matches:  1997: | 4 |
| Organization type: | Not for profit | 1998: | 2 |
| | | Since formation: | 10 |
| | | Service actively screen firms?: | Yes |

Firms featured by service: 49% Start-up, 49% Early, 2% Expansion
Additional services offered: Business financing seminars, research on merger and acquisition activity.

**Company Literature** (This information was obtained from the company's website without independent verification.)
The recycling industry includes hundreds of entrepreneurial product manufacturers, equipment developers and service providers involved in recovering and adding value to materials which otherwise would enter the waste stream. The Northeast Recycling Investment Forum is an annual, one-day event featuring some of the recycling industry's most promising investment opportunities. The Forum includes brief presentation by ten to fifteen start-up, early-stage, and expanding businesses seeking between $100,000 and $5 million in equity financing. Ample networking opportunities and table top displays showcasing the presenting firms' products or services allow Forum attendees to personally interact with the participant firms. The first two forums each attracted over 100 attendees and featured a total of 28 businesses seeking $19.7 million in equity. Of these participant firms, six have said their Forum experience assisted them in securing equity investments totaling $6.5 million. In addition, one firm has been acquired, and three of the 1997 Forum participants are currently negotiating a total of $4.1 million. Besides providing direct exposure to potential investors, the Forum has been commended by participant firms for increasing their self-confidence in approaching investors, and focusing their efforts to attract investors.

**What Sets This Service Apart?** We focus our efforts on the recycling companies in the Northeast.

# Vermont Investor's Forum

**Region: New England**

Mr. Michael Sweatman
Vermont Investor's Forum
c/o Green Mountain Capital
RD 1, Box 1503
Waterbury, VT 05676

tel: (802) 244-8981
fax: (802) 244-8990
e-mail: info@gmtcap.com
http://www.gmtcap.com/vif

| | | |
|---|---|---|
| Classification of service: | A group of angels (annual all day forum) | No. of investors participating: | 60–80 attend forums. Vermont database of 500. |

|  |  |  |  |
|---|---|---|---|
| Classification of service: | A group of angels (annual all day forum) | No. of investors participating: | 60–80 attend forums. Vermont database of 500. |
| Date of formation: | Early 1994 | No. firms seen by investors/yr: | 12–22 |
| Industry preferences: | None | No. of venture forums/yr: | Once |
| Stage of firms preferred: | Seed, start-up, and early stage | No. firms using forum/yr: | All 12 presenters make good investor contacts. |
| Matching methods: | None | $ range sought: Typical max: | $1 mil |
| Primary matching method: | Don't match | Typical min: | $100K |
| No. of employees: Full-time: | | Average: | $100K–250K |
| Part-time: | | Investors invested thru service: | NA |
| Volunteer: | 12 | Successful matches: 1997: | NA |
| Organization type: | Private, not for profit, partly sponsored | 1998: | NA |
| | | Since formation: | NA |
| Firms featured by service: | 20% Seed, 30% Start-up, 30% Early, 20% Expansion | Service actively screen firms?: | Y |
| Additional services offered: | No | | |

**Company Literature**  (This information was obtained from the company's website without independent verification.)
The Vermont Investors Forum Inc. is a nonprofit corporation formed to help support the small business environment in Vermont. To date this has been accomplished through the holding of annual forums. So far there have been 6 annual forums. At each forum 10–12 small, VT businesses are selected to present their business plans to a predominantly private audience.

**What Sets This Service Apart?**   Only one in Vermont, very unstructured.

# Vermont Venture Network

**Region: New England**

Mr. H. Kenneth Merritt
Vermont Venture Network
c/o Merritt & Merritt
P.O. Box 5839
Burlington, VT 05402

tel: (802) 658-7830
fax: (802) 658-0978
e-mail: mail@merritt-merritt.com
http://www.vermontventurenetwork.com

| | |
|---|---|
| Classification of service: | A breakfast/luncheon meeting for investors, entrepreneurs, and others |
| Date of formation: | Jan '89 |
| Industry preferences: | NA |
| Stage of firms preferred: | Seed, start-up, early, and expansion stage |
| Matching methods: | Newsletter/magazine and venture forum |
| Primary matching method: | Newsletter/magazine and venture forums |
| No. of employees: Full-time: | |
| Part-time: | |
| Volunteer: | 2 |
| Organization type: | Not for profit |
| | |
| Firms featured by service: | 25% Seed, 25% Start-up, 25% Early, 25% Expansion |
| Additional services offered: | Database of resources |

| | |
|---|---|
| No. of investors participating: | 300 |
| No. firms seen by investors/yr: | 12 |
| No. of venture forums/yr: | 12 breakfasts |
| No. firms using forum/yr: | 50+ |
| $ range sought: Typical max: | $1M |
| Typical min: | $50K |
| Average: | $250K |
| Investors invested thru service: | NA |
| Successful matches: 1997: | 2 |
| 1998: | 2 |
| Since formation: | 20 |
| Service actively screen firms?: | No |

307

# New Jersey Entrepreneurial Network
**Region: New Jersey and New York**

Mr. Robert D. Frawley
New Jersey Entrepreneurial Network
600 College Road East, Suite 4200
Princeton, NJ 08540

tel: (609) 279-0010
fax: (609) 987-6651
e-mail: rdf@sswhb.com
http://www.njen.com

| | |
|---|---|
| Classification of service: | Breakfast luncheon |
| | |
| Date of formation: | 1991 |
| Industry preferences: | None |
| Stage of firms preferred: | Seed, start-up, and early stage |
| Matching methods: | Venture forums and meetings |
| Primary matching method: | Venture forums/meetings |
| No. of employees: Full-time: | |
| Part-time: | |
| Volunteer: | 14 |
| Organization type: | Not for profit |

| | |
|---|---|
| No. of investors participating: | 9 venture capitalists on board |
| No. firms seen by investors/yr: | NA |
| No. of venture forums/yr: | 10 |
| No. firms using forum/yr: | 11 |
| $ range sought: Typical max: | NA |
| Typical min: | NA |
| Average: | Varies |
| Investors invested thru service: | NA |
| Successful matches: 1997: | NA |
| 1998: | NA |
| Since formation: | NA |
| Service actively screen firms?: | No |

Firms featured by service:  35% Seed, 35% Start-up, 20% Early, 10% Expansion

**Company Literature   (This information was obtained from the company's website without independent verification.)**
The New Jersey Entrepreneurial Network (NJEN) is an nonprofit organization providing educational and informational service to entrepreneurs, investors, and service providers and the general public. A recent survey indicated that of the companies which attended meetings for the purpose of securing outside investment, 11 percent found an investor through NJEN. Meetings are held on the first Wednesday of each month from September and June.

**What Sets This Service Apart?**   No annual fee; active participation of venture capitalists and investors (not just finders and consultants); best lunch on the circuit.

# New Jersey Technology Council

**Region: New Jersey and New York**

Ms. Maxine Ballen
New Jersey Technology Council
500 College Road East, Suite 200
Princeton, NJ 08540

tel: (609) 452-1010
fax: (609) 452-1007
e-mail: Staff@njtc.org
http://www.njtc.org

| | | | |
|---|---|---|---|
| Classification of service: | Not for profit membership organization offering venture forums | No. of investors participating: | 100 |
| | | No. firms seen by investors/yr: | 50 |
| Date of formation: | 1996 | No. of venture forums/yr: | 1 |
| Industry preferences: | Technology | No. firms using forum/yr: | 20 |
| Stage of firms preferred: | Start-up, early, and expansion stage | $ range sought: Typical max: | $10 mil |
| Matching methods: | Venture forums | Typical min: | $100K |
| Primary matching method: | Venture forums | Average: | $2 mil |
| No. of employees: Full-time: | 8 | Investors invested thru service: | 20 |
| Part-time: | 2 | Successful matches: 1997: | 10 |
| Volunteer: | | 1998: | 10 |
| Organization type: | Not for profit | Since formation: | 5 |
| | | Service actively screen firms?: | Yes |
| Firms featured by service: | 50% Start-up, 40% Early, 10% Expansion | | |

**Company Literature** (This information was obtained from the company's website without independent verification.) The mission of the New Jersey Technology Council is to provide recognition, networking, information, and servicing for the state's technology businesses. By collectively representing designated technology-intensive industries and the institutions and servicing companies that support them, the New Jersey Technology Council has the unique ability to offer opportunities, provide access to funding sources, recognize and promote technological innovation and accomplishment, foster technological growth and development, and support public policy consistent with sustained-growth of technology-intensive industries. Three types of membership are offered within the Council including Technology Members, Technology Support Members, and Non-Profit Members, each with its own investment structure. Specific programs are offered for individual industries including Software/Information Technologies, Healthcare, Communication, Consumer Products, Electronics, and Environment. Programs are also offered for peer groups including Human Resources, CFO, CEO, and Sales & Marketing. General membership activities and programs include the annual awards gala; high-tech Hero Breakfasts; roundtables, panel discussions and networking events; legislative reviews; social events; and financing programs such as the New Jersey Venture Fair, the Public Company Showcase and the New Jersey Capital Conference. NJTC is dedicated to directly fostering positive relationship among technology-related companies—a builder exchange, a resource for professional and technical exchange, a resource for professional and technical information.

**What Sets This Service Apart?** This is the only Venture forum in the state of NJ. We've attracted hundreds of companies to exhibit at our fair in the ten years that we have been putting on this event.

# Rochester Venture Capital Group

**Region: New Jersey and New York**

Ms. Cynthia Gary
Rochester Venture Capital Group
1580 Elmwood Ave
PO Box 18926
Rochester, NY 14618

tel: (716) 214-2400
fax: (716) 272-0054
e-mail: cgary@eznet.net

| | |
|---|---|
| Classification of service: | Breakfast/luncheon meeting |
| Date of formation: | early '80 |
| Industry preferences: | No focus, although 40–50% historically has been high-tech |
| Stage of firms preferred: | Start-up and early stage |
| Matching methods: | NA |
| Primary matching method: | NA |
| No. of employees: Full-time: | 0 |
| Part-time: | 0 |
| Volunteer: | All |
| Organization type: | |
| Firms featured by service: | 10% Seed, 20% Start-up, 60% Early, 10% Expansion |

| | |
|---|---|
| No. of investors participating: | 65 paid members, 50 investors |
| No. firms seen by investors/yr: | 10 to 12 |
| No. of venture forums/yr: | Breakfast meetings |
| No. firms using forum/yr: | 10 times a yr |
| $ range sought: Typical max: | $2 mil |
| Typical min: | $250K |
| Average: | $1 mil |
| Investors invested thru service: | NA |
| Successful matches: 1997: | 2 |
| 1998: | 4 |
| Since formation: | NA |
| Service actively screen firms?: | Yes |

## Company Literature (This information was obtained from the company's website without independent verification.)

The Rochester Venture Capital Group (RVCG) was formed in the early 1980s. It provides an excellent forum for entrepreneurs and early stage businesses to present a brief description to their investors and venture fund managers of the purpose of raising early stage that meets. RVCG is an informal group that meets the second Tuesday of each month at the Strathallan from September through June. Typically there are one or two speakers on the program at each meeting. They have approximately 25 minutes to describe the essence of their business and answer questions. Meetings begin at 8:00 A.M., finish about 9:00 A.M. and include breakfast. There are no restrictions on the types of the business selected for the program. Product, service, high tech and no tech businesses are all welcome. Typically the presenters are seeking investments in the range of $25,000 to $1 million. Speakers are encouraged to try to establish contacts for further discussion and formal negotiation. It is often beneficial for the presenters to distribute brochures, brief summary descriptions of their business plans, or samples of their products to those interested.

# Venture Association of New Jersey

**Region: New Jersey and New York**

Ms. Clara Stricchiola
Venture Association of New Jersey
c/o Jay Trien
177 Madison Avenue
Morristown, NJ 07962-1982

tel: (973) 631-5680
fax: (973) 984-9634
e-mail: clara@vanj.com
http://www.vanj.com & http://www.nmanj.com

| | |
|---|---|
| Classification of service: | Breakfast luncheon |
| Date of formation: | 1985 |
| Industry preferences: | No preferences |
| Stage of firms preferred: | Seed, start-up, early, and expansion |
| Matching methods: | Newsletter |
| Primary matching method: | Venture forums |
| No. of employees: Full-time: | 1 |
| Part-time: | |
| Volunteer: | |
| Organization type: | Private |

| | |
|---|---|
| No. of investors participating: | Not tracked |
| No. firms seen by investors/yr: | Formerly 33 |
| No. of venture forums/yr: | 11 |
| No. firms using forum/yr: | Not tracked |
| $ range sought: Typical max: | $7 mil |
| Typical min: | $50K |
| Average: | $250K |
| Investors invested thru service: | Not Tracked |
| Successful matches: 1997: | Not Tracked |
| 1998: | Not Tracked |
| Since formation: | Not Tracked |
| Service actively screen firms?: | No |

**Firms featured by service:** 20% Seed, 20% Start-up, 50% Early, 10% Expansion

**Additional services offered:** Each month three entrepreneurs make five minute presentations, attendees all introduce themselves, we have a guest speaker at each meeting.

**Company Literature** (This information was obtained from the company's website without independent verification.)
Venture Association of New Jersey (VANJ) meets on the third Tuesday of every month (except August) at the Governor Morris; $25 for members, $45 for non-members. It is a forum where three entrepreneurs are each given five minutes to present their companies to potential investors. The VANJ does not endorse any attendee or five-minute presenter, nor do these presentations constitute an offering, which can be made only by written prospects. These presentations give entrepreneurs and investors valuable contacts. VANJ publishes the 6,000-circulation VANJ News.

**What Sets This Service Apart?** An informal opportunity for those looking for checks to meet those who can and want to write checks.

# Western New York Venture Association

**Region: New Jersey and New York**

Mr. John McGowan
Western New York Venture Association
Baird Research Park
1576 Sweet Home Drive
Amherst, NY 14228

tel: (716) 636-3626
fax: (716) 636-3630
e-mail: jmcgowan@acsubuffolo.edu

| | |
|---|---|
| Classification of service: | Breakfast luncheon |
| Date of formation: | 1989 |
| Industry preferences: | None |
| Stage of firms preferred: | Start-up, early, and expansion stage |
| Matching methods: | Venture forums |
| Primary matching method: | Venture forums |
| No. of employees: Full-time: | 0 |
| Part-time: | 0 |
| Volunteer: | 12 |
| Organization type: | Private, not for profit |
| | |
| Firms featured by service: | 10% Seed, 40% Start-up, 40% Early, 10% Expansion |
| Additional services offered: | Coaching of presenters |

| | |
|---|---|
| No. of investors participating: | 15 |
| No. firms seen by investors/yr: | 8 |
| No. of venture forums/yr: | 4 |
| No. firms using forum/yr: | 8 |
| $ range sought: Typical max: | $2 mil |
| Typical min: | $200K |
| Average: | $500K |
| Investors invested thru service: | 5 |
| Successful matches: 1997: | 1 |
| 1998: | 1 |
| Since formation: | 5 |
| Service actively screen firms?: | Yes |

**Company Literature** (This information was obtained from the company's website without independent verification.)
The WNYVA, founded in 1989, is the only not-for-profit organization dedicated to providing a business opportunity and investment forum to the Niagara region. The Association holds a series of networking meeting throughout the year to facilitate the exchange of information between investors and entrepreneurs. WNYVA meetings provide entrepreneurs an opportunity to present their business plans to interested investors in a public forum. Prior to making their presentations entrepreneurs receive valuable coaching and feedback about their business plan from WNYVA directors. Attending meetings can give business owners a greater understanding of what it takes to build a successful business plan. Through the WNYVA, investors have the opportunity to listen to business plan presentations from existing, expanding, and start-up phase companies. All presentations are prescreened by WNYVA directors to maintain high quality. The WNYVA does not, however, endorse or recommend any companies or investment opportunities.

**What Sets This Service Apart?** The only not-for-profit organization dedicated to providing a business opportunity and investment forum in Western New York.

# Center for Innovation

**Region: Northwest**

Mr. Bruce Gjovig
Center for Innovation
PO Box 8372
4300 Dartmouth Drive
Grand Forks, ND 58202

tel: (701) 777-3132
fax: (701) 777-2339
e-mail: gjovig@prairie.nodak.edu
http://www.innovators.net

| | | |
|---|---|---|
| Classification of service: | Business Development Services for Entrepreneurs | |
| Date of formation: | 1984 | |
| Industry preferences: | Manufacturing | |
| Stage of firms preferred: | NA | |
| Matching methods: | NA | |
| Primary matching method: | | |
| No. of employees: Full-time: | 5 | |
| Part-time: | 3 | |
| Volunteer: | | |
| Organization type: | Not for profit; university affiliated | |
| Additional services offered: | Business plan development market research | |

| | |
|---|---|
| No. of investors participating: | Not Applicable |
| No. of firms seen by investors/yr: | Not Applicable |
| No. of venture forums/yr: | Not Applicable |
| No. of firms using forum/yr: | Not Applicable |
| $ range sought: Typical max: | NA |
| Typical min: | $50K |
| Average: | NA |
| Investors invested thru service: | NA |
| Successful matches: 1997: | Not Applicable |
| 1998: | Not Applicable |
| Since formation: | Not Applicable |
| Service actively screen firms?: | No |

**Company Literature** (This information was obtained from the company's website without independent verification.)
The Center for Innovation is dedicated to assisting manufacturers, researchers, and entrepreneurs in exploring and identifying new and emerging markets, commercializing new products and technologies and starting new ventures. Our staff, along with University of South Dakota faculty and students, are available to provide you and your company either marketing assistance, business guidance, strategies for securing funding, and technical expertise. Fees for our services depend largely on the time and complexity of the project and can often be subsidized through local, regional, state, and national funding organizations and resources.

# Enterprise Capital Resources
**Region: Northwest**

Mr. Jim Moore
Enterprise Capital Resources
18521 53rd Ave. NE
Seattle, WA 98155

tel: (206) 363-6260
fax: (206) 682-4859
e-mail: jrmecr@worldnet.att.net

| | |
|---|---|
| Classification of service: | A formal matching service and a breakfast/luncheon meeting |
| Date of formation: | Jan '97 |
| Industry preferences: | None |
| Stage of firms preferred: | Startup, early-stage, and expansion |
| Matching methods: | Internet, newsletter/magazine, investor specified criteria, venture forums, and direct mail targeted |
| Primary matching method: | Investor-specified criteria |
| No. of employees: Full-time: | 3 |
| Part-time: | 2 |
| Volunteer: | |
| Organization type: | Private |
| Firms featured by service: | Seed, 25% Start-up, 50% Early, 25% Expansion |
| Additional services offered: | How to invest; how to find Angel Investors; how to write investor-oriented business plan documents. |

| | |
|---|---|
| No. of investors participating: | 7500 |
| No. firms seen by investors/yr: | 50 |
| No. of venture forums/yr: | Once |
| No. firms using forum/yr: | 10 |
| $ range sought: Typical max: | $2M |
| Typical min: | $5M |
| Average: | $1M |
| Investors invested thru service: | 55 |
| Successful matches: 1997: | NA |
| 1998: | NA |
| Since formation: | 22 |
| Service actively screen firms?: | Yes |

**Company Literature** (This information was obtained from the company's website without independent verification.)
Enterprise Capital Resources (ECR) provides a powerful method for entrepreneurs to reach qualified, accredited, and experienced business angels, informal investors and private venture capitalists, while avoiding the high fees charged be traditional investment bankers and other financial intermediaries. ECR can link you into a capital network of nearly 8,000 private investors who each place $25,000–$1,000,000 per deal. The Private Equity Review (PER), a bimonthly newsletter circulated to ECR staff as the very best among an array of candidate firms. Candidate firms are introduced to ECR by referrals from previously funded ventures, attorneys, accountants, and other financial intermediaries, from interest generated in seminars and speeches given by ECR staff, as well as from direct inquiries at our web site (www.investor connection.com). To become part of the board, promising group ventures being introduced to ECR's nationwide network of investors, send your business plan, private placement memorandum, investment proposal or loan package to ECR for review.

**What Sets This Service Apart?** We screen ventures, select about one out of eight for profiling in Private Equity Review, and provide those not selected with evaluation and advice.

# North Dakota Development Fund

**Region: Northwest**

Mr. Dean Reese
North Dakota Development Fund
1833 East Bismarck Expressway
Bismarck, ND 58504-6708

tel: (701) 328-5310
fax: (701) 328-5320
e-mail: dreese@state.nd.us
http://www.growingnd.com

| | | | |
|---|---|---|---|
| Classification of service: | Equity and subordinated debt funding | No. of investors participating: | NA |
| Date of formation: | 1989 | No. of firms seen by investors/yr: | 30 |
| Industry preferences: | Manufacturing and high-tech | No. of venture forums/yr: | NA |
| Stage of firms preferred: | Start-up, early, and expansion stage | No. firms using forum/yr: | NA |
| Matching methods: | Internet and investors-specified criteria | $ range sought: Typical max: | $500K |
| Primary matching method: | Investor-specified criteria | Typical min: | $50K |
| No. of employees: Full-time: | 3 | Average: | $300K |
| Part-time: | | Investors invested thru service: | NA |
| Volunteer: | | Successful matches: 1997: | 19 |
| Organization type: | Subsidized by state government | 1998: | 21 |
| | | Since formation: | 93 |
| Firms featured by service: | 10% Start-up, 20% Early, 70% Expansion | Service actively screen firms?: | Yes |
| Additional services offered: | No | | |

**Company Literature** (This information was obtained from the company's website without independent verification.)
The North Dakota Development Fund was created in 1999 by North Dakota legislation as an economic development tool. It provides flexible gap financing through debt and equity investments for new or expanding primary sector businesses in North Dakota. As a statewide nonprofit development corporation, the Fund is overseen by a Board of eight key industry executives representing finance, manufacturing, industrial technology and research, and exported services. The Fund makes investments of up to $300K through direct loans, participation loans, subordinated debt, and equity investments. The Board may adjust the limit when deemed appropriate. Development Fund applicants will be required to present a business plan. This plan, at a minimum, should include a history of the company; a description of the product, company, and industry; management team members' resumes; a marketing plan that addresses markets, customers, competition, and niche; historical and projected financials that include balance sheet, income statements and cash flows, and financing requirements with detailed sources and use of funds.

**What Sets This Service Apart?** Low interest rate funding for primary sector businesses using flexible and creative financing terms and conditions.

## Northwest Capital Network

**Region: Northwest**

Mr. Stephen E. Loyd
Northwest Capital Network
P.O. Box 21767
Seattle, WA 98111

tel: (206) 441-3123
fax: (206) 463-6386
e-mail: sloyd@u.washington.edu
http://www.nwcapital.org

| | |
|---|---|
| Classification of service: | A formal matching service |
| Date of formation: | 1989 |
| Industry preferences: | None |
| Stage of firms preferred: | Seed, start-up, early, and expansion stage |
| Matching methods: | Internet, Newsletter, investor-specified criteria, and venture forum |
| Primary matching method: | Investor-specified criteria |
| No. of employees: Full-time: | 2 |
| Part-time: | 6 |
| Volunteer: | 8 |
| Organization type: | Not for profit and university affiliated |
| | |
| Firms featured by service: | 10% Seed, 60% Start-up, 20% Early, 10% Expansion |
| Additional services offered: | Educational seminars for investors and entrepreneurs are offered through the University of Washington. |

| | |
|---|---|
| No. of investors participating: | 853 |
| No. firms seen by investors/yr: | 50–100 |
| No. of venture forums/yr: | NA |
| No. firms using forum/yr: | NA |
| $ range sought: Typical max: | $1M |
| Typical min: | $100K |
| Average: | $400K |
| Investors invested thru service: | NA |
| Successful matches: 1997: | 10+ |
| 1998: | 10+ |
| Since formation: | 100–150 |
| Service actively screen firms?: | No |

**Company Literature**
The Northwest Capital Network (NCN) is a not-for-profit economic development organization offering business angels/investors and entrepreneurs a process to explore business relationships in a confidential manner. NCN introduces business students to the world of entrepreneurship and business start-ups. NCN also provides educational seminars for entrepreneurs, business angels, mentors, and students interested in early-stage, high-growth companies. NCN serves entrepreneurs with high-growth businesses raising less than $2 million in equity—an area not generally served by the investment banking and venture community.

**What Sets This Service Apart?** We are an ACE-Net affiliate: NCN serves the Pacific Northwest as the ACE-Net operator introducing Washington and Oregon investors to early-stage, high-growth companies via the Internet.

316

# Northwest Venture Group
## (Holt & Company)

**Region: Northwest**

Ms. Marilyn Holt
Northwest Venture Group (Holt & Company)
1420 Fifth Avenue, Suite 2200
Seattle, WA 98101

tel: (206) 224-3185
fax: (206) 789-8034
e-mail: mjholt@holtcapital.com
http://www.holtcapital.com

| | | |
|---|---|---|
| Classification of service: | Service matches investors with investments | |
| Date of formation: | 1980 | |
| Industry preferences: | Manufacturing, high-tech, and Internet | |
| Stage of firms preferred: | Seed, start-up, early, and expansion stage | |
| Matching methods: | Investor-specified criteria and direct introductions | |
| Primary matching method: | Personal contacts | |
| No. of employees: Full-time: | 3 | |
| Part-time: | | |
| Volunteer: | Private | |
| | | |
| No. of investors participating: | | NA |
| No. of firms seen by investors/yr: | | NA |
| No. of venture forums/yr: | | Not Applicable |
| No. of firms using forum/yr: | | Not Applicable |
| $ range sought: Typical max: | | $50M |
| Typical min: | | $500K |
| Average: | | $3M |
| Investors invested thru service: | | NA |
| Successful matches: 1997: | | NA |
| 1998: | | NA |
| Since formation: | | NA |
| Service actively screen firms?: | | Yes |

Additional services offered: Venture packaging

**Company Literature** (This information was obtained from the company's website without independent verification.)
Holt & company provides the following intermediately services for high-growth companies in the $1 MM to $80 MM range: capital formation, merger and acquisition, and advisory services. Many entrepreneurs seeking help to grow their business can quickly list myriad of complaints about the process. At Holt & Company, we have taken to heart concerns about service and deliverables in order to create a different type of experience for our clients. We call our approach the "Three R's" for client transactions: Respect, Responsiveness, and Results. The 3 R's form the foundation for delivering quality services with uncompromising integrity. If we aren't the right firm to meet your needs, we'll not only tell you, we'll refer you to someone else. Our goal is to do the right things, not just doing things right. In this way, we can help you achieve your goals.

**What Sets This Service Apart?** We work with entrepreneurs to help make their companies goods investment targets.

## Oregon Entrepreneurs Forum

**Region: Northwest**

Mr. Jim Berchtold,
Oregon Entrepreneurs Forum
2611 SW Third Ave., Suite 200
Portland, OR 97201

tel: (503) 222-2270
fax: (503) 241-0827
e-mail: info@oef.org
http://www.oef.org

| | |
|---|---|
| Classification of service: | One of 19 international MIT Enterprise Forum chapters—but most diverse and full program offering, 3 major events (1300+ attendees), angel investors, luncheon, and evening presentations. |
| Date of formation: | 1991 |
| Industry preferences: | Broad range |
| Stage of firms preferred: | Seed, start-up, early, and expansion stage |
| Matching methods: | Internet, investor-specified criteria, venture forums, and angel presentation private panel reviews |
| Primary matching method: | Venture forums |
| No. of employees: Full-time: | 3 |
| Part-time: | 1 |
| Volunteer: | 100+ |
| Organization type: | |
| Firms featured by service: | 15% Seed, 20% Start-up, 45% Early, 20% Expansion |
| Additional services offered: | Private panel reviews (business plans); public talks (improve company presentations); speak easier and luncheon programs; mentoring services; newsletter. |

| | |
|---|---|
| No. of investors participating: | 60+ Angels + 5 VC's |
| No. firms seen by investors/yr: | 25—40 |
| No. of venture forums/yr: | Annual |
| No. firms using forum/yr: | 20 |
| $ range sought: Typical max: | $5M |
| Typical min: | $25K |
| Average: | $250K+ |
| Investors invested thru service: | NA |
| Successful matches: 1997: | 12 |
| 1998: | 6 |
| Since formation: | 33 |
| Service actively screen firms?: | Yes |
| Organization type: | Not for profit, university affiliated, and have 62 sponsors |

**Company Literature** (This information was obtained from the company's website without independent verification.)

Oregon Entrepreneurs Forum (OEF) is a not-for-profit corporation dedicated to providing opportunities for Oregon entrepreneurs and improving the business climate for emerging, growth-oriented Oregon companies. One of 18 worldwide chapters of the Massacheusetts Institute of Technology Enterprise Forum, OEF is committed to improving the flow of ideas, service, and capital to entrepreneurs; helping connect companies to expertise and other resources; and opening doors for Oregon entrepreneurs. OEF membership is made up of entrepreneurs and business professionals from throughout the state. Membership is diverse and varied—cutting across industries and professional affiliations and ranging from individuals launching new ventures to the senior executives of some of Oregon's most successful corporations.

**What Sets This Service Apart?** Recognized Oregon leader for entrepreneur networking, success of Venture Oregon, quality of private panel reviews, commitment of volunteers

# Rocky Mountain Venture Group

**Region: Northwest**

Mr. Bob Blyth
Rocky Mountain Venture Group
c/o Department of Energy
2300 North Yellowstone
Idaho Falls, ID 83401

tel: (208) 523-1026
fax: (208) 528-7127
http://www.rmvg.org

| | | |
|---|---|---|
| Classification of service: | A breakfast/luncheon meeting for investors, entrepreneurs, and others | |
| | No. of investors participating: | 8 |
| | No. of firms seen by investors/yr: | 15+ |
| Date of formation: | Sep '94 | |
| | No. of venture forums/yr: | 4 |
| Industry preferences: | NA | |
| | No. of firms using forum/yr: | 8+ |
| Stage of firms preferred: | Seed and start-up stage | |
| | $ range sought: Typical max: | $1M |
| Matching methods: | Venture forums and networking | |
| | Typical min: | $50K |
| Primary matching method: | Venture forums and networking | |
| | Average: | $250K |
| | Investors invested thru service: | 9 |
| No. of employees: Full-time: | | |
| Part-time: | 11 | Successful matches: 1997: | 2 |
| Volunteer: | | 1998: | 2 |
| | Since formation: | 8 |
| Organization type: | Not for profit | |
| | Service actively screen firms?: | Yes |
| Firms featured by service: | 10% Seed, 80% Start-up, 10% Early | |
| Additional services offered: | Newsletter and mentoring | |

**What Sets This Service Apart?** Only one in the area, best entrepreneurs network.

## Atlanta Development Authority

**Region: Southeast**

Mr. Kevin Hanna
Atlanta Development Authority
86 Payor Street
Suite 300
Atlanta, GA 30303

tel: (404) 808-4100
fax: (404) 808-9333
e-mail: khanna@atlantadd.com

| | | | |
|---|---|---|---|
| Classification of service: | NA | No. of investors participating: | NA |
| Date of formation: | 1997 | No. of firms seen by investors/yr: | NA |
| Industry preferences: | Commercial real estate | No. of venture forums/yr: | Not Applicable |
| Stage of firms preferred: | Early and expansion stage | No. of firms using forum/yr: | Not Applicable |
| Matching methods: | Internet and newsletter | $ range sought: Typical max: | $250K |
| Primary matching method: | Newsletter/Magazine | Typical min: | NA |
| No. of employees: Full-time: | 30 | Average: | NA |
| Part-time: | | Investors invested thru service: | NA |
| Volunteer: | | Successful matches: 1997: | NA |
| | | 1998: | NA |
| Organization type: | Not for profit | Since formation: | NA |

# Birmingham Venture Club

## Region: Southeast

Mr. Bill Sisson
Birmingham Venture Club
c/o Birmingham Chamber of Commerce
P.O. Box 10127
Birmingham, AL 35202

tel: (202) 323-5461
fax: (202) 250-7669

| | | | |
|---|---|---|---|
| Classification of service: | A breakfast/luncheon | No. of investors participating: | 50 |
| Date of formation: | 1985 | No. of firms seen by investors/yr: | NA |
| Industry preferences: | High tech | No. of venture forums/yr: | 6 |
| Stage of firms preferred: | Seed, start-up, and early stage | No. of firms using forum/yr: | NA |
| Matching methods: | Venture forums | $ range sought: Typical max: | NA |
| Primary matching method: | Venture Forums | Typical min: | $100K |
| No. of employees: Full-time: | | Average: | NA |
| Part-time: | 2 | Investors invested thru service: | NA |
| Volunteer: | | Successful matches: 1997: | NA |
| | | 1998: | NA |
| Organization type: | Not for profit | Since formation: | NA |
| | | Service actively screen firms?: | No |

Firms featured by service: 25% Seed, 25% Start-up, 25% Early, 25% Expansion
Additional services offered: Resource guide membership guide, guest speakers at bimonthly meetings.

**Company Literature**  (This information was obtained from the company's website without independent verification.)
Since 1985, the Birmingham Venture Club has been focusing on just one goal: creating an atmosphere that encourages entrepreneurial development and investments. The club does this in three ways: educating interested persons about the purpose and benefits of venture capital; creating a network for the exchange of information between investors, entrepreneurs, and professionals serving these groups; and stimulating investment capital for ventures that are developed in the Birmingham community. Birmingham Venture Club meetings are structured around a speaker who is a prominent entrepreneur, venture capitalist, or other pertinent professional. Meetings are designed to provide a suitable atmosphere for the exchange of information and the development of a network for business relationships. The club is a nonprofit corporation and is a program of the Birmingham Area Chamber of Commerce.

# Merritt Capital Services

**Region: Southeast**

Mr. Stephen Martin
Merritt Capital Services
400 Fallen Leaf Lane
Rosewell, GA 30075

tel: (770) 650-0495
fax: (770) 650-0495
e-mail: smmartin@merittcap.com
http://www.merittcap.com

| | | | |
|---|---|---|---|
| Classification of service: | A formal matching service | No. of investors participating: | 600+ |
| Date of formation: | 1996 | No. of firms seen by investors/yr: | 4 |
| Industry preferences: | Healthcare, pharmaceutical, software, | No. of venture forums/yr: | Sporadic |
| | medical device, high-tech | No. firms using forum/yr: | Not Applicable |
| Stage of firms preferred: | Start-up and early stage | $ range sought: Typical max: | $8 mil |
| Matching methods: | Internet and investor-specified criteria and | Typical min: | $1 mil |
| | venture forums | Average: | $3 – 4 mil |
| Primary matching method: | Investor-specified criteria | Investors invested thru service: | 12 |
| No. of employees: Full-time: | 3 | Successful matches: 1997: | 1 |
| Part-time: | 1 | 1998: | 4 |
| Volunteer: | | Since formation: | 5 |
| Organization type: | Private | Service actively screen firms?: | Yes |
| Firms featured by service: | 10% Seed, 40% Start-up, 50% Early | | |
| Additional services offered: | Business plan review and editing, advice on strategy and negotiations. | | |

**Company Literature** (This information was obtained from the company's website without independent verification.)
Merritt Capital Services offers venture capital funding assistance and financial planning services to early stage growth businesses where the range of funding needed is between $1 and $10 million. We connect privately held companies seeking money for product introduction business expansion and acquisitions with private investors, appropriate venture firms, and institutional investors. We work with start-ups when the technology is protected and seed funding is already in place. Our focus is on U.S.-based projects in the field of health care and/or communications. We are particularly interested in pharmaceuticals, or E-commerce centered opportunities. We know the investment community and the majority of projects we undertake get funded. We are paid on a performance basis. Merritt Capital charges no advance or up-front fees. Our initial analytical work, overview and consultations are at no cost to our client's. We get paid only at the closing of our clients funding. We represent our client's project on a nonexclusive basis. That means if a client finds funding on their own and not by way of our investor contacts or referrals, the client owes us nothing.

**What Sets This Service Apart?** Experiences in successful start-ups, we care about clients and their projects. No up-front fees—client pays nothing until funding closes, quick response time, small number of clients at any one time.

# Network for Business Acquisitions and Investments (NBA&I)

**Region: Southeast**

Mr. Jerry Martin
Network for Business Acquisitions and Investments (NBA&I)
3873 Roswell Road NW, Suite 4,
Atlanta, GA 30342

tel: (404) 261-2434
e-mail: sylviae@AOL.com

| | |
|---|---|
| Classification of service: | Group of angels |
| Date of formation: | 1995 |
| Industry preferences: | Manufacturing, mid-technology |
| Stage of firms preferred: | Start-up, early, and expansion |
| Matching methods: | Newsletter, investor criteria, forums, and meetings |
| Primary matching method: | Venture forums |
| No. of employees: Full-time: | 1 |
| Part-time: | 2 |
| Volunteer: | 3 |
| Organization type: | Private |

| | |
|---|---|
| No. of investors participating: | 80 |
| No. firms seen by investors/yr: | 120–150 |
| No. of venture forums/yr: | 1–2/yr |
| No. firms using forum/yr: | 50–100 |
| $ range sought: Typical max: | $3 mil |
| Typical min: | $50K |
| Average: | $500K |
| Investors invested thru service: | 40 |
| Successful matches: 1997: | NA |
| 1998: | NA |
| Since formation: | 30 |
| Service actively screen firms?: | Yes |

| | |
|---|---|
| Firms featured by service: | 10% Seed, 25% Start-up, 45% Early, 20% Expansion |
| Additional services offered: | Networking, contacts, database, special events, and so on. |

**Company Literature**  (This information was obtained from the company's website without independent verification.)
The Network for Business Acquisition & Investments (NBA&I) organization was formed by four people in 1995 for the purpose of networking to find quality businesses available for acquisition, merger, and/or investment. Today, this group of 83 members is continuing to identify and match business people wanting to acquire or invest in a business with desired business acquistion, merger, and investment opportunities. In the NBA&I organization there are both individuals and companies looking for the right money-making opportunity. Some are looking because of corporate downsizing, a changing job market, an interest in entrepreneurship, or a general interest in growing a business through acquisition or merger. The purpose of NBA&I is to help members identify quality deals and help make those deals possible. This unique organization helps make deals possible by providing a friendly, organized networking and educational forum where members can learn from each other, and have access to professional advisors who often provide some initial pro bono services. Advisors and resource members are generally limited to one from each discipline, including attorney, investment banker, business plan specialist, venture capital firm, CPA, business financing specialist, SBA lender, asset based lender, and so on. Today, NBA&I is 83 strong and growing. It is looking for new members to continue the growth and to replace members who have become "inactive."

**What Sets This Service Apart?**  Diversity of membership and interests. Fills a void between non-bankable and VC/Institutional eligible. Regular monthly meeting featuring deal presentation, organized, and so on.

# North Florida Venture Capital Network

**Region: Southeast**

Mr. Allan Rossiter
North Florida Venture Capital Network
7400 Baymeadows Way, Suite 201
Jacksonville, FL 32256

tel: (904) 730-4726
fax: (904) 730-4711
e-mail: rossiter@enfc.org
http://www.enfc.org

| | | | |
|---|---|---|---|
| Classification of service: | Group of Angels/Breakfast luncheon/other | No. of investors participating: | 70+ |
| Date of formation: | 1994/1998 | No. firms seen by investors/yr: | 80–100 |
| Industry preferences: | N/A | No. of venture forums/yr: | 1 |
| Stage of firms preferred: | Start-up and early stage | No. firms using forum/yr: | 24 |
| Matching methods: | Investor-specified criteria and venture forums | $ range sought: Typical max: | $5 mil |
| Primary matching method: | Other, deal sheets, personal contacts | Typical min: | $300K |
| No. of employees: Full-time: | 2 | Average: | Varies |
| Part-time: | | Investors invested thru service: | NA |
| Volunteer: | 3+ | Successful matches: 1997: | NA |
| Organization type: | Not for profit | 1998: | NA |
| | | Since formation: | 33 |
| | | Service actively screen firms?: | Yes |

Firms featured by service:   Seed, 50% Start-up, 50% Early

**Company Literature**   (This information was obtained from the company's website without independent verification.)
The North Venture Council Network Inc. (NFCVN) is a Florida incorporated not-for-profit corporation formed in April of 1998 for two purposes: the enhancement of the ability of private and institutional investors to locate promising investment opportunities in emerging growth companies in North Florida, and the enhancement of the ability of North Florida emerging growth companies to locate private and institutional investors interested in making equity investment in such companies. NFVCN is structured to serve the entirety of North Florida from Pensacola to Jacksonville to Ocala and Gainesville. Working closely with entrepreneurial support organizations throughout the region, NFVCN consolidates the entrepreneurial "deal flow" of a 36 county region into a single network.

# Private Investors Network

**Region: Southeast**

Dr. Niren Vyas, Private Investor Network
University of South Carolina at Aiken
471 University Parkway
Aiken, SC 29801

tel: (803) 641-3340
fax: (803) 641-3445
e-mail: nirenv@aiken.sc.edu
http://www.gabn.net/PIN/pin001.htm

| | | |
|---|---|---|
| Classification of service: | A formal matching service | |
| Date of formation: | May '98 | |
| Industry preferences: | Manufacturing | |
| Stage of firms preferred: | Start-up and expansion stage | |
| Matching methods: | Investor-specified criteria | |
| Primary matching method: | Investor-specified criteria | |
| No. of employees: Full-time: | 2 | |
| Part-time: | 2 | |
| Volunteer: | 6 | |
| Organization type: | Not for profit | |
| | | |
| Firms featured by service: | 70% Start-up, 30% Expansion | |
| Additional services offered: | Guidance on other sources of financing | |

| | |
|---|---|
| No. of investors participating; | 55 |
| No. firms seen by investors/yr: | 35 |
| No. of venture forums/yr: | NA |
| No. firms using forum/yr: | NA |
| $ range sought: Typical max: | $500K |
| Typical min: | $50K |
| Average: | $100K |
| Investors invested thru service: | 18 |
| Successful matches: 1997: | 3 |
| 1998: | 2 |
| Since formation: | NA |
| Service actively screen firms?: | No |

**Company Literature** (This information was obtained from the company's website without independent verification.)

Private Investors Network (PIN) is a confidential matching service which brings together entrepreneurs and investors in the state of South Carolina. PIN is operated on a nonprofit basis as a public service of the University of South Carolina-Aiken's Economic Enterprise Institute in cooperation with the South Carolina State Development Board. Investors and entrepreneurs enter the network by completing a brief questionnaire. Once the application and fee have been sent to PIN, the two stage matching process takes place as follows: Stage one, information from the investor and entrepreneur is entered into the computer and answers are compared for similarity on the basis of business category, the company's stage of development, capital requirements, and geographic location. After a first stage match has been determined, the investor receives a copy of the entrepreneur's profile and Executive Summary, neither of which identifies the entrepreneur or his company. The investor reviews the information and indicates by reply card whether or not he or she wishes to contact the entrepreneur. Stage two, if the investor requests contact, he or she will be sent the name, address, and phone number of the entrepreneur. Simultaneously, the entrepreneur will be sent the name, address, and phone number of the investor. After contact is initiated, PIN's involvement with this particular match ends. Both the entrepreneur and investor will continue to be matched with new entries into the database for the remainder of the subscription period, unless they indicate otherwise.

**What Sets This Service Apart?** Not for profit. Match making only. University based.

# South Carolina Recycling Market Development Council

**Region: Southeast**

Mr. Ted Campbell
South Carolina Recycling Market Development Council
South Carolina Department of Commerce
P.O. Box 927
Columbia, SC 29202

tel: (803) 737-0477
fax: (803) 737-0572
e-mail: tcampbel@commerce.state.sc.us
http://www.callsouthcarolina.com/recycling

| | |
|---|---|
| Classification of service: | Other, State Department of Commerce initiative focusing recycling industry support and market development |
| Date of formation: | 1995 |
| Industry preferences: | Recycling-related |
| Stage of firms preferred: | Early and expansion stage |
| Matching methods: | Venture forums |
| Primary matching method: | Venture forums |
| No. of employees: Full-time: | |
| Part-time: | |
| Volunteer: | |
| Organization type: | Subsidized by state government |
| Firms featured by service: | 20% Start-up, 20% Early, 60% Expansion |
| Additional services offered: | Selected businesses are provided with presentation training prior to forum. |

| | |
|---|---|
| No. of investors participating: | 5–10 |
| No. of firms seen by investors/yr: | 15 |
| No. of venture forums/yr: | 1 |
| No. firms using forum/yr: | 12 |
| $ range sought: Typical max: | NA |
| Typical min: | NA |
| Average: | $2 mil |
| Investors invested thru service: | NA |
| Successful matches: 1997: | 4 |
| 1998: | 0 |
| Since formation: | 9 |
| Service actively screen firms?: | Yes |

**Company Literature** (This information was obtained from the company's website without independent verification.)
The Recycling Market Development Advisory Council (RMDAC) is a fourteen member group, consisting primarily of recycling industry representatives. Its mission is to assist in the development of market in South Carolina for recovery materials and products with recycled content with the primary objectives of improved solid waste management, resource conservation, and economic development. Appointed by the Governor, the RMDAC reports annually on the current status of the recycling industry in South Carolina, barriers affecting recycling, and recommendation to facilitate market development. Managed within the Department of Commerce, the Council is well suited to coordinate economic development and recycling programs into a unified recycling market development effort.

# The Central Florida Innovation Corporation

## Region: Southeast

Mr. Ted Rowell
The Central Florida Innovation Corporation
12424 Research Parkway, Suite 350
Orlando, FL 32826

tel: (407) 277-5411
fax: (407) 277-2182
e-mail: cfic@cfic.org
http://www.cfic.org

| | | |
|---|---|---|
| Classification of service: | Other, incubator without walls | |
| Date of formation: | 1995 | |
| Industry preferences: | High-tech | |
| Stage of firms preferred: | Start-up | |
| Matching methods: | Internet, newsletter, investor-specified criteria, and venture forum | |
| Primary matching method: | Other, personal contact | |
| No. of employees: Full-time: | 19 | |
| Part-time: | | |
| Volunteer: | 16 | |
| Organization type: | Not for profit | |
| | | |
| Firms featured by service: | 50% Start-up, 50% Early | |
| Additional services offered: | Mentoring, pro-bono professional services networking, strategic planning, technology transfers. | |

| | |
|---|---|
| No. of investors participating: | 46 |
| No. firms seen by investors/yr: | 25 |
| No. of venture forums/yr: | 11 |
| No. firms using forum/yr: | 25 |
| $ range sought: Typical max: | $5 mil |
| Typical min: | $100K |
| Average: | $3 mil |
| Investors invested thru service: | Clients raised over $50 mil since inception |
| Successful matches: 1997: | NA |
| 1998: | NA |
| Since formation: | 4/year |
| Service actively screen firms?: | Yes |

**Company Literature** (This information was obtained from the company's website without independent verification.)

The Central Florida Innovation Corporation (CFIC), is an engine for economic growth. Our goal is to strengthen the economic base of Central Florida by supporting emerging companies that have a strong probability of succeeding and generating high paying, high-tech jobs in the area. CFIC does this by creating new companies (CFIC licenses technology from local industry and academia with high potential for growth and applies them to commercial market opportunities), strengthening local entrepreneurial business (CFIC works with companies that will be attractive to investors must have the potential to reach $25 million in revenue in 3–5 years), building successful companies (the Emerging Business Network [EBN] is a membership organization that opens doors to consultants, investors, fellow entrepreneurs, and business resources that help build successful companies). The EBN nurtures emerging Central Florida companies through outreach, business consulting, and investor-related services. EBN clients have the potential to reach $2–24 million in annual sales), and actively seeking investment capital (CFIC brings investment capital to emerging growth companies through MILCOM, out-of-state venture capital sources and local private investors. To date, CFIC has successfully raised tens of millions of dollars in out-of-state capital, assisted hundreds of local entrepreneurs, and created new companies. CFIC is a proven, result-oriented organization that is changing the face of technology in Central Florida.

# The South Carolina Technology Alliance

**Region: Southeast**

Mr. Thomas E. Persons, Sr.
The South Carolina Technology Alliance
1201 Main Street
Suite 1913
Columbia, SC 29201

tel: (803) 748-1323
fax: (803) 748-1325
e-mail: Tpersons@scra.org
http://sctech.org

| | |
|---|---|
| Classification of service: | Formal matching service, group of angel investors, Breakfast/luncheon, electronic-only network |
| Date of formation: | 1/1/98 |
| Industry preferences: | High-tech |
| Stage of firms preferred: | Stage and start-up |
| Matching methods: | Internet, newsletter, investor specified criteria, and venture forums |
| Primary matching method: | Internet, Venture forums |
| No. of employees: Full-time: | 8 |
| Part-time: | 2 |
| Volunteer: | 50 |
| Organization type: | Not for Profit, university affiliated, subsidized |
| Firms featured by service: | 20% Seed, 30% Start-up, 10% Early, 20% Expansion, 20% Other |

| | |
|---|---|
| No. of investors participating: | 25 |
| No. firms seen by investors/yr: | 75+ |
| No. of venture forums/yr: | 3 |
| No. firms using forum/yr: | NA |
| $ range sought:  Typical max: | $5 mil |
| Typical min: | $100K |
| Average: | $2 mil |
| Investors invested thru service: | 3 |
| Successful matches:        1997: | NA |
| 1998: | 2 |
| Since formation: | 3 |
| Service actively screen firms?: | Yes |

**Company Literature**   (This information was obtained from the company's website without independent verification.)
South Carolina Technology Alliance was established to complete the following: Prepare the technology-capable workforce, create a business environment that is friendly to technology-intensive companies, invest to expand the base of rapidly growing company and start-up business, invest in world class university research programs that are directly linked to the South Carolina industry.

**What Sets This Service Apart?**   We have the strong support of a group of South Carolina's TOP technology, business and government leaders.

# The Venture Club of Louisville

## Region: Southeast

Mr. Henry Hensley
The Venture Club of Louisville
310 West Liberty Street, Suite 505
Louisville, KY 40202

tel: (502) 589-6868
fax: (502) 583-9176
e-mail: hhenley@rjifs.com
http://www.ventureclub-louisville.org

| | | |
|---|---|---|
| Classification of service: | A breakfast/luncheon meeting for investors, entrepreneurs, and others | No. of investors participating: 50 |
| | | No. firms seen by investors/yr: 36 |
| Date of formation: | 10/1/95 | No. of venture forums/yr: 12 |
| Industry preferences: | Open to all | No. firms using forum/yr: 60 |
| Stage of firms preferred: | Early stage | $ range sought:  Typical max: $5M |
| Matching methods: | Internet, newsletter/magazine, and venture forums | Typical min: $100K |
| | | Average: $500K |
| Primary matching method: | NA | Investors invested thru service: 35 |
| No. of employees:  Full-time: | 1 | Successful matches:  1997: 8 |
| Part-time: | | 1998: 7 |
| Volunteer: | | Since formation: 15 |
| Organization type: | Not for profit | Service actively screen firms?: Yes |
| Firms featured by service: | 20% Seed, 20% Start-up, 50% Early, 10% Expansion | |
| Additional services offered: | 4 seminars per year | |

**Company Literature**   (This information was obtained from the company's website without independent verification.)

The Venture Club of Louisville was begun in autumn 1995 to bring entrepreneurs and investors together in a professional but relaxed forum. The monthly meetings offer both groups the opportunity to make valuable contacts, exchange information, and pursue mutual business opportunities. An important purpose of the Club is to help facilitate and encourage the expansion of business and commercial investment activities in the region. Membership is open to professional venture capitalists, private investors, investment bankers, commercial bankers, entrepreneurs, attorneys, accountants, consultants, and others involved in the investment community. Luncheon meetings are held the first Wednesday of each month at The Seelbach Hotel Medallion Ballroom from noon to 1:30. An informal social time begins at 11:30 A.M. Each meeting features five-minute presentations by entrepreneurs interested in obtaining capital to start or to support growth and expansion of their business; one-minute announcement by fledgling entrepreneurs or about upcoming activities and programs relevant to members; a guest speaker who discusses venture or financial issues, entrepreneurs success stories, or trends affecting the climate for entrepreneurs. Special events are held by the Club from time to time such as seminars to help strengthen and grow the entrepreneur.

# U.S. Investor Network

**Region: Southeast**

Ms. Linda Leake
U.S. Investor Network
P.O. Box 6344
Raleigh, NC 27628-6344

tel: (919) 783-0614
fax: (919) 833-8007
e-mail: president@usinvestor.com
http://www.usinvestor.com

| | | |
|---|---|---|
| Classification of service: | A formal matching service | |
| Date of formation: | 1986 | |
| Industry preferences: | | |
| Stage of firms preferred: | | |
| Matching methods: | Internet and newsletter/magazine | |
| Primary matching method: | Internet | |
| No. of employees:  Full-time: | 3 | |
|   Part-time: | | |
|   Volunteer: | | |
| Organization type: | Not for profit | |
| No. of investors participating: | | NA |
| No. of firms seen by investors/yr: | | NA |
| No. of venture forums/yr: | | NA |
| No. of firms using forum/yr: | | NA |
| $ range sought:  Typical max: | | NA |
|   Typical min: | | NA |
|   Average: | | NA |
| Investors invested thru service: | | NA |
| Successful matches:  1997: | | NA |
|   1998: | | NA |
|   Since formation: | | NA |
| Service actively screen firms?: | | NA |

**Company Literature**  (**This information was obtained from the company's website without independent verification.**)
The U.S. Investor Network is an organization operating in the United States and is designed to serve entrepreneurs and investors. We are a regional operator for the SBA's Ace-Net program and can help you with the application and enrollment process for ACE-Net, where you will be presenting your business plan to hundreds of accredited investors nationwide.

# Houston Venture Capital Association

## Region: Southwest

Ms. Sally Evans
Houston Venture Capital Association
P.O. Box 56644
Houston, TX 77256

tel: (713) 660-7990
fax: (713) 663-6542

| | | | |
|---|---|---|---|
| Classification of service: | An association of private equity funds | No. of investors participating: | 58 |
| Date of formation: | 1982 | No. firms seen by investors/yr: | NA |
| Industry preferences: | No preferences | No. of venture forums/yr: | Not Applicable |
| Stage of firms preferred: | NA | No. firms using forum/yr: | Not Applicable |
| Matching methods: | Referral | $ range sought: Typical max: | NA |
| Primary matching method: | Referral | Typical min: | NA |
| No. of employees: Full-time: | | Average: | NA |
| Part-time: | | Investors invested thru service: | NA |
| Volunteer: | 1 | Successful matches: 1997: | NA |
| Organization type: | Private and not for profit | 1998: | NA |
| | | Since formation: | NA |
| | | Service actively screen firms?: | NA |

Additional services offered:    Quarterly networking breakfast and speakers on timely topics

**Company Literature**    (**This information was obtained from the company's website without independent verification.**)
The Houston Venture Capital Association was founded in the early 1980s to provide networking mechanisms for professional investors in management positions of private equity funds. It's original focus was Houston-based investments funds but now includes funds from around the country who are interested in investment opportunities in the Houston area. The primary activities of the organization include quarterly breakfast, networking meetings which occasionally feature speakers on topics of interest. The organization also provides monetary scholarship funds to graduating high school seniors who have achieved excellence in academics and leadership.

**What Sets This Service Apart?**    Our association is primarily a networking mechanism for professionals in management equity funds. It is not focused on matching investors and investment opportunities.

# MIT Enterprise Forum of Dallas-Fort Worth, Inc.

**Region: Southwest**

Mr. Neil Kaden
MIT Enterprise Forum of Dallas-Forth Worth, Inc.
P.O. Box 830688, LF15
Dallas, TX 75083-0688

tel: (972) 883-6364
fax: (972) 883-6831
e-mail: kadon@alum.mit.edu
http://flash.net/zkaden/Pages/MITEF/mit-ef-at-utd.html

| | |
|---|---|
| Classification of service: | Breakfast luncheon |
| Date of formation: | 1986 |
| Industry preferences: | High-tech |
| Stage of firms preferred: | Early, expansion stage, and mature |
| Matching methods: | Internet and venture forums |
| Primary matching method: | Venture Forums |
| No. of employees: Full-time: | 1 |
| Part-time: | 12 |
| Volunteer: | |
| Organization type: | Not for Profit/university affiliated |
| Firms featured by service: | 25% Early, 50% Expansion, 25% Other |
| Additional services offered: | Networking |

| | |
|---|---|
| No. of investors participating: | 20 |
| No. of firms seen by investors/yr: | 83 |
| No. of venture forums/yr: | 5 |
| No. of firms using forum/yr: | 10 |
| $ range sought: Typical max: | NA |
| Typical min: | NA |
| Average: | NA |
| Investors invested thru service: | |
| Successful matches: 1997: | NA |
| 1998: | NA |
| Since formation: | NA |
| Service actively screen firms?: | Yes |

**Company Literature** (This information was obtained from the company's website without independent verification.)
Formed in 1978 by the MIT Alumni Association in Cambridge, Massachusetts, the MIT Enterprise Forum provides a unique service to small and medium-sized technology-related companies and other entrepreneurs. The Forum has become a focus for constructive analysis of emerging companies in a growing number of metropolitan areas. The Dallas/Fort Worth chapter of the Forum was founded in 1986 by MIT alumni and local business leaders, and joined in association with UT Dallas in 1993. Through presentation of a business plan of experts, the Chief Executive Officer of an emerging company receives vital feedback on his/her strategy, planning product development, production, marketing, and financial orientation. The panelists without pay, and MIT alumni and local business leaders volunteer their time and counsel to the project in a variety of support capacities. In an objective and analytical session, members of the panel comment on the business plan. Each of the panelists reviews the past and ongoing business situation of the Company, as well as its future plans, and offers constructive advice to the Company's CEO. Panelists at each case presentation include leading advisors specifically recruited for the particular case. An audience representing the spectrum of small business and related fields, as well as individuals interested in business development, are present and may offer additional advice or opinions. The Forum presentations are open to the public. The presenting companies are screened from a pool of local Dallas and Fort Worth technology-related business. Activities of the MIT Enterprise Forum at UTD are directed by an Executive Committee. Executive Committee members are experienced business executives who donate their time and services to the Forum. Complementing the human resources made available by MIT, its alumni, and local business people is the financial group of Dallas and Fort Worth business with a history of civic concerns. As co-sponsors, they lend an essential level of community commitment and advice.

**What Sets This Service Apart?** When presenting, CEOs go through the exercise of preparing business case presentations and meet with panelists and attendees. They often discover new options for their companies.

# MIT Enterprise Forum of Texas, Inc.

**Region: Southwest**

Ms. Dottie Kerr
MIT Enterprise Forum of Texas, Inc.
PO Box 96758
Houston, TX 77213-6758

tel: (713) 685-3891
http://www.mitetx.org

| | | | |
|---|---|---|---|
| Classification of service: | Education and networking forum | No. of investors participating: | NA |
| Date of formation: | 1978 | No. of firms seen by investors/yr: | 7 |
| Industry preferences: | Technology | No. of venture forums/yr: | 1 |
| Stage of firms preferred: | Start-up, early, and expansion stage | No. of firms using forum/yr: | NA |
| Matching methods: | Venture forums and studies and clinics with | $ range sought: Typical max: | $10 mil |
| | feedback | Typical min: | $1 mil |
| Primary matching method: | Venture forums | Average: | $3 mil |
| No. of employees: Full-time: | 0 | Investors invested thru service: | NA |
| Part-time: | 1 | Successful matches: 1997: | NA |
| Volunteer: | 40 | 1998: | NA |
| Organization type: | Private, not for profit and university affiliated | Since formation: | NA |
| | | Service actively screen firms?: | Yes |
| Firms featured by service: | 50% Start-up, 10% Early, 40% Expansion | | |
| Additional services offered: | Roster of members, notice of programs, discount on program attendance fees. | | |

**Company Literature** (This information was obtained from the company's website without independent verification.)
The Houston-based MIT Enterprise Forum of Texas, Inc. is one of 18 licensed, autonomous chapters of the MIT Enterprise Forum, Inc., founded in Cambridge Massachusetts, in 1978. Since 1984, the local organization has offered a basic group of services which include professional seminars, start-up clinics, business plan workshops, case presentations, and networking opportunities with peers, business specialists and venture capitalists. In the United Stated, Canada, Mexico and Israel, the Forum works in partnership with various law and accounting firms, financial institutions, and corporations to help entrepreneurs and technology-based companies grow. Additionally, the Executive Office of the Forum sponsors Technology Policy Conferences in collaboration with local, national, and international governments to disseminate up-to-date policy information about the commercialization of state-of-the-art technology.

**What Sets This Service Apart?** Companies present their business plans or case studies and get feedback from a panel of selected relevant experts and an informed audience.

# Southwest Venture Forum

**Region: Southwest**

Delania Teems
Southwest Venture Forum
Edwin L. Cox School of Business, SMU
P.O. Box 750333
Dallas, TX 75275-0333

tel: (214) 768-3689
fax: (214) 768-3604
e-mail: dteems@mail.cox.smu.edu
http://www.smu.edu/

| | | | |
|---|---|---|---|
| Classification of service: | A breakfast/luncheon meeting for investors, entrepreneurs, and others | No. of investors participating: | Several dozen |
| | | No. firms seen by investors/yr: | 12 |
| Date of formation: | 1985 | No. of venture forums/yr: | 6 |
| Industry preferences: | Fast growth | No. firms using forum/yr: | 12 |
| Stage of firms preferred: | Seed, start-up, early, and expansion stage | $ range sought: Typical max: | $5M |
| Matching methods: | Venture Forums | Typical min: | $1M |
| Primary matching method: | Venture forums | Average: | $1.5M–2M |
| No. of employees: Full-time: | 0 | Investors invested thru service: | NA |
| Part-time: | 0 | Successful matches: 1997: | NA |
| Volunteer: | 10 | 1998: | NA |
| Organization type: | Private, not-for-profit, and university affiliated | Since formation: | NA |
| | | Service actively screen firms?: | Yes |
| Firms featured by service: | 10% Seed, 20% Start-up, 40% Early, 30% Expansion | | |
| Additional services offered: | Networking | | |

**What Sets This Service Apart?** Deals are screened by advisory board of Venture Capitalists'; 350 persons in attendance at forums.

# Colorado Capital Alliance, Inc.
## Region: The Great Plains

Ms. Marcia Schirmer
Colorado Capital Alliance, Inc.
P.O. Box 19169
Boulder, CO 80308-2169

tel: (303) 499-9646
fax: (303) 494-4146
e-mail: ecainc@earthlink.net
http://www.angelcapital.com

| | |
|---|---|
| Classification of service: | A formal matching service |
| Date of formation: | 1997 |
| Industry preferences: | Cover all, high in software high tech |
| Stage of firms preferred: | Seed, start-up, early, and expansion stage |
| Matching methods: | Internet, newsletter, investor criteria, forums, training |
| Primary matching method: | Customized computer matching |
| No. of employees: Full-time: | 0 |
| Part-time: | 2–5 |
| Volunteer: | 0 |
| Organization type: | Not for profit |
| Firms featured by service: | 30% Seed, 47% Early, 23% Expansion |
| Additional services offered: | Investor seminars ("Art of Successful Angel Investing") Business plan preparation. |

| | |
|---|---|
| No. of investors participating: | 30–70 (varies) |
| No. firms seen by investors/yr: | 100–160 |
| No. of venture forums/yr: | 1–2 per year |
| No. firms using forum/yr: | 200 |
| $ range sought: Typical max: | $750K |
| Typical min: | $100K |
| Average: | $200K |
| Investors invested thru service: | 10 |
| Successful matches: 1997: | 3 |
| 1998: | 7 |
| Since formation: | 16 |
| Service actively screen firms?: | No |

**Company Literature** (This information was obtained from the company's website without independent verification.)

The Colorado Capital Alliance is a not-for-profit angel network that matches private investors with high growth ventures. It provides an efficient, confidential, and cost-effective way for investors to review entrepreneurs' business summaries—only in the investor's area of interest. The CCA has facilitated over $4 million dollars in direct and indirect investments since its inception in 1997. The Alliance also hosts educational seminars for private investors and entrepreneurs. The goal of the seminar is to provide information and training that will maintain the high quality of deal flow in the CCA database as well as increase the number of successful and profitable angel investments. The CCA is the recipient of a national SBA Vision 2000 award, a Denver Business Journal award for innovation, and its book *Business Angels: A Guide to Private Investing*, recently reviewed in *Money* magazine, has sold throughout the world. The book has gained national attention as a one-of-a-kind, clearly written book that advises investors how to investigate, invest in, and work with young companies. It also advises entrepreneurs how to make a presentation to investors, assist investors in their background studies, negotiate terms, and work together to build a company. *Business Angels* can be ordered directly from the CCA website or by calling (303) 440-1356 and leaving a fax number.

**What Sets This Service Apart?** Personal service, investor seminars, business plan development, book we published on *Business Angels*.

# Montana Private Capital Network

**Region: The Great Plains**

Mr. Jon Marchi
Montana Private Capital Network
P.O. Box 430
Polson, MT 59860-0430

tel: (406) 883-5470
fax: (406) 883-5677
http://www.mbc.umt.edu/mpcn.html

| | |
|---|---|
| Classification of service: | A formal matching service |
| Date of formation: | 1992 |
| Industry preferences: | None |
| Stage of firms preferred: | Seed, start-up, early, and expansion |
| Matching methods: | Newsletter, investor-specified criteria, and venture forums |
| Primary matching method: | Investor-specified criteria |
| No. of employees: Full-time: | |
| Part-time: | 2 |
| Volunteer: | |
| Organization type: | Not for profit, university affiliated, subsidized by Government |
| Firms featured by service: | 50% Seed, 20% Start-up, 10% Early, 20% Expansion |

| | |
|---|---|
| No. of investors participating: | 60 |
| No. firms seen by investors/yr: | 10 to 20 |
| No. of venture forums/yr: | 1 |
| No. firms using forum/yr: | 100 |
| $ range sought: Typical max: | $1 mil |
| Typical min: | $500K |
| Average: | $300K |
| Investors invested thru service: | 12 |
| Successful matches: 1997: | NA |
| 1998: | NA |
| Since formation: | 7 |
| Service actively screen firms?: | No |

**Company Literature** (This information was obtained from the company's website without independent verification.)

Montana Private Capital Network (MPCN) is a unique computerized database that uses software from the Massachusetts Institute of Technology to match investors and entrepreneurs with similar business interests. During these first stage matches, information on the identity of the entrepreneur and investor is confidential. When a first-stage match is made, the investor receives an anonymous business summary and information from the entrepreneur's application form. At the same time, the entrepreneur is notified that he or she has matched with an investor. MPCN has now successfully completed 2267 first-stage matches. Every entrepreneur enrolled in the database is now one step closer to finding the right "angel" for their business. There have been 133 second stage matches completed as well. A second-stage match occurs when an investor decides he wants to pursue a venture he has been matched up with. At that point, both the investor and entrepreneur receive information on how to contact one another. Further negotiations take place between the two parties. The third-stage process has succeeded in placing over $1,600,000 in Montana businesses by MPCN investors with an additional $877,500 leveraged by the investments for a total of $2,477,500. With the assistance of the Montana Department of Commerce CDBG Technical Assistance Program, we are exploring the opportunity of becoming an ACE-Net operator for the state of Montana. This program will provide entrepreneurs and growing business a link to a nationwide network of investors who can review their proposals.

336

# The Rockies Venture Club

## Region: The Great Plains

Ms. Maita Lester
The Rockies Venture Club
190 East 9th Avenue, Suite 320
Denver, CO 80203

tel: (303) 831-4174
fax: (303) 832-4920
e-mail: MAITA@EARTHLINK.net
http://www.rockiesventureclub.org

| | |
|---|---|
| Classification of service: | Dinner meetings |
| Date of formation: | 1984 |
| Industry preferences: | None |
| Stage of firms preferred: | Seed, start-up, early, and expansion |
| Matching methods: | Newsletter and venture forums and monthly meetings |
| Primary matching method: | None |
| No. of employees: Full-time: | 0 |
| Part-time: | 0 |
| Volunteer: | 21 Board, 20 Committees |
| Organization type: | Not for profit |

| | |
|---|---|
| No. of investors participating: | 100 |
| No. firms seen by investors/yr: | None |
| No. of venture forums/yr: | 1 |
| No. firms using forum/yr: | Not tracked |
| $ range sought: Typical max: | $5 mil |
| Typical min: | $50K |
| Average: | Not Tracked |
| Investors invested thru service: | Not Tracked |
| Successful matches: 1997: | NA |
| 1998: | NA |
| Since formation: | NA |
| Service actively screen firms?: | No, except for annual forum |

Additional services offered: Membership benefits include: discounted prices at all events, a 5-minute presentation slot at monthly meetings to talk about any subjects, membership directory, monthly newsletter, free use of display tables to present information about your company.

**Company Literature** (This information was obtained from the company's website without independent verification.)
The Rockies Venture Club (RVC) is a nonprofit, volunteer organization that celebrates the spirit of entrepreneurship in the Rocky Mountain region. Founded in 1983, RVC is the only networking organization that connects entrepreneurs, service professionals, investors, venture capitalists and other funding sources. Dramatic changes in the Rocky Mountain business climate will have a profound effect on emerging businesses. How will these changes impact your business, competitors, suppliers, and customers? Insights, information, and new connections are vital to entrepreneurs, investors, bankers, consultants, accountants, lawyers, and marketers. The RVC provides a unique open forum where emerging businesses can network with qualified funding sources and professional service providers, and where potential investors can learn of growing businesses through the RVC's presentation series and monthly forums.

**What Sets This Service Apart?** Networking!

## Wayne Brown Institute
**Region: The Great Plains**

Mr. Bradley B. Bertoch
Wayne Brown Institute
170 South Main Street #1210
Salt Lake City, UT 84101

tel: (801) 595-1141
fax: (801) 595-1181
e-mail: waynebrown@venturecapital.org
http://www.venturecapital.org

| | | | |
|---|---|---|---|
| Classification of service: | Other, cooperative venturing organization | No. of investors participating: | 100+ |
| Date of formation: | 1983 | No. of firms seen by investors/yr: | 45–60 |
| Industry preferences: | High-tech | No. of venture forums/yr: | 3–4 |
| Stage of firms preferred: | Seed, start-up, early, and expansion | No. firms using forum/yr: | 45–60 |
| Matching methods: | Investor-specified criteria and venture forums | $ range sought: Typical max: | $5–7 mil |
| Primary matching method: | Investor-specified criteria/venture forum | Typical min: | $0.5–1.5 mil |
| No. of employees: Full-time: | 2 | Average: | $1–3 mil |
| Part-time: | 2 | Investors invested thru service: | 100+ |
| Volunteer: | hundreds | Successful matches: 1997: | 30 |
| | | 1998: | 10 |
| Organization type: | Private/not for profit | Since formation: | 60 |
| Firms featured by service: | 30% Seed, 30% Start-up, 30% Early, 10% Expansion | Service actively screen firms?: | Yes |
| Additional services offered: | Venture, analysis of business plans, mentoring. | | |

**Company Literature** (This information was obtained from the company's website without independent verification.)
Established in 1983, the Wayne Brown Institute is a nationally recognized organization focusing on developing quality deal flow for the venture, corporate, and private investor. As a nonprofit educational organization, the Institute focuses on helping emerging high-technology businesses find the resources they need to raise capital. The Institute has developed a selection process in which almost 60 percent of participating companies raise capital totaling almost $450 million. The Institute has accomplished this as follows: By being one of the largest suppliers of venture capital conferences in the country. The Institute focus on venture in Utah, Hawaii, and New York. ninety percent of its revenue for operations is from private sources. By having many major professional service firms, corporations, and venture capitalists as long-term supporters and sponsors, it helped develop and is currently commercializing revolutionary technology for new venture analysis. The Institute's mission is "Improve the Human Condition by Commercializing Technology Through Entrepreneurship." It should be noted that the Wayne Brown Institute is not an entrepreneurship driven organization. It is a venture capital driven organization. The Institute is predicated on the belief that entrepreneurs must conform to the needs of the Investor, rather than the Investor conforming to the wants of the entrepreneur. In order to create financial deals, the Institute has had to understand the Investor; remain through private sponsorship; and afford entrepreneurship a genuine opportunity to raise capital.

**What Sets This Service Apart?** Investor focus, experience, contacts.

# Appendix Two:
# Further Helpful Resources

In this section of the book, you will find many helpful resources to aid your entrepreneurial endeavors, regardless of whether you are an entrepreneur, business angel, venture capitalist, or student in this area. All these references should be available at your local library, local university library, or the publisher listed for each source, although many also have useful websites that we encourage you to explore. These references were all accurate at the time of publication, and some may appear in more than one section for obvious reasons.

We are greatly indebted to Carol Elsen of the Harvard University Graduate School of Business for her contributions to this section.

## Directories of Venture Capital and Private Investors

This section includes resources that help identify, locate, and categorize companies (as well as organizations, individuals, and other resources) in an industry.

*Pratt's Guide to Venture Capital Sources.* Wellesley, Mass.: Venture Economics. Annual.
This directory contains information on more than twelve hundred venture capital companies, including some Canadian, European,

---

The primary reference for this appendix is Elsen, C. J. *Baker Library Industry Guide: Venture Capital and Private Equity.* Cambridge, Mass.: Harvard University Graduate School of Business, 1999. On the Web at http://www.library.hbs.edu/industry/venture-print.htm

and Asian-Pacific ones. Entries are arranged by state or country and list project preferences, type of financing, minimum investment, preferred investment, and contact person. The introductory chapters give a useful overview of the venture capital industry, with chapters on "Background on Venture Capital," "How to Raise Venture Capital," "Sources of Business Development Financing," and "Perspectives."

*Directory of Private Equity Investors.* New York: Securities Data Publishing. Annual.
This directory profiles seven hundred capital sources in the field of private equity. There are articles on private equity and detailed profiles of the larger investors. Several sections contain short directory listings for investment advisors, public pension plans, corporate pension plans, endowments and foundations, insurance companies, and financial corporations. There are indexes by company name, personnel, location (by state), investment interest, preferred investment size, and assets under management.

*Corporate Finance Sourcebook.* New Providence, N.J.: National Register Publishing Company. Annual.
This directory is a comprehensive guide to capital investment sources and financial services, including cash managers, U.S. and international venture capital firms, lenders, lessors, commercial and investment banks and bankers, intermediaries, corporate real estate services, merchant banking, business insurance brokers, securities analysts, and CPAs. Information for each firm varies, depending on types of activity. More than thirty-five hundred firms are covered. Also included is a three-year "finance retrospective," listing all corporate public offerings.

*Directory of Alternative Investment Programs.* Wellesley, Mass.: Asset Alternatives, Inc. Annual.
The Directory of Alternative Investment Programs on CD-ROM features hard-to-find information on private equity investors. This directory has detailed profiles of the private investment programs of five hundred of the largest U.S. pension funds (public and corporate), endowments, foundations, banks, and finance and insurance companies. The database allows searching by investor

information (type of institution and geographic location), type of program (including asset buyouts and corporate finance, direct investment, real estate funds, energy funds, mezzanine, and so on), portfolio characteristics (total assets, how active the investment program is, and so on), and commitments (funds in which invested, type of fund, commitment amount, total fund size). What sets this directory apart from other similar resources is the information on the funds in which each organization invests.

*EVCA Yearbook.* London: Ernst and Young; European Venture Capital Association. Annual.
This is a comprehensive survey of the European private equity and venture capital industry. Statistics on European private equity are listed overall and by country. There is also a directory of the members of the European Venture Capital Association, listed by country.

FinanceHub. http://FinanceHub.com/vc/vctab.html
FinanceHub's Venture Capital site allows the investor to search for venture capital seekers; seekers may add their entries to this database. There are also links to VC firms and articles on how to get venture capital.

*Fitzroy Dearborn International Directory of Venture Capital Funds.* Chicago: Fitzroy Dearborn. Annual.
This directory covers more than one thousand funds and is arranged in five sections: general companies; high technology and medical funds; minority and socially useful funds; strategic partners; and venture capital funds outside the United States. Entries include address, phone, e-mail, year founded, average and minimum investment, industry group preferences, and portfolio companies. There are alphabetical, geographic, personnel, and category (investment preference) indexes.

*Galante's Venture Capital and Private Equity Directory.* Wellesley, Mass.: Asset Alternatives, Inc. Annual.
This directory covers a wide variety of organizations, including venture capital, mergers and acquisitions, LBO, merchant banking firms, corporate pension funds, and small business investment

companies (SBICs) and associations. International in scope, the directory covers fifteen hundred firms and includes various ranked lists and industry statistics. The introductory section includes articles on the history of venture capital and the current state of the industry. Separate sections cover U.S. private equity firms, U.S. indexes, and international private equity firms. The indexing is a strong feature of Galante's, covering company names, location by country and city, funding stage preference, industry stage preference, and geographic preference and investment funds. Company entries include the usual logistics: names, addresses, investment criteria, and preferences. Added features are website, investment pace and policies, and a description of the firm's focus. The CD-ROM version is searchable by firm name, geographic location, type of firm, size (capital managed, number of employees), and activity level (actively seeking, will consider, not seeking); investment or buyout size; means of compensation; funding stage preferences (R&D, seed, bridge, LBO, distressed debt, and so on); and geographic preferences.

*Going Public: Guide to Technology Finance.* (Special issue of *Red Herring.*) San Francisco: Herring Communications. Monthly.
This special issue features ranked lists of the top twenty-five technology IPOs, technology venture capital firms, and technology investment banks, as well as many articles.

*Guide to Venture Capital in Asia.* Hong Kong: AVCJ Holdings Limited. Annual.
Sections include a history and prospective of venture capital in seventeen countries in the Asia Pacific region, details of the industry by country, and profiles of eight hundred worldwide venture capital firms operating in Asia. Company name, location, fund, and name indexes are included. There is a geographical index as well as a listing of venture capital associations in Asia. Charts and graphs.

*PricewaterhouseCoopers Money Tree Survey.* Quarterly.
http://209.67.194.61/index.asp (or the company's main venture capital site: www.pw.com/vc)

These surveys represent the merger of the Price Waterhouse National Venture Capital Survey with the Coopers and Lybrand Money Tree Survey. The quarterly surveys include overviews of venture capital and private equity in the United States and statistics by industry, by state, and by firm.

*Top VCs on the Internet.* Capital Venture. http://www.capitalventure .com/cvvclinks.htm
Capital Venture has links to top venture capital firms on the Web.

*The Venture Report Guide to Venture Capital in the UK and Europe: How and Where to Raise Risk Capital.* Oxford, England: Venture Capital Report. Annual. On the Web at http://www.vcr1978.com
Introductory sections include detailed information on preparing business plans and personal experiences of entrepreneurs. Profiles of UK venture capital firms include firm history, sources of funds, fees, decision-making process, key management, and profiles of investments. There are indexes of investees, people, and investors.

## Associations and Organizations

This section offers descriptions of and links to associations and organizations that can be sources of information and contacts for the general venture capital and private equity industries. Names, addresses, phone numbers, and descriptive information are provided for all organizations, along with links to and descriptions of their websites, where available. The matching services documented in Appendix One fit this section.

## North America

AEEG: American Entrepreneurs for Economic Growth. 1655 N. Fort Myer Drive, Suite 700, Arlington, VA 22209, 703/351-5246. On the Web at http://www.aeeg.org
With ten thousand members, AAEG is the largest national organization of venture-backed companies and other entrepreneurial enterprises. The association focuses on the public policy issues that affect emerging growth companies.

Capital Venture. On the Web at http://www.capitalventure.com/
Capital Venture, a "trade association" for venture capital and related professionals, with chapters in Atlanta, Boston, and Hong
Kong, provides links to venture capital firms on the Web. Also included are Capital Venture happenings, private equity 101 (an
overview of venture capital), private equity jobs listings, and information on how to get a job in venture capital.

Capital Association. 1881 Yonge Street, Suite 706, Toronto, Ontario, M4S 3C4, 416/487-0519. On the Web at http://www.cvca
.ca/contact.html
The website lists association events, has links to member firms, and
offers statistics on the Canadian venture capital industry.

Center for Venture Research. University of New Hampshire, Whitte-
more School of Business and Economics, Durham, NH 03824,
603/862-3341. On the Web at http://ace-net.sr.unh.edu/pub/
The Angel Capital Electronic Network, sponsored by the Small
Business Administration's Office of Advocacy, is an Internet-based
listing service offering information to angel investors on small, dynamic, growing businesses seeking to raise $250,000 to $5 million
in equity financing. The pioneering researchers of the business
angel field, William E. Wetzel Jr., Jeffrey E. Sohl, and John Freear,
are based at this center and assisted us with this book, in particular with the list of matching services.

Ewing Marion Kauffman Foundation. 4900 Oak Street, Kansas
City, MO 64112-2776, 816/932-1000. On the Web at http://www
.emkf.org/index.html
The Kauffman Center for Entrepreneurial Leadership promotes
the growth of entrepreneurship in America. The Center's Entrepreneur Training Institute sponsors education, training, and research initiatives targeted to the needs of adult entrepreneurs and
entrepreneurship support systems. Through the Institute for Entrepreneurship Education, a variety of experience-based education efforts work to encourage the entrepreneurial spirit in
students from kindergarten through community college. The
Public Sector and Community Entrepreneurship segment focuses
on entrepreneurship in the nonprofit sector, public policy issues

related to entrepreneurship, and the community infrastructure that supports entrepreneurs.

NASBIC: National Association of Small Business Investment Companies. 666 11th St. N.W., Suite 750, Washington DC 20001, 202/628-5055. On the Web at http://www.nasbic.org/
"The National Association for Small Business Investment Companies' goal is to build and maintain a strong and profitable small business investment company (SBIC) industry."

National Association of Investment Companies. 1111 14th St. NW, Suite 700, Washington DC 20005, 202/289-4336. On the Web at http://www.envista.com/naic/index.html

National Venture Capital Association. 1655 N. Fort Myer Drive, Suite 700, Arlington, VA 22209, 703/351-5269. On the Web at http://www.nvca.org/
The mission of the NVCA, which was founded in 1973, is to define, serve, and represent the interests of the venture capital and private equity industries.

## Asia

Australian Venture Capital Association. Level 2, 111 Harrington Street, The Rocks, Sydney, NSW 2000, Australia, 612/9251-3911.

Hong Kong Venture Capital Association. c/o 15/F, Wanchai Commercial Centre, 194-204 Johnston Road, Wanchai, Hong Kong, 852/2838-9626. On the Web at http://www.hkvca.com.hk
Features information on membership and includes a directory of officers and association members.

Indian Venture Capital Association. c/o Gujarat Venture Finance Ltd., 1/4, Premchang House Annexe, B/h, Popular House, Ashram Road, Admedabad 380 009, India, 9179/658-0335.

Korea Venture Capital Association. Rm. 1201, Ssangma Building, 24-5 Yoido-dong, Yongdungpo-ku, Seoul 150 010, Korea, 822/785-0602/4.

Singapore Venture Capital Association. 331 North Bridge Road, #05-04/06 Odeon Towers, Singapore 188720, 65/339-9090.

Taipei Venture Capital Association. Rm. 301, 142 Ming Chuan East Road, Section 3, Taipei, Taiwan, 8862/713-2219.

Thai Venture Capital Association. 10/F, Maneeya Center, 518/ 5 Ploenchit Road, Patumwan, Bangkok 10330, Thailand, 662/ 255-6816. On the Web at http://www.supertrade.com/venture capital/index.html
Includes a list of members in English. The rest of the site is in Thai.

Venture Capital Club of Indonesia. c/o PT Binaniagatama Perkasa, 3/F, Kanindo Plaza, Jl. Jend. Gatot Subroto Kav.23, Jakarta 12950, Indonesia, 6221/525-8386.

Venture Enterprise Center. Landic Nagai Building, 4/F, 3-9-9, Tsukiji, Chuo-ku, Tokyo 104, Japan, 813/3545-4081.

## Europe

AIFI: Italian Venture Capital Association. Via Cornaggia 10, I-20123 Milan, Italy, 39 2 80 55 901.

Asociacion Espanola de Entidades de Capital Riesgo (ASCRI), Castello 36-5A, E28001 Madrid, Spain, 34 1 577 47 59.

Association Française des Investisseurs en Capital Risque (AFIC). Avenue Marceau 76, F 75008, Paris, France, 33 1 472 099 09.

Associacao Portuguesa de Capital de Risco (APCRI), Campo Grande 28-3E, 1700 Lisboa, Portugal, 351 1 795 0022.

Belgian Venturing Association. 9052 Zwynaarde (Gent) Belgium, 32 9 221 33 64.

British Venture Capital Association. Essex House, 12-13 Essex Street, London WC2R 3AA, 44 171 240 3846. On the Web at http://www.brainstorm.co.uk/BVCA/Welcome.html

The BVCA website has brief background and statistical information on venture capital in the UK and includes a list of members (without addresses).

Bundesverband deutscher Kapitalbeteiligungsgesellschaften (BVK). Karoliner Platz 10-11, 14052 Berlin 19, Germany, 49 30 302 91 81.

Czech Venture Capital Association (CVCA). c/o DBG Eastern Europe, Jungmannova 34, CZ-110 00 Prague 1, Czech Republic, 42 2 24 09 84 00.

European Venture Capital Association. Keibergpark, Minervastraat 6, Box 6, B-1930 Zaventem, Belgium, 32 2 715 00 20. On the Web at http://www.evca.com
Includes a directory of member companies, searchable by company name and country.

Finnish Venture Capital Association. c/o SITRA, Uudenmaankatu 16-20 B, PO Box 329, SF 00120, Helsinki Finland, 358 0 618 991.

Hungarian Venture Capital Association. Csorst u. 3., H-1123 Budapest, Hungary, 36 1 201 9284.

Irish Venture Capital Association (IVCA). c/o Delta Partners, South County Business Park, Leopardstown, Dublin 18, 353 1 294 0870.

Nederlandse Vereniging van Participatiemaatschappijen. Prinses Beatrixlaan 5, Postbus 93093, 2509 AB The Hague, The Netherlands, 31 70 347 06 01.

Norwegian Venture Capital Association. Postboks 1863 Vika Nedre Vollgate, N-0123 Olso, Norway, 47 2 33 1212.

Russian Venture Capital Association (RVCA). Stroenye 3, podjezd 3, Krasina Street 7, 123056 Moscow, 95 255 98 11.

Svenska Riskkapitalforeningen Foreningen. S 11786 Stockholm, Sweden, 46 8 775 40 12.

Swiss Private Equity and Corporate Finance Association. Bahnhof-strasse 17, CH-8702 Zollikon Switzerland, 41 1 392 09 05.

## Middle East

Israel Venture Association (IVA). Eliahu House, 2 Ibn Gvirol Street, Tel Aviv 64077, Israel, 972 3 696 8224.

## Trade Journals

The following trade publications cover the venture capital and entrepreneurship arenas.

*Asian Venture Capital Journal.* Hong Kong: Asian Venture Capital Journal Limited. Monthly. On the Web at http://www.asiaventure.com/
"The Asian private equity news source." The website offers a free sample issue, but access to current articles and archives requires a subscription.

*Buyouts.* New York: Securities Data Publishing. Twenty-five issues/year.
"The newsletter for managed buyouts, leveraged acquisitions and special situations."

*European Venture Capital Journal.* London: Securities Data Publishing. Bimonthly.
News and analysis of Europe's private equity markets.

*Institutional Investor.* New York: Institutional Investor. Monthly.
"The magazine for finance and investment." Each January issue has investment banking deals of the previous year.

*Investment Dealer's Digest.* New York: IDD. Weekly.
This financial community news magazine has listings of new equity and debt registrations and issues as well as securities in registration.

*Investor's Business Daily.* Los Angeles: Investor's Business Daily Inc. Daily.

National coverage of daily financial and economic news. The website has today's issue. Other features are available by subscription.

*The IPO Reporter.* New York: Securities Data Publishing. Weekly.
Covers the life cycles of IPOs, with news, tables, and IPO initiation prices and trading, as well as IPOs in the pipeline.

*NASBIC News.* Washington, D.C.: National Association of Small Business Investment Companies. Biweekly.
News from the National Association of Small Business Investment Companies on its activities, members, and legislative and regulatory issues.

*Private Equity Analyst.* Wellesley, Mass.: Asset Alternatives, Inc.; Monthly.
"The newsletter serving investors and managers of alternative assets." Although this publication is not indexed in commercial databases, it is a must read for anyone interested in the field of private equity.

*Private Equity Week.* New York: Investment Dealers' Digest. Weekly.
This weekly newsletter offers a look at the deal activity taking place in the private equity market.

*The Red Herring.* San Francisco: Herring Communications. Monthly. On the Web at http://www.herring.com/
*Red Herring* reports on companies and trends influencing technology and business. Tracks technology IPOs and IPOs in registration. The special "Going Public: Guide to Technology Finance" issue features ranked lists of the top twenty-five technology IPOs, technology venture capital firms, and technology investment banks as well as many articles. The website includes current, past, and special issues.

*Start-Up.* Zaventem, Belgium: European Seed Capital Fund Network. Monthly.
"The newsletter for Europe's seed capital network."

*Upside, the Magazine for Technology Investment.* Foster City, Calif.: Upside Publishing Co. Monthly. On the Web at http://www.upside .com/
Articles on people, finance, and current issues in the technology industry. The website has the current issue, special issues, and a seven-day archive of features.

*UK Venture Capital Journal.* New York: Securities Data Publishing. Bimonthly. On the Web at http://www.upside.com/
Articles from this bimonthly publication are available via One-Source. "Contains news, analysis and insights about the UK venture capital industry."

*Venture Capital Journal.* New York: Securities Data Publishing. Monthly.
"News and analysis of the private equity markets."

## Literature

This section includes resources that present a broad view of the industry, including descriptions of the nature of the industry, its current state, history, and the outlook for the future. It can also include resources that combine information from several sections of the guide (statistics, news, directories) to present an overall picture of the industry.

Capital Venture, a "trade association" for venture capital, provides Private Equity/Venture Capital 101, an overview and explanation of venture capital.

*Fitzroy Dearborn International Directory of Venture Capital Funds.* Chicago: Fitzroy Dearborn. Annual.
Introductory articles in this directory offer background information on the venture capital industry.

Frontiers of Entrepreneurship Research. On the Web at http://www.Babson.edu/entrep/fer/
For those interested in academic research in the entrepreneurship field, this site features the latest research presented at the

annual Babson College–Kauffman Foundation Entrepreneurship Conference.

*Pratt's Guide to Venture Capital Sources.* Wellesley, Mass.: Venture Economics. Annual.
The introductory chapters are a useful overview of the venture capital industry, with chapters on "Background on Venture Capital," "How to Raise Venture Capital" and "Sources of Business Development Financing."

"Venture Capital." Roosevelt, Jonathan. On the Web at http://www.capitalventure.com/article1.htm
This article explains the basics of venture capital investing.

*Venture Capital 101.* Capital Venture. On the Web at http://www.capitalventure.com/cvindustry.htm

*Venture Capital at the Crossroads.* Bygrave, William D., and Timmons, Jeffrey A. Boston: Harvard Business School Press, 1992.
This is one of the best books written on the evolution of the U.S. venture capital industry—a must read.

"What Is Venture Capital?" Arlington, Va.: National Venture Capital Association. On the Web at http://www.nvca.org/def.html
This article from the National Venture Capital Association is an overview of the venture capital industry.

## Useful Links

This section has further resources that entrepreneurs in particular can use to find and secure funding.

U.S. Small Business Administration (SBA). On the Web at http://www.sba.gov/
The SBA has a wealth of information online, from how to start a business to how to finance its growth.

Bloomberg Financial Markets.
Scaled-down version available on the Web at http://www.bloomberg.com/

Covers all the major financial sectors and markets around the world, with news, prices, and analytics. Includes investment banking equity league tables and IPO information.

Entreprenet. On the Web at http://www.enterprise.org/enet/
This site features information and links for entrepreneurs, including business plan advice.

Envista Private Equity Links. On the Web at http://www
.privateequity.com/
Envista has links to sources of information on private equity, including private equity firms, a global calendar of private equity events (sponsored by numerous organizations, among them NASBIC, Venture Capital Institute, and Asset Alternatives), service providers (law firms, M&A firms, investment banks), research and publishing firms, online research tools, and resources for entrepreneurs.

Fortune's Ultimate Resource Guide. On the Web at http://cgi
.pathfinder.com/yourco/resources/index.html
This site has excellent links to the latest online resources for funding and developing your entrepreneurial firm. These include links to venture capital and angel capital sources, commercial small-business lenders, federal grant and technical assistance programs, state incentive programs, business incubators, and industrial research parks.

NVST.com.
This site has information relevant to start-up firms and offers entrepreneur-investor matching.

Venture Capital: On the Net (1000). On the Web at http://www
.gen.com/ani/venturemks.htm
This site features numerous links to other Venture Capital sites on the Web.

Venture Capital and Principal Investment Club. Boston: HBS Venture Capital and Principal Investment Club. On the Web at http://wasat.hbs.edu/venture_cap/

If you are a Harvard Business School alum, keep in touch with the members and activities of this student club. Addresses and links to venture capital firms and special deals on subscriptions.

Venture Capital Resource Library. On the Web at http://www .vfinance.com/
This site is an easy way to research the venture capital market for your firm.

## Statistics

This section includes resources that present statistics about the venture capital industry as a whole or a substantial segment of it. It can include sources of statistics on production, stock or financial performance, operations, employment, and other categories. This section may be particularly helpful for academic researchers.

*Annual Statistical Review.* Toronto: Canadian Venture Capital Association. On the Web at http://www.cvca.ca/statistical_review/ index.html
Includes detailed statistics on the Canadian venture capital industry: investments by stage of development, revenue of investees, sector, investee location, number of employees in investee companies, number of investments, and amount invested (private versus public companies).

*EVCA Yearbook.* London: Ernst and Young; European Venture Capital Association. Annual.
This is a comprehensive survey of the European private equity and venture capital industry. Statistics on European private equity are listed overall and by country. There is also a directory of the members of the European Venture Capital Association, listed by country.

*PricewaterhouseCoopers Money Tree Survey.* Quarterly. On the Web at http://www.pwcmoneytree.com
These surveys represent the merger of the Price Waterhouse National Venture Capital Survey with the Coopers and Lybrand Money Tree Survey. The quarterly surveys include overviews of

venture capital and private equity in the United States and statistics by industry, by state, and by firm.

*Pratt's Guide to Venture Capital Sources.* Wellesley, Mass.: Venture Economics. Annual.
Basic statistics are reported on U.S. venture capital by region, industry, and year.

Venture Industry Data: Quarterly Statistics. VentureOne. Quarterly. On the Web at http://www.v1.com/research/venturedata/stats/index.htm
VentureOne's Industry Monitor (deals and amounts) and State of the Market (quarterly commentary on trends) offer a sampling of statistical information from VentureOne publications.

## Career Resources

For those who have been motivated by this book to become venture capitalists, here are some helpful guides and resources. But remember, the odds are unfortunately stacked against you, so make sure that you give it your best shot.

Bloomberg Financial Markets. Job postings are available on the Web at http://www.bloomberg.com/fun/jobs.html/
The online and Web versions of Bloomberg have international job postings for sales, traders, analysts, analytics, portfolio managers, and in finance and banking.

Kauffman Fellows. On the Web at http://www.emkf.org/Entrepreneurship/programs_for_entrepreneurs/index.html
The Kauffman Fellows program is a venture capital fellowship designed to immerse fellows in the venture capital process. The program is conducted by venture capitalists, entrepreneurs, and scholars and is sponsored by the Ewing Marion Kauffman Foundation.

"How to Get a Job in Venture Capital." Lenet, Scott. *Wharton Journal,* Feb. 5, 1996. On the Web at http://www.capitalventure.com/article3 (Capital Venture)

Outlines venture capital basics and presents strategies for getting a job in the field.

*Information Sources About Private Equity.* Lerner, Joshua. On the Web at http://www.people.hbs.edu/jlerner/info.html
Advice on finding out about private equity companies and additional sources of information.

*The Insider's Guide to Jobs in Venture Capital.* San Francisco: Wet Feet Press, 1998.
Get the inside scoop on what a venture capital career is really like from this popular Wet Feet Press "Industry Insider." Learn about venture capital lingo, firm culture, and workplace diversity. Follow a partner or analyst around for a day, find out about the recruiting process, and see if you have what it takes to measure up in this industry. Includes ranked lists of top firms and interview tips.

## Research Awards

Doctoral students in the field of entrepreneurship should consider competing for the Heizer Award, one of the most prestigious doctoral dissertation awards that can be won in any of the social or economic sciences.

The Heizer Award was established in 1976 through the joint efforts of Edgar F. Heizer Jr., then president of the Heizer Corporation (and founder and first chairman of the National Venture Capital Association), and Dr. Charles W. Hofer, then associate professor of strategy and entrepreneurship at Northwestern University.

The Heizer Award is offered each year through the support of the Entrepreneurship Division of the Academy of Management. The principal focus of the Heizer Award is on research that deals with the founding, financing, management, development, and growth of high potential new ventures; or with venture capital investing; or with corporate entrepreneurship. Research dealing primarily with small business, family business, minority business, or with the traditional management practices of large, established firms are specifically *excluded* from consideration for the Heizer Award.

Dissertations completed in calendar year N will qualify for the Heizer Award in calendar year N + 1. Twenty-five-page abstracts of any dissertation being submitted for the Heizer Award should be sent to the Chair-Elect of the Entrepreneurship Division of the Academy of Management by April 1 of the year N + 1. Finalists for the Heizer Award will be required to send six copies of their complete dissertation to the judging panel by June 1 of the year involved. The winner of the Heizer Award will also be required to send one copy of his or her dissertation to Mr. Edgar F. Heizer Jr. and one copy to Dr. Charles W. Hofer, who maintains a file of all Heizer Award winners.

It should be noted that even though the Heizer Award is offered every year, it is only awarded if a majority of the judging panel feels the best entry in a particular year meets the historic standards of excellence established for the Award. Thus, in the twenty-four years in which the Heizer Award has been offered, it has been actually awarded only seventeen times. Put differently, in seven different years no Heizer Award was given because no dissertation was deemed worthy in that year. On the other hand, a Certificate of Distinction is given if more than one dissertation meets the Heizer Award's high standards in a given year. To date, six Certificates of Distinction have been awarded in the twenty-four years of the Heizer Award competition.

For more information on the Heizer Award, or on past winners of the Award, the reader may contact Dr. Charles W. Hofer, Regents Professor of Strategy and Entrepreneurship at the University of Georgia. Hofer not only helped found the Heizer Award with Heizer, he also serves as the liaison between Heizer and the Academy of Management's Entrepreneurship Division. Hofer's address and telephone and fax numbers are as follows:

Dr. Charles W. Hofer
Terry College of Business
University of Georgia
Athens, GA 30602
Telephone: 706/542-3724
Fax: 706/542-3743

Or:
Dr. Charles W. Hofer
Venture Resource Associates
4445 Stonington Circle
Dunwoody, GA 30338
Telephone: 770/455-4555
Fax: 770/455-4280

# Appendix Three: Writing a Winning Business Plan

To help entrepreneurs turn the knowledge this book has presented into fruitful action, this Appendix gives practical advice on how to develop an effective business plan.

## General Advice for Entrepreneurs

Before we analyze the business plan, which is often one of the most time-consuming aspects of the fundraising process, let's review some general pieces of advice that every entrepreneur should follow. These conclusions are from our extensive review of the entrepreneurship literature and the feedback we received from successful entrepreneurs.

- *Know when to seek outside funds.* Acquiring equity capital should be a strategic decision, undertaken once a firm has verified its growth potential and found a *real* need for funds. The longer an entrepreneur waits to raise funds, the better. Once a firm has a track record, the entrepreneur will be able to surrender less equity for outside money. Bootstrapping and personal funds are good ways to build a firm to position it for outside investors. Amid today's Internet craze, however, high-tech start-ups have the rare luxury of seeking outside investors while their ideas are still in their infancy because of the unprecedented investor interest in the sector.
- *Decide how much you are willing to surrender.* Before initiating the search for funds, entrepreneurs should determine roughly

how much they are willing to offer in the form of firm equity to attract an outside investor. Having realistic expectations of the cost of finance avoids surprises and potential wasted effort later on.

- *Determine the ideal investor for your firm.* Benefits and advantages vary with the type of investor, as this book has clearly shown. Entrepreneurs in search of an outside investor should determine whether financial input is all they desire, or whether experienced management advice or a new coworker is also a high priority. For those firms in the early stage, in addition to finance, business angels may offer many hands-on benefits that venture capitalists cannot. But mature firms, which have built a track record in a fast-growing market and have a balanced management team, may benefit more from the large cash infusion and strategic guidance of a venture capitalist. Clearly, entrepreneurs need to first assess their own firm (stage, growth potential, market, competition, management team) to determine which type of investor they are most likely to secure, and then decide what they need in such an investor beyond a fund infusion. Recruiting investors who understand your industry gives you added support, guidance, and empathy if your industry takes a seasonal slump or as your firm struggles to be competitive in its market.

- *Use your network contacts.* To find potential investors, particularly business angels, entrepreneurs must exploit their business and personal networks to the fullest, as detailed in Chapter Five. With many potential angels in your geographic area, getting the word out is often the best way to find an interested investor. Alternatively, formal matching services can be approached, although they remain at this time a factor in only a small portion of funding matches. To lure venture capitalists, a professional referral is mandatory to gain attention.

- *Refine your sales pitch.* Different things motivate investors, as we have thoroughly discussed throughout this book, particularly in Chapter Seven. Before appealing to the investor type of your choice, know what in general motivates them most and then tailor your business plan and sales pitch accordingly. If you are fortunate to already have a specific investor in mind, be it an angel or a venture capitalist, find out what his or her interests are, other ventures funded recently, and the primary criteria, and then tailor your plan to emphasize these features. Angels often seek excitement and the opportunity to use their own creativity and skills; make sure that your investment opportunity embodies these requirements. Should this particular approach not work for the investor you have in mind, find another investor—there are plenty of fish in the sea!

• *Emphasize the uniqueness of your firm.* No one wants to invest hard-earned dollars in a firm lacking a unique aspect that sets it apart from the competition and gives it the edge that will potentially bring in millions in revenue. Entrepreneurs should communicate their unique vision for the firm and go to pains to clarify its competitive position. A unique edge of some sort is of vital importance.

• *Emphasize the people aspects of your firm.* Investors tend to invest more in people than in ideas. A stellar entrepreneur with a lackluster idea, though not ideal, will have the smarts and experience to change things around to attain success. Especially for angel investors (who often want to work with the entrepreneur), having confidence in the entrepreneur is one of the most important characteristics to attract investment. If the people do not have (and cannot show) a high degree of integrity, motivation, and experience, investors will usually pass on the deal.

• *Know your limitations.* If attempts to attract an outside investor result in an entrepreneur modifying the business plan and the outlook beyond what he or she is comfortable with, the entrepreneur has to decide whether acquiring an outside investor is really worth it, and whether the right type of investor has been focused on thus far. If an entrepreneur is not entirely happy with what is being presented to potential investors, this is sure to be a cause for aggravation at a later stage, after the funds have been secured.

• *Borrow added credibility.* Start-up firms and their young entrepreneurs often lack credibility. Though this is an inherent part of the situation, it can be partly overcome by securing support and backing from experienced and credible outside individuals. First, an entrepreneur may establish a board of directors and fill it with a number of talented and experienced outsiders who can lend their advice and reputations within the community to the young unproven venture. Second, a board of technical advisors may be established, especially for technical firms, to lend added insight and credibility. Third, entrepreneurs should create professional advisory relationships with respected legal and accounting firms. Forwarding financial statements that have been verified by a respected Big Six accounting firm can certainly lend added credibility and comfort to investors and others. If you negotiate hard, the fees for such an accounting firm may not be much higher than for a no-name firm (Welles, 1994). Fourth, any public relations exposure that a small firm can get is an added bonus. Though being featured in a national publication such as *Forbes* may be unlikely, news coverage in trade magazines and the local press can certainly help to expose the business and possibly attract potential investors, or at least give the firm added credibility to lure investors. Fifth, if a firm already has outside equity investors, this can improve the odds of gaining a second round of funds from angels, venture capitalists, and even banks. Already having some sort of outside backing adds credibility to the venture ("If others have seen fit to invest in the firm, then my hunch may be right").

• *Follow a rifle-shot approach (leave the shotgun at home).* When selecting angel investors to approach, select only a few (who may be potentially interested) to approach. Tailoring your sales pitch to just a few (in whom you are interested as well) is a surefire road to funding success, as opposed to using a shotgun approach to reach many investors at once. "Quality over quantity" rules in the search for equity funds. Additionally, if a shotgun attempt at seeking finance is not received favorably by angels in your area, it is difficult to go back to some of them later with a more refined and tailored second attempt. Similarly, when approaching venture capitalists, make sure that you use a referral source for each investment firm considered, and tailor your approach to their investment requirements and motivations. This is particularly important in the highly inbred venture capital community because one rejection of a business plan usually reduces the chances that other venture capitalists will find it attractive.

• *Target lead investors.* Increasingly, angels are investing in groups to improve diversification of risk and skills and to afford larger investment opportunities otherwise outside of their grasp. In every such angel syndicate, there is at least one prominent investor who the others respect and follow. Entrepreneurs must try to target these individuals and gain their approval. Similarly, in venture capital firms, where investment decisions are made in committees, targeting a particular partner who is seen as sympathetic may allow the entrepreneur to gain an internal champion and build momentum (Wasserman, 1999). Also, there are often patterns of deference between different venture capital firms, where support by one firm can increase the support from others.

• *Get your foot in the door.* Most investment opportunities seen by business angels and venture capitalists are rejected before these people even meet the entrepreneur. Once an entrepreneur gains an investor's attention, then the chances of securing funds have already increased dramatically (Riding, 1998).

• *Check out potential investors.* Due diligence is a two-way street. Although entrepreneurs may be hesitant to check out potential investors for fear of possibly turning away committed funds, it is imperative that they learn as much as possible about the person to whom they are selling part of their company. Every entrepreneur should ask:

- Are the investor's motivations in line with what we can realistically offer?
- Is the investor's personality compatible with mine?
- Does the investor share the same goals I have?
- What other firms has the investor funded in the past? How did they turn out?
- How active was the investor in those firms?
- Did the investor make constructive contributions?
- What do entrepreneurs in those firms (especially those that failed) say about the investor?
- Did the investor stick with the firms in times of trouble?
- What industries does the investor have experience in?
- Does the investor understand this firm's industry sector? Can he or she contribute to this area?
- How helpful will this investor be in trying to obtain future rounds of financing?
- Does this investor have the expertise, contacts, and reputation to attract other potential investors and build the firm?

• *Set guidelines with your investors.* Before the investment agreement is drawn up, the entrepreneur and investor must establish guidelines to clarify each person's role in the venture. The timing and amount of assistance from the investor should be agreed upon so that the entrepreneur knows realistically how much value-added assistance to expect, and the investor feels as if there is a role to play in the firm. Lay it all out on the table before signing on the dotted line.

• *Set up a formal communication channel.* Once the investment has been made, the entrepreneur should establish a formal channel of communication so that contact with the investor(s) remains frequent and can lead to valuable assistance (Gruner, 1998).

• *Be persistent.* Although most investors are very choosy about the deals they fund, it is important to remember that there are at least a few committed investors out there for every deal. If negotiations with one investor do not turn out as planned, ask him or her to kindly refer your investment opportunity to another potentially interested investor. Angels are often quite happy to do this (Riding, 1998), especially if the opportunity was rejected by them for lack of sector knowledge or inability to contribute certain investor skills. Persistence pays—often very handsomely—in pursuing entrepreneurial funds.

• *Conduct a reality check.* If multiple attempts to obtain funds fail, the investment opportunity may not yet be developed enough to seek outside funds. Reliance on other sources may be more appropriate for the time being. If continued attempts fail over time, it is important to recognize that all the money in the world may not be able to save a bad idea.

## Writing a Persuasive Business Plan

Crafting a good business plan is a difficult task, usually involving weeks (if not months) of endless drafting and rewriting. But a clear and professional plan is crucial for any business since it is the main selling tool in the fundraising process. A good business plan must have immediate impact if it is to gain interest and follow-up. Potential investors receive dozens, if not hundreds, of proposals per month. Luckily for first-time entrepreneurs, many books have been written on how to put together a good business plan. Many of these sources are, in our opinion, excellent and certainly comprehensive. We could make up our own guide here, but we do not

think that we can do any better. The Internet alone offers countless free (and excellent) business plan guides; any local bookstore
should offer a wide selection too. Take a look through them and
decide which style of plan is most to your liking—but remember
to keep it short and concise!

For starters, we urge entrepreneurs to review some of the
sources that we liked:

- "How to Write a Great Business Plan," by William Sahlman, in
  the *Harvard Business Review,* July 1997.
- *Anatomy of a Business Plan,* by Linda Pinson and Jerry Jinnett
  (Fullerton, Calif.: Martketplace Press, 1999).
- *Business Plans That Work,* edited by Susan M. Packsack
  (Chicago: CCH, 1998).
- *How to Write a Business Plan,* by Mike McKeever (Berkeley,
  Calif.: Nolo Press, 1994).
- *Inc. Magazine's How to Really Create a Successful Business Plan—Step
  by Step,* by David E. Gumpert (Boston: Inc. Publishing, 1996).
- *Online Business Planning: How to Create a Better Business Plan Us-
  ing the Internet, Including a Complete, Up-to-Date Resource Guide,*
  by Robert T. Gorman (Franklin Lakes, N.J.: Career Press,
  1999).
- *The Complete Book of Business Plans: Simple Steps to Writing a Pow-
  erful Business Plan,* by Joseph Covello and Brian Hazelgren
  (Naperville, Ill.: Sourcebooks, 1994).
- *The Entrepreneur's Guide to Building a Better Business Plan: A Step
  by Step Approach,* by Harold McLaughlin (New York: Wiley,
  1992).
- *Total Business Planning: a Step-by-Step Guide with Forms,* by
  E. James Burton (New York: Wiley, 1999).

Try the Internet, too:

- "How to Start a Business: Business Plan," Small Business Development Center, available at
  http://www.inreach.com/sbdc/book/bizplan.html
- "Creating an Effective Business Plan," American Express Small
  Business Exchange, available at http://www.americanexpress
  .com/smallbusiness/

- "The Business Plan—Road to Success: A Tutorial and Self-Paced Activity," Small Business Administration, available at http://www.sba.gov/starting/indexbusplans.html

Most of these guides are not written with business angel investors in mind; banks and venture capitalists are the common funding targets. In light of this, let's look at some of the aspects of a general business plan that should be emphasized, depending on the type of investor sought.

Here is what business angels specifically look for in a business plan:

- An opportunity to add their own skills and creativity to the venture
- A trustworthy entrepreneur with a compatible personality
- A firm in a niche market
- An early-stage venture whose development they can still shape
- Healthy financial projections
- A venture that is within driving distance for the investor

This is what venture capitalists look for in a business plan:

- An experienced and well-balanced management team with a sound track record
- A firm with a unique concept or idea that meets an unmet consumer need
- A target market with almost unlimited growth potential
- A proven niche product with almost unlimited growth potential
- Strong competitive position
- Very healthy, but realistic, financial projections
- A firm that is usually developed and looking for expansion funds (not a start-up)
- Preferably a high-tech firm, but also firms in other sectors
- Detailed financial statements (preferably with milestone charts)
- A potential equity stake of around 30 percent of the company in exchange for funds (though there is much variation)
- Potential exit routes identifiable at the time of investment

Lastly, what should every business plan have? Business plan manuals stress different content styles, and there is no universal best. Depending on their own preferences and types of business, entrepreneurs should select the style that most appeals to them and allows them to present their opportunity in the best light. But in general, all business plans tend to be variations of the one we feature here, which happens to be a simpler variation of a plan featured by the Small Business Development Center, one we particularly favor.

## Sample Table of Contents for a Business Plan

Cover letter
Cover sheet
Table of contents
Executive summary
    Business concept
        Name
        Product or service
        Market and competition
        Management experience and expertise
    Business goals
    Summary of financial needs
    Earnings projections
Market analysis
    Total market analysis
    Industry trends
    Target market
    Market competition
Product or service analysis
    Product line or service description
    Proprietary nature
    Competitive threats
Marketing strategy
    Overall strategy
    Pricing policy
    Selling, distribution, servicing methods
Management
    Officers, organizational chart, and responsibilities

Résumés of key personnel
Composition of board of directors or advisors
Financial plan
Historical analysis
Budget projections
Income statement
Balance sheets
Cash flow
Capital expenditures
Explanation of projections
Key business ratios
Explanation of financing needs and anticipated use of funds

## Twenty General Tips on Business Plan Preparation

Every business plan is a sales tool. It must look professional and read well to be effective. Here are some general guidelines that every entrepreneur must follow to develop the overall form of a business plan:

1. Develop your business plan yourself, rather than hiring someone else to do it.
2. Keep the full plan as short as possible, focusing on key issues, not extraneous details.
3. Put yourself in the mind of the target investors.
4. Start with a short, compelling, and concise one-page executive summary to attract immediate attention.
5. Get straight to the point!
6. Articulate concisely a simple but powerful plan for an innovative solution to an emerging but important consumer problem that is still unmet.
7. Be specific about your market and your firm's fit within the environment. Show that you really understand the target market.
8. Leave out technical jargon; use plain English.
9. Be clear in your key assumptions, using independent sources to back them up.
10. Be realistic in all your projections.

11. Openly address risks and problems, and how they can best be overcome. Any good investor can identify them and will not invest until they are addressed.

12. Demonstrate that you have a management team that has the experience and balance to make the venture a success.

13. Include milestone charts for past events within the firm, and those projected for the future.

14. Clearly discuss the firm's financing needs, by addressing (Posner, 1993):

    How much money you need, being very specific about the amount sought
    What you plan to use the money for
    How this money will improve the business
    How the business will pay the money back
    If Plan A does not work, what the backup plan is

15. Prepare a time schedule for additional funds that are likely to be needed.

16. Show that you fully understand the needs and interests of investors. The entrepreneur must learn to think in terms of the investors' risks.

17. List possible exit strategies for investors.

18. Solicit comments and criticism from everyone you know.

19. Revise, revise, revise.

20. Try not to let the process of fundraising adversely affect your firm's ongoing operations.

Even though we feel that these tips are some of the most important ones an entrepreneur needs to follow in preparing a business plan, this list is clearly not exhaustive. In summary: try to write a short, concise, and thorough business plan addressing a solution to an unmet need in a growing and potentially profitable market. Such a plan may sound more ideal than real, but then investors (especially venture capitalists) have high standards that must be met before their checkbook is put to good use.

# A Final and Amusing Reality Check on Business Plans

In his 1996 Harvard Business School case study, "Some Thoughts on Business Plans," William Sahlman, one of the most respected academics in the entrepreneurship area, presents a unique reality check for some of the phrases we often see in business plans. Here is an excerpt:

## Translation Glossary for Business Plans

| Business Plan Phrase | What It Really Means |
|---|---|
| We conservatively project . . . | We read a book that said we had to have sales of $50 million in five years, and we reverse engineered the numbers. . . . |
| We took our best guess and divided by 2. . . . | We accidentally divided by 5. . . . |
| We project a 10 percent margin. . . . | We did not modify any of the assumptions in the business plan template we downloaded from the Internet. . . . |
| The project is 98 percent complete. . . . | To complete the remaining 2 percent will take as long as to create the initial 98 percent but will cost twice as much. . . . |
| We have a six-month lead. . . . | We have not tried to find out how many other people also have a six-month lead. . . . |
| We only need a 10 percent market share. . . . | So too do all the other fifty entrants getting funded. . . . |

| | |
|---|---|
| Customers are clamoring for our product. . . . | We have not yet broached the issue of them paying for it. Also, all of our current customers are relatives. . . . |
| We are the low-cost producer. . . . | We have not produced anything yet, but we are confident that we will be able to. . . . |
| We have no competition. . . . | Only Microsoft, Netscape, IBM, and Sun have announced plans to enter the business. . . . |
| Our management team has a great deal of experience. . . . | . . . in consuming the product or service. . . . |
| A select group of investors is considering the plan. . . . | We mailed a copy of the plan to everyone in *Pratt's Guide to Venture Capital Sources.* . . . |
| We seek a value-added investor. . . . | We are looking for a passive, dumb-as-rocks investor. . . . |
| If you invest on our terms, you will earn a 68 percent IRR. . . . | If everything that could conceivably ever go right does go right, you might get your money back. . . . |

*Source:* Sahlman (1996).

# Glossary

*Acquisition*  Procurement of control, possession, and ownership of a firm by another larger firm or corporation.

*Agent*  A person who is contracted to perform work or a duty on behalf of another party (the "principal").

*Alliances*  Cooperative agreements with one or more companies to use and maximize complementary resources for mutual benefit.

*Antidilution provisions*  Contractual measures that allow investors to keep a constant share of a firm's equity in light of subsequent equity issues. These may give investors preemptive rights to purchase new stock at the offering price.

*Archangel*  Usually an outsider hired by a syndicate of angel investors to perform due diligence on investment opportunities and coordinate allotment of investment duties among members. Archangels typically have no financial commitment to the syndicate.

*Asset-backed loan*  Loan, typically from a commercial bank, that is backed by asset collateral, often belonging to the entrepreneurial firm or the entrepreneur.

*Automatic conversion*  Immediate conversion of an investor's priority shares to ordinary shares at the time of a company's underwriting before an offering of its stock on an exchange.

*Average IRR*  The arithmetic mean of the internal rate of return.

*BATNA (best alternative to a negotiated agreement)*  A no-agreement alternative reflecting the course of action a party to a negotiation will take if the proposed deal is not possible.

*Board rights*  Allowing an investor to take a seat on a firm's board of directors.

*Bootstrapping*  Means of financing a small firm by employing highly creative ways of using and acquiring resources without raising equity from traditional sources or borrowing money from the bank.

*Break-even point*   The level of sales where revenue is equal to operating expenses, resulting in zero net income.

*Business angel*   Private investors, often with entrepreneurial experience, who invest some of their own money and experience in small entrepreneurial ventures. The United States has almost three million angel investors, who invest around $50 billion annually in young firms. Business angels are the oldest, largest, most often used, and most important source of outside funds for entrepreneurial firms. The business angel market is exploding in size, particularly in the United States.

*Business plan*   A detailed summary of a business that includes its objectives and projections over a three-to-five-year period. The plan is often the main selling tool in a firm's fundraising process.

*Business risk*   Uncertainty as to whether a firm will be able to generate sales, cash flows, and earnings.

*Buyback provision*   An agreement mandating that a firm purchase a leaving entrepreneur's stock at a preset price.

*Capital gains*   Profits from the sale of assets. This is the difference between the price paid for shares (or other assets) and the price for which they are eventually sold.

*Capital structure*   The mix of a firm's debt (short-term and long-term) and owners' equity (used to fund the firm's operations).

*Capital under management*   The amount of funds a venture capital firm has available for venture investments.

*Captive funds*   A venture capital firm owned by a larger financial institution, such as a bank.

*Cash flows*   The flow of cash in and out of a business. This is quite different from profit and loss in that a firm may have a negative cash flow (for a time) but still be profitable, or a firm may have a positive cash flow and still lose money (for a time). Managing cash flow is crucial in an entrepreneurial firm to meet varying short-term cash needs.

*Collateral*   Assets that are pledged to secure a loan. The lender has a lien on these assets and can claim them if the borrower defaults on the loan.

*Commitment*   A limited partner's obligation to furnish a certain amount of funds to a venture capital fund.

*Convertible*   A financial instrument that can be converted into another type of financial security, often ordinary shares, under conditions agreed to when the original deal is completed.

*Convertible debt*   Debt convertible to ordinary shares under conditions originally agreed on between the entrepreneur or firm and the debt lender.

*Corporate venturing*   Strategic investment by a large firm or corporation in a young and smaller firm to encourage development of new technologies, products, techniques, and (potentially) eventual acquisition.

*Deal flow*   The number of potential investment opportunities to which an investor is exposed.

*Demand rights*   Allowing investors to force their firm to file a registration statement for an IPO offering. This allows investors to exit their entrepreneurial investments and realize gains.

*Development capital*   Equity capital raised for an entrepreneurial firm to help it to grow.

*Distribution*   Disbursement of realized cash or stock to a venture capital fund's limited partners upon termination of the fund.

*Due diligence*   Rigorous investigation and evaluation of an investment opportunity before committing funds. This process includes review of its management team, business conditions, projections, philosophy, and investment terms and conditions.

*Early stage*   A stage of development in which a firm is usually expanding and already producing and delivering products or services. Often less than five years old, early-stage firms may not yet be profitable.

*Employment contracts*   Agreements that specify under which circumstances a venture's board can fire the entrepreneur or the entrepreneur can quit.

*Entrepreneur*   Typically an owner of an unquoted business that this enterprising person started or is trying to grow. Entrepreneurs are those seeking business angel funds and venture capital.

*Entrepreneurial firm*   The term given to those young firms that have the propensity to grow more than 20 percent annually and attain revenue projections of more than $10 million in five years. Constituting fewer than 10 percent of all start-up firms, most are considered to be middle-market firms; approximately the top 1 percent of the fastest growing are termed high-potential firms. Entrepreneurial firms are the only firms funded with outside equity capital.

*Equity*   An ownership stake in a business that can be bought by an investor with risk capital.

*Equity gap*   A stage of business financing, usually involving less than $500,000, in which outside funds are difficult to obtain. This absence of small amounts of risk capital is due to the high fixed costs of appraisal and monitoring that institutional investors must assume, making it uneconomic for them to invest in young and small firms. The gap is further worsened by banks' reluctance to make unsecured loans to small ventures. Business angels make investments that fall in the equity gap, partly relieving this unfortunate situation.

*Exit route*   The means by which an investor can exit an investment and realize returns.

*Factoring*   A procedure in which a firm can sell its accounts receivable invoices to a factoring firm, which pays a percentage of the invoices immediately, and the remainder (minus a service fee) when the accounts receivable are actually paid off by the firm's customers.

*Financial risk*   The uncertainty that a firm will be able to generate the cash flows needed to meet its contractual financial obligations.

*Flotation*   When a firm's shares start trading on a formal stock exchange, such as the NASDAQ or the NYSE. This is probably the most profitable exit route for entrepreneurs and their financial backers.

*Fund providers*   Institutional investors, such as pension funds and corporations, or very wealthy individuals, that invest large sums of money in venture capital funds. These investors are formally called limited partners.

*Fund size*   The total sum of capital committed to a venture capital fund by its general partners and limited partners.

*Gatekeeper*   A person or organization that advises limited partners as to which venture capital funds they should invest in.

*General partners (GPs)*   The partners of a venture capital firm who run and oversee its venture capital funds and raise new funds from limited partners. They typically receive 20 percent of a fund's capital gains and an annual 3 percent management fee on the funds under management.

*High-potential firms*   Although they make up less than 1 percent of all start-ups annually, these entrepreneurial firms have anticipated annual growth rates in excess of 50 percent and five-year revenue projections in excess of $50 million. These ventures are of the greatest interest to venture capitalists and other equity investors and will be among the Microsofts, Disneys, and Blockbuster Videos of the next decade.

*Holding period*   The length of time an investment remains in the investor's portfolio.

*IPO (initial public offering)*   Sale or distribution of an entrepreneurial firm's stock to the public for the first time.

*IRR (internal rate of return)*   Discount rate of an investment that makes its net present value (NPV) equal to zero. This is one of the most common figures used to assess an investment's performance.

*Intellectual property*   A venture's intangible assets, such as patents, copyrights, trademarks, and brand name.

*Interests*   Underlying concerns or deeper dimensions of value that a party may hold in the negotiations process.

*Investee firm*   A company in which an investor has made an equity investment. Typically called a portfolio firm when invested in by a venture capital fund.

*Issues*   Items on the table for explicit agreement in the negotiation process. These may include the amount to be invested, equity granted, and terms of payback.

*LBO (leveraged buyout)*   An investment strategy involving acquisition of a product or business from a public or private company using a high degree of debt and little or no equity.

*Later stage*   Also called the expansion stage, firms at this level of development are mature and profitable and often still expanding. Those with continued high-growth rates may get listed on a stock exchange.

*Lead investor*   The main coordinating investor in a group of investors, whether it is a syndicate of angels or a number of venture capital firms co-investing on a particular deal.

*Lemon*   An investment that has a poor or negative rate of return. An old venture capital adage claims that "lemons ripen before plums."

*Lifestyle firms*   Category comprising around 90 percent of all startups. These firms merely afford a reasonable living for their founders, rather than incurring the risks associated with high growth. These ventures typically have growth rates below 20 percent annually, have five-year revenue projections below $10 million, and are primarily funded internally—only very rarely with outside equity funds.

*Limited partners (LPS)*   Outside fund providers that invest a share of their assets in venture capital funds. These fund providers include pension funds, corporations, individuals and families, financial and insurance firms, endowments and foundations, and foreign investors. On termination of a venture capital fund, these investors typically receive their principal investments back, plus 80 percent of the fund's capital gains (minus the annual management fee).

*Liquidation*   Sale of all of a firm's assets for distribution to creditors and shareholders in order of priority.

*Liquidation preferences*   Allowing investors to force the liquidation of a venture, even against the wishes of management.

*Listing*   Placing a firm's shares in trade on a stock exchange.

*Living dead*   The term given to venture capital investments that are not generating very healthy returns but are managing to survive.

*Management fee*   An annual fee of around 3 percent of the funds under management, paid to the overseeing venture capital firm for its services and administrative expenses.

*Matching services*   Organizations that match investors looking for investment opportunities with entrepreneurs looking for investment funds. Appendix One of this book contains a list of over seventy such services around the United States.

*Middle-market firms*   Firms with growth prospects of more than 20 percent annually and five-year revenue projections between $10 million and $50 million. Less than 10 percent of all start-ups annually, these entrepreneurial firms are the backbone of the U.S. economy and attractive to business angel investors.

*Net present value (NPV)*   A firm or project's net contribution to wealth. This is the present value of current and future income streams, minus initial investment.

*Noncompete clause*   Prohibiting an entrepreneur from competing with his or her former firm for a certain amount of time.

*Options* or *share options*   Financial instruments that give the holder the right to buy another underlying security, such as common equity shares.

*Performance or forfeiture provisions*   Agreements that require entrepreneurs to surrender part of their equity to investors in the event of the firm failing to reach previously agreed financial targets and milestones. These provisions allow investors to protect their investment if it performs poorly and align the incentives of the entrepreneurs with those of the investors.

*Piggyback rights* Enabling investors to include their shares in the official registration filing when the firm files a registration statement for an IPO. This allows investors to avoid the full expenses of registering shares themselves.

*Plum* An investment that has a very healthy rate of return. The inverse of an old venture capital adage (see *Lemons*) claims that "plums ripen later than lemons."

*Positions* A party's stand on various issues in the negotiations process.

*Preference shares* Shares of a firm that encompass preferential rights over ordinary common shares, such as the first right to dividends and any capital payments.

*Principal* A person or party who delegates work and responsibilities to another person or party (the "agent"), who performs that work on the principal's behalf. Principals and agents are central to agency theory and separation of ownership and control common in most modern firms.

*Ratchets* A financial arrangement that allows one party to increase the share of their equity stake in a venture depending on the performance of the enterprise. Venture capitalists often use such agreements to increase their equity stake (and thus gain more control) in investments that are performing poorly.

*Redeemable shares* Equity shares that a venture can repurchase at a future point for a predetermined price.

*Return on investment (ROI)* An annual rate of return on an investor's investment. If the investment has been exited, then the *realized* rate of return can be calculated; if not, the *potential* rate of return estimates the forecasted future cash-out value.

*Risk capital* Financial assets invested in a high-risk venture, typically in the early and unproven stages.

*Screening* Scanning investment opportunities that are "rolling in" to find one or more that match the investor's criteria and preferences. The small minority of opportunities surviving the screening stage enter the due-diligence process before final investment becomes a strong possibility.

*Seed stage* Stage in which the entrepreneur has only a concept for a potentially profitable business opportunity that still has to be developed and proven.

*Snowballing*   The process of using contact with one business angel to find many more such investors through personal referral. Angels in particular often personally know many others, some of whom may be interested in new investment opportunities.

*Staging*   The process of providing an investment amount in increments dependent on time or performance quotas being reached. Staging gives investors the option to revalue, abandon, or expand commitment to the investment.

*Start-up*   A new business that is usually completing its product development and initial marketing. It can be of any size, but usually small.

*Stock options* or *grants*   Financial instruments that allow the holder to convert the instrument (after a predetermined date) into a certain number of the firm's equity shares for a predetermined price.

*Sweat equity*   Equity shares of a venture given to its founder(s) in recognition of his or her effort (sweat) expended to start and build the venture.

*Supermajority rights*   Control rights of a venture separate from the rights to residual value. These protect the minority ownership and allow them to exert some influence.

*Syndication*   A number of investors offering funds together as a group on a particular deal. A lead investor often coordinates such deals and represents the group's members. Within the last few years, syndication among angel investors (an angel alliance) has become more common, enabling them to fund larger deals closer to those typifying a small venture capital fund.

*Takedown schedule*   The plan stated in the fund prospectus or offering memorandum specifying the actual transfer of funds from the venture capital fund's limited partners to the general partners' control.

*Trade sale*   The sale of one firm to another firm. This is the most common exit route for business angel and venture capital investments.

*Unquoted firm*   A firm that is not listed on an organized stock exchange.

*Venture capital*   Financial capital supplied to young and innovative ventures, where both the risks and the potential returns are high. The venture capital offered by business angels tends to be more speculative and early-stage than that traditionally provided by the formal venture capital industry.

*Vesting schedules* Timetables for stock grants and options mandating that entrepreneurs earn (vest) their equity stakes over a number of years, rather than upon conversion of the stock options. This guarantees to investors and the market that the entrepreneurs will stick around, rather than converting and cashing in their shares.

*Virgin angels* High net-worth individuals, often with entrepreneurial backgrounds, who wish to make their first investment in an unquoted entrepreneurial venture but have not yet done so.

*ZOPA (zone of possible agreement)* The range of investment terms or amounts open to possible negotiation, ranging from the lowest the entrepreneur is willing to accept (the minimum) to the most the investor is willing to pay (the maximum).

# Bibliography

Acs, Z. J., and Phillips, B. D. "Why Does the Relative Share of Employment Stay Constant?" Paper presented at the Babson College–Kauffman Foundation Research Conference, Babson College, Babson Park, Mass., Apr. 16–19, 1997.

Advisory Council on Science and Technology (ACOST). *The Enterprise Challenge: Overcoming Barriers to Growth in Small Firms.* London: HMSO, 1990.

Aghion, P., and Bolton, P. "An Incomplete Contracts Approach to Financial Contracting." *Review of Economic Studies,* 1992, *59,* 473–494.

Alvarez, F., and others. "Financing Issues in the Twenty-First Century." Paper presented at the Babson College–Kauffman Foundation Research Conference, Babson College, Babson Park, Mass., Apr. 16–19, 1997.

Amit, R., Glosten, L. R., and Muller, E. "Does Venture Capital Foster the Most Promising Entrepreneurial Firms?" *California Management Review,* 1990, *32*(3), 102–111.

Aram, J. D. "Attitudes and Behaviors of Informal Investors Toward Early-Stage Investments, Technology-Based Ventures and Coinvestors." *Journal of Business Venturing,* 1989, *4,* 333–347.

Armstrong, J. S., and Overton, T. S. "Estimating Nonresponse Bias in Mail Surveys." *Journal of Marketing Research,* 1977, *14,* 396–402.

Atkin, R., and Esiri, M. *Informal Investment—Investor and Investee Relationships.* London: Business Development Centre, University of Greenwich, 1993.

Audretsch, D. B. *Innovation and Industry Evolution,* Cambridge, Mass.: MIT Press, 1995.

"Bank and Nonbank Competition for Small Business Credit: Evidence from the 1987 and 1993 National Surveys of Small Business Finances." *Federal Reserve Bulletin,* Nov. 1996, pp. 983–995.

Barney, J. B., Busenitz, L. W., Fiet, J. O., and Moesel, D. "Determinants of a New Venture Team's Receptivity to Advice from Venture Capitalists." In *Frontiers of Entrepreneurship Research.* Babson Park, Mass.: Babson College, 1994.

Barry, C. B., Muscarella, C. J., Peavy, J. W., III, and Vetsuypens, M. R. "The Role of Venture Capital in the Creation of Public Companies." *Journal of Financial Economics,* 1990, *27,* 447–471.

Bates, T. "Entrepreneur, Human Capital Inputs, and Small Business Longevity." *Review of Economics and Statistics,* 1990, *72,* 551–559.

Baty, G. B. *The Initial Financing of the New Research-Based Enterprise in New England.* Boston: Federal Reserve Bank of Boston, 1964.

Baty, G. B. *Entrepreneurship for the 1990s.* Upper Saddle River, N.J.: Prentice-Hall, 1991.

Benjamin, G. A., and Margulis, J. *Finding Your Wings: How to Locate Private Investors to Fund Your Venture.* New York: Wiley, 1996.

Berglof, E. "A Control Theory of Venture Capital Finance." *Journal of Law, Economics, & Organisation,* 1994, *10*(2), 247–267.

Berle, A. A., and Means, G. C. *The Modern Corporation and Private Property.* New York: Macmillan, 1932.

Bester, H. "Screening vs. Rationing in Credit Markets with Imperfect Information." *American Economic Review,* 1985, *75*(4).

Bhide, A. "Bootstrap Finance: The Art of Start-ups." *Harvard Business Review,* Nov.–Dec. 1992, pp. 109–117.

Bhide, A. "Deficient Governance." *Harvard Business Review,* Nov.–Dec. 1994, pp. 129–139.

Binks, M. R., and Ennew, C. T. "Assessing the Importance of the Relationship Between Banks and Their Small Business Customers." Paper presented at the Babson College–Kauffman Foundation Research Conference, Babson College, Babson Park, Mass., Apr. 16–19, 1997.

Binks, M. R., Ennew, C. T., and Reed, G. V. "Information Asymmetries and the Provision of Finance to Small Firms." *International Small Business Journal,* 1992, *11*(1), 35–46.

Birch, D., Haggerty, A., Parsons, W., and Rossel, C. *Entrepreneurial Hot Spots.* Boston: Cognetics, 1993.

Blanton, K. "Market Economy." *Boston Globe,* Oct. 25, 1998, pp. G1, G3.

Bowden, A. "Who Wants to Be a Millionaire?" *Investors Chronicle,* June 24, 1994.

British Venture Capital Association (BVCA). *The Sensor, no. 2.* London: BVCA, 1993.

British Venture Capital Association (BVCA). "Report on Investment Activity 1993." London: BVCA, 1994.

British Venture Capital Association (BVCA). "Report on Investment Activity." London: BVCA, 1995.

Brodsky, N., and Burlingham, B. "My Life as an Angel." *Inc.,* July 1997, p. 42.

Brophy, D. J. "Financing the New Venture: A Report of Recent Research." In D. L. Sexton and J. D. Kasarda (eds.), *The State of the Art of Entrepreneurship*. Boston: PWS-Kent, 1992.

Brophy, D. J., and Shulman, J. M. "A Finance Perspective on Entrepreneurship Research." *Entrepreneurship, Theory & Practice*, Spring 1992, *16*(3).

Brouwer, M., and Hendrix, B. "Two Worlds of Venture Capital: What Happened to U.S. and Dutch Early Stage Investment?" *Small Business Economics*, 1998, *10*, 333–368.

Bruno, A. V. "A Structural Analysis of the Venture Capital Industry." In D. L. Sexton and R. W. Smilor (eds.), *The Art and Science of Entrepreneurship*. Cambridge, Mass.: Ballinger, 1986.

Bruno, A. V., and Tyebjee, T. T. "The Entrepreneur's Search for Capital." *Journal of Business Venturing*, 1985, *1*, 64–74.

Bruton, G., Fried, V., and Hisrich, R. "CEO Dismissal and the Role of the Venture Capitalist." In *Frontiers of Entrepreneurship Research*. Babson Park, Mass.: Babson College, 1994.

Bruton, G., Fried, V., and Hisrich, R. "Venture Capitalist and CEO Dismissal." *Entrepreneurship, Theory & Practice*, 1998.

Buckland, R., and Davis, E. W. (eds.). *Finance for Growing Enterprises*. London: Routledge, 1995.

Busenitz, L. W., and Fiet, J. O. "Venture Capital Firm Resources and Their Long-Term Effect on Venture Disposition." Paper presented at the Babson College–Kauffman Foundation Research Conference, University of South Carolina, May 12–15, 1999.

Busenitz, L. W., Moesel, D. D., and Fiet, J. O. "The Impact of Post-Funding Involvement by Venture Capitalists on Long-Term Performance Outcomes." Paper presented at the Babson College–Kauffman Foundation Research Conference, Babson College, Babson Park, Mass., Apr. 16–19, 1997.

Bygrave, W. D. "The Structure of the Investment Networks of Venture Capital Firms." *Journal of Business Venturing*, 1987, *3*, 137.

Bygrave, W. D. *The Portable MBA in Entrepreneurship*. New York: Wiley, 1994.

Bygrave, W., Johnstone, G., Matchett, M., and Roedel, J. "Venture Capital High-Tech Investments: Can We Differentiate the Best from Worst?" Paper presented at the Babson College–Kauffman Foundation Research Conference, University of South Carolina, May 12–15, 1999.

Bygrave, W. D., and Shulman, J. M. "Capital Gains Tax: Bane or Boom for Venture Capitalists." In *Frontiers of Entrepreneurship Research*. Babson Park, Mass.: Babson College, 1988.

Bygrave, W. D., and Timmons, J. A. "Networking Among Venture Capital Firms." In *Frontiers of Entrepreneurship Research*. Babson Park, Mass.: Babson College, 1986.

Bygrave, W. D., and Timmons, J. A. *Venture Capital at the Crossroads*, Boston: Harvard Business School Press, 1992.

Cable, D. M., and Shane, S. "A Prisoner's Dilemma Approach to Entrepreneur–Venture Capitalist Relationships." *Academy of Management Review*, 1997, *22*(1), 142–176.

Campbell, N. "The Interface Between Business Angels and Venture Capitalists in Scottish Technology-Based Companies." Paper presented at the Babson College–Kauffman Foundation Research Conference, University of South Carolina, May 12–15, 1999.

Carter, R. B., and Van Auken, H. E. "Venture Capital Firms' Preferences for Projects in Particular Stages of Development." *Journal of Small Business Management*, Jan. 1994, pp. 60–73.

Cary, L. *The* Venture Capital Report *Guide to Venture Capital in the UK & Europe*. (7th ed.) Henley-on-Thames: Venture Capital Report, 1995.

Chan, G. "Manna Makers: 'Angel Investors' Bestow Precious Investment Capital on the Chosen Few." *Sacramento Bee*, Apr. 26, 1999.

Conlin, E. "Adventure Capital." *Inc.*, Sept. 1989, pp. 32–42.

Coleman, S., and Cohn, R. "Small Firms' Use of Financial Leverage: Evidence from the 1993 National Survey of Small Business Finances." Paper presented at the Babson College–Kauffman Foundation Entrepreneurship Research Conference, University of South Carolina, May 12–15, 1999.

Coveney, P. "Informal Investment in Britain: An Examination of the Behaviours, Characteristics, Motives and Preferences of British Business Angels." Unpublished master's thesis, Oxford University, 1994.

Coveney, P. "Informal Investment in Britain: An Examination of the Investment Activity, Characteristics and Preferences of British Business Angels." Unpublished doctoral thesis, Oxford University, 1996.

Coveney, P., and Moore, K. *Business Angels*. London: Wiley, 1998.

Cruz, H. "You Might Not Recognize the Neighborhood Millionaire." *Sarasota Herald-Tribune*, June 6, 1999, pp. 1–2d.

Cullen, L. R. "On the Side of Angels." *Money*, Dec. 1998, pp. 130–136.

De Bare, I. "Young Tech Millionaires Now Face the Rest of Their Lives." *Minneapolis Star Tribune*, June 20, 1999, p. D6.

De Meza, D., and Webb, D. "Entrepreneurial Wealth, The Level of Investment and Credit Policy." *London School of Economics (LSE) Financial Markets Group, Discussion Paper no. 228*. 1995.

Deakins, D. *Entrepreneurship and Small Firms*. London: McGraw-Hill, 1996.

Dean, B, V., and Giglierno, J. J. "Multistage Financing of Technical Start-up Companies in Silicon Valley." *Journal of Business Venturing*, 1990, *5*, 375–389.

Dennis, W. J., Jr. "More Than You Think: An Inclusive Estimate of Business Entries." *Journal of Business Venturing*, 1997, *12*, 175–196.

Dixon, R. "Venture Capitalists and the Appraisal of Investments." *Omega*, 1991, pp. 333–344.

Duggins, R. "Strategic Analysis of the Venture Capital Industry." *Venture Capital Report*, Apr. 1993, pp. 1–4.

Duxbury, L., Haines, G., and Riding, A. "A Personality Profile of Canadian Informal Investors." *Journal of Small Business Management*, 1996, *34*(2),44–55.

Eglin, R. "Small Businesses That Are Too Big and Important to Ignore." *Management Today*, Mar. 1994, pp. 17–18.

Ehrlich, S. B., Noble, A. F., Moore, T., and Weaver, R. R. "After the Cash Arrives: A Comparative Study of Venture Capital Firms and Private Investor Involvement in Entrepreneurial Firms." *Journal of Business Venturing*, 1994, *9*, 67–82.

Eisenhardt, K. M. "Agency Theory: An Assessment and Review." *Academy of Management Review*, 1989, *14*(1), 57–74.

European Venture Capital Association (EVCA). *EVCA '94 Yearbook*. London: KPMG, 1994.

Evanson, D. R. *Where to Go When the Bank Says No: Alternatives for Financing Your Business*. New York: Bloomberg Press, 1998.

Fama, E., and Jensen, M. C. "Separation of Ownership and Control." *Journal of Law & Economics*, 1983, *26*, 301–325.

Fiet, J. O. "Network Reliance by Venture Capital Firms: An Empirical and Theoretical Test." In *Frontiers of Entrepreneurship Research*. Babson Park, Mass.: Babson College, 1991.

Fiet, J. O. "Reliance upon Informants in the Venture Capital Industry." *Journal of Business Venturing*, 1995a, *10*, 195–223.

Fiet, J. O. "Risk Avoidance Strategies in Venture Capital Markets." *Journal of Management Studies*, 1995b, *32*(4), 551–574.

Fiet, J. O. "Fragmentation in the Market for Venture Capital." *Entrepreneurship, Theory & Practice*, Winter 1996, pp. 5–20.

"15 High-Tech Startups to Get Seed Capital." *Business Times* (Singapore), Apr. 12, 1999, p. 14.

"Financial Services Used by Small Businesses: Evidence from the 1993 National Survey of Small Business Finances." *Federal Reserve Bulletin*, July 1995, pp. 629–667.

"The Financing of Technology-Based Small Firms." Bank of England, Oct. 1996. (Downloaded from Internet.)

"The First Billion Takes a Lifetime . . . Except in the Internet Age." *Forbes,* Apr. 1999, p. 246.

Foote, D. "Show Us the Money! *Newsweek,* Apr. 19, 1999, pp. 43–44.

Freear, J., Sohl, J. E., and Wetzel, W. E. "Raising Venture Capital: Entrepreneurs' View of the Process." In *Frontiers of Entrepreneurship Research.* Babson Park, Mass.: Babson College, 1990.

Freear, J., Sohl, J. E., and Wetzel, W. E. "Raising Venture Capital to Finance Growth." In *Frontiers of Entrepreneurship Research.* Babson Park, Mass.: Babson College, 1991.

Freear, J., Sohl, J. E., and Wetzel, W. E. "The Investment Attitudes, Behavior and Characteristics of High Net Worth Individuals." In *Frontiers of Entrepreneurship Research.* Babson Park, Mass.: Babson College, 1992a.

Freear, J., Sohl, J. E., and Wetzel, W. E. "The Truth About Angels More Than a Myth." (Working paper.) Durham: Center for Venture Research, University of New Hampshire, 1992b.

Freear, J., Sohl, J. E., and Wetzel, W. E. "Summary: Angel Profiles: A Longitudinal Study." In *Frontiers of Entrepreneurship Research.* Babson Park, Mass.: Babson College, 1993.

Freear, J., Sohl, J. E., and Wetzel, W. E. "Angels and Non-Angels: Are There Differences?" *Journal of Business Venturing,* 1994a, *9,* 109–123.

Freear, J., Sohl, J. E., and Wetzel, W. E. "The Private Investor Market for Venture Capital." *The Financier: ACMT,* 1994b, *1*(2), 7–15.

Freear, J., Sohl, J. E., and Wetzel, W. E. "Angels: Personal Investors in the Venture Capital Market." *Entrepreneurship & Regional Development,* 1995a, *7,* 85–94.

Freear, J., Sohl, J. E., and Wetzel, W. E. "Who Bankrolls Software Entrepreneurs." In *Frontiers of Entrepreneurship Research.* Babson Park, Mass.: Babson College, 1995b.

Freear, J., Sohl, J. E., and Wetzel, W. E. "The Informal Venture Capital Market: Milestones Passed and the Road Ahead." Paper presented at the fourth State of the Art in Entrepreneurship Research Conference, May 9–11, 1996.

Freear, J., and Wetzel, W. E. "Equity Financing for New Technology-Based Firms." In *Frontiers of Entrepreneurship Research.* Babson Park, Mass.: Babson College, 1988.

Freear, J., and Wetzel, W. E. "Equity Capital for Entrepreneurs." In *Frontiers of Entrepreneurship Research.* Babson Park, Mass.: Babson College, 1989.

Freear, J., and Wetzel, W. E. "Who Bankrolls High-Tech Entrepreneurs?" *Journal of Business Venturing,* 1990, *5,* 77–89.

Freear, J., and Wetzel, W. E. "The Informal Venture Capital Market in the Year 2000." Paper presented at the Third Annual International Research Symposium on Small Business Research, Florida State University, Tallahassee, Apr. 24–26, 1991.

Freear, J., and Wetzel, W. E. "The Informal Venture Capital Market in the 1990s." In D. L. Sexton and J. D. Kasarda (eds.), *The State of the Art of Entrepreneurship.* Boston: PWS-Kent, 1992.

Fried, V. H., and Hisrich, R. D. "Venture Capital from the Investors' Perspective." In *Frontiers of Entrepreneurship Research.* Babson Park, Mass.: Babson College, 1989.

Gartner, W. B., Starr, J. A., and Bhat, S. "Predicting New Venture Survival: An Analysis of 'Anatomy of a Start-up.'" (Cases from *Inc.* magazine.) *Journal of Business Venturing,* 1998, *14,* 215–232.

Gaston, R. J. *Finding Private Venture Capital for Your Firm: A Complete Guide.* New York: Wiley, 1989.

Gaston, R. J., and Bell, S. E. "The Informal Supply of Capital." Washington, D.C.: Office of Economic Research, U.S. Small Business Administration, 1988.

Gay, K. (1996) Alternative Funding, *Black Enterprise,* 26(12).

Gifford, S. "Limited Attention and the Role of the Venture Capitalists." *Journal of Business Venturing,* 1997, *12,* 459–482.

Gompers, P. A. "Grandstanding in the Venture Capital Industry." *Journal of Financial Economics,* 1996, *42*(1), 133–156.

Gordon, S. "Touched by an Angel: They've Got a Billion Dollars to Invest—and If Your Company Is Too Small for the Venture Capitalists But Too Big to Borrow from the In-Laws, Angel Investors Could Be the Answer to Your Prayers." *National Post* (Canada), May 1, 1999, p. 24.

Gordon, J., and Grover, M. B. "Celestial Cast of Characters." *Forbes,* Nov. 2, 1998.

Gorman, M., and Sahlman, W. A. "What Do Venture Capitalists Do?" *Journal of Business Venturing,* 1989, *4,* 231–248.

Green, M. B. (ed.). *Venture Capital: International Comparisons.* London: Routledge, 1991.

Gruner, S. "The Trouble with Angels." *Inc.,* Feb. 1998, p. 46.

Gujarati, D. N. *Basic Econometrics.* London: McGraw-Hill, 1995.

Gupta, A. K., and Sapienza, H. J. "The Pursuit of Diversity by Venture Capital Firms: Antecedents and Implications." In *Frontiers of Entrepreneurship Research.* Babson Park, Mass.: Babson College, 1988.

Haar, N. E., Starr, J., and MacMillan, I. C. "Informal Risk Capital Investors: Investment Patterns on the East Coast of the U.S.A." *Journal of Business Venturing,* 1988, *3,* 11–29.

Hale, D. "For New Jobs, Help Small Business." *Wall Street Journal,* Aug. 10, 1992, p. B10.

Hall, P. "Investment Evaluation in UK Venture Capital Funds: The Appraisal of Risk and Return." Unpublished M.B.A. thesis, City College, London, 1988.

Hall, J., and Hofer, C. W. "Venture Capitalists' Decision Criteria in New Venture Evaluation." *Journal of Business Venturing*, 1993, *8*, 25–41.

Harper, D. A. *Entrepreneurship and the Market Process: An Enquiry into the Growth of Knowledge.* London: Routledge, 1996.

Harrison, R. T., Dibben, M. R., and Mason, C. M. "The Role of Trust in the Informal Investor's Investment Decision: An Exploratory Analysis." *Entrepreneurship, Theory & Practice,* Summer 1997, pp. 63–81.

Harrison, R. T., and Mason, C. M. "Informal Investment Networks: A Case Study from the United Kingdom." *Entrepreneurship & Regional Development,* 1991a, pp. 269–279.

Harrison, R. T., and Mason, C. M. "Informal Venture Capital in the UK and the USA: A Comparison of Investor Characteristics and Decision-Making." In *Frontiers of Entrepreneurship Research.* Babson Park, Mass.: Babson College, 1991b.

Harrison, R. T., and Mason, C. M. "International Perspectives on the Supply of Informal Venture Capital." *Journal of Business Venturing,* 1992a, *7*, 459–475.

Harrison, R. T., and Mason, C. M. "The Roles of Investors in Entrepreneurial Companies: A Comparison of Informal Investors and Venture Capitalists." *Venture Finance Research Project.* (Working paper no. 5.) University of Southampton and Ulster Business School, Southampton, U.K., 1992b.

Harrison, R. T., and Mason, C. M. "Developments in the Promotion of Informal Venture Capital in the UK." *International Journal of Entrepreneurial Behaviour & Research,* 1996a, *2*(2), 6–33.

Harrison, R. T., and Mason, C. M. *Informal Venture Capital: Evaluating the Impact of Business Introduction Services.* London: Woodhead-Faulkner, 1996b.

Hart, O. *Firms, Contracts, and Financial Structures.* Oxford: Oxford University Press, 1995.

Hart, O., and Holmstrom, B. "The Theory of Contracts." In T. F. Bewley (ed.), *Advances in Economic Theory, Fifth World Congress.* Cambridge University Press, 1987.

Hart, O., and Moore, J. "Incomplete Contracts and Renegotiation." *Econometrica,* 1988, *56*(4), 755–785.

Hart, O., and Moore, J. "Property Rights and the Nature of the Firm." *Journal of Political Economy,* 1990, *98*(6).

"Helping High-Tech Firms Take Off Series: High-Tech Heartache." *Chicago Sun Times,* Apr. 20, 1999, p. 49.

Hisrich, R. D. (ed.). *Entrepreneurship, Intrapreneurship, and Venture Capital.* Burr Ridge, Ill.: Irwin, 1986.

Hisrich, R. D., and Jankowicz, A. D. "Intuition in Venture Capital Decisions: An Exploratory Study Using a New Technique." *Journal of Business Venturing,* 1990, *5,* 49–62.

Hoffman, C. A. *The Venture Capital Investment Process: A Particular Aspect of Regional Economic Development.* Ph.D. dissertation, University of Texas at Austin, 1972.

Huey, J. "Working up to the New Economy." *Fortune,* June 27, 1994.

Huntsman, B., and Hoban, J. P. "Investment in New Enterprise: Some Empirical Observations on Risk, Return, and Market Structure." *Financial Management,* Summer 1980, pp. 44–51.

*International Herald Tribune,* Mar. 10, 1997, p. 3.

"Internet Economy Surges: Study Shows Internet Generated an Estimated $301 B in the U.S. Last Year." *CNNfn,* June 10, 1999. [www.cnnfn.com]

Jensen, M. C. "The Modern Industrial Revolution, Exit, and the Failure of Internal Control Systems." *Journal of Finance,* July 1993.

Jensen, M. C., and Meckling, W. H. "Theory of the Firm: Managerial Behavior, Agency Costs and Ownership Structure." *Journal of Financial Economics,* 1976, *3,* 305–360.

Keating, R. J. "The Entrepreneurial Economy: A Monthly Review of the Economy from the Small Business Survival Committee." Jan. 13, 1999. [http://www.sbsc.org/]

Keeley, R. H., and Knapp, R. W. "New Company Evolution: A Comparison of Large and Small Start-ups." In *Frontiers of Entrepreneurship Research.* Babson Park, Mass.: Babson College, 1993.

Keeley, R. H., and Knapp, R. W. "Founding Conditions and Business Performance: 'High Performers' vs. Small vs. Venture Capital-Backed Start-ups." In *Frontiers of Entrepreneurship Research.* Babson Park, Mass.: Babson College, 1994.

Keeley, R. H., Roure, J. B., and Loo, R. "New Ventures Which Obtain Funding and Those Which Do Not: What's the Difference?" In *Frontiers of Entrepreneurship Research.* Babson Park, Mass.: Babson College, 1991.

Keeley, R. H., and Turki, L. A. "New Ventures: How Risky Are They?" In *Frontiers of Entrepreneurship Research.* Babson Park, Mass.: Babson College, 1992.

Kelly, P., and Hay, M. "Serial Investors: An Exploratory Study." (Working paper.) London: London Business School, 1996.

Kelly, P., and Hay, M. "Deal-Makers": A Reputation That Attracts Quality." Paper presented at the Babson College–Kauffman Foundation
Entrepreneurship Research Conference, University of South Carolina, May 12–15, 1999.

Kent, C. A., Sexton, D. L., and Vesper, K. H. (eds). *Encyclopaedia of Entrepreneurship.* Upper Saddle River, N.J.: Prentice-Hall.

Knight, R. M. "Summary: Criteria Used by Venture Capitalists: A Cross
Cultural Analysis." In *Frontiers of Entrepreneurship Research.* Babson
Park, Mass.: Babson College, 1992.

KPMG Management Consulting. *Investment Networking.* Glasgow: Scottish
Enterprise, 1992.

Krasner, O. J., and Tymes, E. R. "Informal Risk Capital in California." In
*Frontiers of Entrepreneurship Research.* Babson Park, Mass.: Babson
College, 1983.

Kudlow, L. "Soaring! Dow 10,000 Reflects Enlightened Policy on Taxes,
Regulation." *San Diego Union-Tribune,* Apr. 4, 1999.

Landstrom, H. "Co-operation Between Venture Capital Companies and
Small Firms." *Entrepreneurship & Regional Development,* 1990, *2,*
345–362.

Landstrom, H. "The Relationship Between Private Investors and Small
Firms: An Agency Theory Approach." *Entrepreneurship & Regional
Development,* 1992, *4,* 199–223.

Landstrom, H. "Informal Risk Capital in Sweden and Some International
Comparisons." *Journal of Business Venturing,* 1993, *8,* 525–540.

Landstrom, H. "A Pilot Study of the Investment Decision-Making Behavior of Informal Investors in Sweden." *Journal of Small Business Management,* July 1995, pp. 67–76.

Landstrom, H., and Winborg, J. "Small Business Managers' Attitudes To-
wards and Use of Financial Sources." In *Frontiers of Entrepreneurship
Research.* Babson Park, Mass.: Babson College, 1995.

Lange, J., Warhuus, J. P., and Levie, J. "Entrepreneur/Banker Interaction
in Young Growing Firms: A Large Scale International Study." Paper
presented at the Babson College–Kauffman Foundation Entrepreneurship Research Conference, University of South Carolina,
May 12–15, 1999.

Lax, D. A., and Sebenius, J. K. *The Manager as Negotiator.* New York: Free
Press, 1986.

Leland, H. E., and Pyle, D. H. "Informational Asymmetries, Financial
Structure, and Financial Intermediation." *Journal of Finance,* 1977,
22(2).

Lonsdale, C. "Government and the UK Equity Gap: The Need for a Policy Overhaul," *Venture Capital Report,* Mar. 1996.

Lorenz, E. "Neither Friends Nor Strangers: Informal Networks of Sub-contracting in French Industry." In E. Gambretta (ed.), *Trust: The Making and Breaking of Cooperative Relations.* Oxford: Basil Blackwell, 1988.

Lumme, A., Mason, C., and Suomi, M. "The Returns from Informal Venture Capital Investments: Some Evidence from Finland." In *Frontiers of Entrepreneurship Research.* Babson Park, Mass.: Babson College, 1996.

MacDonald, M. *Creating Threshold Technology Companies in Canada: The Role for Venture Capital.* Ottawa: Science Council of Canada, 1991.

MacMillan, I. C., Kulow, D. M., and Khoylian, R. "Venture Capitalists' Involvement in Their Investments: Extent and Performance." *Journal of Business Venturing,* 1988, *4,* 27–47.

MacMillan, I. C., Siegel, R., and Subbanarasimha, P. N. "Criteria Used by Venture Capitalists to Evaluate New Venture Proposals." *Journal of Business Venturing,* 1985, 1, 119–128.

MacMillan, I. C., Zemann, L., and Subbanarasimha, P. N. "Criteria Distinguishing Successful from Unsuccessful Ventures in the Venture Screening Process." *Journal of Business Venturing,* 1987, *2,* 123–137.

Malik, O. "Internet Breakthroughs." *Forbes,* May 26, 1999a.

Malik, O. "Who's Next." *Forbes,* May 26, 1999b.

Manigart, S., and others. "Venture Capitalists, Rates of Return and Valuation: A Comparative Study of the U.S., UK, France, Belgium and Holland." Paper presented at the Babson College–Kauffman Foundation Research Conference, Babson College, Babson Park, Mass., Apr. 16–19, 1997.

Martin, R. "The Growth and Geographical Anatomy of Venture Capitalism in the United Kingdom." *Regional Studies,* 1989, *25*(5), 389–403.

Mason, C. M. "Informal Investment in the UK: Knowns and Unknowns." Presentation to a Department of Trade and Industry Informal Investment Seminar, London, Oct. 18, 1993.

Mason, C. M. "Informal Venture Capital: Is Policy Running Ahead of Knowledge?" *International Journal of Entrepreneurial Behaviour & Research,* 1996a, *2*(1), 4–14.

Mason, C. M. (ed.). *International Informal Venture Capital Research Newsletter,* 1996b, vol. 4.

Mason, C. M., and Harrison, R. T. "Informal Risk Capital: A Review and Research Agenda." *Venture Finance Research Project.* (Working paper no. 1.) University of Southampton and Ulster Business School, Southampton, U.K., 1990.

Mason, C. M., and Harrison, R. T. "Venture Capital, the Equity Gap and the 'North-South' Divide in the United Kingdom." In M. B. Green (ed.), *Venture Capital: International Comparisons*. London: Routledge, 1991.

Mason, C. M., and Harrison, R. T. "The Supply of Equity Finance in the UK: A Strategy for Closing the Equity Gap." *Entrepreneurship & Regional Development*, 1992, *4*, 357–380.

Mason, C. M., and Harrison, R. T. "Promoting Informal Venture Capital: An Evaluation of a British Initiative." In *Frontiers of Entrepreneurship Research*. Babson Park, Mass.: Babson College, 1993a.

Mason, C. M., and Harrison, R. T. "Strategies for Expanding the Informal Venture Capital Market." *International Small Business Journal*, 1993b, *11*(4), 23–38.

Mason, C. M., and Harrison, R. T. "Why Business Angels Say No: A Case Study of Opportunities Rejected by an Informal Investor Syndicate." *Venture Finance Research Project*. (Working paper no. 7.) University of Southampton and Ulster Business School, Southampton, U.K., 1994.

Mason, C. M., and Harrison, R. T. "Informal Venture Capital and the Financing of Small and Medium-Sized Enterprises." *Journal of SEAANZ*, 1995, *3*(1, 2), 33–56.

Mason, C. M., and Harrison, R. T. "Informal Venture Capital: A Study of the Investment Process, the Post-Investment Experience and Investment Performance." *Entrepreneurship & Regional Development*, 1996a, *8*, 105–125.

Mason, C. M., and Harrison, R. T. "The UK Clearing Banks and the Informal Venture Capital Market." *International Journal of Bank Marketing*, 1996b, *14*(1), 5–14.

Mason, C. M., and Harrison, R. T. "Business Angels in the UK: A Response to Stevenson & Coveney." *International Small Business Journal*, Jan./Mar. 1997. (Downloaded from the Internet.)

Mason, C. M., and Harrison, R. T. "The Rates of Return from Informal Venture Capital Investments: Some UK Evidence." Paper presented at the Babson College–Kauffman Foundation Entrepreneurship Research Conference, University of South Carolina, May 12–15, 1999.

Mason, C. M., Harrison, R. T., and Allen, P. "Informal Venture Capital: A Study of the Investment Process, the Post-Investment Experience and Investment Performance." *Venture Finance Research Project*. (Working paper no. 12.) University of Southampton and Ulster Business School, Southampton, U.K., 1995.

Mason, C. M., Harrison, R. T., and Chaloner, J. "Informal Risk Capital in the UK: A Study of Investor Characteristics, Investment Preferences and Investment Decision-Making." *Venture Finance Research Project*.

(Working paper no. 2.) University of Southampton and Ulster Business School, Southampton, U.K., 1991a.

Mason, C. M., Harrison, R. T., and Chaloner, J. "The Operation and Effectiveness of LINC: Part 1, a Survey of Investors." (Working paper.) Urban Policy Research Unit, University of Southampton, Southampton, U.K., 1991b.

Mason, C. M., and Rogers, A. "Understanding the Business Angel's Investment Decision." *Venture Finance Research Project.* (Working paper no. 14.) University of Southampton and Ulster Business School, Southampton, U.K., 1996.

Mason, C. M., and Sackett, N. *BVCA: Report on Business Angel Investment Activity 1995/6.* London: British Venture Capital Association, 1996.

Mason, C. M., and others. "The Perception of Opportunity by European Venture 'Angels.'" In *Frontiers of Entrepreneurship Research.* Babson Park, Mass.: Babson College, 1994.

Mayfield, W. M. "The Determination of the Developmental Process of the Relationship Between the Informal Investor and the Entrepreneur: An Exploratory Study." Unpublished doctoral thesis, Glasgow Caledonian University, Glasgow, Scotland, 1999.

Mayfield, W. M., and Bygrave, W. D. "The Formation and Organization of Mega-Angel Syndicates." Paper presented at the Babson College–Kauffman Foundation Research Conference, University of South Carolina, May 12–15, 1999.

Mayfield, W. M., Hynes, B., and O'Cinneide, B. "Celtic Cousins: Insights into Small Business Maturation in Scotland and Ireland." Paper presented at the Babson College–Kauffman Foundation Research Conference, Babson College, Babson Park, Mass., Apr. 16–19, 1997.

Mitchell, J. E. "Small Firms: A Critique." *Three Banks Review,* 1980, pp. 50–61.

Moore, B. "Financial Constraints to the Growth and Development of Small, High-Technology Firms." Cambridge, England: Small Business Research Centre, 1993.

Moore, B. "Financial Constraints to the Growth and Development of Small High-Technology Firms." In A. Hughes and D. J. Storey (eds.), *Finance and the Small Firm.* London: Routledge, 1994.

Moore, B., and Segaghat, N. "Factors Constraining the Growth of Small High-Technology Companies: A Case Study of the Cambridge Sub-Region." (Working paper no. 21.) Small Business Research Centre, University of Cambridge, England, 1992.

Mourkheiber, Z. "Three Men and a Web Idea." *Forbes,* May 17, 1999.

Murray, G. C. *Change and Maturity in the UK Venture Capital Industry, 1991–95.* London: BVCA, 1991.

Murray, G. C. "An Evaluation of the First Three Years of the European Seed Capital Fund (ESCF) Initiative." Paper presented to a conference on Studies in the New Europe, University of Nottingham, England, 1992.

Murray, G. C. "The Second 'Equity Gap': Exit Problems for Seed and Early Stage Venture Capitalists and Their Investee Companies." *International Small Business Journal*, 1994, *12*(4), 59–76.

Murray, G. C. "Evolution and Change: An Analysis of the First Decade of the UK Venture Capital Industry." *Journal of Business Finance & Accounting*, 1995a, *22*(8), 1077–1106.

Murray, G. C. "A Synthesis of Six European Case Studies of Successfully Exited, Venture Capital Financed, New Technology Based Firms." (Working paper.) Warwick Business School, Warwick, U.K., 1995b.

Murray, N. "Finding the Right Partner: Private Investor Networks." In *Sharing Experience: The NatWest Guide to Informal Investment*. London: National Westminster Bank, 1998.

Murray, G. C., and Lott, J. "Summary: Have UK Venture Capital Firms a Bias Against Investment in Technology-Related Companies?" In *Frontiers of Entrepreneurship Research*. Babson Park, Mass.: Babson College, 1992.

Muzyka, D., Birley, S., and Leleux, B. *Trade-offs in the Investment Decisions of European Venture Capitalists.* (Working paper.) London: Imperial College, 1995.

Muzyka, D., Birley, S., Leleux, B., Rossell, G., and Bendixen, F. "Financial Structure and Decisions of Venture Capital Firms: A Pan-European Study." In *Frontiers of Entrepreneurship Research*. Babson Park, Mass.: Babson College, 1993.

Myers, S. "The Capital Structure Puzzle." *Journal of Finance*, 1984, *39*, 572–592.

Myers, S. C., and Majluf, N. S. "Corporate Financing and Investment Decisions When Firms Have Information That Investors Do Not Have." *Journal of Financial Economics*, 1984, *13*, 187–221.

Nance-Nash, S. "Brevity, Bullets and No B.S." *Forbes*, Feb. 18, 1999.

Neiswander, D. K. "Informal Seed Stage Investors." In *Frontiers of Entrepreneurship Research*. Babson Park, Mass.: Babson College, 1985.

"Next Millennium May Usher in 'Entrepreneurial Age' According to New Ernst & Young-Commissioned Survey." *Business Wire*, 1998.

Nittka, I. "A Comparison of Companies Seeking Venture Capital over the Internet in the U.S.A., U.K., and Germany." Paper presented at the Babson College–Kauffman Foundation Research Conference, University of South Carolina, May 12–15, 1999.

Norton, E. "Venture Capital as an Alternative Means to Allocate Capital: An Agency-Theoretic View." *Entrepreneurship Theory and Practice,* Winter 1995, pp. 19–29.

Norton, E., and Tenenbaum, B. H. "Factors Affecting the Structure of U.S. Venture Capital Deals." *Journal of Small Business Management,* July 1992.

Norton, E., and Tenenbaum, B. H. "The Effects of Venture Capitalists' Characteristics on the Structure of the Venture Capital Deal." *Journal of Small Business Management,* Oct. 1993.

NVCA. *National Venture Capital Association Annual Report.* N.J.: Venture Economics Information Services, 1998.

NVCA. *National Venture Capital Association Yearbook.* N.J.: Venture Economics Information Services, 1999.

Ou, C. "Holdings of Privately-Held Business Assets by American Families: Findings from the 1983 Consumer Finance Survey." Unpublished manuscript. Washington, D.C.: Office of Economic Research, U.S. Small Business Administration, 1987.

Pence, C. C. *How Venture Capitalists Make Investment Decisions.* Michigan: UMI Research Press, 1982.

Pesenti, S. "Valuing Privately Owned Companies: Valuation Techniques." (Teaching note.) London: London Business School, 1993.

Pettit, R. R., and Singer, R. F. "Small Business Finance: A Research Agenda." *Financial Management,* 1985, *14*(3), 47–59.

Podolny, J., and Feldman, A. "Is It Better to Have Status or to Know What You Are Doing? An Examination of Position and Capability in Venture Capital Markets." *Academy of Management,* 1997, vol. 26.

Posner, B. G. "How to Finance Anything." *Inc.,* Feb. 1993, p. 54.

Postma, P. D., and Sullivan, M. K. "Informal Risk Capital in the Knoxville Region." Unpublished report. University of Tennessee, 1990.

Pratt, G. "Venture Capital in the United Kingdom." *Bank of England Quarterly Review,* 1990, *30,* 78–83.

Ravid, A., and Spiegel, M. "Optimal Financial Contracts for a Start-up with Unlimited Operating Discretion." *Journal of Finance & Quantitative Analysis,* 1997, *32*(3), 269–286.

Rea, R. H. "Factors Affecting Success and Failure of Seed Capital/Start-up Negotiations." *Journal of Business Venturing,* 1989, *4,* 149–158.

Reid, G. C. "Fast Growing Small Entrepreneurial Firms and Their Venture Capital Backers: An Applied Principal-Agent Analysis." *Small Business Economics,* 1996, *8*(3), 235–248.

Reitan, B., and Sorheim, R. "The Private Venture Capital Market in Norway: Investor Characteristics, Behavior and Preferences." Paper presented at the Babson College–Kauffman Foundation Entrepreneurship Research Conference, University of South Carolina, May 12–15, 1999.

Reynolds, P. D., and White, S. B. (eds.). *The Entrepreneurial Process: Economic Growth, Men, Women, and Minorities.* Westport, Conn.: Quorum, 1997.

"Richest Americans in History." *Forbes,* Aug. 8, 1998.

Riding, A. "Where Angels Don't Fear to Tread: Financing Early-Stage Growth." *Financial Post* (Canada), Mastering Enterprise: Part 3, Mar. 18, 1998, p. ME4.

Riding, A., and Short, D. "On the Estimation of the Investment Potential of Informal Investors: A Capture-Recapture Approach." *Journal of Small Business and Entrepreneurship,* 1987, 5(4), 26–40.

Riding, A., and others. *Informal Investors in Canada: The Identification of Salient Characteristics.* Ottawa: Carleton University, 1993.

Rigby, M. "What Is the Venture Capital Investor Looking for in a Prospective Deal?" *Venture Capital Report,* Mar. 1997, pp. 1–4.

Riquelme, H., and Rickards, T. "Hybrid Conjoint Analysis: An Estimation Probe in New Venture Decisions." *Journal of Business Venturing,* 1992, 7, 505–518.

Robbie, K., Wright, M., and Chiplin, B. *The Monitoring of Venture Capital Firms.* Paper Presented at the Babson College–Kauffman Foundation Research Conference, Babson College, Babson Park, Mass., Apr. 16–19, 1997.

Robbie, K., Wright, M., and Chiplin, B. "The Monitoring of Venture Capital Firms." *Entrepreneurship, Theory & Practice,* 1998.

Roberts, E. B. *Entrepreneurs in High-Technology: Lessons from MIT and Beyond.* New York: Oxford University Press, 1991.

Robinson, R. B., Jr. "Emerging Strategies in the Venture Capital Industry." *Journal of Business Venturing,* 1987, 2, 53–77.

Robinson, R. J., and Van Osnabrugge, M. "Do Venture Capitalists Behave Differently When Investing in High Tech Ventures?" (Working paper.) Harvard Business School, 1999.

Robinson, R. J., and Van Osnabrugge, M. "The Importance of Structure Within Entrepreneurial Firms." Unpublished manuscript, Harvard University, 1999.

Robinson, R. J., and Van Osnabrugge, M. "Venture Capital's Angelic Revolution." Unpublished manuscript, Harvard University, 1999.

Robinson, R. J., & Van Osnabrugge, M. *Do Venture Capitalists Behave Differently When Investing in High-Tech Ventures?* Boston, Mass.: Harvard Business School Working Paper #99-131, 1999.

Robinson, R. J., Van Osnabrugge, M., and Coveney, P. F. "Forecasting the

Unknowable: Measuring the Deal Space in Entrepreneurial Investments." Unpublished manuscript, Harvard University, 1999.

Roll, R., and Ross, S. "On the Cross-Sectional Relationship Between Expected Returns and Betas." *Journal of Finance,* 1994, *49,* 101–121.

Rosenstein, J., Bruno, A. V., Bygrave, W. D., and Taylor, N. T. "Do Venture Capitalists on Boards of Portfolio Companies Add Value Besides Money?" In *Frontiers of Entrepreneurship Research.* Babson Park, Mass.: Babson College, 1989.

Rosenstein, J., Bruno, A. V., Bygrave, W. D., and Taylor, N. T. "How Much Do CEOs Value the Advice of Venture Capitalists on Their Boards?" In *Frontiers of Entrepreneurship Research.* Babson Park, Mass.: Babson College, 1990.

Ross, S. "On the Economic Theory of Agency and the Principle of Similarity." In M. Balch, D. McFadden, and S. Wu (eds.), *Essays on Economic Behavior Under Uncertainty.* New York: Elsevier, 1974.

Ross, S. "The Determination of Financial Structures: The Incentive Signalling Approach." *Bell Journal of Economics,* 1977, *8,* 23–40.

Ross, S. "The Current Status of the Capital Asset Pricing Model." *Journal of Finance (Papers and Proceedings),* 1978.

Ruhnka, J., Feldman, H., and Dean, T. "The 'Living Dead' Phenomenon in Venture Capital Investments." *Journal of Business Venturing,* 1992, *7*(2), 137–155.

Ruhnka, J., and Young, J. "Some Hypotheses About Risk in Venture Capital Investing." *Journal of Business Venturing,* 1991, *6,* 116–133.

Sahlman, W. A. "Note of Free Cash Flow Valuation Models: Identifying the Critical Factors That Affect Value." (Teaching note.) Cambridge, Mass.: Harvard Business School, 1987.

Sahlman, W. A. "Aspects of Financial Contracting in Venture Capital." *Journal of Applied Corporate Finance,* 1988, *1*(2), 23–36.

Sahlman, W. A. "A Method for Valuing High-Risk, Long-Term Investments: 'The Venture Capital Method.'" (Business school note.) Cambridge, Mass.: Harvard Business School, 1989.

Sahlman, W. A. "The Structure and Governance of Venture-Capital Organizations." *Journal of Financial Economics,* 1990, *27,* 473–521.

Sahlman, W. A. "How to Write a Great Business Plan," *Harvard Business Review,* July 1997.

Sahlman, W. A. "Some Thoughts on Business Plans." (Case study.) Cambridge, Mass.: Harvard Business School, 1996.

Sahlman, W. A., and Stevenson, H. H. "Capital Market Myopia." In *Frontiers of Entrepreneurship Research.* Babson Park, Mass.: Babson College, 1985.

Sandberg, W. R., Schweiger, D. M., and Hofer, C. W. "Determining Venture Capitalists' Decision Criteria: The Use of Verbal Protocols." In *Frontiers of Entrepreneurship Research*. Babson Park, Mass.: Babson College, 1987.

Sapienza, H. J. "When Do Venture Capitalists Add Value?" *Journal of Business Venturing*, 1992, *7*, 9–29.

Sapienza, H. J., and Korsgaard, M. "The Role of Procedural Justice in Entrepreneur–Venture Capitalist Capital Relations." *Academy of Management Journal*, 1996, *39*, 544–574.

Sapienza, H. J., Manigart, S., and Herron, L. "Summary: Venture Capitalist Involvement in Portfolio Companies: A Study of 221 Portfolio Companies in Four Countries." In *Frontiers of Entrepreneurship Research*. Babson Park, Mass.: Babson College, 1992.

Sapienza, H. J., Manigart, S., and Vermeir, W. "Venture Capitalist Governance and Value Added in Four Countries." *Journal of Business Venturing*, 1996, *11*, 439–469.

Sapienza, H. J., and Timmons, J. A. "The Roles of Venture Capitalists in New Ventures: What Determines Their Importance?" *Academy of Management Best Papers Proceedings*, 1989, pp. 74–78.

Sappington, D. E. "Incentives in Principal-Agent Relationships." *Journal of Economic Perspectives*, 1991, *5*(2), 45–66.

Sareen, A. "No End in Demand for Internet IPOs." *Forbes*, Mar. 1, 1999.

SBSC. "Small Business Fact of the Week: Land of Entrepreneurs." Small Business Survival Committee, July 1, 1998. [http://www.sbsc.org/]

SBSC. "National Small Business Week." May 25, 1999. [http://www.sbsc.org/]

Schumpeter, J. A. *The Theory of Economic Development*. Cambridge, Mass.: Harvard University Press, 1951.

Sebenius, J. K. "Introduction to Negotiation Analysis: Creating and Claiming Value." (Course note N2-898-0854.) Cambridge, Mass.: Harvard Business School, 1997.

Sexton, D. L., and Kasarda, J. D. *The State of the Art of Entrepreneurship*. Boston: PWS-Kent, 1992.

Sexton, D. L., and Smilor, R. W. (eds.). *The Art and Science of Entrepreneurship*. Cambridge, Mass.: Ballinger, 1986.

Shepherd, D. A., Zacharakis, A., and Baron, R. A. "Venture Capitalists' Expertise: Real or Fallacious." In *Frontiers of Entrepreneurship Research*. Babson Park, Mass.: Babson College, 1998.

Short, D. M., and Riding, A. L. "Informal Investors in the Ottawa-Carleton Region: Experiences and Expectations." *Entrepreneurship & Regional Development*, 1989, *1*, 99–112.

Singleton, C., Wilson, N., and Peel, M. "Banking Relationships and Financial Constraints to Growth: An Empirical Study of Small Businesses." Paper presented at the Babson College–Kauffman Foundation Research Conference, Babson College, Babson Park, Mass., Apr. 16–19, 1997.

Small Business Administration. "Fact of the Week." Apr. 14, 1999. [www.sbsc.org]

"Small Business Entrepreneurship 101: Zeroing in on Outside Source of Small Loans." *Los Angeles Times,* May 20, 1998.

Smith, D. G. "How Early Stage Entrepreneurs Evaluate Venture Capitalists." Paper presented at the Babson College–Kauffman Foundation Research Conference, University of South Carolina, May 12–15, 1999.

Smith, K. G., Ganon, M. J., and Sapienza, H. J. "Selection Methodologies for Entrepreneurial Research." *Entrepreneurship, Theory & Practice,* Fall 1989.

Smith, R., and Kiholm, J. *Entrepreneurial Finance.* New York: Wiley, forthcoming.

Sohl, J. E. "The Early-Stage Equity Market in the USA." *Venture Capital,* 1999, *1*(2), 1–20.

Soja, T. A., and Reyes, J. E. *Investment Benchmarks: Venture Capital.* 1990.

Spragins, E. E. "Heaven Sent." *Inc.,* Feb. 1991, p. 85.

"Start-up Firms Have Discovered a New Exit Strategy: Easy Way Out." *Economist,* Feb. 20, 1999, p. 22.

Steinberg, C. "Friends or Foes? Forge a Win-Win Relationship with Venture Capitalists." *Success,* Oct. 1996, p. 10.

Stevenson, H. *Britain's 100 Fastest Growing Private Companies.* Templeton College, Oxford: Oxford Executive Research Briefings, 1997.

Stevenson, H., and Coveney, P. *Survey of Business Angels: Fallacies Corrected and Six Distinct Types of Angel.* Henley-on-Thames, England: Venture Capital Report, 1994.

Storey, D. J. *Understanding the Small Business Sector.* London: Routledge, 1994.

Storey, D. J., and Westhead, P. "Financing Technology-Based Firms in the United Kingdom." (Working paper no. 28.) Warwick Business School, 1995.

Sullivan, M. K. "Entrepreneurs as Informal Investors: Are There Distinguishing Characteristics?" In *Frontiers of Entrepreneurship Research.* Babson Park, Mass.: Babson College, 1991.

Sullivan, M. K., and Miller, A. "Applying Theory of Finance to Informal Risk Capital Research: Promise and Problems." In *Frontiers of Entrepreneurship Research.* Babson Park, Mass.: Babson College, 1990.

Surlemont, B., Leleux, B., and Denis, S. "Enabling Entrepreneurship: The Role of Personal and Corporate Bankruptcy Legislation in Europe, USA, and Japan." Paper presented at the Babson College–Kauffman Foundation Entrepreneurship Research Conference, University of South Carolina, May 12–15, 1999.

Sweeting, R. C. "UK Venture Capital Funds and the Funding of New Technology-Based Businesses: Process and Relationships." *Journal of Management Studies,* 1991, *28*(6), 601–622.

Swift, C. "Financing the Rapidly Growing Firm: Recent Canadian Experience." In *Frontiers of Entrepreneurship Research.* Babson Park, Mass.: Babson College, 1989.

Talton, J. "In Midst of Boom, One of Charlotte's Pockets Still Empty." *Charlotte Observer,* May 3, 1999.

Tashiro, Y. "Japanese Business Angels." In *Frontiers of Entrepreneurship Research.* Babson Park, Mass.: Babson College, 1998.

Tewksbury, J. G., Crandall, M. S., and Crane, W. E. "Measuring the Societal Benefits of Innovation." *Science,* Aug. 8, 1980, vol. 209.

Timmons, J. A. "Planning and Financing the New Venture." Acton, Mass.: Brick House, 1990.

Timmons, J. A. *New Venture Creation: Entrepreneurship for the 21st Century.* Homewood, Ill.: Irwin, 1994.

Timmons, J. A., and Bygrave, W. D. "Venture Capital's Role in Financing Innovation for Economic Growth." *Journal of Business Venturing,* 1986, *1,* 161–176.

Timmons, J. A., and Sapienza, H. J. "Venture Capital: The Decade Ahead." In D. L. Sexton and J. D. Kasarda, *The State of the Art of Entrepreneurship.* Boston: PWS-Kent, 1992.

Townsend, R. M. "Optimal Contracts and Competitive Markets with Costly State Verification." *Journal of Economic Theory,* 1979, *21,* 265–293.

Tyebjee, T. T., and Bruno, A. V. "Venture Capital Decision Making: Preliminary Results from Three Empirical Studies." In *Frontiers of Entrepreneurship Research.* Babson Park, Mass.: Babson College, 1981.

Tyebjee, T. T., and Bruno, A. V. "A Model of Venture Capitalist Investment Activity." *Management Science,* 1984, *30*(9), 1051–1066.

Usem, J. "Start-up Chasers Track New-Biz Storm." *Inc.,* Apr. 1997, p. 22.

Van Osnabrugge, M. "The Financing of Entrepreneurial Firms in the UK." Unpublished doctoral dissertation, Oxford University, 1998.

Van Osnabrugge, M. "A Comparison of Business Angel and Venture Capitalist Investment Procedures: An Agency Theory-Based Analysis."

Paper presented at the Babson College–Kauffman Foundation Entrepreneurship Conference, University of South Carolina, May 12–15, 1999a.

Van Osnabrugge, M. "Do Serial and Non-Serial Investors Behave Differently? An Empirical and Theoretical Analysis." *Entrepreneurship, Theory & Practice,* 1999b, *22*(4), 23–42.

Van Osnabrugge, M. "A Comparison of Business Angel and Venture Capitalist Investment Procedures: An Agency Theory-Based Analysis." *Venture Capital: An International Journal of Entrepreneurial Finance,* forthcoming.

Van Osnabrugge, M., and Robinson, R. J. *Financing Entrepreneurship: Business Angels and Venture Capitalists Compared.* Boston: Harvard Business School. Working Paper #99-132, 1999a.

Van Osnabrugge, M., and Robinson, R. J. *The Influence of a Venture Capitalist's Source of Funds.* Boston: Harvard Business School. Harvard Business School Working Paper #99-133, 1999b.

"Venture Capital in the United Kingdom." *Bank of England Quarterly Bulletin,* Feb. 1990.

Wasserman, N. *Venture Capital Negotiations: A 360 Degree View."* (Working paper.) Cambridge, Mass.: Harvard Business School, 1999.

Weicher, J. C. "The Rich and the Poor: Demographics of the U.S. Wealth Distribution." *Federal Reserve Bank of St. Louis Review,* July 17, 1997, *4*(79), p. 25.

Welles, E. O. "How a Start-up Positioned Itself to Appeal to Investors and Landed $2 Million in Venture Capital." *Inc.,* Mar. 1994, p. 72.

Wetzel, W. E. "Project I-C-E: An Experiment in Capital Formation." In *Frontiers of Entrepreneurship Research.* Babson Park, Mass.: Babson College, 1982a.

Wetzel, W. E. "Risk Capital Research." In C. A. Kent, D. L. Sexton, and K. H. Vesper (eds.), *Encyclopedia of Entrepreneurship.* Upper Saddle River, N.J.: Prentice-Hall, 1982b.

Wetzel, W. E. "Angels and Informal Risk Capital." *Sloan Management Review,* Summer 1983, pp. 23–34.

Wetzel, W. E. "Entrepreneurs, Angels, and Economic Renaissance." In R. D. Hisrich (ed.), *Entrepreneurship, Intrapreneurship, and Venture Capital.* Homewood, Ill.: Irwin, 1986a.

Wetzel, W. E. "Informal Risk Capital: Knowns and Unknowns." In D. L. Sexton and R. W. Smilor (eds.), *The Art and Science of Entrepreneurship.* Cambridge, Mass.: Ballinger, 1986b.

Wetzel, W. E. "The Informal Venture Capital Market: Aspects of Scale and Market Efficiency." *Journal of Business Venturing,* 1987, *2,* 299–313.

Wetzel, W. E. Statements to the House Banking, Finance, and Urban Affairs Committee, Subcommittee of Economic Growth and Credit Formation. Roundtable Hearing, Nov. 16, 1993.

Wetzel, W. W. "Economic Policy in an Entrepreneurial World: Seven Treacherous Misconceptions and Half-Truths." *Venture Capital Report,* Apr. 1996, pp. 1–4.

Wetzel, W. E., and Freear, J. "Starting a Private Investor Network: Reflections on the History of VCN." In R. T. Harrison and C. M. Mason (eds.), *Informal Venture Capital: Information, Networks and Public Policy.* Hemel Hempstead, England: Woodhead-Faulkner, 1993.

Wetzel, W. E., and Freear, J. "Promoting Informal Venture Capital in the United States: Reflections on the History of the Venture Capital Network." In R. Harrison and C. M. Mason (eds.), *Informal Venture Capital: Information, Networks, and Public Policy.* Hemel Hempstead, England: Woodhead-Faulkner, 1994.

Wetzel, W. E., and Seymour, C. R. "Informal Risk Capital in New England." Washington D.C.: Office of Advocacy, U.S. Small Business Administration, 1981.

Wetzel, W. E., and Wilson, I. G. "Seed Capital Gaps: Evidence from High-Growth Ventures." In *Frontiers of Entrepreneurship Research.* Babson Park, Mass.: Babson College, 1985.

Wilmsen, S. "Loan to On-line Firm Gets Out-of-Sight Returns." *Boston Globe,* April 9, 1999a, p. C1.

Wilmsen, S. "MBAs Are the Latest Net Gain." *Boston Sunday Globe,* May 9, 1999b, p. A24.

Wilson, J. *The New Venturers.* Reading, Mass.: Addison-Wesley, 1985.

Wilson, H. I. "Sources of Start-up and Early-Stage Capital Available to High Technology Entrepreneurs in the UK: A Regional Study." In *Frontiers of Entrepreneurship Research.* Babson Park, Mass.: Babson College, 1994.

Winborg, J., and Landstrom, H. "Financial Bootstrapping in Small Businesses: A Resource-Based View of Small Business Finance." Paper presented at the Babson College–Kauffman Foundation Research Conference, Babson College, Babson Park, Mass., Apr. 16–19, 1997.

Wright, M., and Robbie, K. "Summary: Venture Capitalists Target Rates of Return and Investment Appraisal." In *Frontiers of Entrepreneurship Research.* Babson Park, Mass.: Babson College, 1995.

Wright, M., and Robbie, K. "Venture Capitalists, Unquoted Equity Investment Appraisal and the Role of Accounting Information." *Accounting and Business Research,* 1996, *26*(2), 153–168.

Wright, M., Robbie, K., and Ennew, C. "Venture Capitalists and Serial Entrepreneurs." *Journal of Business Venturing,* 1997, *12,* 227–249.

Zacharakis, A. L., and Meyer, G. D. "The Venture Capitalist Decision: Understanding Process Versus Outcome." In *Frontiers of Entrepreneurship Research.* Babson Park, Mass.: Babson College, 1995.

Zacharakis, A. L., and Meyer, G. D. "A Lack of Insight: Do Venture Capitalists Really Understand Their Own Decision Process?" *Journal of Business Venturing,* 1998, *13,* 57–76.

# Name Index

# Subject Index

## A

Acceptance by entrepreneurs, funding offers, 101, 150–151, 181

Acceptance rates, investment proposal, 146–147

The Access to Capital Electronic Network (ACE-Net), SBA, 263–264, 330

Accountants, roles of, 152, 165, 172, 362

Accounts receivable factoring, 29, 376

ACE-NET (The Angel Capital Electronic Network), 82, 344

Acquisitions. *See* Trade sales or acquisitions

Advice: for entrepreneurs, 359–364; on finding angels, 92–93, 144; on finding entrepreneurs, 93–94; giving business strategy, 192, 238; postinvestment regrets and, 210–212; and tips for prospective angels, 235–239

Advisers: gatekeeper, 376; lawyers and accountants, 152, 165, 172, 243, 362; technical, 361–362

Advisory Council on Science and Technology (ACOST), 70

Agency relationship: comparison of business angel and venture capitalist, 97–99, 162, 163; venture capitalist information signals and, 102, 103

Agreement: contingency, 230; lockup, 153, 243; setting guidelines before, 363–364. *See also* Contracts

Alignment of entrepreneurs, 177–178

Alliances, angel, 43–46, 75, 80, 136, 380. *See also* Syndication

Alliances, business, 31–33; definition of, 373; reasons for finding, 32

Altruism, 117, 118–119

Amazon.com, 42, 202, 207; financial history of, 59, 60

Amis Ventures, 207

American Entrepreneurs for Economic Growth (AEEG), 343

Amounts, investment. *See* Size: of the investment

Analysis by investors. *See* Due diligence

Angel alliances. *See* Syndication

Angel investors. *See* Business angel investors

Angel role models, 15, 42, 43, 44

Angel syndicates. *See* Syndication

Anonymity of business angels, 46, 77, 80, 84

Antidilution provisions, 179, 373

Apple Computer, 42, 48, 66, 207

Arch Venture Partners, 168

Archangel role, 45, 373

Arizona Technology Incubator/Arizona Technology Venture Fund, 266

Asia Pacific region, 342; associations and organizations in, 345–346

Assets, entrepreneurial firm: valuation of, 216–223

Assistance, managerial. *See* Monitoring the investment

Associations and organizations: directories of, 339–343; resources on, 343–348

Atlanta Development Authority, 320

Awareness: of business angel investing, 73; by venture capitalists of fund providers, 105. *See also* Information; Resources

## B

Backup business plan, 237, 242

Balance sheet valuation, 222

Baltimore Washington Venture Group, 284

Band of Angels syndicate, 44

Bankruptcy laws, 13

Banks, 29, 75, 252; compared to venture capitalists, 52; lending practices of, 31, 52–55, 180; percentage of financing by, 53

Bargaining range and alternatives, 226–228

Barter investors, 87

Ben Franklin Technology Center of Southeastern Pennsylvania, 285

Benchmark ratio, 220

Birmingham Venture Club, 321

Board of directors: credibility lent by, 361; investor membership in, 192–193, 238

Board rights, 178, 187, 373

North Dakota Development Fund, 315
North Florida Venture Capital Network, 324
The Northeast Recycling Investment Forum, 305
Northwest Capital Network, 168, 316
Northwest region matching services, 313–319
Northwest Venture Group (Holt & Company), 317
Novice investors, questions of, 239–246

**O**

128 Venture Capital Group, 295
Offers. *See* Funding offers
One-product firms, 237
Opportunity attrition. *See* Investment opportunities
Orange Coast Venture Group, 271
Oregon Entrepreneurs Forum, 318
Ownership: and control issues, 95–97; investor level of, 183–184

**P**

Partner investors, 86, 136–137
Partners: business alliance, 32–33; negotiation, 230–232
Partnerships, venture capital. *See* Co-investing; Syndication
Patents, 129–130
Patient capital, 203
Peers (business angels), 88
Pennsylvania Private Investors Group, 289
Pension funds (public and corporate), 97
Performance or forfeiture provisions, 178, 378
Personal differences among investor types, 106–111. *See also* Investment criteria
Personal networks, 78, 240, 360. *See also* "Three Fs" (founder, family, and friends)
Piggyback rights, 180, 379
Plum (investment), 379
Portfolios: diversification of, 238–239, 252; returns for, 208; size of business angel, 67–70, 93, 181–182; size of venture capitalist, 67–70, 180, 181–182; and specialization, 149–150, 156–157, 206
Positions, negotiation, 225–226
*Pratt's Guide to Venture Capital Sources,* 10, 91, 339–340, 351, 354
Preference matters, investor. *See* Business angel investors; Motivations of business angels
Preference shares, 210, 379
Price to earnings ratio (P/E), 216, 217–218, 221
*PricewaterhouseCoopers Money Tree Survey,* 342–343, 353

Private investors. *See* Business angel investors; Investors
Private Investors Network (PIN), 279, 325
Problem solving. *See* Bootstrapping; Negotiation
Product development techniques, 26
Product markets. *See* Sectors, industry
Productive resources, 209
Professional angels, 85, 170
Professional networks, 78–79
Profitability of investments, 206–210; financial characteristics and potential, 130–131, 138, 160–162; and IPOs, 56–60
Projections, financial: investors' use of, 160–161; realism of entrepreneur, 161–162
Prominent angels. *See* Entrepreneurial angels
Proposals, business. *See* Investment proposals
Prospective angels, ten investment tips for, 235–239
Public stock offerings. *See* Initial public offerings (IPOs)
Put rights, contract, 179

**Q**

Questions and reflections, investor, 235–246

**R**

Rachet (antidilution adjustment), 179, 379
Ratios and multiples, 216–219; free cash flow, 218–219; gearing ratio, 55; historic versus future, 219; P/E, 217–218, 221
Realism: of exit strategies, 135; of financial projections, 161–162, 242
Reality check, 364; on business plans, 370–371
Recordkeeping, 31
Recruitment of employees by investors, 190–191, 198, 212
*The Red Herring,* 349
Referral sources: accepting independent references from, 159–160; investors as, 364; use of by entrepreneurs, 150–151, 362, 364; use of by investors, 147–149, 241, 243
Reflections and questions, investor, 239–246
Regrets, investors' postinvestment, 158, 210–212
Rejection, proposal, 146, 364
Replacement of entrepreneurs, 186–187
Reports, due diligence, 152
Reputation and performance: of the entrepreneurs, 147–149, 243–244; of venture capitalists, 100–101, 157
Research: costs of due diligence, 163–164; and development, 26, 56; to find business angels, 46, 83–84; industry sector, 157–158